# FREE Test Taking Tips DVD Offer

To help us better serve you, we have developed a Test Taking Tips DVD that we would like to give you for FREE. **This DVD covers world-class test taking tips that you can use to be even more successful when you are taking your test.**

All that we ask is that you email us your feedback about your study guide. Please let us know what you thought about it – whether that is good, bad or indifferent.

To get your **FREE Test Taking Tips DVD**, email freedvd@studyguideteam.com with "FREE DVD" in the subject line and the following information in the body of the email:

    a. The title of your study guide.

    b. Your product rating on a scale of 1-5, with 5 being the highest rating.

    c. Your feedback about the study guide. What did you think of it?

    d. Your full name and shipping address to send your free DVD.

If you have any questions or concerns, please don't hesitate to contact us at freedvd@studyguideteam.com.

Thanks again!

# NES Study Guide Elementary Education Subtest 1 and 2

## NES Prep and Practice Test Questions
## [2nd Edition]

TPB Publishing

Interested in buying more than 10 copies of our product? Contact us about bulk discounts:
bulkorders@studyguideteam.com

ISBN 13: 9781628459234
ISBN 10: 1628459239

# Table of Contents

# Quick Overview

As you draw closer to taking your exam, effective preparation becomes more and more important. Thankfully, you have this study guide to help you get ready. Use this guide to help keep your studying on track and refer to it often.

This study guide contains several key sections that will help you be successful on your exam. The guide contains tips for what you should do the night before and the day of the test. Also included are test-taking tips. Knowing the right information is not always enough. Many well-prepared test takers struggle with exams. These tips will help equip you to accurately read, assess, and answer test questions.

A large part of the guide is devoted to showing you what content to expect on the exam and to helping you better understand that content. In this guide are practice test questions so that you can see how well you have grasped the content. Then, answer explanations are provided so that you can understand why you missed certain questions.

Don't try to cram the night before you take your exam. This is not a wise strategy for a few reasons. First, your retention of the information will be low. Your time would be better used by reviewing information you already know rather than trying to learn a lot of new information. Second, you will likely become stressed as you try to gain a large amount of knowledge in a short amount of time. Third, you will be depriving yourself of sleep. So be sure to go to bed at a reasonable time the night before. Being well-rested helps you focus and remain calm.

Be sure to eat a substantial breakfast the morning of the exam. If you are taking the exam in the afternoon, be sure to have a good lunch as well. Being hungry is distracting and can make it difficult to focus. You have hopefully spent lots of time preparing for the exam. Don't let an empty stomach get in the way of success!

When travelling to the testing center, leave earlier than needed. That way, you have a buffer in case you experience any delays. This will help you remain calm and will keep you from missing your appointment time at the testing center.

Be sure to pace yourself during the exam. Don't try to rush through the exam. There is no need to risk performing poorly on the exam just so you can leave the testing center early. Allow yourself to use all of the allotted time if needed.

Remain positive while taking the exam even if you feel like you are performing poorly. Thinking about the content you should have mastered will not help you perform better on the exam.

Once the exam is complete, take some time to relax. Even if you feel that you need to take the exam again, you will be well served by some down time before you begin studying again. It's often easier to convince yourself to study if you know that it will come with a reward!

# Test-Taking Strategies

## 1. Predicting the Answer

When you feel confident in your preparation for a multiple-choice test, try predicting the answer before reading the answer choices. This is especially useful on questions that test objective factual knowledge. By predicting the answer before reading the available choices, you eliminate the possibility that you will be distracted or led astray by an incorrect answer choice. You will feel more confident in your selection if you read the question, predict the answer, and then find your prediction among the answer choices. After using this strategy, be sure to still read all of the answer choices carefully and completely. If you feel unprepared, you should not attempt to predict the answers. This would be a waste of time and an opportunity for your mind to wander in the wrong direction.

## 2. Reading the Whole Question

Too often, test takers scan a multiple-choice question, recognize a few familiar words, and immediately jump to the answer choices. Test authors are aware of this common impatience, and they will sometimes prey upon it. For instance, a test author might subtly turn the question into a negative, or he or she might redirect the focus of the question right at the end. The only way to avoid falling into these traps is to read the entirety of the question carefully before reading the answer choices.

## 3. Looking for Wrong Answers

Long and complicated multiple-choice questions can be intimidating. One way to simplify a difficult multiple-choice question is to eliminate all of the answer choices that are clearly wrong. In most sets of answers, there will be at least one selection that can be dismissed right away. If the test is administered on paper, the test taker could draw a line through it to indicate that it may be ignored; otherwise, the test taker will have to perform this operation mentally or on scratch paper. In either case, once the obviously incorrect answers have been eliminated, the remaining choices may be considered. Sometimes identifying the clearly wrong answers will give the test taker some information about the correct answer. For instance, if one of the remaining answer choices is a direct opposite of one of the eliminated answer choices, it may well be the correct answer. The opposite of obviously wrong is obviously right! Of course, this is not always the case. Some answers are obviously incorrect simply because they are irrelevant to the question being asked. Still, identifying and eliminating some incorrect answer choices is a good way to simplify a multiple-choice question.

## 4. Don't Overanalyze

Anxious test takers often overanalyze questions. When you are nervous, your brain will often run wild, causing you to make associations and discover clues that don't actually exist. If you feel that this may be a problem for you, do whatever you can to slow down during the test. Try taking a deep breath or counting to ten. As you read and consider the question, restrict yourself to the particular words used by the author. Avoid thought tangents about what the author *really* meant, or what he or she was *trying* to say. The only things that matter on a multiple-choice test are the words that are actually in the question. You must avoid reading too much into a multiple-choice question, or supposing that the writer meant something other than what he or she wrote.

## 5. No Need for Panic

It is wise to learn as many strategies as possible before taking a multiple-choice test, but it is likely that you will come across a few questions for which you simply don't know the answer. In this situation, avoid panicking. Because most multiple-choice tests include dozens of questions, the relative value of a single wrong answer is small. As much as possible, you should compartmentalize each question on a multiple-choice test. In other words, you should not allow your feelings about one question to affect your success on the others. When you find a question that you either don't understand or don't know how to answer, just take a deep breath and do your best. Read the entire question slowly and carefully. Try rephrasing the question a couple of different ways. Then, read all of the answer choices carefully. After eliminating obviously wrong answers, make a selection and move on to the next question.

## 6. Confusing Answer Choices

When working on a difficult multiple-choice question, there may be a tendency to focus on the answer choices that are the easiest to understand. Many people, whether consciously or not, gravitate to the answer choices that require the least concentration, knowledge, and memory. This is a mistake. When you come across an answer choice that is confusing, you should give it extra attention. A question might be confusing because you do not know the subject matter to which it refers. If this is the case, don't eliminate the answer before you have affirmatively settled on another. When you come across an answer choice of this type, set it aside as you look at the remaining choices. If you can confidently assert that one of the other choices is correct, you can leave the confusing answer aside. Otherwise, you will need to take a moment to try to better understand the confusing answer choice. Rephrasing is one way to tease out the sense of a confusing answer choice.

## 7. Your First Instinct

Many people struggle with multiple-choice tests because they overthink the questions. If you have studied sufficiently for the test, you should be prepared to trust your first instinct once you have carefully and completely read the question and all of the answer choices. There is a great deal of research suggesting that the mind can come to the correct conclusion very quickly once it has obtained all of the relevant information. At times, it may seem to you as if your intuition is working faster even than your reasoning mind. This may in fact be true. The knowledge you obtain while studying may be retrieved from your subconscious before you have a chance to work out the associations that support it. Verify your instinct by working out the reasons that it should be trusted.

## 8. Key Words

Many test takers struggle with multiple-choice questions because they have poor reading comprehension skills. Quickly reading and understanding a multiple-choice question requires a mixture of skill and experience. To help with this, try jotting down a few key words and phrases on a piece of scrap paper. Doing this concentrates the process of reading and forces the mind to weigh the relative importance of the question's parts. In selecting words and phrases to write down, the test taker thinks about the question more deeply and carefully. This is especially true for multiple-choice questions that are preceded by a long prompt.

## 9. Subtle Negatives

One of the oldest tricks in the multiple-choice test writer's book is to subtly reverse the meaning of a question with a word like *not* or *except*. If you are not paying attention to each word in the question, you can easily be led astray by this trick. For instance, a common question format is, "Which of the following is…?" Obviously, if the question instead is, "Which of the following is not…?," then the answer will be quite different. Even worse, the test makers are aware of the potential for this mistake and will include one answer choice that would be correct if the question were not negated or reversed. A test taker who misses the reversal will find what he or she believes to be a correct answer and will be so confident that he or she will fail to reread the question and discover the original error. The only way to avoid this is to practice a wide variety of multiple-choice questions and to pay close attention to each and every word.

## 10. Reading Every Answer Choice

It may seem obvious, but you should always read every one of the answer choices! Too many test takers fall into the habit of scanning the question and assuming that they understand the question because they recognize a few key words. From there, they pick the first answer choice that answers the question they believe they have read. Test takers who read all of the answer choices might discover that one of the latter answer choices is actually *more* correct. Moreover, reading all of the answer choices can remind you of facts related to the question that can help you arrive at the correct answer. Sometimes, a misstatement or incorrect detail in one of the latter answer choices will trigger your memory of the subject and will enable you to find the right answer. Failing to read all of the answer choices is like not reading all of the items on a restaurant menu: you might miss out on the perfect choice.

## 11. Spot the Hedges

One of the keys to success on multiple-choice tests is paying close attention to every word. This is never truer than with words like almost, most, some, and sometimes. These words are called "hedges" because they indicate that a statement is not totally true or not true in every place and time. An absolute statement will contain no hedges, but in many subjects, the answers are not always straightforward or absolute. There are always exceptions to the rules in these subjects. For this reason, you should favor those multiple-choice questions that contain hedging language. The presence of qualifying words indicates that the author is taking special care with his or her words, which is certainly important when composing the right answer. After all, there are many ways to be wrong, but there is only one way to be right! For this reason, it is wise to avoid answers that are absolute when taking a multiple-choice test. An absolute answer is one that says things are either all one way or all another. They often include words like *every*, *always*, *best*, and *never*. If you are taking a multiple-choice test in a subject that doesn't lend itself to absolute answers, be on your guard if you see any of these words.

## 12. Long Answers

In many subject areas, the answers are not simple. As already mentioned, the right answer often requires hedges. Another common feature of the answers to a complex or subjective question are qualifying clauses, which are groups of words that subtly modify the meaning of the sentence. If the question or answer choice describes a rule to which there are exceptions or the subject matter is complicated, ambiguous, or confusing, the correct answer will require many words in order to be expressed clearly and accurately. In essence, you should not be deterred by answer choices that seem excessively long. Oftentimes, the author of the text will not be able to write the correct answer without

offering some qualifications and modifications. Your job is to read the answer choices thoroughly and completely and to select the one that most accurately and precisely answers the question.

## 13. Restating to Understand

Sometimes, a question on a multiple-choice test is difficult not because of what it asks but because of how it is written. If this is the case, restate the question or answer choice in different words. This process serves a couple of important purposes. First, it forces you to concentrate on the core of the question. In order to rephrase the question accurately, you have to understand it well. Rephrasing the question will concentrate your mind on the key words and ideas. Second, it will present the information to your mind in a fresh way. This process may trigger your memory and render some useful scrap of information picked up while studying.

## 14. True Statements

Sometimes an answer choice will be true in itself, but it does not answer the question. This is one of the main reasons why it is essential to read the question carefully and completely before proceeding to the answer choices. Too often, test takers skip ahead to the answer choices and look for true statements. Having found one of these, they are content to select it without reference to the question above. Obviously, this provides an easy way for test makers to play tricks. The savvy test taker will always read the entire question before turning to the answer choices. Then, having settled on a correct answer choice, he or she will refer to the original question and ensure that the selected answer is relevant. The mistake of choosing a correct-but-irrelevant answer choice is especially common on questions related to specific pieces of objective knowledge. A prepared test taker will have a wealth of factual knowledge at his or her disposal, and should not be careless in its application.

## 15. No Patterns

One of the more dangerous ideas that circulates about multiple-choice tests is that the correct answers tend to fall into patterns. These erroneous ideas range from a belief that B and C are the most common right answers, to the idea that an unprepared test-taker should answer "A-B-A-C-A-D-A-B-A." It cannot be emphasized enough that pattern-seeking of this type is exactly the WRONG way to approach a multiple-choice test. To begin with, it is highly unlikely that the test maker will plot the correct answers according to some predetermined pattern. The questions are scrambled and delivered in a random order. Furthermore, even if the test maker was following a pattern in the assignation of correct answers, there is no reason why the test taker would know which pattern he or she was using. Any attempt to discern a pattern in the answer choices is a waste of time and a distraction from the real work of taking the test. A test taker would be much better served by extra preparation before the test than by reliance on a pattern in the answers.

# FREE DVD OFFER

Don't forget that doing well on your exam includes both understanding the test content and understanding how to use what you know to do well on the test. We offer a completely FREE Test Taking Tips DVD that covers world class test taking tips that you can use to be even more successful when you are taking your test.

All that we ask is that you email us your feedback about your study guide. To get your **FREE Test Taking Tips DVD**, email freedvd@studyguideteam.com with "FREE DVD" in the subject line and the following information in the body of the email:

- The title of your study guide.
- Your product rating on a scale of 1-5, with 5 being the highest rating.
- Your feedback about the study guide. What did you think of it?
- Your full name and shipping address to send your free DVD.

# Introduction

**Function of the Test**

The National Evaluation Series (NES) tests are teacher certification tests intended to evaluate teacher's qualifications in over thirty different areas. The Elementary Education I & II subtests are designed to assess the qualifications of elementary school teachers in five different subject areas: Reading/Language Arts and Social Studies on Elementary Education Subtest I and Mathematics, Science, and Arts/Fitness/Health on Elementary Education Subtest II.

Like all of the NES tests, the NES Elementary Education Subtests are offered nationwide by Pearson Education. Various states and professional bodies require the tests for licensing and hiring purposes, including Arizona, New Mexico, Oregon, and Washington. Accordingly, the typical test taker is a current elementary school teacher seeking to be licensed or renew a license, a prospective elementary school teacher, or elementary school teacher entering a state where the tests are required. Scores are typically used only for licensing and hiring purposes.

**Test Administration**

The NES tests are administered by computer at Pearson VUE testing centers. Prospective takers may register to take the test at any time that a center is open throughout the year. There is no limit to the amount of times a test taker may attempt to pass the subtests; however, test takers who do not pass one of the Elementary Education subtests must wait at least thirty days before they can register to take one of the subtests again. Individuals with documented disabilities may receive appropriate accommodations under the Americans with Disabilities Act.

No reference materials are provided during the exams. Scaled scores are provided to test takers immediately upon completion of the tests, while more detailed reports are mailed to test takers a couple weeks later.

**Test Format**

Each of the two subtests consists of about seventy-five questions. The first subtest is conducted in ninety minutes and the second in 105 minutes, with no breaks or interruptions in either. A test taker may schedule an individual subtest or both, depending on their needs. The content is based on competencies identified by Pearson and based on national content standards in the respective subject areas.

A breakdown of the content of the two tests follows:

| Test | Subject Area | % of Test | Time |
|---|---|---|---|
| Elementary Education I | Reading & English Language Arts | 62 | 90 |
| | Social Studies | 38 | |
| Elementary Education II | Mathematics | 50 | 105 |
| | Science | 38 | |
| | The Arts, Health, and Fitness | 12 | |

**Scoring**

The NES Elementary Education Subtests are scored by summing the number of correct answers provided by the test taker and then converting that raw score to a scaled score between 100 and 300. There is no penalty for guessing incorrectly, aside from the missed opportunity to provide another correct response. Pearson sets a National Benchmark scaled score of 220 as a passing score on the test, but each state that requires the exam is free to set its own benchmark. For instance, Arizona and Washington have adopted the National Benchmark score of 220 as its passing score for all NES tests, while Oregon and New Mexico have adopted their own state-specific benchmark scores. Oregon's benchmark score is 227 on Subtest I and 228 on Subtest II. New Mexico recently switched from the National Benchmark to match Oregon's 227 and 228 benchmarks on the two respective subtests.

**Recent/Future Developments**

In September of 2016, Pearson added fifteen minutes to the time allowed for completing the NES Elementary Education Subtest II exam, taking it from one hour and thirty minutes to one hour and forty-five minutes. No other recent changes have been announced by Pearson for the NES Elementary Education tests. However, New Mexico did recently adopt its own, higher benchmark passing scores, replacing the National Benchmark that it previously had used.

# Reading and English Language Arts

## *Foundations of Language and Literacy*

### Phonological Awareness

Well before children are able to read and write, they begin to develop basic listening skills and gradually begin to imitate and produce the sounds they hear. Since language is used to communicate one's needs, react to situations, share experiences, and develop an understanding of the surrounding world, these beginning stages form the foundation of a child's literacy development. Before a child reaches the preschool years, they begin to develop the ability to recognize and manipulate the sounds in their environment.

Generally speaking, *phonological awareness* is the ability to identify and manipulate specific units of oral language, including words, syllables, onsets, and rimes. The beginning stages of phonological awareness occur when a child is able to listen to and understand the words that people speak and read and when they are further able to recognize the various sounds within these words. Phonological awareness is also defined as the ability to sound out various words by connecting the sounds heard to familiar sounds and to manipulate those sounds in order to create new sounds and words. A child is demonstrating phonological awareness when they are able to do the following:

- Appropriately recognize and apply words that rhyme—*cat, bat, sat*
- Identify initial letters—the *c* in *cat*
- Identify middle letters—the *a* in *cat*
- Identify ending letters—the *t* in *cat*
- Separate simple words into their individual sounds or phonemes—c/a/t *cat*

There are many strategies educators can use to strengthen a child's phonological awareness. One effective strategy to strengthen a child's awareness of word units is clapping out the number of syllables in a word. Familiar and enjoyable songs, such as "Bingo," help children to identify individual phonemes within a word and strengthen their spelling skills, listening comprehension, and rhythm. Other strategies may include word games that challenge children to think of rhyming words or words that share the same initial, middle, or ending sounds. Creating fun and engaging ways for children to strengthen their phonological awareness will build the framework for future literary success.

### Phonemes, Syllables, Onsets, and Rimes

A *phoneme* is commonly referred to as a sound or a group of sounds that differentiate one word from another in a spoken language. Phonemes are language-specific sound units that do not carry inherent meanings, but are simply known as the smallest unit in a language. For example, there are phonemes

unique to the English language that do not necessarily exist in other spoken languages. In English, although there are only twenty-six letters, there are forty-four phonemes:

| Forty-Four Phonemes in English | | | |
|---|---|---|---|
| **Consonant Sounds** | | **Vowel Sounds** | |
| /b/ | boy | /a/ | bat |
| /d/ | desk | /e/ | head |
| /f/ | fall | /i/ | dish |
| /g/ | game | /o/ | rock |
| /h/ | hand | /u/ | muck |
| /j/ | joy | /a/ | bake |
| /k/ | king | /e/ | meet |
| /l/ | life | /i/ | like |
| /m/ | map | /o/ | moat |
| /n/ | nail | /yoo/ | cube |
| /p/ | park | /e/ | alarm |
| /r/ | run | /oo/ | doom |
| /s/ | sock | /oo/ | nook |
| /t/ | tail | /ou/ | mouse |
| /v/ | veil | /oi/ | toy |
| /w/ | water | /o/ | call |
| /y/ | yawn | /u/ | herd |
| /z/ | zebra | /a/ | hair |
| /ch/ | chalk | /a/ | star |
| /sh/ | shallow | | |
| /th/ | thorn | | |
| /wh/ | whale | | |
| /zh/ | leisure | | |
| /ng/ | sing | | |

Mastery of all forty-four phonemes in oral and written communication is a strong predictor of future reading readiness.

*Syllables* are defined as one complete unit of pronunciation. Every syllable contains only one vowel sound that can be created by one or more than one vowel. Syllables can consist of vowels that stand alone or combine with consonants. The study of syllables and how they operate help children to become stronger readers and will aid in spelling proficiency. Educators will often introduce new words that contain more than one syllable by teaching children to say and write the syllable. Segmenting a word into its individual syllables, as well as blending syllables into whole words, allows children to see the key parts of a word and provides opportunities for them to strengthen their reading skills.

In the English language, there are six different types of syllables, four of which are syllable combinations:

- Closed syllables: syllables that end in a consonant, as in *bat*, or *it*
- Open syllables: syllables that end with a vowel, as in *he*, *she*, or *we*
- Vowel-consonant-e syllables: syllables that end with a silent *e*, as in *ate*, *wife*, or *mile*
- Vowel team syllables: syllables that work in combination to create a new sound, as in *mouth* or *join*

- Consonant + le syllables: syllables that contain a consonant and end with an *le*, as in *turtle*
- R-Controlled syllables: syllables that contain a vowel followed by the letter *r*, where the *r* controls how the vowel is pronounced, as in *bird* or *word*

A word is broken up into two pieces: onset and rime. The *onset* is the initial phonological unit of any word, whether it is a consonant or a consonant cluster. The *rime* is the string of letters that follows the onset, usually consisting of a vowel or variant vowels along with one or more consonants. Many words in the English language share common features or patterns. These *word families* often share the same letter combinations that form the same or similar sounds. When introducing word families, educators will often initiate activities involving onsets and rimes to help children accurately recognize, read, and spell simple words. The study of onsets and rimes has shown to improve a child's overall literacy skills, increase reading fluency, and strengthen spelling skills. The following word family list illustrates words separated into onset and rime:

| Word | Onset | Rime |
|------|-------|------|
| sun | s | Un |
| sunny | s | unny |
| sunshine | s | unshine |

## Blending, Segmenting, Substituting, and Deleting Phonemes, Syllables, Onsets, and Rimes

The ability to break apart a word into its individual phonemes is referred to as *segmenting*. Segmenting words can greatly aid in a child's ability to recognize, read, and spell an entire word. In literacy instruction, *blending* is when the reader connects segmented parts to create an entire word. Segmenting and blending practice work together like pieces of a puzzle to help children practice newly-acquired vocabulary. Educators can approach segmenting and blending using a multi-sensory approach. For example, a child can manipulate letter blocks to build words and pull them apart. An educator may even ask the child to listen to the word being said and ask him or her to find the letter blocks that build each phoneme, one at a time:

/m/ /u/ /g/

/b/ /a/ /t/

/r/ /u/ /n/

Once children are able to blend and segment phonemes, they are ready for the more complex skill of blending and segmenting syllables, onsets, and rimes. Using the same multi-sensory approach, children may practice blending the syllables of familiar words on a word wall, using letter blocks, paper and pencil, or sounding them out loud. Once they blend the words together, students can then practice segmenting those same words, studying their individual syllables and the letters and sounds that create the words. Educators may again read a word out loud and ask children to write or build the first syllable, followed by the next, and so on. The very same practice can be used to identify the onset. Children can work on writing and/or building this sound followed by the word's rime. Word families and rhyming words are ideal for this type of exercise so that children can more readily see the parts of each word. Using words that rhyme can turn this exercise into a fun and engaging activity.

Once children have demonstrated the ability to independently blend and segment phonemes, syllables, onsets, and rimes, educators may present a more challenging exercise that involves *substitutions* and *deletions*. As these are more complex skills, children will likely benefit from repeated practice and modeling. Using word families and words that rhyme when teaching this skill will make the activity more enjoyable, and it will also greatly aid in a child's overall comprehension.

| Substitution and Deletion Using Onset and Rime | | | | |
|---|---|---|---|---|
| **Word** | **Onset Deletion** | **Rime Deletion** | **Onset Substitution** | **Rime Substitution** |
| run | un | r | fun | rat |
| bun | un | b | gun | bat |
| sun | un | s | nun | sat |

| Substitution and Deletion Using Phonemes | | |
|---|---|---|
| **Word** | **Phoneme Substitution** | **Phoneme Deletion** |
| sit | sat | si |
| bit | bat | bi |
| hit | hat | hi |

| Substitution and Deletion Using Syllables | | |
|---|---|---|
| **Word** | **Syllable Substitution** | **Syllable Deletion** |
| cement | lament or, cedar | ce |
| moment | statement, or motive | mo |
| basement | movement, or baseball | base |

## Active Listening

To develop active listening skills, several important areas require focus and conscious effort. Before a speech or dialogue even begins, removing any distractions sets a positive and respectful tone. Those with active listening skills offer undivided attention, acknowledge the presenter's message by asking

relevant questions and provide encouraging feedback when appropriate. Maintaining eye contact, smiling, and using posture that signifies respect are also effective characteristics of active listening, but perhaps one of the most important ways to improve active listening skills is to keep an open mind and defer judgment until the speaker has completed the entire message.

Active listening skills are an important part of children's family, social, and academic life, and they will eventually become an equally important part of their professional lives. Recognizing the importance of active listening and strengthening these skills assists students in achieving personal, academic, and professional success.

## Stages of Language Acquisition

There are many factors that influence a child's language acquisition. A child's physical age, level of maturity, home and school experiences, general attitudes toward learning, and home languages are just some of the many influences on a child's literacy development. However, a child's *language acquisition* progresses through the following generalized stages:

| Stage | Examples | Age |
|---|---|---|
| Preproduction | does not verbalize/ nods yes and no | zero to six months |
| Early production | one to two word responses | six to twelve months |
| Speech emergence | produces simple sentences | one to three years |
| Intermediate fluency | simple to more complex sentences | three to five years |
| Advanced fluency | near native level of speech | five to seven years |

While this applies to language acquisition in one's home language, the very same stages apply to English language learners (ELLs). Since effective communication in any given language requires much more than a mere collection of vocabulary words that one can accurately translate, paying particular attention to each stage in language acquisition is imperative. In addition to vocabulary knowledge, language acquisition involves the study and gradual mastery of intonation, a language's dialects—if applicable— and the various nuances in a language regarding word use, expression, and cultural contexts. With time, effort, patience, and effective instructional approaches, both students and educators will begin to see progress in language acquisition.

*Second language acquisition* does not happen overnight. When educators take the time to study each stage and implement a variety of effective instructional approaches, progress and transition from one stage to the next will undoubtedly be less cumbersome and more consistent. In the early stages of language acquisition, children are often silently observing their new language environment. At these early stages, listening comprehension should be emphasized with the use of read alouds, music, and visual aids. Educators should be mindful of their vocabulary usage by consciously choosing to speak slowly and to use shorter, less complex vocabulary. Modeling during these beginning stages is also very effective. If the educator has instructed the class to open a book for instance, they can open a book as a

visual guide. If it is time to line up, the educator can verbally state the instruction and then walk to the door to begin the line.

During the *pre-production stage*, educators and classmates may assist ELLs by restating words or sentences that were uttered incorrectly, instead of pointing out errors. When modeling the correct language usage instead of pointing out errors, ELL learners may be less intimidated to practice their new language.

As students progress into the *early production stage*, they will benefit from exercises that challenge them to produce simple words and sentences with the assistance of visual cues. The educator should ask students to point to various pictures or symbols and produce words or sentences to describe the images they see. At the early production and speech emergent stages, ELL students are now ready to answer more diverse questions as they begin to develop a more complex vocabulary. Working in heterogeneous pairs and small groups with native speakers will help ELL students develop a more advanced vocabulary.

At the *beginning and intermediate fluency stages*, ELLs may be asked questions that require more advanced cognitive skills. Asking for opinions on a certain subject or requiring students to brainstorm and find ways to explain a given phenomenon are other ways to strengthen language proficiency and increase vocabulary.

When a child reaches the *advanced fluency stage*, he or she will be confident in social and academic language environments. This is an opportune time to introduce and/or increase his or her awareness of idiomatic expressions and language nuances.

*World-Class Instructional Design and Assessment (WIDA)* is a consortium of various departments of education throughout the United States that design and implement proficiency standards and assessments for English language learners and Spanish language learners. Primarily focusing on listening, speaking, reading, and writing, WIDA has designed and implemented English language development standards and offers professional development for educators, as well as educational research on

instructional best practices. The five English language proficiency standards according to WIDA are as follows:

**English Language Proficiency Standards—WIDA**

1. Within a school environment, ELL students require communication skills for both social and instructional purposes.

2. Effective communication involving information, ideas, and concepts are necessary for ELL students to be academically successful in the area of Language Arts.

3. Effective communication involving information, ideas, and concepts are necessary for ELL students to be academically successful in the area of Mathematics.

4. Effective communication involving information, ideas, and concepts are necessary for ELL students to be academically successful in the area of Science.

5. Effective communication involving information, ideas, and concepts are necessary for ELL students to be academically successful in the area of Social Studies.

According to WIDA, mastering the understanding, interpretation, and application of the four language domains—listening, speaking, reading, and writing—is essential for language proficiency. Listening requires ELL students to be able to process, understand, interpret, and evaluate spoken language. Speaking proficiently allows ELL students to communicate their thoughts, opinions, and desires orally in a variety of situations and for a variety of audiences. The ability to read fluently involves the processing, understanding, interpreting, and evaluating of written language with a high level of accuracy, and writing proficiency allows ELL students to engage actively in written communication across a multitude of disciplines and for a variety of purposes.

Since language acquisition involves the ELL students, their families, their classmates, educators, principals and administrators, as well as test and curriculum developers, WIDA strives to ensure that the English Language Proficiency Standards reflect both the social and academic areas of language development.

## Visual and Oral Elements

Depending on home life and first language acquisition, children generally enter the primary years of school with a basic foundation of oral development as well as basic phonemic awareness. It is imperative to a young child's continued success in language development that educators provide students with language-rich lessons and activities throughout the instructional day.

### Visual Instructional Techniques

Studies continue to show a strong correlation between language development and the use of visual aids. From the primary years of education through the post-secondary years, the use of visual aids as a way to enhance reading comprehension has proven to be very effective. In the primary grades, picture books provide students with visual cues that help them to decode unknown words and strengthen reading comprehension. Visual aids support and clarify meaning, helping to make the learning and reading process more enjoyable and more interactive. When educators engage the students in a *picture walk*, skimming through picture books prior to reading, children become more motivated to read. Even reluctant readers, struggling readers, and English language learners are more apt to pick up a picture book and attempt to read it from cover to cover, enjoying the graphics and using them as powerful clues to the text's overall meaning.

Graphic novels are also becoming a popular addition to classroom and school libraries. With a structural approach that is similar to comic books, graphic novels have a strong appeal to children in the middle school years, teen years, and beyond. The visual images within graphic novels help children to make immediate connections to a story's plot and help them to understand potentially more challenging information.

As a universal learning tool, visual aids help all learners to comprehend the meaning behind the words and strengthen their ability to retain information over a longer period of time.

## Oral Instructional Techniques

When children are just learning to read, they benefit greatly from shared reading and oral reading experiences. Having a teacher or a classmate read a book aloud helps emergent readers connect their phonemic awareness skills to a growing understanding and application of print awareness. This will begin to form the foundation for more advanced reading skills in later years.

Oral reading also helps children strengthen their use of vocabulary and advances their vocabulary inventory. Educators and more advanced readers who model oral reading fluency—including rate, accuracy, and prosody—demonstrate to young readers that the process of reading is highly interactive and meaningful. Educators who spend significant time engaging in classroom discussions and asking and answering questions help children develop social interaction skills, listening comprehension skills, and oral communication skills. When early and intensive instruction focuses on oral language development, educators set the groundwork for future reading success.

## Oral and Visual Instructional Techniques

Multimedia presentations, such as PowerPoint or SlideShare, have been traditionally most effective at the higher education levels. However, as young children are more and more exposed to a world of technology, educators at the primary years are beginning to employ multimedia presentations in the classroom.

If carefully planned out, multimedia presentations can be used to enhance comprehension on virtually any subject. Using powerful graphic imagery that is directly relevant to the topic—coupled with effective textual language or audio—has been particularly effective in a growing number of classrooms.

Presenting students with the challenge of creating their own multimedia presentations can also be very rewarding for educators and students alike. Either independently, in pairs, or in groups, children take the learning process into their own hands with the opportunity to demonstrate the knowledge of a given subject by employing relevant written text and graphics.

# *Phonics, Word Analysis, Spelling, and Fluency*

## Phonics and Word Analysis

*Phonics* is the study of sound-letter relationships in alphabetic writing systems, such as the English language, and it is paramount to a child's future ability to read and write. Phonics helps children

recognize and identify letter symbols and translate these symbols into their corresponding sound units, phonemes. The study of phonics concerns itself with the *Alphabetic Principle*—the systematic relationships that exist between letters and sounds—as well as with *Phonemic Awareness*—the understanding that letters correspond with distinct sounds and that there are specific rules governing the placement of letters in the English language.

As children become more familiar with recognizing the names and shapes of each letter, called *graphemes*, they begin to verbally practice their corresponding sounds—the phonemes. Although this sounds straightforward, it can pose significant challenges to both the children and teachers.

For example, when children learn that the letter *y* is pronounced /wigh/, but that it can make other various sounds, including /ee/, /i/, and /igh/—depending on letter placement—it may take repeated practice in order for children to pronounce and read this one letter accurately. Some examples would be the words, *happy, gym,* and *cry.* Although each word contains the same vowel, *y*, the placement of the *y* in each word differs, which affects the letter's pronunciation.

For this reason, there is an ongoing debate in literacy circles regarding the appropriate instructional approach for teaching phonics. Should educators teach letter shapes with their corresponding names or letter shapes with their corresponding sound or sounds? Is it possible to combine instruction to include shapes, names, and sounds, or should each of these skills be taught in isolation with a cumulative approach—shape, sound/s, and name? Some experts believe that when children are introduced to letter names and shapes in isolation of their corresponding sounds, children can become quickly confused, which can delay reading acquisition. Therefore, the answer to what approach to take lies with a keen understanding of a student's background knowledge in English and each child's specific needs. In order to create effective phonics instruction and help students strengthen literacy development, it is strongly suggested that educators are sensitive and aware of these unique challenges to English language acquisition.

It is widely accepted that letter-sound relationships are best taught systematically, introducing one relationship at a time and gradually increasing in complexity. Effective instruction in the initial stages of phonics awareness involves explicit introduction of the most important and the most frequently used letter-sound relationships. For instance, short vowels should be introduced and practiced ahead of long vowels, and lowercase letters should be introduced ahead of uppercase as they occur the most often. Letters that frequently appear in simple words, such as /a/, /m/, and /t/ would be logical starting points.

The following guide offers an introduction of phonics instruction:

| Introduction | Examples |
|---|---|
| Initial consonants | s, t, m, n, p |
| Short vowel and consonant | -it, -in, -at, -an |
| Consonant blends | -st, -bl, -dr |
| Digraphs | -th, -ph, -sh, -ch |
| Long vowels | ear, eat, oar, oat |
| Final (silent) e | site, mine, lane |
| Variant vowels and diphthongs | -au, -oo, -ow, -ou, -oi |
| Silent letters and inflectional endings | -kn, -gn, -wr, es, s |

Effective phonics instruction begins with focusing on the overall literacy experiences of the students and connecting these experiences to further their literacy development. Best practices in teaching will work to establish a student's prior phonics knowledge, if there is any at all. Educators can differentiate their instruction based on their students' unique needs and background knowledge of phonics. Creating phonics activities that ensure students are actively engaged and motivated is key to overall success in literacy development.

Once children have mastered the relationship that exists between the names, shapes, sounds of letters, and letter combinations, educators may begin a more implicit instructional approach by incorporating the children's current phonics awareness with simple basal readers that focus on basic monosyllabic words. Grouping monosyllabic words according to their initial sounds continues to be an effective approach to instruction as the students advance in their understanding and application of phonics. When educators combine or further this practice with that of identifying the names of the initial letters in the words, children are likely to have more success with overall literacy development. A word wall with simple consonant-vowel-consonant words in alphabetical order acts as a visual reference to help strengthen a child's literacy development:

**Word Wall**

| A | B | C |
|---|---|---|
| add | ball | car |
| age | bean | clean |
| ant | black | cub |

At this stage, educators begin laying the foundation for reading readiness. Children begin listening to others read and start to recognize familiar sounds within the words being read. They independently practice sounding out words and will soon learn how to independently segment, blend, and manipulate the individual sounds in each newly acquired word.

When a child demonstrates phonological awareness and a clear understanding of how phonics works, they are ready to further their literacy development with *word analysis*. Word analysis is an effective study that helps students acquire new vocabulary. *Morphemes* are when words are broken down into their smallest units of meaning. Each morpheme within words carry specific meanings, therefore adding to children's understanding of entire words. When children begin to recognize key morphemes— especially prefixes and suffixes—they are beginning to demonstrate word analysis skills, which is a critical foundation in literacy development.

Word analysis helps children to read and comprehend complex reading materials, including informational texts. It is essential for vocabulary development. Word analysis skills also help children clarify the meaning of unknown words, figurative language, word relationships, and nuances in word meaning with the use of context clues.

Some effective instructional strategies to teach word analysis skills include Universal Design for Learning (UDL), studying words according to a subject theme, using diagrams and graphic organizers, and pre-teaching and reviewing new vocabulary on a regular basis. UDL involves the modeling of how to analyze new words by breaking them down into their individual morphemes and studying each morpheme separately. Once each morpheme in a given word has been identified and defined, students put the morphemes back together in order to understand the word in its entirety. The following is a word analysis study of the word *astronaut*:

| Word | Morpheme 1 | Morpheme 2 | Word Meaning |
|---|---|---|---|
| astronaut | astro—Greek origin, roughly translates to anything relating to the stars and outer space | naut—Greek origin, roughly translates to "sailor" | a sailor of outer space |

Studying words according to a shared theme is another effective word analysis strategy. For instance, when studying mathematics, educators may focus on words that contain the same prefix, such as *kilometer*, *kilogram*, and *kilowatt*. Common suffixes in science include *microscope*, *telescope*, and *macroscope*.

Diagrams and graphic organizers provide students with visual clues to contrast and compare word meanings. From organizational charts and mind maps to Venn diagrams and more, visual aids help students readily see and analyze the similarities and differences in various word meanings.

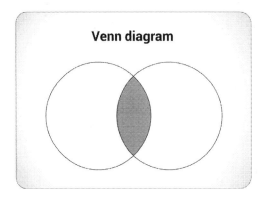

With the introduction to new topics of discussion or a new theme to any subject area, it is likely that there will also be an introduction to new, unfamiliar words. Both educators and students will benefit from a formal introduction to these new words prior to the lesson. Pre-teaching new vocabulary increases vocabulary acquisition and allows children to become comfortable and familiar with new terms ahead of the lesson. Pre-teaching new vocabulary has also been shown to reduce unnecessary stress and time that would otherwise be taken to stop lessons in order to explain unfamiliar words.

## Letter-Sound Correspondences

When children begin to learn the various letter-sound correspondences, their phonemic awareness begins to overlap with their awareness of orthography and reading. One of the widely accepted strategies to employ when introducing children to letter-sound correspondences is to begin with those correspondences that occur the most frequently in simple English words. In an effort to help build confidence in young learners, educators are encouraged to introduce only a few letter-sound combinations at a time and provide ample opportunities for practice and review before introducing new combinations. Although there is no formally established order for the introduction of letter-sound correspondences, educators are encouraged to consider the following general guidelines, but they should also keep in mind the needs, experiences, and current literacy levels of the students. The following is intended as a general guide only:

| | | | | |
|---|---|---|---|---|
| 1. a | 6. n | 11. g | 16. l | 21. x |
| 2. m | 7. c | 12. h | 17. e | 22. v |
| 3. t | 8. d | 13. i | 18. r | 23. y |
| 4. p | 9. u | 14. f | 19. w | 24. z |
| 5. o | 10. s | 15. b | 20. k | 25. j |
| | | | | 26. q |

As a generally accepted rule, short vowels should be introduced ahead of long vowels, and uppercase letters should be mastered before the introduction of their lowercase counterparts.

Spelling conventions in the English language are primarily concerned with three areas: mechanics, usage, and sentence formation.

## Mechanics

For primary students who are just beginning to master the alphabetic principle, educators should first concentrate on proper letter formation, the spelling of high-frequency words and sight words, and offer classroom discussions to promote the sharing of ideas. When children begin to write in sentences to share their thoughts and feelings in print, educators may consider the introduction of an author's chair, in which students read their writing out loud to their classmates.

Although the phonetic spelling or invented spelling that primary students employ in these early stages may not be the conventional spelling of certain words, it allows primary students to practice the art and flow of writing. It works to build their confidence in the writing process. This is not the time for educators to correct spelling, punctuation, or capitalization errors as young learners may quickly lose interest in writing and may lose self-confidence.

One strategy to employ early on to help students with proper spelling is to ensure there is an easily accessible and updated word wall that employs high-frequency words and sight words. Students should be encouraged to refer to the word wall while they write.

## Usage

Usage concerns itself with word order, verb tense, and subject-verb agreement among other areas. As primary children often have a basic knowledge of how to use oral language effectively in order to communicate, this area of spelling conventions may require less initial attention than the mechanics of spelling. During read-aloud and shared reading activities, educators may wish to point out punctuation marks found in print, model how to read these punctuation marks, and periodically discuss their importance in the reading and writing process.

When children begin to engage in writing exercises, educators may wish to prompt self-editing skills by asking if each sentence begins with a capital and ends with a period, question mark, or exclamation point.

## Sentence Formation

Verbs, nouns, adverbs, and adjectives all play significant roles in the writing process. However, for primary students, these concepts are fairly complex to understand. One instruction approach that may prove effective is to categorize a number of simple verbs, nouns, adverbs, and adjectives on index cards by color coordination. Educators can then ask one child to choose a noun card and another student to choose a verb card. The children can then face the class and read their words starting with the noun and then the verb. The students can even try reading the verb first followed by the noun. A class discussion can follow, analyzing whether or not the sentences made sense and what words might need to be added to give the sentence more meaning.

## Distinguishing High-Frequency Sight Words from Decodable Words

Beginning readers enter primary school years with many challenges involving literacy development. Tackling the alphabetic principle and phonemic awareness helps children to recognize that specific sounds are usually comprised of specific letters, or a combination thereof, and that each letter or combination of letters carries a specific sound. However, these young readers are also faced with the challenge of sight word mastery. *Sight words* do not necessarily follow the alphabetic principle and appear quite often in primary reading material. Some sight words are decodable, but many are not, which requires the additional challenge of memorizing correct spelling. Some of these non-decodable sight words include words such as *who, the, he, does,* and so on. There are approximately one hundred sight words that appear throughout primary texts.

The goal for primary teachers is to help emergent readers to recognize these sight words automatically, in order to help strengthen reading fluency. One effective instructional approach is to provide children daily opportunities to practice sight words in meaningful contexts and to establish a clearly visible, large print word wall that children can freely access throughout the day. Dr. Edward William Dolch was a well-known and respected children's author and professor who, in the late 1940s, published a list of sight words he believed appeared most frequently in children's literature for grades kindergarten through second grade. Now known as the Dolch Word List, these sight words are still widely used in primary classrooms throughout the United States. Organized by grade and frequency, the Dolch Word List consists of 220 words in total, with the first one hundred known as the "Dolch 100 List." Dr. Edward Fry, a university professor, author, and expert in the field of reading, published another commonly used high-frequency word list approximately a decade later. Although similar in many ways to the Dolch List, the Fry Word List primarily focuses on sight words that appear most frequently in reading material for third to ninth grade. Other high-frequency word lists now exist, but the Dolch and Fry word lists are still widely used in today's elementary classrooms. The debate, however, is whether to teach high-frequency sight words in isolation or as part of the integrated phonics program.

Unlike many sight words, *decodable words* follow the rules of phonics and are spelled phonetically. They are spelled precisely the way they sound—as in words like *dad* and *sit*. When a child has mastered his or her phonics skills, these decodable words can also be easily mastered with continued opportunities to practice reading. Activities involving segmenting and blending decodable words also help to strengthen a child's decoding skills. Some educators will find that it is beneficial to integrate lessons involving decodable words and high-frequency sight words, while others may see a need to keep these lessons separate until children have demonstrated mastery or near mastery of phonemic awareness. Some activities that encourage the memorization of sight words and strengthen decoding skills involve the use of flash cards, phonemic awareness games, air writing, and card games, such as *Bingo* and *Go Fish*.

Both Dolch and Fry word lists are organized according to frequency and grade level. It is widely accepted that educators follow a cumulative approach to reading instruction, introducing high-frequency sight words that are also phonetically decodable. Should words appear in the lesson that are not phonetically decodable, educators may wish to use this as an opportunity to evaluate the children's phonemic awareness skills and determine whether or not students are ready for lessons that integrate non-decodable sight words. For instance, an educator might challenge a student to study the parts of the non-decodable sight word by asking whether or not there are parts of the word that are phonetically decodable and parts that are not. This approach gives students the opportunity for guided word study and acts as a bridge between phonemic awareness skills and sight word memorization.

Determining what lists of words to introduce to students varies greatly and depends on an initial and ongoing spelling assessment of each child to determine his or her current spelling and reading levels. Effective instructional approaches also involve the intentional selection of words that demonstrate a specific spelling pattern, followed by multiple opportunities to read, spell, segment, and blend these word families. Students will benefit the greatest with ongoing formative and summative assessments of their decoding skills as well as their ability to apply their word knowledge to and memorize non-decodable sight words.

With the reinforcement of high-frequency word walls, daily opportunities to read, write, and engage in meaningful word games and activities, children will gradually begin to develop their reading and spelling skills and learn to become more fluent and capable readers.

## Roots and Affixes to Decode Unfamiliar Words

The study of *morphology* concerns itself with the segmenting of words into their respective affixes and roots. It also involves the studying of a word's origins. Children who study morphology expand their vocabulary knowledge as they begin to understand that words are connected by similar spelling patterns and similar meaning.

*Affixes* are parts of words that are bound to the root word either in front, following, or in the middle of the word itself. Since affixes do contain meanings, they are considered morphemes, but they are unable to exist without being attached to the root words.

*Prefixes* are affixes that appear in front of root words, such as *dis*appear or *un*able. Generally speaking, prefixes denote negation, direction, or intensity. For example, in the word *disappear*, the prefix *dis* means *not* or *opposite of*. Therefore, *disappear* can be defined as *to not appear*. In the word *inject*, the prefix *in* refers to *inside* or *towards*, and in the word *excruciate*, the *ex* works as an intensifier referring to the pain as being *thorough*.

*Suffixes* are affixes that appear at the end of root words. There are two types of suffixes: inflectional and derivational. *Inflectional suffixes* can change the number, tense, or degree of the word, such as the word *loud* changing to *loudest*. *Derivational suffixes* change the parts of speech of a given word. The word *slow* functions as an adjective in this sentence: *The slow turtle walks*. When the suffix *-ly* is added to the end of *slow*, the part of speech is automatically changed to an adverb: *The turtle walks slowly*.

*Infixes*—affixes that appear in the middle of a word—are the least conventional and most rare of all affixes. An example is the word *cupful*. This consists of the root word, *cup*, and the suffix, *-ful*. In order to pluralize this word, an *s* would need to be strategically placed directly following the letter *p* to form *cupsful*. The *s* acts as an infix, inserting itself and its meaning in the middle of the word.

*Root words* are referred to as free morphemes that can stand alone and carry an independent meaning without the need of any affixes. Some examples are the root words *help*, *kind*, and *shy*, which clearly hold their own meaning, but can also be attached to affixes, as in *helpful*, *unkind*, and *shyness*.

When students are invited to become word detectives, the study of root words and affixes is of prime importance. There are several instructional approaches to the study of root words and affixes, including a multi-sensory guided approach in which children can physically pull apart the affixes to be left with the root word and then manipulate the root word by playing with a variety of suffixes and prefixes. The following table begins with the original word containing both a prefix and suffix. The word is pulled

apart into its individual components—root, prefix, and suffix. Then, it is given a new prefix and suffix to form a new word, carrying a completely new meaning:

| Original Word | Root Word | Prefix | Suffix | New Prefix | New Suffix | New Word |
|---|---|---|---|---|---|---|
| inactive | act | in | ive | de | ate | deactivate |
| disbelieving | believe | dis | ing | un | able | unbelievable |
| unbearable | bear | un | able | for | ing | forbearing |

Effective instruction for root, prefix, and suffix study should involve the active exploration of words, with ample opportunity for children to read the words in meaningful context. Typically, a formal study of root words and affixes is introduced by the 4th grade, but it may be introduced earlier, depending on the students' understanding of basic phonics and spelling patterns. It is important for educators to keep in mind that new vocabulary terms, verb forms, plurals, and compound words may present a challenge for some students.

A formal study of root words, prefixes, and suffixes strengthens a child's knowledge of word meanings, expands vocabulary knowledge, and advances his or her understanding and application of various spelling patterns. Children will learn more about how affixes affect the spelling of the root word and can completely alter its meaning, which ultimately strengthens their ability to read, write, and spell accurately and effectively. As children become familiar with various affixes, they will begin to decipher the meaning of unfamiliar words that share the same affixes and roots.

## Common Phonics and Word-Recognition Approaches for ELLs

Phonics instruction and word-recognition exercises involve a number of skills, including print awareness, alphabetic knowledge, phonological and phonemic awareness, the alphabetic principle, decoding, the memorization of high-frequency words, and reading practice. As language acquisition is highly complex, there seems to be some debate in the educational field regarding the best instructional approaches for ELL students. Some educators argue that phonics should be taught in isolation and not in context, while others stress the need for a more integrated approach. When faced with what instructional approach to implement, educators who take the time to learn about each child's home language, literacy development, and exposure to the English language will be in the best position to decide on whether a student would benefit from an isolated phonics approach or one that is more integrated. The following are the three different instructional approaches to phonics:

### Synthetic Phonics
Educators implement an explicit approach, teaching individual letter-sound correspondence and helping students to blend letters into words.

### Embedded Phonics
Educators teach letter-sound correspondence during the reading of a text.

### Analogy-Based Phonics
Educators teach students to use parts of words that they already know to help decode words that they don't know. Analogy-Based phonics involves the use of story time, tutoring in small groups, and various

language-based activities. Educators share various books and stories with decodable words with students and provide opportunities for children to spell words and write simple sentences with letter-sound correspondence.

The amount of time allotted for phonics and word recognition instruction varies greatly from classroom to classroom. Educators who pay particular attention to the ages of the ELL students and their current level of English language proficiency will be in the best position to decide on an appropriate approach to phonics instruction. However, generally speaking, younger ELL students in the primary grades will benefit from explicit practice with phonemic awareness and the alphabetic principle. Exposure to print awareness will increase in complexity as the child progresses in his or her understanding and application of phonemic awareness skills. Decoding practice, exposure to word families, spelling patterns, onsets and rimes, and structural analysis—including affixes and root words—should be gradually introduced as the child becomes more able to read simple words and simple sentences independently.

When working with ELL students, educators must be sensitive to each child's background knowledge, home language, and experiences involving literacy. In order to become proficient in the English language, ELL students must develop a clear understanding of the relationship that exists between letters and sounds in the English alphabetic system, and this may be in complete opposition to the rules they have already mastered in their home language. For example, some languages use the same or similar alphabet as English, but some of the phonemes might be pronounced differently, causing confusion. The English language may also have letter combinations that do not exist in the student's home language, adding to the confusion. Complicating matters even further, some languages do not utilize an alphabetic writing system, such as the Chinese language, which is *logographic*, relying on characters that represent a word or idea, rather than relying on letters to produce a sound. Therefore, a formal study of phonics is critical to ELL students' literacy development.

One approach for educators to consider is the highlighting of similarities and differences between the student's home language and that of English. For instance, many *cognates* exist between English and Spanish that can act as a bridge to strengthen a child's English language acquisition. Since cognates share the same or similar meaning, spelling, and pronunciation in two different languages, ELL students can quickly add these new words to their vocabulary inventory. Some effective approaches to integrate cognate awareness into lessons include read alouds, student reading activities, and word sorts.

As children read aloud, ELL students are encouraged to raise their hand when they think they've come across a cognate. The reading can momentarily stop while the class discusses the similarities and differences between the pronunciation, spelling, and meaning of each cognate. During a student reading activity, ELL students are encouraged to locate two, three, or more cognates they encounter in their reading and to write them down in their notebooks. These cognates can then be added to the classroom's word wall and further explored. In pairs, students can be given a number of cards with Spanish and English cognates. The students then sort the cards appropriately and discuss their meaning, spelling, and pronunciation. These approaches not only build vocabulary knowledge and confidence for ELL students by actively including their home language in lessons, but they also help to build social bonds in the classroom. Since language acquisition is also very social, when children develop and strengthen positive friendships within and outside the classroom, language acquisition will likewise develop and strengthen. Other effective classroom approaches to help ELL students with phonics and word-recognition skills include the use of word walls and posters throughout the classroom.

As children progress with their phonemic awareness skills, educators may introduce word studies by helping children classify and sort words according to the same or similar spelling patterns. Word study increases children's vocabulary and acts as a bridge from reading to writing as children transfer their newly-acquired words into print. Introducing children to a variety of reading and writing genres and formats will also help to strengthen their reading and writing skills. For example, learning to follow recipes provides children with opportunities to read and engage in hands-on activities to demonstrate their understanding by following a recipe's steps. Personal journals continue to be an effective practice that stimulates creative writing and helps children to express their thoughts and opinions in writing, without worrying too much about grammar, spelling, and punctuation. Personal journals can also be used as reading practice as children pick and choose sections to read aloud to the entire class, in pairs, or in small groups.

It is important for educators to recognize that some written languages are not read from left to right, and some are not even read from top to bottom. Therefore, it is also important for educators to teach print conventions and book awareness, including the direction in which the words in books are read and how to handle and hold a book. These lessons can be taught explicitly or may be simply modeled by the educator during shared reading time.

| Syllabication Patterns | Examples |
| --- | --- |
| 1. Open—Syllables that stand by themselves, or that have a single vowel at the end of the syllable | he, my, apron |
| 2. Closed—Syllables containing short vowel sounds that are spelled with a single vowel letter and end with one or more consonants | am, dog, rabbit |
| 3. Vowel + Consonant + e—Syllables that contain one-letter long vowels, followed by one consonant and a silent e | base, nose, shake |
| 4. Vowel Team—Comprised of two, three, or four letters that create long vowels, short vowels, or diphthongs | thieves, boil, suit |
| 5. R-Controlled—Vowels that are followed by the letter r, with the r controlling the vowel's pronunciation | bird, word, herd |
| 6. Consonant + le—Found exclusively at the end of words in which the vowel or combination of vowels is followed by a consonant, and the consonant is followed by an le | tackle, title, puzzle |

A *syllable* is defined as a unit of spoken language that consists of one vowel sound that may or may not be surrounded by consonants. Syllables form part of a word or may even form the entire word itself. There are both *monosyllabic words* that contain only one syllable, such as the word *sit*, and *polysyllabic words* containing more than one syllable, such as the words *today* or *yesterday*.

Generally speaking, there are six *syllable-spelling conventions* in the English language. Learning these conventions will help to strengthen a student's spelling and pronunciation accuracy. The study of

syllables also helps to strengthen their literacy development in many other ways. It allows students to chunk longer words into manageable parts, instead of simply guessing at the word or ignoring it altogether, thereby strengthening reading fluency. Children who are exposed to syllable study will also have a better understanding of short and long vowel sounds, diphthongs and consonant blends, r-controlled vowels, prefixes, suffixes, and compound words.

*Syllabication* is the process of separating a word into its individual syllables. It is an essential skill in learning how to accurately pronounce words. Syllabication involves learning various syllabic patterns and rules in the English language; therefore, repeated practice is best. Since every syllable has one vowel sound, the study of syllabication must be preceded with a firm understanding of how English vowel sounds operate. For instance, short vowels sound much different than long vowels, and some vowel sounds are formed using more than one vowel, as in the sounds *ou* or *oi*.

To help children master syllabication, educators will need to introduce and practice the various *syllabication patterns*:

| Rule/Pattern | Examples |
| --- | --- |
| 1. Monosyllabic words are never divided. | house, car, eat, run |
| 2. Compound words are divided between the individual words that make up the compound word. | base/ment; up/stairs; out/side |
| 3. Divide a word directly after its prefix. | pre/view; de/text; un/seen |
| 4. Divide a word directly before its suffix. | ac/tion; trac/tion |
| 5. If a word ends in a consonant + le, divide directly before this consonant. | tur/tle; cy/cle |
| 6. If there are two consonants directly in the middle of the word, divide between the consonants. | rab/bit; sis/ter |
| 7. Keep consonant blends and digraphs together. | fast/ing; bun/ches |
| 8. In words containing the letter combinations ck or the letter x, syllables are generally divided directly before the ck or the x. | ni/ckel; ta/xi |
| 9. If a single consonant is positioned between two vowels and the first vowel is short, divide directly after the consonant. | nev/er; hab/it |
| 10. If a single consonant is positioned between two vowels and the first vowel is long, divide directly before the consonant. | ma/jor; lat/er; |
| 11. When two vowels in a word make individual sounds, divide between the two vowels. | ri/ot; li/on |

While these syllabication patterns are helpful in order to gain a clearer understanding of how syllables operate, they are by no means exhaustive. As children gradually strengthen their awareness and application of syllables, educators may introduce them to more complex patterns.

## Fluency

*Reading fluency* has been traditionally defined as a student's ability to read accurately, quickly, and with appropriate expression. This definition only accounts for reading aloud, however, so it has been expanded to include silent reading. *Silent reading fluency* is the ability to read more than one word at a time without having to vocalize one's reading. If readers are able to derive the accurate meaning and

message from a reading passage without involving too much labor of reading mechanics, they are said to be reading with fluency. Reading fluency is automatic, with less attention and effort spent on decoding, allowing the reader to concentrate fully on reading comprehension. When a reader reaches the fluency stage, reading becomes much more of an enjoyable activity.

Generally, fluent readers do not require the need to reread passages for understanding and have developed a fairly large inventory of sight-word vocabulary. Fluent readers are usually able to self-correct and employ a number of reading strategies. Signs that a child is having difficulty with reading fluency include reading slowly, focusing on only one word at a time, needing to reread the passage for understanding, and stopping often to decipher and decode unknown words. There are three main focus areas that relate to reading fluency: accuracy, rate, and prosody. When children read accurately with steady, consistent speed and appropriate expression, reading comprehension is likely to strengthen.

Areas of Fluency:

## Accuracy
Accuracy refers to the frequency of pronunciation errors a student might make when reading. When students make frequent pronunciation errors while reading, guess at the pronunciation of unknown words, or ignore words altogether, they are showing signs of *dysfluency*. Reading accurately requires the reader to read words correctly with minimal to no errors. When errors do occur, readers who read with accuracy are generally able to self-correct and continue reading without interrupting the flow of the reading.

## Rate
Rate refers to a student's ability to recognize words automatically without having to spend any time on decoding them. This manifests in their ability to read texts at a steady and consistent rate. Both accurate reading and reading at a consistent rate greatly strengthen a reader's overall reading comprehension.

## Prosody
Prosody refers to appropriate expression when reading—showing emotions, such as excitement, panic, or sorrow that accurately matches the intended emotions of the text. Readers may be able to read texts with accuracy and at a steady and consistent rate, but if they are unable to vocalize any expression in their reading or if the expression used does not match the intended expression of the text, their overall comprehension will be negatively affected. Readers who engage in an emotional or personal level with the text will experience greater reading comprehension and fluency.

## Impact of Fluency on Comprehension

In reading fluency, specific instructional strategies will help strengthen a student's ability to read text accurately, at a consistent rate, and with appropriate expression, and they will also help to strengthen reading comprehension. When students experience dysfluency in their reading, their overall comprehension will be negatively impacted. With an inability to make connections in their reading, children are unable to grasp the meaning in the text. When children are more focused on decoding individual words rather than on comprehending the text's message, much of their cognitive efforts are spent on deciphering the pronunciation of individual words, with little left to devote to comprehension of the text itself.

As children's reading fluency strengthens, they are able to interact on a much higher level with a variety of texts. It is important for educators to recognize that reading fluency acts as a bridge to reading

comprehension and that time devoted to the individual components of reading fluency benefits a child's overall reading comprehension.

# *Reading Comprehension and Vocabulary*

## Promoting Students' Comprehension of Informational Text and Literature

### Promoting Literacy Development

It is widely accepted that the more classroom opportunities a child has for listening, speaking, reading, and writing, the more these skills will strengthen. Educators, who frequently read to emergent readers using exaggerated pauses, inflections, tones, and pronunciation, report encouraging signs of progress in student literacy development and independent reading skills.

### *Directed Reading-Thinking Activities*

Prior to the introduction of a challenging text, educators may spend time with the class predicting what the text might be about. By paying attention to the features of the book or text, students can begin to formulate ideas about the overall content. Educators may try to extend this discussion, prompting children to consider what the setting of the book or written piece might be, what events might take place, and what types of characters they might encounter. When an educator focuses on prediction skills prior to reading, children begin to strengthen their ability to connect literature to real life.

After reading, educators may begin another class discussion, prompting children to consider whether their predictions were accurate and why or why not this was so. For instance, an educator may point out that a child's own life experiences may have prompted her to predict a certain outcome. When children relate literature to their own lives in this way, reading becomes a more enjoyable and meaningful activity. Post-reading activities may also involve small groups of children acting out various scenes or retelling the story in their own words, which also helps the educator to assess children's overall comprehension. Post-reading activities should include discussions regarding various literary elements such as cause and effect or the author's points of view.

### *Monitoring Comprehension*

Self-monitoring one's comprehension is a valuable lifelong skill for students to learn. Teaching self-monitoring takes advantage of students' natural ability to recognize when they understand the reading and when they do not. Students will need to learn to:

- Identify exactly the part of the text where the difficulty occurs
- Identify the specific problem and restate the difficult text in their own words
- Reread previous portions of the text to gain clues about the problematic piece
- Scan future portions of the text for information that helps resolve the question

### *Metacognition*

Skilled readers have learned to think about thinking. This is called metacognition. Using metacognitive strategies is a skill that gives students control over their learning while they read and may involve the use strategies such as:

- Identifying purpose for reading the selection
- Previewing the text
- Matching their reading speed to the challenge level of the selection

- Asking themselves comprehension questions
- Resolving comprehension problems independently or with help
- Checking themselves for understanding after reading the selection

## KWL Activities

Good reading teachers know how to help students activate their prior knowledge and draw from personal curiosity to set them up for the learning task. Students can create a KWL (Know/Want to know/Learned) chart to get ready for any unit of instruction. Teachers guide students to identify what they already know about a given topic. They then help them generate questions about the topic. After the instruction takes place, teachers help students analyze what they have learned.

## Comprehension of Informational Text

Informational text is written material that has the primary function of imparting information about a topic. It is often written by someone with expertise in the topic and directed at an audience that has less knowledge of the topic. Informational texts are written in a different fashion from storytelling or narrative texts. Typically, this type of text has several organizational and structural differences from narrative text. In informational texts, there are features such as charts, graphs, photographs, headings and subheadings, glossaries, indexes, bibliographies, or other guidance features. With the aid of technology, embedded hyperlinks and video content are also sometimes included. Informational material may be written to compare and contrast, be explanatory, link cause and effect, provide opinion, persuade the reader, or serve a number of other purposes. Finally, informational texts typically use a different style of language than narrative texts, which instead, focus more on storytelling. Historically, informational texts were not introduced until students were ready to read to learn versus still learning to read. However, research is now suggesting that informational text can be developmentally appropriate for children at a much younger age.

One very effective strategy for increasing comprehension of informational text is *reciprocal teaching*. Reciprocal teaching is a method of small group teaching that relies on students assuming different roles to practice four reading strategies particularly helpful for readers of informational texts. Predicting, summarizing, questioning, and clarifying will lead students to understand and apply what they read. Skilled readers have acquired a set of techniques that make informational reading effective for them. They begin by previewing text selections and making educated guesses as to what the content will include. They then identify the purpose for reading the text and can explain why the content will be important to know. They are able to filter the reading selection to screen out the trivial points and focus on the most important facts. Using critical thinking skills, they monitor their own understanding of the information by asking themselves questions about what they have read. They use multiple methods to determine the meaning of unknown vocabulary. Finally, they can concisely and succinctly form an overall summary of what they have learned from the text.

## Predicting

Predicting requires thinking ahead and, after reading, verifying whether predictions were correct. This method engages students with the text and gets them to pay attention to details that tell them whether their predictions might be coming true. The goal is to help students learn to base their predictions on clues from the text. They should not only state what they predict but also be able to comment on the specifics of the text that lead them to make those predictions.

## Summarizing

Through summarizing, students learn to identify the main ideas and differentiate them from the less important information in the text. It helps them remember what they read and retell the central concepts in their own words. As students learn to break down larger chunks of information into more concise sentences, they use analytical thinking skills and hone their critical reading capabilities.

## Questioning Techniques

Questioning has immeasurable value in the reading process. Answering questions about a text gives purpose for reading to students and focuses them on reading to learn information. Similarly, generating questions about a text for others to answer enables a student to analyze what is important to learn in the text and glean summarizing skills. Keeping Bloom's Taxonomy in mind, teachers can scaffold students toward increased critical thinking capabilities. Bloom's Taxonomy shows the hierarchy of learning progressing through the following stages:

- Remembering
- Understanding
- Applying
- Analyzing
- Evaluating
- Creating

## Clarifying

This is the post-reading phase where students learn to clear up any misunderstandings and unanswered questions. Strategies for clarifying include defining any unknown words, rereading at a slower pace, reviewing previous segments of the text, referring to their summaries, and skimming future portions of the text.

## Comprehension of Literature

Comprehension of literature comes through teaching students about story structure and the complexities of literary elements that comprise a good tale. Comprehension is enhanced when students learn to identify and analyze the characters, settings, events, problems, themes, and resolutions that are found in the stories. Teachers should keep in mind the following concepts when teaching story structure:

- Narrative Strategies
- Flashback
- Point of View
- Characterization
- Figurative Language
- Mood
- Theme
- Style
- Making Inferences
- Author's Purpose
- Generating Questions
- Main Ideas

## Narrative Strategies

All narrative literature is centered on the plot of the story or the sequence of events that make the story happen. Authors use various narrative strategies to unfold their plot and make it grab the reader's attention. Writers give their stories action. Good authors are descriptive with their words. Narrative writers inspire readers to keep reading the story by adding an element of suspense. To help understand the characters and their relationships with one another, authors use dialogue between characters. The author may describe gestures and facial expressions to help develop the characters' personalities. These narrative techniques engage the reader, pull him or her into the story, and enhance the believability of the literature.

## Flashback

Sometimes an author needs to give the reader more information about a character or the story's events, but the information doesn't fit well into the story itself. In such situations, the author might introduce a flashback into the plot. A flashback is a scene set earlier than the main story.

## Point of View

Writers can choose the point of view of one character (first person), a narrator who gives the point of view (thoughts and feelings) of one or a few characters (third person limited), or from a narrator who gives the point of view of all the characters in the story (third person omniscient).

## Characterization

The writer wants the reader to be as connected as possible to the characters of the story. If the author directly makes comments about the personality of the character, it is called direct characterization. If instead, the author allows the reader to learn about the character naturally through the course of the story, it is called indirect characterization.

## Figurative Language

Figurative language is used when a writer wants to illustrate a point that is not literal in meaning. Phrases that mean something other than what they literally state are called figures of speech. Examples of these are metaphors, hyperboles, similes, etc.

## Mood

Authors use elements of literature to achieve a certain mood to their writing. The mood can be light and airy, comical, dark and oppressive, or any number of other emotions. The mood of a selection of literature will determine some of the meaning of the words and phrases.

## Theme

In any selection of literature, the author is trying to convey a main idea or central theme. Sometimes the writer explains the main point clearly, while at other times, the reader must use critical thinking and analysis to determine the underlying theme of the writing.

## Style

Each writer's own style is conveyed in his or her word choice, use of sentence structure, and the way punctuation adds to the story. The writer's style injects a certain personality, attitude, and voice into the writing.

## Making Inferences

When readers put together clues from the writing to "guess" that a particular idea is a fact, it is called making inferences. Making inferences helps read "between the lines" of a selection to derive meaning that is intended by the author but not explicitly written.

## Author's Purpose

There are endless reasons why authors might write a particular narrative piece to a certain audience. They might be simply trying to entertain readers, to enlighten them about a specific concept, to give information about historical or current events, to spark imagination, or to help readers resolve a problem.

## Generating Questions

Asking questions as a reader reads requires an interactive relationship with the text and can deepen understanding. The reader is constantly honing metacognitive skills as more and more questions are asked.

## Main Ideas

Typically, in a piece of narrative writing there are only a couple of ideas that the author is trying to convey to the reader. It is important to understand and discern the difference between a topic and a main idea. A topic might be "horses," but the main idea should be a complete sentence such as, "Racehorses run faster when they have a good relationship with the jockey."

## Integrating Knowledge and Ideas

Visual learning is a powerful tool for helping students integrate new ideas with their prior knowledge. Research shows that most students need to be able to see information to be able to learn it well.

## Graphic Organizers

One highly effective method of integrating knowledge and ideas is the use of graphic organizers. These may be sequencing charts, graphs, Venn diagrams, timelines, chain of events organizers, story maps, concept maps, mind maps, webs, outlines, or other visual tools for connecting concepts to facilitate understanding. This strategy helps students to examine, analyze, and summarize selections they have read and can be used individually or collaboratively in the classroom.

## Helping Students Identify and Evaluate Common Types of Text

### The Importance of Teaching Varied Types of Text

Reading is fundamental to learning. Reading nurtures imagination, critical thinking, communication skills, and social competence. Many children are drawn to the allure of reading and often their attention is captivated by a certain type of book or books about a particular personal interest. It is important to introduce them to an eclectic selection of text types. Cultural knowledge, a more intricate worldview, and a host of new vocabulary can be built through the experience of diverse literature. Reading a wide range of writing styles brings students into contact with many characters and lifestyles. Reading varied texts sparks different emotions in a child and teaches a variety of means of expression. In this way, children deepen social and emotional skills. In short, reading a wide variety of texts produces a well-rounded education and prepares children for their experience of the world.

## Literary Genre

Genre is a method of categorizing literature by form, content, style, and technique. When selections of literature share enough characteristics and literary elements, they are classified into the same genre. Genre is more than just a categorization system, though; genre identifies literature by its communicative purpose. Authors write to accomplish any of a variety of social purposes: to inform, to explain, to entertain, to persuade, to maintain relationships, and so on. All types of texts fall into one of the following five genres: fiction, nonfiction, poetry, drama, and folklore. Each of these has a variety of subgenres. A particular piece of writing may fall into more than one genre or subgenre.

## Fiction

Fiction is imaginative text that is invented by the author. Fiction is characterized by the following literary elements:

- *Characters* — the people, animals, aliens, or other living figures the story is about
- *Setting* — the location, surroundings, and time the story takes place in
- *Conflict* — a dilemma the characters face either internally or externally
- *Plot* — the sequence and the rise and fall of excitement in the action of a story
- *Resolution* — the solution to the conflict that is discovered as a result of the story
- *Point of View* — the lens through which the reader experiences the story
- *Theme* — the moral to the story or the message the author is sending to the reader

### Historical Fiction

Historical fiction is a story that occurs in the past and uses a realistic setting and authentic time period characters. Historical fiction usually has some historically accurate events mixed and balanced with invented plot and characters.

### Science Fiction

Science fiction is an invented story that occurs in the future or an alternate universe. It often deals with space, time travel, robots, or aliens, and highly advanced technology.

### Fantasy

Fantasy is a subgenre of fiction that involves magic or supernatural elements and/or takes place in an imaginary world. Examples include talking animals, superheroes rescuing the day, or characters taking on a mythical journey or quest.

### Mystery and Adventure

Mystery fiction is a story that involves a puzzle or crime to be solved by the main characters. The mystery is driven by suspense and foreshadowing. The reader must sift through clues and distractions to solve the puzzle with the protagonist. Adventure stories are driven by the risky or exciting action that happens in the plot.

### Realistic and Contemporary Fiction

Realistic fiction depends on the author portraying the world without speculation. The characters are ordinary, and the action could happen in real life. The conflict often involves growing up, family life, or learning to cope with some significant emotion or challenge.

## Non-Fiction Literature

Non-fiction literature is text that is true and accurate in detail. Nonfiction can cover virtually any topic in the natural world. Nonfiction writers conduct research and carefully organize facts before writing. Nonfiction has the following subgenres:

- Informational Text — This is text written to impart information to the reader. It may have literary elements such as charts, graphs, indexes, glossaries, or bibliographies.

- Persuasive Text —This is text that is meant to sway the reader to have a particular opinion or take a particular action.

- Biographies and Autobiographies — This is text that tells intimate details of someone's life. If an author writes the text about someone else, it is a biography. If the author writes it about himself or herself, it is an autobiography.

- Communicative text — This is text used to communicate with another person. This includes such texts as emails, formal and informal letters, and tweets. This content often consists of two-sided dialogue between people.

## Drama

Drama is any writing that is intended to be performed in front of an audience, such as plays, and TV and movie scripts. Dialogue and action are central to convey the author's theme.

- Comedy — Comedy is any drama designed to be funny or lighthearted.
- Tragedy — Tragedy is any drama designed to be serious or sad.

## Poetry

This is text that is written in verse and has a rhythmic cadence. It often involves descriptive imagery, rhyming stanzas, and beautiful mastery of language. It is often personal, emotional, and introspective. Poetry is often considered a work of art.

## Folklore

Folklore is literature that has been handed down from generation to generation by word of mouth. Folklore is not based in fact but in unsubstantiated beliefs. It is often very important to a culture or custom.

- Fairy Tales — These are usually written for children and often carry a moral or universal truth. They are stories written about fairies or other magical creatures.

- Fables — Similar to fairy tales, fables are written for children and include tales of supernatural people or animals that speak like people.

- Myths — These tales are often about the gods, include symbolism, and may involve historical events and reveal human behavior. Sometimes they tell how historical things came about.

- Legends — Exaggerated and only partially truthful, these are tales of heroes and significant events.

- Tall Tales — Often funny stories and sometimes set in the Wild West, these are tales that contain extreme exaggeration and were never true.

<u>Helping Students Evaluate Literature</u>

Teaching students how to identify quality literature is essential. Students need to know how to choose a good book and, after reading it, how to form sound judgment—based on solid evidence—about the book. Here are some questions that students can ask that will help them evaluate the books they've read.

- Did I enjoy the book? What made it enjoyable?
- Do I feel the story and characters were believable?
- Was the conflict resolved in a way that wasn't too simple?
- What was the climax and did it fit with the storyline?
- Did the action of the characters fit with their personalities?
- Was there a lesson or moral to the story? What was the theme?
- Were the characters well-developed? Did I get to know them and bond with them?
- What was the setting of the book and was it well-developed? Could I "see" it?
- Did the characters seem like they were from the time and location of the story?
- Did the book envelop my mind? Was I wrapped up in reading it?
- Did the author write with purpose and if so, what was that purpose?
- Did the dialogue between characters seem real, like what someone would actually say?
- Was it worthwhile to read the book?

## Inferences Made from Text Supported with Appropriate Evidence

Although related to predictions and the finding of factual information, *inferences* refer to the ability to make logical assumptions based on contextual clues. People of all ages make inferences about the world around them on a daily basis but may not be aware of what they are doing. Even young children may infer that it is likely cold outside if they wake up and their bedroom is chilly or the floor is cold. While being driven somewhere on the highway and a child notices a person at the side of the road with a parked car, that child will likely infer that the individual is having car problems and is awaiting some assistance. Therefore, the challenge for educators is not necessarily teaching children how to infer, but rather demonstrating how this skill they already use can be transferred into the study of various texts.

One effective introductory strategy may be to set up scenarios within the classroom and challenge the children to infer what is happening. For instance, the educator may arrive at school pretending to have a cold without saying anything. By placing a personal box of tissues on the desk along with a nasal spray and frequently sneezing, the teacher is challenging the students to infer that he or she not feeling well. Once the children begin to understand that making inferences is indeed similar to detective work by collecting key evidence, the educator can now introduce more inanimate objects like photographs, pictures, or diagrams void of explanatory language. The children's task would be to study the visual aids to try to infer what the subject is about. Educators can assist the children initially by asking questions aloud, modeling how to arrive at a logical inference. For example, the teacher might hold up a picture of a school in which all children are gathered in the playground and grouped according to their classes. Upon closer examination, the children might spot a fire truck parked at the side of the road and may infer that the school had a fire drill or an actual fire.

As the children progress in their ability to infer based on picture clues, it is time to transfer their new skill to texts. Educators may wish to begin with inference challenges in which students are prompted to write short stories about specific events—without directly mentioning the event. For instance, if a child is interested in swimming, they may write about the ideal temperature of the water, backstroke,

freestyle, full laps, and so on without ever mentioning the word *swimming*. Other children in the class will then be prompted to read the short story and infer what the text is about. The children must examine the clues in the text, make an inference, and support the inference with evidence from the text:

> In the second paragraph, it says that the water was relatively warm, so it was easy to finish a full lap. This must mean that the person was swimming in the water.

The more initial practice children receive before moving into more complicated texts, the most success they will have in making accurate inferences and, in turn, the more fun they will have acting as text detectives.

## Summarization of Information

While summarizing information from a text seems like an easy concept at first, it is more complex than one thinks. *Summarizing* involves the ability to extract the most important elements in writing, to eliminate elements of lesser importance, to reorganize the information, to rewrite information in one's own words, and, finally, to condense the writing into a significantly smaller text than that of the original. Thus, learning to summarize consists of many individual skills that all converge and overlap. There are two forms of summary: (1) summaries that aid the reader in understanding the text and (2) summaries that aid others in their understanding of the text.

Summarizing should be explicitly taught beginning in the primary school years with continual reinforcement and gradual introduction to more complex texts as students progress. In order to summarize effectively, children need to demonstrate the following abilities:

- Text comprehension
- Identification of main idea
- Elimination of inconsequential information
- Ability to condense
- Ability to paraphrase
- Ability to organize writing in a logical order

### Personal Summaries

Educators are encouraged to first assist children in summarizing texts as a means to strengthen personal comprehension. For instance, when children are able to identify a text's main idea, state that idea in their own words, and back up that main idea with supporting evidence, they are learning to summarize, and their comprehension undoubtedly strengthens.

Summarizing for oneself is also an invaluable tool for studying and memorizing, which children will use throughout their academic careers. When students summarize for themselves, the goal is to strengthen overall comprehension of the text, arrive at the author's point of view, and isolate the main idea. Since the summary is intended to be only for the student, there is no need to pay particular attention to spelling, grammar, or sentence structure. Students are learning to make personal notes for the purpose of comprehension strengthening and, possibly, memorization for upcoming tests.

### Summaries for Others

Once children have demonstrated a clear ability to summarize a variety of texts for their own understanding, educators may begin to introduce them to the skill of *summarizing for others*. This

involves a more complex approach to summarization. Now that students have ownership of the given text, they inherit the challenge of explaining the text's meaning to an audience. In addition to extracting the main idea, eliminating unimportant text elements, reorganizing and condensing the text, and paraphrasing, students must now pay close attention to the summary's length, the mechanics of writing, and the audience. For example, are students writing to classmates to help them better understand the text? Are they writing the summary for their teacher, in an effort to demonstrate their ability to summarize? Since this type of summarization involves a polished finish, children must also employ proofreading and revision skills.

Educators who are introducing summarization for the first time should focus on less complex texts that involve familiar subject matter, and the texts should be well organized, with titles, possible subtitles, and easily identifiable main ideas. Allowing children to refer to the text as often as possible while learning to summarize is also an important teaching strategy. Children at the early stages of summarizing should not be expected to have memorized and clearly understood what they have read. Sometimes children need to reread the same text several times before beginning a summarization. By explicitly teaching children how to recognize signaling devices, educators help them summarize and isolate a text's main idea. Some signaling devices may be found in an introductory or summary statement or specific words or phrases that have been placed in italics, bold print, or are underlined.

The more advanced students become with summarizing texts, the greater their comprehension and ability to apply what they learn will be.

## Analysis of Characters, Setting, and Plot

When it comes to the study of stories or literary texts, it is important for children to gain an understanding and awareness of text structures and organization. All literary texts involve various story elements, including characters, setting, and plot. Being able to identify these elements and show their relationship to one another is key to understanding the story.

### Characters
A story may have both main characters and minor characters, but all characters, regardless of their level of importance, work to provide the story's framework. Therefore, it is important for students to be able to list and describe all characters that appear throughout a story. The following questions aid students in this endeavor:

- What do the characters look like?
- How old are they?
- What language or languages do they speak?
- What is their personality like?
- How do they relate to one another?
- Do you know of anyone like this in your life?
- Have you come across a similar character in another story?
- How are they the same?
- How are they different?

The more children identify with various characters in a story, the stronger their overall comprehension will be.

## Setting

The setting is very important to a story's framework and may even change periodically as the story unfolds. Understanding when and where a story takes place helps children visualize the various scenes and relate the story's setting to a time and place in their own lives or to a similar setting in another story. Questions that aid in the understanding of setting include the following:

- What country are the characters in?
- What year or era is it?
- Does the story take place in a suburban, urban, or rural location?
- Is the setting similar or different to where you live?
- How is it similar?
- How is it different?
- Does this setting remind you of a setting in another story?
- How are the settings similar? How are they different?
- Would you like to visit this setting? Give clear reasons why or why not.

A story's setting is critical to helping children make sense of a character's language, dress, attitude, relationships with others, and character traits. Building a stronger understanding of each character within a story will assist young readers in their overall text comprehension.

## Plot

Generally speaking, the plot of a literary text involves the introduction of a key problem at the beginning of a story, which is usually resolved by the story's end. Educators build a bridge that strengthens students' story comprehension by helping children connect the story's plot to a familiar scenario in another story or by helping children connect the problem in the text with a problem they have encountered in their own lives. For instance, the plot can involve dealing with a bully, battling the elements of nature, or learning to overcome personal obstacles. The more children are able to relate to a story's plot, the greater their comprehension and appreciation of the story will be.

When teaching children about the various elements in literary texts, the use of visual aids, such as story maps, can provide invaluable assistance to a child's overall understanding:

## Structural Elements of Literature Across Genres

There are several *genres* of literature including poetry, fiction, nonfiction, and drama. Each genre has specific structural elements. Although there are elements that are shared by more than one genre of literature—such as character, setting, and plot, which are found in both fiction and drama—there are also clear differences in other genres. For instance, the structural elements in nonfiction often consist of cause and effect, sequence, or compare and contrast.

### Structural Elements in Drama

A drama, or a play, is almost exclusively delivered as a dialogue and performed live on a stage. The audience observes the story unfolding as opposed to reading it in a book. The actors or actresses in a drama follow written scripts, which are divided into acts and further divided into scenes. The only written material generally given to the audience is the cast of characters, which lists all the character names with an accompanying brief description of their role in the play. This is the only written assistance the audience will receive, so it is imperative that they read through the cast of characters and then carefully follow each scene in the play to understand the story.

Stage directions in a drama refer to the directions or descriptions given to the actors in each scene. They are often presented in italics or in parentheses to differentiate the directions from the dialogue. Stage directions may tell actors where to stand, what direction to face, how to deliver lines, and whom to address.

### Structural Elements in Poetry

Generally speaking, *rhyme* goes hand and hand with the study of poetry and involves the repetition of similar sounds. Sounds may rhyme at the end of every two or more lines, referred to as *end rhyme*, or

may even rhyme in the middle of a line, referred to as *internal rhyme*. The following offers examples of both:

I went to school *today*,

Not wanting to leave the *house*,

And as I passed the *day*,

I remained as quiet as a *mouse*.


In rain or *shine*, your house or *mine*,

We'll meet *again*, my dear *friend*.

The first poem demonstrates the example of end rhyme. The second example demonstrates internal rhyme.

*Meter* is the rhythm of the syllables within a poem. Each type of meter equates to the specific number of syllables and, possibly, the way the syllables are stressed. There are five basic meters: *iambic, trochaic, spondaic, anapestic,* and *dactylic*. Recognizing the meter within poetry helps readers understand the poem's rhythm and guides the reader in how to read the poem with the poet's intended emphasis. Meter also helps poets develop and maintain the structural elements within the poem.

## Organizational Structures of Informational Text

Organizational structures found in informational text differ from structures found in fictional works. It is important for educators to teach children how to recognize and use these structures to further their knowledge of a given discipline.

### Cause and Effect

When an author unfolds a cause and effect relationship within a given text, readers must work to uncover what has happened and why. Sometimes, the cause and effect relationships are melancholy, but they can also be positive. Before asking children to locate the cause and effect relationship within an informational text, it is first important to define the terms and then provide key examples with which the students can relate. For instance, a teacher might ask the children what happens after it rains. There will undoubtedly be a variety of responses, from *the ground becomes wet* to *the flowers grow*. From this simple exercise, educators can begin to model the relationship between the *cause*—why something happened—and the *effect*—what happened as a result.

Showing pictures, photographs, and other visual aids, and gradually encouraging children to use key graphic organizers will also help them solidify their understanding of cause and effect relationships. Teaching key vocabulary words that specifically relate to cause and effect are also effective instructional strategies. Educators should ensure that these vocabulary lists become incorporated into classroom word walls and personal dictionaries.

### Problem and Solution

Similar to cause and effect, the *problem and solution pairing* that often appears in informational texts refers to something that has happened that requires a solution. Although both cause and effect and

problem and solution involve related events that occur before and after, cause and effect situations do not necessarily seek a solution to a problem. They seek to identify the impact one or more events have had on something else. In contrast, the problem and solution pairing in a text refers specifically to a problem that has occurred that requires a solution:

| Problem | Solution |
|---|---|
| Scraped a knee | Wash, dry, and apply bandage |
| Unprepared for upcoming test | Practice and study |
| No clean clothes to wear | Do some laundry |

## Contribution of Structural Elements to the Development of Literary Text

The structure or framework of any given literary text is significant to the overall quality of the work. *Structure* refers to how the literary work is organized by introduction, expansion of ideas, and interrelation of all the literary elements. If the structure of a literary work is inexistent or poorly developed, the individual elements will appear chaotic, which makes the challenge of comprehending and enjoying the literary work difficult.

Although there are different elements in literature depending on the genre, generally an author will introduce and develop characters, establish a theme, provide a plot, develop the setting, establish the conflict, and present the resolution. These elements must be strategically introduced and developed, paying particular attention to placement within the story's framework. A properly developed structure connects these individual elements so that the reader develops a deep appreciation for the story and arrives at a clear understanding of the author's message. A well-organized structure also helps readers connect background knowledge to new information as it unfolds, and it helps strengthen a reader's retention of important literary details.

## Locating Information

In informational texts, certain features function to organize the information and also act as guides, which in turn supports the reader's overall comprehension.

*Headings* include titles and subtitles that identify the topic of study. They also help a reader to arrive at a clearer understanding with regard to the text's main idea. Headings can help readers make connections between background knowledge and the information in the text, which helps them make predictions before reading begins. Headings also strategically organize a text into sections so that one section at a time can be studied.

*Sidebars* are found in the right or left margins of informational texts. Sidebars often provide the reader with helpful, additional information about a topic that appears on that particular page. By providing examples, interesting facts, definitions of key terms, and more, sidebars emphasize important information that the author wishes to convey.

*Hyperlinks* are in-text links to specific website addresses that a reader may wish to visit to further their understanding of a specific topic. When authors insert hyperlinks into modern informational texts, they create a text that is more interactive, providing further resources for children to strengthen their comprehension of a given topic.

## Tiers of Vocabulary

Language is used for effective communication and can be thought of as a social tool. However, since communication is also used in educational and professional circles, language must be flexible enough to meet the challenges of each social structure.

*Conversational language* is the everyday language spoken at home, with family, and with friends. It is a relaxed form of communication that may carry regional dialects, slang, and even sayings that may only be known by those who are part of those intimate social circles.

*Academic language* refers to the understanding and application of key vocabulary terms in order to achieve academic success. From their introduction to formal education, students become acquainted with this language tier. It prompts higher-level thinking and challenges students to research, analyze, and push the boundaries of thought, belief, and imagination.

*Domain-specific languages* are now widely used to refer to computer-based languages—called DSLs— but they are also known as any language system that has been specifically designed to perform a task in a given domain. In domain-specific languages, people are able to communicate concepts unique to that particular domain, avoid redundancy, and stay focused and on target.

# *Understanding Different Texts and Graphic Sources*

## Literary Text vs. Oral, Staged, or Filmed Version

Many of today's students are saturated with technology in their everyday lives. With the availability of iPads, iPods, personal computers, and smartphones, children as early as the primary grades are not only familiar with modern technology, but are becoming confident practitioners. Therefore, integrating technology in the classroom is a logical approach to helping children connect to the learning process and engage their interests.

With regard to English language arts instruction, technology can provide ample opportunities for educators to help strengthen students' critical thinking, oral communication, and reading comprehension skills. Since stories have always been used as a way of helping to explain the world and our place in it, they continue to be an integral part of any society's culture. The same story can be shared orally, in print, in film, or onstage, and each presentation provides similarities and differences with regard to the story's elements and to the audience's interpretation. By allowing children to compare and contrast various presentations of the same story, educators can increase students' motivation in English language arts.

Isolated scenes in films or documentaries can be used to begin a class discussion on a given topic. Children can openly discuss what version of the story they prefer and why. They can become detectives as they watch carefully for differences and similarities in the story's elements, such as setting, plot, and character traits. Educators who introduce a film or stage version of a literary work may wish to introduce the elements of lighting, dialogue, or special effects and begin a class discussion about how these elements, much like points of view, setting, and details in print, are critical to a film's structure.

If used strategically and with careful planning, the use of films, plays, and various technology-based story presentations can prove to be a very effective instructional strategy that strengthens students' understanding and appreciation of English language arts.

## Multiple Informational Texts Addressing the Same Topic

When children begin to research topics for formal reports, presentations, or class discussions, it is important that they understand that information on a given topic comes in a variety of formats and is presented by many different points of view. Information is shared orally and is found in print and digital format, but not all information on a given topic will be the same. For instance, one text about the benefits of farming may completely contradict information found in another text. There are many reasons why contradictory information is found in two or more texts. Helping students consider the time period the text was written, the level of expertise of the author or authors, cultural points of view, and the author's purpose will help them strengthen their critical thinking skills, as well as allow them to develop their own interpretation and evaluation of the information.

It is critical that children begin to critique information found in print, online, or told orally and not just accept it at face value. These critical thinking skills will serve them well throughout their academic career and will play a fundamental role in their personal and professional lives.

## Key Claims from Textual Evidence

The ability to identify significant claims made by the author and to support those claims with evidence found within the text is integral to the development of reading comprehension and critical thinking skills. Educators need to introduce key vocabulary words and phrases that authors use when stating and supporting claims. These vocabulary terms can be added to an ever-changing and expanding classroom word wall, incorporated into personal dictionaries and captured on charts to further classroom discussions. Once children begin to identify key words and phrases as indicators of claims and claim evidence, they are ready to begin the more complex task of evaluating these claims.

When children can identify claims and show evidence that supports the claims, educators may wish to initiate a class discussion on whether or not these claims are valid. For instance, prompting a reader's background knowledge and personal experiences on the topic, examining the author's expertise on the subject, weighing any possible cultural or personal bias the author may have, and comparing/contrasting the author's claims to claims made by other authors on the same subject will help children develop objectivity as they read.

## Key Details, Moral, and/or Theme of a Literary Text

*Literary analysis* of a text involves the study of character development, setting, mood, plot, point(s) of view, figurative language, and other literary elements. The *study of informational text* involves nonfictional elements, such as the author's purpose, major ideas or concepts, and more. All of these individual components in a text often interrelate and form the text's overall theme or message. Some common universal themes found in literature include disappointment, courage, overcoming obstacles, loneliness, and good triumphing over evil. In informational texts, the themes or messages vary greatly, but they usually involve subjects that pertain to the natural or social world. When children reach the stage in their literacy development that allows them to begin literary analysis exercises, they are beginning to take their reading comprehension beyond the surface details to arrive at an even deeper understanding of the text by studying these individual themes and messages.

When first introducing literary analysis, it is important for educators to select texts that carry themes children can relate to. Educators are encouraged to consider themes that depict similar life experiences or interests. Although many themes in texts are universal in nature, the younger the students are, the

more important it is to choose texts that have themes with which they can identify, that appeal to their interests, and that inspire discussion and debate. As children progress and strengthen their literacy skills, they will be able to apply these skills to a wider variety of themes.

An ideal strategy to introduce literary analysis is to hold class discussions at the beginning and ending of texts, as well as periodically throughout the reading of a given text. Educators may prompt these class discussions with key questions that help students to make connections between the events and characters in a fictional text and the students' life experiences. Class discussions allow children to hear multiple ideas, which works to strengthen overall comprehension and build an appreciation of alternate points of view. These key questions also prompt children to consider their own feelings as they read the text, helping them to connect on a personal or emotional level, which strengthens overall comprehension. Class discussions should also challenge children a little further by asking them to explain why they feel a certain way about a message in the text. Once children have had ample opportunity to practice and master this skill, the next step is to teach children how to support their thoughts, feelings, and ideas by finding textual evidence that supports their views.

Learning to find supporting evidence within a text is a very complex skill that can initially cause some confusion and frustration. One strategy to employ that may assist children in learning how to find key information is the introduction of graphic organizers. The following is an example of a graphic organizer that is split into three sections:

| Student Answer | Text Evidence (quotation and page number) | Explanation |
|---|---|---|
|  |  |  |

Searching for supportive evidence involves more than merely finding a quotation. The above graphic organizer guides students to connect the specific quotation(s) to their interpretation and further provides students the opportunity to explain, in their own words, how their answers and the quotations are connected. Forming credible and logical responses to questions and supporting those responses with appropriate quotations from the text are considered very advanced literary skills, which take students to a much deeper understanding of literature.

## Key Details and the Central Idea of an Informational Text

Informational texts appear in several forms, including expository texts, persuasive texts, procedural texts, and nonfiction narratives. As early as kindergarten, children are encouraged to read a variety of informational texts. Placing an assortment of texts in the classroom library, hanging posters on classroom walls that promote a wide range of topics, and providing children with ample time and opportunity to explore any number of subjects, has shown to have a very positive impact on reading comprehension and overall literacy skill development. Informational texts provide children an opportunity to explore and develop a better understanding of the world around them. Taking this one step further, by allowing children to choose topics of informational texts that pique their curiosity,

educators help children develop a more positive attitude toward reading and writing. All informational texts typically include five key elements:

- The author's purpose(s)
- A major idea(s)
- Supporting detail(s)
- Visual or graphic aid(s)
- Vocabulary

## Author's Purpose

*Expository texts* typically share information about a given topic. *Persuasive texts* aim to convince readers to think or act a certain way, and *procedural texts* generally give step-by-step or "how-to" instructions in a given discipline. *Nonfiction narratives* tell a true story, perhaps to inspire, educate, bring awareness to a subject, or simply chronicle an important historical event. In order for students to become independent readers and draw their own conclusions about what they read, it is critical that they learn to discern the *author's purpose*.

One obvious approach to teaching children how to reveal an author's purpose is to simply ask children why they think the author wrote this information. These types of open-ended class discussions allow children to express their ideas, explore theories, and consider what others have to say on the subject. Educators can record various answers and then ask the children to return to the text as detectives, looking for clues that support each theory.

Another approach to uncovering the author's purpose is for students to take a closer look at the written structure of the text and the vocabulary usage. For example, is the text's structure written in chronological order, simply listing events as they occurred? Does the text open up with a problem that is then resolved? Is the author using cause/effect or compare/contrast vocabulary? Learning about the structure of the text gives great insight into the author's purpose.

When children develop reading fluency, they are able to read a text with minimal to no errors, with consistent speed, and with appropriate expression, and they learn to connect with what they are reading on a personal level. As children read through an informational text, educators may ask how the students are feeling. Did they begin feeling one way and end up feeling another by the end of the text? When children examine their own personal feelings with regard to what they have read, they will be in a better position to explore the author's purpose.

Once children have had several opportunities to explore the author's purpose using a variety of informational texts, prompting them to write their own informational texts will help them to develop and strengthen a better understanding about writing with a purpose. Perhaps they can write a procedural text that lists the steps in how to ride a bike, or they can write a persuasive paper to try to convince their teacher that extra free time during the school day stimulates learning.

Learning to identify an author's purpose connects children with their reading on a deeper level. Instead of believing everything they read, they will begin to understand that there are many reasons why authors write, and they will further understand that they possess the ability to draw their own conclusions and make their own decisions on any given topic.

## Major Idea

Some children struggle with identifying the main idea of an informational text. Identifying the main idea of a text requires that the reader understand the entire text and is able to zero in on one central, overarching idea amongst a sea of other information. The ability to sort through the entire text and arrive at the main idea takes a considerable amount of effort and practice for beginning readers.

Before prompting students to locate the main idea of a given text or passage, educators must first explain what the main idea actually is. Here are some guidelines, tips, and tricks to follow that will help children identify the main idea:

| Identifying the Main Idea |
| --- |
| The most important part of the text |
| Text title and pictures may reveal clues |
| Opening sentences and final sentences may reveal clues |
| Key vocabulary words that are repeatedly used may reveal clues |

Providing students with simple lists of related vocabulary may be a logical starting point when teaching how to recognize a main idea. For instance, on a large chart, educators may list several fruits, vegetables, snacks, and meals, and then prompt the children to explain what they have in common. This also works well with a set of images, pictures, or photographs that all represent the same idea. After repeated practice, children will begin to strengthen their ability to center in on the main idea that connects all the elements on the list.

Once children begin to identify and demonstrate a clear understanding of the main idea in simple lists, educators may wish to introduce simple texts that gradually increase in complexity.

## Supporting Details

Supporting details of texts are defined as those elements of a text that help readers make sense of the main idea. They either qualitatively and/or quantitatively describe the main idea, strengthening the reader's understanding.

Using simple sentences is an effective instructional approach when introducing children to supporting details. Educators may write out a simple sentence and ask the children to underline the main idea, as in the sentence that follows:

The *apple* is hard, red, and juicy.

Once the main idea, the apple, is accurately identified, educators can now ask children to locate words that describe or support this main idea and highlight/circle each supporting word:

The *apple* is hard, red, and juicy.

Simple sentence exercises will gradually become simple paragraphs and, eventually, full texts in which children are challenged with the task of locating the main idea and the supporting details. Children must learn to differentiate between trivial and supporting details by evaluating whether or not the detail in

question further quantifies or qualifies the main idea. If the detail does neither, it is likely not important enough to be considered a supporting detail and can be left alone.

Graphic organizers can also be a helpful tool when working with main ideas and supporting details. There are many graphic organizers that help students to organize their analysis into clear and visible representations. The following are examples of graphic organizers that are commonly used when teaching the main idea and supporting details.

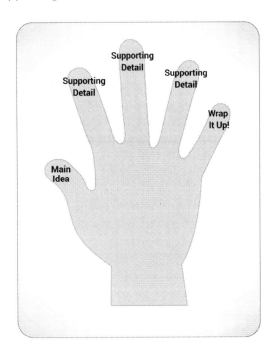

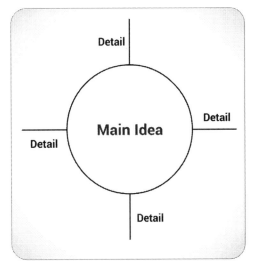

Children who demonstrate the ability to accurately identify a text's main idea and supporting details can further strengthen these skills by attempting to write their own texts with a main idea and supporting details. Likewise, graphic organizers can be used as tools that help children to organize their thoughts and ideas before they begin this writing process.

## Visual or Graphic Aids

Authors of informational texts will often employ the use of visual or graphic aids in strategic locations throughout the text in order to strengthen the reader's understanding of the topic at hand. Visual aids can provide an overview of key information, illustrate relationships among important text elements, and summarize the main idea. Visual aids are generally colorful and catch students' attention; they help to simplify what could be potentially complicated information. There are a multitude of visual aids that are frequently used in informational texts, including models, graphs, charts, tables, maps, drawings, photographs, and time lines. Some visual aids also involve a side bar, which defines key vocabulary necessary to understand the topic.

In most instances, children merely need to look at the visual aid to make an instant connection. The implementation of graphic aids in writing reduces instructional time and strengthens comprehension. During read alouds and guided reading sessions, educators may wish to model how to extract meaning from visual aids by connecting the graphic to specific elements in the text. Before reading begins, educators have students skim through the pages to find the visual aids and predict what the text may be about based on the text's graphics. Therefore, visual aids may often help students to identify the text's main idea.

The time it requires to read and process the written text is considerably longer than the time it takes to derive meaning from the graph. Helping students to identify and derive meaning from visual aids will help to strengthen their reading comprehension skills and overall literacy development.

## Vocabulary

Vocabulary used throughout informational texts is generally quite different than vocabulary found in fictional print. For this reason, it is imperative that educators help children strengthen and increase their vocabulary inventory so that they can eventually become successful at reading and understanding informational text.

For instance, educators can point out *signal words* throughout texts to help children more readily and accurately identify the author's purpose. There are specific vocabulary words that authors employ that spotlight the author's intent. For instance, if authors wish to list examples to support a main idea, they may use vocabulary such as *for example*, *such as*, or *as illustrated*. When displaying the chronological order of events, authors may use *first*, *lastly*, *before*, and *finally*. Some common compare and contrast vocabulary words include *but*, *same as*, *similar to*, *as opposed to*, and *however*. There are several key phrases that signal cause and effect relationships, including *because of*, *as a result of*, and *in order to*.

Using word walls and personal dictionaries, sorting vocabulary words according to theme, introducing text maps, and teaching children to become familiar with sidebars and glossaries in informational texts, educators will help expand their students' vocabulary and strengthen their ability to read and comprehend informational texts successfully.

## Relationships Among Individuals, Events, Ideas, and Concepts

Very rarely are elements within an informational text unrelated. Part of an author's responsibility is to connect a series of elements from the beginning of a text right through to the text's summary. The more successful an author is at relating the various elements, the easier the text is to comprehend. Educators may assist children in analyzing these relationships by first explaining that a relationship involves two or more characters, events, ideas, or concepts that have an impact on one another. There are key words or phrases in informational texts that may signal this relationship, including *therefore*, *because*, and *as a*

*result*. Identifying these relationships will help children to comprehend the text's message, the author's point of view, and may even help to explain elements in the text that occur later on.

## Identifying Similarities and Differences

By taking character analysis one step further, students can compare and contrast the similarities and differences between the points of view of two or more characters in a story. The ability to consider various points of view helps children strengthen their critical thinking skills in both academic and social settings.

Educators should consider using a variety of instructional approaches when comparing and contrasting points of view. One strategy educators can implement is a class debate or partner debate. A debate brings students to center stage as they learn to defend the point of view of various characters within a story while listening to classmates defend the points of view of other characters. Friendly debating has been proven to strengthen a student's ability to reason, apply logic, communicate with self-expression, listen to others, and organize thoughts and opinions. Debating also helps children develop an appreciation for opposing points of view and, therefore, works to build stronger bonds both in and out of the classroom. By taking on the point of view of a character in a story with the added responsibility of defending that point of view with evidence, students broaden their own thought processes and challenge the world around them in more depth.

Visual aids are another strategy that educators use when comparing and contrasting points of views, especially when examining characters in stories. Venn diagrams are especially effective as they provide a clear space for unique perspectives, with a common overlapping section for similarities. There are several visual aids available for use in the classroom depending on the age and ability of the students. From the earliest of primary education to the upper level high school grades, visual aids continue to be a powerful instructional tool. The visual aid below demonstrates opposing and shared characteristics of characters:

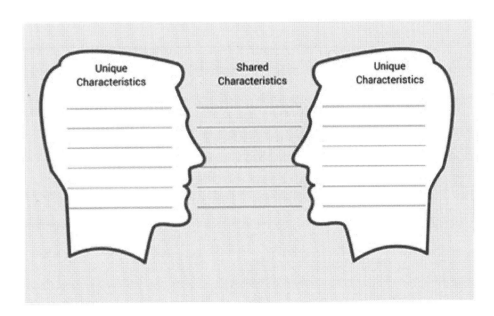

## Author's Point of View

An important reading comprehension skill is identifying the points of view that exist in literature. In literature, the *point of view* refers to the lens through which readers see the story unfold. Readers are often able to understand the overall story more fully when they are able to determine from what angle the story is told. The point of view of the main character or of several characters helps readers interpret character traits, understand how each character relates to the other, and determine how those relationships relate to the story's plot. In literary works, there are four main points of view to consider:

- Third person omniscient
- Third person limited
- First person
- Objective

### Third Person Omniscient

*Third person* refers to the use of the third person singular in writing, as in *he* or *she*. *Omniscient* is defined as all knowing. When the author employs *third person omniscient*, each character's perspective is revealed, allowing readers to consider and evaluate the points of view of all the characters within a story.

### Third Person Limited

The difference between this point of view and third person omniscient is that *third person limited* only reveals the thoughts, feelings, and opinions of one character, thereby creating a more intimate impact on the reader and leaving the points of view of other characters a mystery to uncover. This point of view also employs the third person singular forms of *he* and *she* when speaking directly about a specific character.

### First Person

Regarded in literature as the most intimate approach to point of view development, *first person* is written in first person singular, using the pronouns *I, me,* and *my*. When authors apply this point of view, readers develop a clear understanding of the true inner feelings of that particular character and strengthen their understanding of how the character relates to the story's plot and to supporting characters.

### Objective

The *objective point of view* reveals no feelings, thoughts, or opinions of characters; it remains void of emotional elements. This point of view focuses on facts, data, historical information, and quotations for reference. Authors who write in the objective point of view write as outside observers describing events as they happen.

To help students develop an awareness of which point of view the author is applying, educators may wish to model the thinking process required to locate point of view evidence. Beginning with a character analysis in chart form, for instance, educators and students can list all characters within a story and discuss the character traits of each one. Teachers may then ask the students why they believe characters possess certain traits and may then facilitate this understanding by referring to specific areas in the story that reveal these traits.

Using various excerpts from familiar stories to develop a character analysis also helps children strengthen point of view awareness. Working as literary detectives, students should be prompted to

look for the pronouns *he, she,* and *I* and then focus on the key vocabulary surrounding these pronouns. The ability to identify key vocabulary used to evoke emotion, as well as vocabulary used to simply state facts, will be very useful in developing a student's ability to recognize points of view within a story:

| Emotional Vocabulary | Factual Vocabulary |
|---|---|
| Fear: apprehensive, cautious, concerned, hesitant, uneasy, watchful | Facts: details, knowledge, information, proof |
| Anger: annoyed, cranky, critical, frustrated, irritated | Data: as evidenced by statistics |
| Sadness: disappointed, heartbroken, gloomy, depressed | Historical Information: recorded, an account of |
| Happy: amused, inspired, joyful, pleased | Quotations: testimony, witness, verification, affidavit |

## Impact of Point of View on Overall Structure of Texts

Generally speaking, the majority of informational texts involves a third person point of view. It is widely accepted in academic circles that the use of any other point of view for information purposes is likely to have a negative impact on the text's quality. Third person point of view removes the author from associating the information with a personal bias and allows the reader to evaluate the content objectively. Third person point of view strengthens informational texts with the use of validated research, facts, and statistics from a variety of credible sources. The more factual evidence that is presented in informational texts along with the employment of third person points of view, the more likely the work will be accepted as a reliable informational resource.

However, there are informational texts that use first person points of view for specific reasons. For example, informational texts that are written with the intent to persuade a reader's feelings, opinions, actions, or reactions will often use first person points of view. By giving the text a personal connection, authors can stress their expertise and experience with regard to the event or topic, which may carry weight on how readers relate to the information. Although this may prove to be advantageous to the author, the drawbacks to employing first person point of view include the potential for readers to evaluate the work as too subjective and, therefore, unreliable.

In contrast, first person point of view is the most frequently used in literary works. With the narrator playing an active role in the story's plot, readers are able to connect on an intimate level with the thoughts, emotions, and opinions being expressed.

It is important for authors to consider the main intent of their writing. The messages they wish to convey, the emotions they may wish to evoke, and the overall impressions they want to leave on their readers should ultimately guide authors toward the employment of a specific point of view.

## Written, Visual, and Oral Information from Texts and Multimedia Sources

Students in a modern classroom have access to a wide variety of instructional resources. From teacher-led instruction and classroom activities, traditional textbooks, encyclopedias, nonfiction magazines, and customized classroom libraries to desktop computers, iPads, tablets, laptops, online tutorials, and smart boards, there is a plethora of information waiting to be discovered. Learning how to integrate traditional written, visual, and oral information to other information provided on a multimedia platform can prove challenging, but it is well worth the effort. Since the vast majority of children from the primary school years and older are well equipped at using a variety of technology-based resources, educators who integrate technology in the classroom will likely succeed in helping children to progress both academically and socially. The classroom is as much a social setting as it is academic, and as society changes, so must the instructional approaches.

Time management is one of the initial tasks facing educators when setting up their academic year. Educators are responsible for teaching a wide range of subjects, specific domains within each subject, and numbers of skills within each domain. Designing long-range plans that take all of this into account and forming a framework for the academic year is the most logical starting point.

From this framework, educators can determine how to teach each discipline with an effective, time management approach. Taking the number of students, the possible varying academic and social levels, socioeconomic differences, and language barriers into account, teachers can begin to develop differentiated instructional approaches that cater to all the needs in the classroom. It is at this stage that both traditional resources and technology must find a way to complement each other in the classroom.

For instance, one effective approach is to instruct children to ensure that every research project involves a minimum of two textbook sources as well as a minimum of two technology-based sources. When introducing new topics or reinforcing a lesson, educators are still highly encouraged to use visual aids in the classroom, including word walls, personal dictionaries, and classroom labels. Modeling the effective use of hand-held books, reference guides, and magazines also provides children the opportunity to see how valuable written information continues to be in the world of education.

In order for children to experience a well rounded, quality education, instructional days should be divided between effective, quality instruction, independent exploration and learning, and positive social interaction. Since the needs of children vary in each classroom, as well as their academic and social levels, each educator's decision on how to divide instructional time will also vary. However, having access to technology is paramount in every classroom and at every grade level.

Technology in the classroom helps children to become more actively engaged and encourages independent learning with the use of student-centered, project-based activities. From virtual math tools to collaborative class blogs, there are many ways for students to effectively engage in technology in the classroom.

Although technology plays an important role in the modern classroom, it is still important for educators to guide children, helping them use the technology in an effective, efficient, and responsible manner. Teaching children about cyber-bullying, copyright, plagiarism, and digital footprints will inevitably strengthen their ability to responsibly and safely conduct themselves online.

Educators also use technology for lesson planning, assessments, and evaluation. With a number of online programs available, educators are able to provide students, colleagues, administration, and parents with effective feedback and to develop and evaluate high-quality formative and summative assessments in an efficient manner.

By combining the use of technology along with teacher-centered instruction and traditional textbooks, educators will undoubtedly help to create a classroom with children who are actively engaged throughout the instructional day.

## Visual and Multimedia Elements in Texts

Graphic novels, comic books, fiction, folktales, myths, and poetry often include visual elements in the story. Whether in the form of drawings, photographs, sound, video, or animation, these visual elements work to strengthen the reader's understanding and interpretation of the author's message, help to set the story's tone, bring characters into perspective, and, possibly, provide the reader with alternative interpretations of the story's main idea.

Hyperlinks included in informational texts provide the reader with additional sources of information that strengthen the author's message. Informational texts also employ the use of graphs, charts, diagrams, and maps, which either work to compare and contrast information, demonstrate cause and effect, show a chronological timeline of events, or display trends and patterns.

Effective instructional approaches to literature incorporate how to interpret the various forms of visual and multimedia elements that exist within literary and informational texts. Modeling how to use visuals in various texts appropriately will undoubtedly strengthen students' reading comprehension and critical thinking skills.

# *Processes, Conventions, and Modes of Written and Oral Communication*

## Common Types of Writing

### Opinion/Argument

In the early elementary grades, students begin to write simple *opinion pieces*. Acting as a precursor to argumentative and persuasive writing, opinion pieces allow children to express how they feel on a certain subject based on preferences, express their likes and dislikes, and use personal knowledge, without relying too heavily on supporting evidence. Educators encourage children to write opinion pieces with the use of personal journals as well as reflective pieces, connecting personal experiences to various stories read.

In the middle school years and beyond, students will be required to write *argumentative* or *persuasive* pieces of writing, which must involve logical and relevant proof for a claim or an assertion. Regarded as a more sophisticated form of writing, argumentative or persuasive writing works to change the point of view of the readers or ignite a call-to-action response. This form of writing does not shy away from contradicting points of view but, instead, brings them to light and then works to disprove or discredit each opposing claim. Some examples of argumentative or persuasive writing include essays, reviews, and letters to the editor.

### Informative

Informative writing comes in many forms, including directions, instructions, definitions, summaries, and more. *Informative writing* works to relay information and advance the reader's understanding of a given subject. If written correctly, the vast majority of informative writing is written in third person to distance the author from relying on personal bias, instead relying on objective facts, historical evidence, and statistics.

<u>Narrative</u>

Almost always written in first person, *narratives* include autobiographies, memoirs, and even fictional stories. Their general purpose is to entertain readers, but some also focus on morals, values, or life lessons. By conveying personal experiences on a given subject or by opening up one's life to the audience, narrative writers create a more intimate connection with readers.

## Purpose, Key Components, and Subgenres of Writing

Effective writing, whether for the purpose of persuading, entertaining, or advancing a reader's knowledge, must be well planned and organized. In order to create a powerful piece of writing, authors must adhere to specific structural designs, apply a functional and logical order to their writing, and employ key elements.

The following chart outlines three types of writing and their respective purposes, the structural elements unique to each type of writing, and some examples of subgenres:

| | Opinion/Persuasive | Narrative | Informative |
|---|---|---|---|
| Purpose | To persuade, influence, or prompt a call-to-action response | To entertain or to share a moral when writing fictional narratives<br><br>To share factual information when writing nonfiction narratives | To convey information and advance a reader's knowledge of a given topic |
| Key components | Opening statement and point of view<br><br>Well organized paragraphs with supportive evidence and/or examples<br><br>Strong concluding statement that reinforces point of view | Fictional narratives: plot, characters, setting, point of view, tone<br><br>Nonfictional Narratives: introductory paragraph<br><br>Body: including details and descriptions of events and individuals<br><br>Conclusion | Introduction<br><br>Headings and Subheadings<br><br>Body<br><br>Conclusion<br><br>Works Cited |
| Subgenres | Speeches, letters, reviews, advertisements, essays | Fictional narratives: folktales, fantasy, science-fiction, mystery, drama<br><br>Nonfictional narratives: autobiographies, biographies, memoirs | How-to books, cookbooks, instructional manuals, textbooks |

## Engaging Oral Presentations

Oral presentations can cause panic in a classroom as children scramble to figure out how, when, where, why, and what to speak about. However, if given proper guidance, appropriate time, and constructive feedback, the panic will soon fade, and in turn, students will learn how to give powerful oral presentations.

In order to be effective, educators should follow best practices, including sharing a well-designed rubric with the class, discussing the importance of each skill listed, answering any questions the children might have, and providing ongoing and constructive feedback while children develop their presentations.

Key areas to develop oral presentations:

## Volume

Children should consider where the presentation would be held. Will it be indoors, outdoors, in an auditorium, or in the classroom? Learning to match the volume of the presentation with the location and size of the audience will greatly improve the presentation.

## Articulation

Pronouncing words clearly is another aspect of effective communication, especially during an oral presentation. Slurred words, rushed words, mumbling, or leaving out the beginning or ending of sentences will have a negative impact on the message, and the presenter risks losing the interest of the audience.

## Awareness of Audience

Facing the audience at all times is paramount to the success of an oral presentation. If possible, walking around the room and maintaining eye contact with the audience have proven to be effective techniques. Welcoming questions from the audience, restating questions for everyone to hear, and providing honest and thoughtful responses, also play a key role in ensuring a successful oral presentation.

## Writing Pieces for Specific Purposes

*Aristotle's Rhetorical Triangle* is perhaps the best visual representation to demonstrate the importance of effective writing. Three key areas require the writer's full attention and should be balanced accordingly throughout the writing process:

*Ethos* refers to the writer's credibility: What are the writer's qualifications regarding the subject of the writing? Is the author using an objective or subjective approach? Are the sources, evidence, and examples in the writing relevant and credible?

*Pathos* refers to the writer's ability to engage and connect with the intended audience: What details and imagery does the author use to ignite and excite the emotions, imagination, values, and beliefs of the audience?

*Logos* refers to the validity of the author's message: Is the author's message clearly discernible? Is it logical and well organized?

Each of these three areas are critical to the quality of the writing and require the author's full attention and consideration throughout the writing process, from the preliminary stages to the final published work. Writers are tasked with the responsibility of choosing appropriate language to connect with an audience and choosing a style that maintains interest, which helps the audience understand the writer's purpose and accept the writer's intent. Did the writer succeed, for instance, in entertaining, informing, or persuading the audience?

## Clear and Coherent Writing

## Coherent Writing

*Coherent writing* uses a logical order and consists of information that is both relevant to the topic and reliable. Coherent writing ensures that the language usage appropriately activates the audience's

background knowledge and keeps the audience interested. For writing to be considered coherent, the author must also consider the structure and its relevance to the writing goal.

## Writing Clarity

Although separate and distinct in definition, both coherent writing and writing clarity are interrelated and impact each other. For writing to be fully coherent, it must also be written clearly and for writing to be written clearly, it needs to be coherent. *Writing clarity* refers to the conventions of the English language. Has the author paid considerable attention to the spelling, grammar, and punctuation? For example, the misspelling of a word can confuse a reader and negatively impact writing clarity. The use of visual aids in the form of graphs, diagrams, maps, and charts can also greatly strengthen the writing clarity by allowing students to see examples of what they are reading.

## Evaluation of a Piece of Writing

Traditionally, evaluating a student's writing has been a one-sided affair performed by the educator at the end of the writing process. This is no longer the customary practice since research has clearly shown the importance of formative assessments, as well as the importance of including the students as welcomed and respected self-evaluators. However, no evaluation or assessment should take place unless the instructions given for a particular writing assignment have been made clear, and the students have received quality, comprehensive writing instruction, in general. Assuming these requirements have been met, assessment and evaluation can take on many forms.

Formative assessments help keep the students focused and on task, and they also help to drive instruction. For example, educators are able to determine a child's individual needs, as well as common errors made by many students in the class. During formative assessments, children receive constructive feedback, and educators focus on the individual needs of each student. Formative assessments may also require students to perform self-evaluation using a guided rubric, which helps advance writing skills and develop autonomy. Summative assessments are equally important and also come in many forms. Some summative assessments are curriculum-based to ensure the appropriate standards are being met. Others may be anecdotal, wherein educators write endnotes that highlight areas that require improvement, praise the student's effort and progress, and provide next-step instructions.

Regardless of the type of assessments used, it is critical to a student's continued success that each assessment be personal, meaningful, well understood, and constructive, providing a clear pathway for his or her continued advancement in the writing process.

## Planning, Revising, and Editing

*Planning* is the precursor to writing. This brainstorming stage is when writers consider their purpose and think of ideas that they can use in their writing. Graphic organizers are excellent tools to use during the planning stage. Graphic organizers can help students connect the writing purpose to supporting details, and they can help begin the process of structuring the writing piece. Brainstorming can be done independently, in partners, or as a whole-class activity.

As students begin writing their first draft of a writing piece, they need to continuously revise and edit their work. *Revisions* take place during and after the writing process. As students revise their writing, they are encouraged to frequently refer back to the planning stage. This helps ensure that they are staying focused and are remaining on topic. During the revising and editing stage, educators prompt students to reread their work several times and to focus on one aspect of their writing each time.

For example, the first review may be to examine the writing content, while the second review may focus on spelling, grammar, and punctuation. Another helpful strategy during this stage is to have students display the graphic organizers they used during the planning stage and read their work aloud to the class, in small groups, or with a partner to receive constructive feedback and to welcome other perspectives and ideas. Students are able to refer to the planning stage as the classmate reads and can make connections as to whether or not the writer has stayed on topic.

## Appropriate Revisions to Writing

Writing is a multi-step process in which a student must consider the message and the audience. Likewise, revisions should focus on specific areas. If revision requirements are too vague or all requirements are combined into one task, students can become confused and overwhelmed. Breaking up revisions into specific categories will help students to recognize, understand, and correct specific errors.

One revision task should focus solely on the conventions of the English language, including spelling, punctuation, and grammar. Another task should focus on language usage, wherein students consider the writing style chosen and evaluate whether or not this style is appropriate for delivering the intended message to the intended audience. The writing structure is another area of focus that allows the student to evaluate the introduction, body, and conclusion. Does the writing clearly introduce the topic, does the body gradually strengthen the writer's point of view with relevant and reliable sources and examples, and does the conclusion restate the writer's message in a concise and effective manner? Students should be actively involved in all revisions along with the educators in order for the revisions to make sense.

## Conventions of Standard English Grammar, Usage, Mechanics, and Spelling

When learning to speak, listen, read, or write in any language, students are tasked with multiple challenges. The study of the English language is no exception. The conventions of Standard English are complex and require comprehensive study and continual practice.

### Parts of Speech

Words within the English language play very unique roles in the formation of coherent sentences. Each English word is categorized into a specific part of speech that carries a unique function. For instance, in order to create simple English language sentences, writers are required to incorporate a noun and a verb. However, when sentences become more complex, additional parts of speech are required.

The following chart outlines the parts of speech, along with a brief description of their function within an English sentence and concrete examples.

| Part of Speech | Function | Examples |
| --- | --- | --- |
| Noun | Identifies a person, place, or thing—can be concrete or abstract | Love, thought, man, woman, child, school, home, integrity, America |
| Pronoun | Replaces a noun | He, she, it, they |
| Verb | Depicts an action or state of being | Run, jump, fly, is, are |

| Adjective | Modifies nouns | Great idea, interesting thought, tall girl |
| --- | --- | --- |
| Adverb | Modifies verbs, other adverbs, and adjectives | He has an *extremely* shy demeanor. She *quickly* ran away. They walked *very* clumsily together. |
| Preposition | Almost always combined with other key words in a sentence in order to indicate a time, location, or movement | *At* nine o'clock, *beside* the nightstand, *toward* the door |
| Conjunction | Connects words, clauses, or sentences, with related meaning | She *and* I have similar tastes in food. The teacher handed us the assignment, *but* we refused to accept it. The dogs ran and played, *while* the cats sat and stared. |
| Interjection | Brief exclamations that are added to sentences for emphasis or effect | *Wow*! I had no idea you could sing! "*Boo*!" she screamed, as she jumped out from behind the door. |

Although an explicit approach to teaching the various parts of speech plays an integral role in the primary grades, it is equally as important that a child learns to recognize these parts of speech when reading and gradually learn to apply them to writing tasks. Being able to recognize and appropriately use various parts of speech demonstrates a growing command of the English language and its conventions.

## Correction of Errors

Usage and mechanics are often mistakenly used as interchangeable terms in the educational field. In writing, *usage* refers to a student's ability to choose appropriate words that clearly express an idea, thought, or opinion, or accurately summarize information. Therefore, usage is a very important component of learning to be an effective writer. *Mechanics* involve the writer's ability to use capitalization, ending punctuation, apostrophes, and commas properly. For writing to be both coherent and fluent, mechanics play an important role. *Spelling* is a little less complicated to understand, as it refers to the student's ability to spell decodable and non-decodable words accurately. Learning how and when to correct errors in usage, mechanics, and spelling can be a source of frustration for educators, but it need not be. By creating a logical balance and manageable plan for correcting student writing, educators will help children to be more effective, lifelong writers. The key is balance.

Traditionally, English language educators have focused a great deal of evaluation and feedback on correcting mistakes in usage, mechanics, and spelling alone. Although it is widely accepted that these components are necessary in order to write fluent and coherent sentences, too much focus on correcting these areas—and not enough attention paid to the creative side of writing—may have a negative impact on the writing process.

For example, instead of emphasizing or highlighting every spelling error, educators should ensure that their corrections reflect the task. In other words, if children are given a writing assignment that must incorporate their spelling words, they will undoubtedly expect the educator to correct and evaluate how well they spelled these key words. However, since the assignment also asked the children to use a creative approach to this writing assignment, educators would be doing students a disservice if they did not also offer praise and feedback on the children's writing creativity.

Developing a writing checklist with well-defined goals and sharing this checklist with the class helps educators keep the correction process clear and specific, and it provides children with the opportunity to self-correct and edit their work prior to submission. Using a standardized system of symbols that helps children focus on spelling, capitalization, or word choice is also an effective strategy. Displaying these symbols in a readily-accessible place in the classroom will allow them to self-correct and help their peers with the correction process.

For writing to be meaningful and for students to advance in their writing skills, educators should follow a balanced approach to correcting student work with frequent, timely, and appropriate feedback that reflects the task.

## Sentence Types

When children begin to connect letters to words and, gradually, words to sentences, those sentences are generally very simple, consisting of one subject and one verb. However, as children advance in their writing fluency, it is paramount to introduce more complex sentences.

*Simple sentences* are sentences that consist of one subject and one verb:

> I run.

> She eats.

> They play.

At this stage, educators may prompt children to add some more detail to the simple sentences with adjectives or adverbs:

> I run *quickly*.

> She eats *very well*.

> They play *together*.

*Compound sentences* contain two independent clauses connected by a conjunction:

> I run, but she runs marathons.

*I run* is an *independent clause*. *She runs marathons* is another independent clause. Each clause could be a complete sentence that stands on its own. However, they are connected with the coordinating conjunction, *but*.

*Complex sentences* are structures in which two clauses exist, but one clause is *dependent* on the other—that is, it cannot form a sentence in its own right and requires the assistance of the independent clause in order for the sentence to be coherent. Here's an example:

Although he passed the exam, he remained very sad.

*He remained very sad* is an independent clause, but *Although he passed the exam* is not, as it is dependent on the second part of the sentence in order for the sentence to be coherent.

*Compound-complex sentences* are structures that employ two or more independent clauses along with at least one dependent clause:

Though I preferred long distance running, I started speed walking, and I enjoyed it very much.

*Though I preferred long-distance running* is a dependent clause that relies on the independent clause *I started speed walking*. The second independent clause is *I enjoyed it very much*, making this sentence compound-complex.

## English Used in Stories, Dramas, or Poems

### Register

Despite the fact that a standardized form of English is used in published academic and scientific language, several varieties of spoken and written English also exist. There are differences in how one speaks at home, with friends, to teachers, and to colleagues. In each social setting, a person's *register*—his or her level of formality—will likely change in order to appropriately address the audience. Written registers also vary, depending on a number of factors. For instance, when writing a research paper for professional purposes, formal language will be used, but when writing a letter to a friend, a person is more apt to employ a more casual register. The following statements indicate differences in register:

*Call me back when you get this message.*

*I look forward to hearing back from you at your earliest convenience.*

Although both statements express the writer's desire to further communicate with the receiver of the message, the degree of formality, the register, is strikingly different.

### Dialect

A language also has several dialects, which are dependent on a great many factors. *Dialects* have specific grammatical rules and patterns that often differ from the standard rules of the language. For instance, within Britain, Canada, and the United States, there are several dialects of the English language. One need only travel from Newfoundland, in eastern Canada, to Louisiana, in the southern United States, to witness a striking difference in how the English language is spoken.

Written dialects and registers also exist. They vary, based on the type of written work, when it was created, where it was written, by whom it was written, for what purposes, and for what audience it was intended. Authors of dramas, stories, and poetry employ the use of dialect for a multitude of reasons. For instance, when authors wish to develop a clear picture of the setting and characters within a drama, dialect plays a significant role. Here are some examples of dialect:

"Bess, you is my woman now..."—from George Gershwin's opera, *Porgy and Bess*

"That ain't no matter."—from Mark Twain's novel, *Huckleberry Finn*

With the careful and skillful placement of written dialect, the author conveys the character's personality, situation, and social class.

## Literal Meaning of Unknown Words

As children advance in their reading fluency, written material will likewise become more complex. Students transition from reading works in which the meaning is literal and direct, to works that require a more critical thinking approach. Educators can facilitate this transition by modeling and demonstrating how to use context clues, syntax, roots, and suffixes to derive meaning from texts.

### Context Clues

There are many types of clues found within sentences that help to clarify the meaning of unfamiliar words. Sometimes sentences provide a clear and direct definition of an unfamiliar word:

> Anglophones, *also known as native English speakers,* are found in every corner of the globe.

Teaching children phrases that are used to compare and contrast can also be an effective instructional approach:

> The workday today was laborious *as opposed to* yesterday, which was relaxed and easy going.

If children were unfamiliar with the word *laborious*, they would quickly decipher that it means the opposite of *relaxed* and *easy going*, thanks to the use of the phrase *as opposed to*.

### Syntax

There is a certain order to the way in which words are placed in a sentence. For instance, many English sentences follow the pattern of noun + verb + object. The more acquainted children become with syntax, the stronger their ability to recognize parts of speech and how they are interrelated.

### Roots and Affixes

Having even a rudimentary understanding of root words and affixes can greatly increase a reader's ability to decipher unknown words. The study of word origins helps children to understand that words are not just arbitrarily put together, but they are often formed like pieces of a puzzle. The following are examples:

- Astronaut
  - Astro: star or celestial body (Greek)
  - Naut: sailor (Greek origin)
- Portable
  - Port: carry
  - Able: ability, capacity

## Figurative Language

Figurative language is a specific style of speaking or writing that uses tools for a variety of effects. It entertains readers, ignites imagination, and promotes creativity. Instead of writing in realistic terms or

literal terms, figurative language plays with words and prompts readers to infer the underlying meaning. There are seven types of figurative language:

| Type | Definition | Example |
| --- | --- | --- |
| Personification | Giving animate qualities to an inanimate object | The tree stood tall and still, staring up at the sky. |
| Simile | The comparison of two unlike things using connecting words | Your eyes are as blue as the ocean. |
| Metaphor | The comparison of two unlike things without the use of connecting words | She was in the twilight of her years. |
| Hyperbole | An over-exaggeration | I could eat a million of these cookies! |
| Alliteration | The patterned repetition of an initial consonant sound | The bunnies are bouncing in baskets. |
| Onomatopoeia | Words that are formed by using the very sound associated with the word itself | "Drip, drip, drip" went the kitchen faucet. |
| Idioms | Common sayings that carry a lesson or meaning that must be inferred | That math work was a piece of cake! |

## Interpretation

Since idioms and hyperboles are commonly used in everyday speech, educators may wish to introduce them early.

I'm so tired that I could sleep forever!—Hyperbole

He's not playing with a full deck!—Idiom

Other forms of figurative language can be found in poetry and in children's stories. As educators come across figurative speech, they can prompt children's critical thinking skills by asking what they think the author meant by those words or that particular sentence. Giving concrete examples of each style and challenging children to attempt writing their very own creative sentences will strengthen their understanding and application of figurative language.

## Relationship Between Word Choice and Tone

The words authors choose to use must always be well thought out. Although words carry specific meanings, they also carry *connotations*—emotional feelings that are evoked by the words. Connotation creates the tone of the writing. Some words can be said to be loaded words or trigger words that ignite strong emotional responses in readers. These two sentences offer examples:

My grandfather is a robust, elderly man.

My grandfather is a chubby, old man.

In the first sentence, the adjectives used to describe the grandfather instill positive emotions in the reader. However, in the second sentence, the adjectives instill negative emotions. The *mood* of a writing piece refers to the emotions—positive or negative—the reader feels during and after reading. *Tone* refers to the author's purposeful choice of words, designed to evoke those feelings.

## Word Choice, Order, and Punctuation

Language is a powerful communication tool that advances thought and facilitates social change. Some features of language that play key roles in communication include word choice, order, and punctuation.

For example, an author can write two sentences that carry a similar meaning but evoke opposing emotions based on word choice. For instance, to write that a person is *intelligent* is a compliment, but to rewrite that sentence and replace *intelligent* with *smart aleck* changes the compliment to an insult. The order of words can also be effective in writing. Instead of beginning a sentence with the subject, authors can begin with the predicate, which instills a sense of mystery and wonder in the reader. The same can be true of fictional stories in which the author begins at the end or in the middle and works backward to unravel the tale. These writing styles create a powerful, dramatic effect on the stories.

Punctuation can also play a key role in how a reader interprets a passage:

He did do his homework?

He did do his homework!

With the mere change in ending punctuation, the author changes the reader's interpretation of the sentence. Although both sentences use identical words and order, the first sentence infers nothing more than an innocent inquiry, whereas the second infers an emotional, perhaps defensive response.

# Practice Questions

1. When children begin to negotiate the sounds that make up words in their language independently, what skill/s are they demonstrating?
    a. Phonological awareness
    b. Phonemes
    c. Phoneme substitution
    d. Blending skills

2. What is phonics?
    a. The study of syllabication
    b. The study of onsets and rimes
    c. The study of sound-letter relationships
    d. The study of graphemes

3. Word analysis skills are NOT critical for the development of what area of literacy?
    a. Vocabulary
    b. Reading fluency
    c. Spelling
    d. Articulation

4. What area of study involves mechanics, usage, and sentence formation?
    a. Word analysis
    b. Spelling conventions
    c. Morphemes
    d. Phonics

5. How do the majority of high-frequency sight words differ from decodable words?
    a. They do not rhyme.
    b. They do not follow the Alphabetic Principle.
    c. They do not contain onsets.
    d. They contain rimes.

6. Reading fluency involves what key areas?
    a. Accuracy, rate, and prosody
    b. Accuracy, rate, and consistency
    c. Prosody, accuracy, and clarity
    d. Rate, prosody, and comprehension

7. When students study character development, setting, and plot, what are they studying?
    a. Word analysis
    b. Points of view
    c. Literary analysis of a text
    d. Fluency

8. The author's purpose, major ideas, supporting details, visual aids, and vocabulary are the five key elements of what type of text?
    a. Fictional texts
    b. Narratives
    c. Persuasive texts
    d. Informational texts

9. When students use inference, what are they able to do?
    a. Make logical assumptions based on contextual clues
    b. Independently navigate various types of text
    c. Summarize a text's main idea
    d. Paraphrase a text's main idea

10. Story maps, an effective instructional tool, do NOT help children in what way?
    a. Analyze relationships among characters, events, and ideas in literature
    b. Understand key details of a story
    c. Follow the story's development
    d. Read at a faster pace

11. Which text feature does NOT help a reader locate information in printed or digital text?
    a. Hyperlink
    b. Sidebar
    c. Glossary
    d. Heading

12. Read the following passage to answer the question below:

> *He is a kind and generous man who wants nothing more than the best for his community,* thought Michael as the board members discussed the nominees for head of council. Lana June, however, was far more critical. *He is just saying those things to get elected,* she thought.

What is the author's point of view?
    a. First person
    b. Third person limited
    c. Third person omniscient
    d. Objective

13. What do *quantitative*, *qualitative*, and *reader* and *task* measure?
    a. Text complexity
    b. Genres of writing
    c. Points of view
    d. Reading comprehension

14. Autobiographies and memoirs are examples of what form of writing?
    a. Fiction
    b. Narrative
    c. Informational text
    d. Research papers

15. Rating scales, student logs, and the POWER method are effective assessment practices for what area of literacy development?
   a. Reading
   b. Writing
   c. Spelling
   d. Listening

16. Which effective writing area engages and connects with the audience, igniting emotion?
   a. Ethos
   b. Logos
   c. Pathos
   d. Kairos

17. When children begin to leave spaces between words with a mixture of uppercase and lowercase letters, what developmental stage of writing are they demonstrating?
   a. Emergence of beginning sound
   b. Strings of letters
   c. Words represented by consonants
   d. Transitional phase

18. First-hand accounts of an event, subject matter, time period, or an individual are referred to as what type of source?
   a. Primary sources
   b. Secondary sources
   c. Direct sources
   d. Indirect sources

19. The following is an example of what type of sentence?
   Although I wished it were summer, I accepted the change of seasons, and I started to appreciate the fall.

   a. Compound
   b. Simple
   c. Complex
   d. Compound-Complex

20. Read the following sentence to answer the question below:
   The teacher directed the children's attention to the diagram, but the children couldn't understand the information.

This is an example of what type of sentence?
   a. Complex
   b. Compound
   c. Simple
   d. Compound-Complex

21. Read the following sentences to answer the question below:
    Give me a shout back when you can.

    Please return my call at your earliest convenience.

What is the main difference in these two sentences?
    a. Point of view
    b. Dialect
    c. Accent
    d. Register

22. What type of literary device is being used in this sentence?
    I worked a billion hours this week!

    a. Idiom
    b. Metaphor
    c. Hyperbole
    d. Alliteration

23. What are the three tiers of vocabulary?
    a. Conversational, academic, and domain-specific language
    b. Informal, formal, and academic
    c. Social, professional, and academic
    d. Phonics, fluency, and rate

24. Volume, articulation, and awareness of audience help with what practice?
    a. Effective instruction
    b. Communication
    c. Active listening
    d. Oral presentations

25. Offering a presenter with undivided attention and asking relevant and timely questions are examples of what skill set?
    a. Active listening skills
    b. Effective speaking
    c. Formal communication
    d. Informal communication

# Answer Explanations

**1. A:** Phonological Awareness refers to a child's ability to understand and use familiar sounds in his or her social environment in order to form coherent words. Phonemes are defined as distinct sound units in any given language. Phonemic substitution is part of phonological awareness—a child's ability to substitute specific phonemes for others. Blending skills refers to the ability to construct or build words from individual phonemes by blending the sounds together in a unique sequence.

**2. C:** When children begin to recognize and apply sound-letter relationships independently and accurately, they are demonstrating a growing mastery of phonics. Phonics is the most commonly used method for teaching people to read and write by associating sounds with their corresponding letters or groups of letters, using a language's alphabetic writing system. Syllabication refers to the ability to break down words into their individual syllables. The study of onsets and rimes strives to help students recognize and separate a word's beginning consonant or consonant-cluster sound—the onset—from the word's rime—the vowel and/or consonants that follow the onset. A grapheme is a letter or a group of letters in a language that represent a sound.

**3. D:** Breaking down words into their individual parts, studying prefixes, suffixes, root words, rimes, and onsets, are all examples of word analysis. When children analyze words, they develop their vocabulary and strengthen their spelling and reading fluency.

**4. B:** Spelling conventions is the area of study that involves mechanics, usage, and sentence formation. Mechanics refers to spelling, punctuation, and capitalization. Usage refers to the use of the various parts of speech within sentences, and sentence formation is the order in which the various words in a sentence appear. Generally speaking, word analysis is the breaking down of words into morphemes and word units in order to arrive at the word's meaning. Morphemes are the smallest units of a written language that carry meaning, and phonics refers to the study of letter-sound relationships.

**5. B:** Although some high-frequency sight words are decodable, the majority of them are not, so they do not follow the Alphabetic Principle, which relies on specific letter-sound correspondence. High-frequency sight words appear often in children's literature and are studied and memorized in order to strengthen a child's spelling and reading fluency. High-frequency sight words, as well as decodable words, may or may not rhyme and may or may not contain onsets and rimes.

**6. A:** Reading fluency involves how accurately a child reads each individual word within a sentence, the speed at which a child reads, and the expression the child applies while reading. Therefore, accuracy, rate, and prosody are the three key areas of reading fluency.

**7. C:** Literary analysis of a fictional text involves several areas of study, including character development, setting, and plot. Although points of view refer to a specific area of study in literary analysis, it is only one area. Word analysis does not involve the study of elements within a fictional text.

**8. D:** Informational texts generally contain five key elements in order to be considered informative. These five elements include the author's purpose, the major ideas, supporting details, visual aids, and key vocabulary. Narratives are accounts—either spoken or written—of an event or a story. Persuasive texts, such as advertisements, use persuasive language to try to convince the reader to act or feel a certain way. Informational texts strive to share factual information about a given subject in order to advance a reader's knowledge.

**9. A:** When a person infers something, he or she is demonstrating the ability to extract key information and make logical assumptions based on that information. The information provided is not direct, but implied. Being able to navigate a variety of texts independently has nothing to do with inference; it demonstrates a student's reading comprehension and fluency. Successfully summarizing and paraphrasing texts are advanced literacy skills that demonstrate a student's reading comprehension and writing proficiency.

**10. D:** Story maps are a specific type of visual aid that helps younger children develop a clearer understanding of a story being read. Story maps may represent the beginning, middle, and ending of a story, or they may be used to develop a clearer picture of each character's personality and traits, unfold the story's plot, or establish the setting.

**11. C:** Informational texts organized with headings, subheadings, sidebars, hyperlinks and other features help strengthen the reader's reading comprehension and vocabulary knowledge. A glossary defines terms and words used within a text.

**12. C:** Third person is a term used to refer to a specific point of view in literature. A third person omniscient point of view develops the point of view of each character within a given story and allows the reader to understand each character's feelings as well as their interpretation of a story's events. Third person limited only offers insight into one character, usually the main character. Character analysis is the intimate study of one character within the story—the character's physical characteristics, personality traits, and relationships to the story's elements and other characters. The story's plot refers to the story's main events; it usually reveals the problem and how it might be resolved. A genre of writing is the specific style of writing the author employs—fiction, non-fiction, mystery, narrative, or informational text.

**13. A:** These are all measures of a text's complexity. Quantitative measures determine a text's level of difficulty. There are several ways to measure this level of difficulty, some of which are sentence length, number of unfamiliar words, and even syllable count within words. Qualitative measures examine a text's attributes, including clarity of language, figurative versus literal language, and a text's overall meaning. Since each reader has unique background knowledge, skill set, and level of reading motivation, reader and task refers to how likely a reader is to engage in and comprehend a given text. Thus, all three of these components comprise a text's complexity. A genre of writing is simply the style of writing that the author employs. Authors will always reveal a given point of view in fictional writing. Sometimes, the author offers readers several points of view, and sometimes, the points of view are limited. Reading comprehension refers to how well a student demonstrates understanding or mastery of the text.

**14. B:** Narratives are personal accounts of a time period, event, or an individual, with the purpose of documenting, recording, or sharing such factual information. By contrast, fiction is a genre of writing that is fabricated. Informational texts are academic texts used to further a student's mastery of a given subject, and research papers are written reports students write to demonstrate their understanding of a given area of study that has been researched.

**15. B:** There are several effective assessments to evaluate a child's overall writing progress. Rating scales, student logs, and the POWER method are just some of these assessment methods. Although

educators can create rating scales and student logs to assess and help students assess reading and spelling, the POWER method is specific to writing:

P—Prewriting

O—Organizing

W—Writing a rough draft

E—Evaluating

R—Revise and Rewrite

**16. C:** Pathos refers to the author's appeal to the audience or reader's emotions. Ethos refers to the level of credibility of a piece of writing. Logos refers to the author's appeal to the audience or reader's logic. Kairos refers to the most opportune moment to do something. Therefore, the correct answer is pathos.

**17. C:** There are eight developmental writing stages:

- Scribbling
- Letter-like symbols
- Strings of letters
- The emergence of beginning sounds
- Words represented by consonants
- Initial, middle, and final sounds
- Transitional phase
- Standard spelling

When children begin to leave visible spacing between words, even if those words are incorrectly spelled or if there is a mixture of upper and lower case letters, they are considered to be at the *Words represented by consonants* stage.

**18. A:** Firsthand accounts are given by primary sources—individuals who provide personal or expert accounts of an event, subject matter, time period, or of an individual. They are viewed more as objective accounts than subjective. Secondary sources are accounts given by an individual or group of individuals who were not physically present at the event or who did not have firsthand knowledge of an individual or time period. Secondary sources are sources that have used research in order to create a written work. Direct and indirect sources are not terms used in literary circles.

**19. D:** Since the sentence contains two independent clauses and a dependent clause, the sentence is categorized as compound-complex:

Independent clause: *I accepted the change of seasons*

Independent clause: *I started to appreciate the fall*

Dependent clause: *Although I wished it were summer*

**20. B:** Since the sentence contains two independent clauses connected by a conjunction, it is referred to as a compound sentence.

Independent clause: *The teacher directed the children's attention to the diagram*

Independent clause: *The children couldn't understand the information*

Conjunction: *But*

**21. D:** The first sentence is written quite informally and gives a clear impression that the exchange is on a socially relaxed level. The second sentence is written quite formally and gives a clear impression that the exchange is academic or professional in nature. Although both sentences carry the same message—to respond to the messenger as quickly as possible—the register, or level of formality, is very different.

Accent refers to the way in which certain words are pronounced by an individual and is usually dependent on where a person resides. Dialect refers to how groups of people from a specific geographical region manipulate their language. Point of view refers to a person's interpretation of or feelings toward an event. In literature, a point of view refers to a character's interpretation of or feelings toward an event.

**22. C:** When authors use hyperbole, they are using extreme exaggeration to strongly state a point or evoke a specific emotion in the reader. Idioms can be in the form of words, phrases, or sentences that are expressed figuratively, but they carry a literal meaning that readers must infer. Metaphors are literary devices that compare two unlike entities, as in "The United States is a melting pot." Alliteration is a poetic device that repeats the beginning consonant sound throughout a sentence or phrase strictly for entertainment—"The **b**all **b**ounced along the **b**lue **b**alcony."

**23. A:** The three tiers of vocabulary are as follows:

Conversational: informal, more relaxed

Academic: more professional, with vocabulary intended to challenge critical thinking skills

Domain-specific language: a unique vocabulary inventory that focuses around a given discipline or computer language

**24. D:** In order for oral presentations to be effective, the presenter's volume should match the size of audience and the location of the presentation. The presenter should also practice articulation—how clearly the words are being said. The third most important element of oral presentations is how well the presenter is engaging the audience. Making eye contact, moving around the room, and involving the audience, when appropriate, are all part of audience awareness skills.

**25. A:** Active listening skills are very important in all forms of communication, whether one is at home, among friends, in school, or at work. An active listener is one who pays close attention to what is being said, maintains eye contact, uses body language to indicate respect, asks relevant questions, and shares information that directly pertains to the subject.

# Mathematics

## Numbers Sense and Mathematical Operations

### Base-10 Numerals, Number Names, and Expanded Form

Numbers used in everyday life are constituted in a base-10 system. Each digit in a number, depending on its location, represents some multiple of 10, or quotient of 10 when dealing with decimals. Each digit to the left of the decimal point represents a higher multiple of 10. Each digit to the right of the decimal point represents a quotient of a higher multiple of 10 for the divisor. For example, consider the number 7,631.42. The digit one represents simply the number one. The digit 3 represents $3 \times 10$. The digit 6 represents $6 \times 10 \times 10$ (or $6 \times 100$). The digit 7 represents $7 \times 10 \times 10 \times 10$ (or $7 \times 1000$). The digit 4 represents $4 \div 10$. The digit 2 represents $(2 \div 10) \div 10$, or $2 \div (10 \times 10)$ or $2 \div 100$.

A number is written in expanded form by expressing it as the sum of the value of each of its digits. The expanded form in the example above, which is written with the highest value first down to the lowest value, is expressed as: $7,000 + 600 + 30 + 1 + .4 + .02$.

When verbally expressing a number, the integer part of the number (the numbers to the left of the decimal point) resembles the expanded form without the addition between values. In the above example, the numbers read "seven thousand six hundred thirty-one." When verbally expressing the decimal portion of a number, the number is read as a whole number, followed by the place value of the furthest digit (non-zero) to the right. In the above example, 0.42 is read "forty-two hundredths." Reading the number 7,631.42 in its entirety is expressed as "seven thousand six hundred thirty-one and forty-two hundredths." The word *and* is used between the integer and decimal parts of the number.

### Composing and Decomposing Multi-Digit Numbers

Composing and decomposing numbers aids in conceptualizing what each digit of a multi-digit number represents. The standard, or typical, form in which numbers are written consists of a series of digits representing a given value based on their place value. Consider the number 592.7. This number is composed of 5 hundreds, 9 tens, 2 ones, and 7 tenths.

Composing a number requires adding the given numbers for each place value and writing the numbers in standard form. For example, composing 4 thousands, 5 hundreds, 2 tens, and 8 ones consists of adding as follows: $4,000 + 500 + 20 + 8$, to produce 4,528 (standard form).

Decomposing a number requires taking a number written in standard form and breaking it apart into the sum of each place value. For example, the number 83.17 is decomposed by breaking it into the sum of 4 values (for each of the 4 digits): 8 tens, 3 ones, 1 tenth, and 7 hundredths. The decomposed or "expanded" form of 83.17 is $80 + 3 + .1 + .07$.

### Place Value of a Given Digit

The number system that is used consists of only ten different digits or characters. However, this system is used to represent an infinite number of values. The place value system makes this infinite number of values possible. The position in which a digit is written corresponds to a given value. Starting from the decimal point (which is implied, if not physically present), each subsequent place value to the left

represents a value greater than the one before it. Conversely, starting from the decimal point, each subsequent place value to the right represents a value less than the one before it.

The names for the place values to the left of the decimal point are as follows:

| ... | Billions | Hundred-Millions | Ten-Millions | Millions | Hundred-Thousands | Ten-Thousands | Thousands | Hundreds | Tens | Ones |
|---|---|---|---|---|---|---|---|---|---|---|

*Note that this table can be extended infinitely further to the left.

The names for the place values to the right of the decimal point are as follows:

| Decimal Point (.) | Tenths | Hundredths | Thousandths | Ten-Thousandths | ... |
|---|---|---|---|---|---|

*Note that this table can be extended infinitely further to the right.

When given a multi-digit number, the value of each digit depends on its place value. Consider the number 682,174.953. Referring to the chart above, it can be determined that the digit 8 is in the ten-thousands place. It is in the fifth place to the left of the decimal point. Its value is 8 ten-thousands or 80,000. The digit 5 is two places to the right of the decimal point. Therefore, the digit 5 is in the hundredths place. Its value is 5 hundredths or $\frac{5}{100}$ (equivalent to .05).

## Base-10 System

### Value of Digits
In accordance with the base-10 system, the value of a digit increases by a factor of ten each place it moves to the left. For example, consider the number 7. Moving the digit one place to the left (70), increases its value by a factor of 10 ($7 \times 10 = 70$). Moving the digit two places to the left (700) increases its value by a factor of 10 twice ($7 \times 10 \times 10 = 700$). Moving the digit three places to the left (7,000) increases its value by a factor of 10 three times ($7 \times 10 \times 10 \times 10 = 7,000$), and so on.

Conversely, the value of a digit decreases by a factor of ten each place it moves to the right. (Note that multiplying by $\frac{1}{10}$ is equivalent to dividing by 10). For example, consider the number 40. Moving the digit one place to the right (4) decreases its value by a factor of 10 ($40 \div 10 = 4$). Moving the digit two places to the right (0.4), decreases its value by a factor of 10 twice ($40 \div 10 \div 10 = 0.4$) or ($40 \times \frac{1}{10} \times \frac{1}{10} = 0.4$). Moving the digit three places to the right (0.04) decreases its value by a factor of 10 three times ($40 \div 10 \div 10 \div 10 = 0.04$) or ($40 \times \frac{1}{10} \times \frac{1}{10} \times \frac{1}{10} = 0.04$), and so on.

### Exponents to Denote Powers of 10
The value of a given digit of a number in the base-10 system can be expressed utilizing powers of 10. A power of 10 refers to 10 raised to a given exponent such as $10^0$, $10^1$, $10^2$, $10^3$, etc. For the number $10^3$, 10 is the base and 3 is the exponent. A base raised by an exponent represents how many times the base is multiplied by itself. Therefore, $10^1 = 10$, $10^2 = 10 \times 10 = 100$, $10^3 = 10 \times 10 \times 10 = 1,000$, $10^4 = 10 \times 10 \times 10 \times 10 = 10,000$, etc. Any base with a zero exponent equals one.

Powers of 10 are utilized to decompose a multi-digit number without writing all the zeroes. Consider the number 872,349. This number is decomposed to $800,000 + 70,000 + 2,000 + 300 + 40 + 9$. When utilizing powers of 10, the number 872,349 is decomposed to $(8 \times 10^5) + (7 \times 10^4) + (2 \times 10^3) + (3 \times 10^2) + (4 \times 10^1) + (9 \times 10^0)$. The power of 10 by which the digit is multiplied corresponds to the

number of zeroes following the digit when expressing its value in standard form. For example, $7 \times 10^4$ is equivalent to 70,000 or 7 followed by four zeros.

## Rounding Multi-Digit Numbers

Rounding numbers changes the given number to a simpler and less accurate number than the exact given number. Rounding allows for easier calculations which estimate the results of using the exact given number. The accuracy of the estimate and ease of use depends on the place value to which the number is rounded. Rounding numbers consists of:

- Determining what place value the number is being rounded to
- Examining the digit to the right of the desired place value to decide whether to round up or keep the digit
- Replacing all digits to the right of the desired place value with zeros

To round 746,311 to the nearest ten thousands, the digit in the ten thousands place should be located first. In this case, this digit is 4 (7<u>4</u>6,311). Then, the digit to its right is examined. If this digit is 5 or greater, the number will be rounded up by increasing the digit in the desired place by one. If the digit to the right of the place value being rounded is 4 or less, the number will be kept the same. For the given example, the digit being examined is a 6, which means that the number will be rounded up by increasing the digit to the left by one. Therefore, the digit 4 is changed to a 5. Finally, to write the rounded number, any digits to the left of the place value being rounded remain the same and any to its right are replaced with zeros. For the given example, rounding 746,311 to the nearest ten thousand will produce 750,000. To round 746,311 to the nearest hundred, the digit to the right of the three in the hundreds place is examined to determine whether to round up or keep the same number. In this case, that digit is a one, so the number will be kept the same and any digits to its right will be replaced with zeros. The resulting rounded number is 746,300.

Rounding place values to the right of the decimal follows the same procedure, but digits being replaced by zeros can simply be dropped. To round 3.752891 to the nearest thousandth, the desired place value is located (3.75<u>2</u>891) and the digit to the right is examined. In this case, the digit 8 indicates that the number will be rounded up, and the 2 in the thousandths place will increase to a 3. Rounding up and replacing the digits to the right of the thousandths place produces 3.753000 which is equivalent to 3.753. Therefore, the zeros are not necessary and the rounded number should be written as 3.753.

When rounding up, if the digit to be increased is a 9, the digit to its left is increased by 1 and the digit in the desired place value is changed to a zero. For example, the number 1,598 rounded to the nearest ten is 1,600. Another example shows the number 43.72961 rounded to the nearest thousandth is 43.730 or 43.73.

## Solving Multistep Mathematical and Real-World Problems

### Problem Situations for Operations

Addition and subtraction are *inverse operations*. Adding a number and then subtracting the same number will cancel each other out, resulting in the original number, and vice versa. For example, $8 + 7 - 7 = 8$ and $137 - 100 + 100 = 137$. Similarly, multiplication and division are inverse operations. Therefore, multiplying by a number and then dividing by the same number results in the original number, and vice versa. For example, $8 \times 2 \div 2 = 8$ and $12 \div 4 \times 4 = 12$. Inverse operations are used to work backwards to solve problems. In the case that 7 and a number add to 18, the inverse operation

of subtraction is used to find the unknown value ($18- 7 = 11$). If a school's entire 4th grade was divided evenly into 3 classes each with 22 students, the inverse operation of multiplication is used to determine the total students in the grade ($22 \times 3 = 66$). Additional scenarios involving inverse operations are included in the tables below.

There are a variety of real-world situations in which one or more of the operators is used to solve a problem. The tables below display the most common scenarios.

## Addition & Subtraction

|  | Unknown Result | Unknown Change | Unknown Start |
|---|---|---|---|
| Adding to | 5 students were in class. 4 more students arrived. How many students are in class? $5 + 4 =?$ | 8 students were in class. More students arrived late. There are now 18 students in class. How many students arrived late? $8+? = 18$ Solved by inverse operations $18- 8 =?$ | Some students were in class early. 11 more students arrived. There are now 17 students in class. How many students were in class early? $? +11 = 17$ Solved by inverse operations $17- 11 =?$ |
| Taking from | 15 students were in class. 5 students left class. How many students are in class now? $15- 5 =?$ | 12 students were in class. Some students left class. There are now 8 students in class. How many students left class? $12-? = 8$ Solved by inverse operations $8+? = 12 \; \rightarrow 12- 8 =?$ | Some students were in class. 3 students left class. Then there were 13 students in class. How many students were in class before? $?- 3 = 13$ Solved by inverse operations $13 + 3 =?$ |

|  | Unknown Total | Unknown Addends (Both) | Unknown Addends (One) |
|---|---|---|---|
| Putting together/ taking apart | The homework assignment is 10 addition problems and 8 subtraction problems. How many problems are in the homework assignment? $10 + 8 =?$ | Bobby has $9. How much can Bobby spend on candy and how much can Bobby spend on toys? $9 =? +?$ | Bobby has 12 pairs of pants. 5 pairs of pants are shorts, and the rest are long. How many pairs of long pants does he have? $12 = 5+?$ Solved by inverse operations $12- 5 =?$ |

| | Unknown Difference | Unknown Larger Value | Unknown Smaller Value |
|---|---|---|---|
| Comparing | Bobby has 5 toys. Tommy has 8 toys. How many more toys does Tommy have than Bobby? $5 + ? = 8$ Solved by inverse operations $8 - 5 = ?$ Bobby has \$6. Tommy has \$10. How many fewer dollars does Bobby have than Tommy? $10 - 6 = ?$ | Tommy has 2 more toys than Bobby. Bobby has 4 toys. How many toys does Tommy have? $2 + 4 = ?$ Bobby has 3 fewer dollars than Tommy. Bobby has \$8. How many dollars does Tommy have? $? - 3 = 8$ Solved by inverse operations $8 + 3 = ?$ | Tommy has 6 more toys than Bobby. Tommy has 10 toys. How many toys does Bobby have? $? + 6 = 10$ Solved by inverse operations $10 - 6 = ?$ Bobby has \$5 less than Tommy. Tommy has \$9. How many dollars does Bobby have? $9 - 5 = ?$ |

## Multiplication and Division

| | Unknown Product | Unknown Group Size | Unknown Number of Groups |
|---|---|---|---|
| Equal groups | There are 5 students, and each student has 4 pieces of candy. How many pieces of candy are there in all? $5 \times 4 = ?$ | 14 pieces of candy are shared equally by 7 students. How many pieces of candy does each student have? $7 \times ? = 14$ Solved by inverse operations $14 \div 7 = ?$ | If 18 pieces of candy are to be given out 3 to each student, how many students will get candy? $? \times 3 = 18$ Solved by inverse operations $18 \div 3 = ?$ |

| | Unknown Product | Unknown Factor | Unknown Factor |
|---|---|---|---|
| Arrays | There are 5 rows of students with 3 students in each row. How many students are there? $5 \times 3 = ?$ | If 16 students are arranged into 4 equal rows, how many students will be in each row? $4 \times ? = 16$ Solved by inverse operations $16 \div 4 = ?$ | If 24 students are arranged into an array with 6 columns, how many rows are there? $? \times 6 = 24$ Solved by inverse operations $24 \div 6 = ?$ |

|  | **Larger Unknown** | **Smaller Unknown** | **Multiplier Unknown** |
|---|---|---|---|
| Comparing | A small popcorn costs $1.50. A large popcorn costs 3 times as much as a small popcorn. How much does a large popcorn cost? $1.50 \times 3 =?$ | A large soda costs $6 and that is 2 times as much as a small soda costs. How much does a small soda cost? $2 \times ? = 6$ Solved by inverse operations $6 \div 2 =?$ | A large pretzel costs $3 and a small pretzel costs $2. How many times as much does the large pretzel cost as the small pretzel? $? \times 2 = 3$ Solved by inverse operations $3 \div 2 =?$ |

## Remainders in Division Problems

If a given total cannot be divided evenly into a given number of groups, the amount left over is the remainder. Consider the following scenario: 32 textbooks must be packed into boxes for storage. Each box holds 6 textbooks. How many boxes are needed? To determine the answer, 32 is divided by 6, resulting in 5 with a remainder of 2. A remainder may be interpreted three ways:

- Add 1 to the quotient
  How many boxes will be needed? Six boxes will be needed because five will not be enough.

- Use only the quotient
  How many boxes will be full? Five boxes will be full.

- Use only the remainder
  If you only have 5 boxes, how many books will not fit? Two books will not fit.

## Strategies and Algorithms to Perform Operations on Rational Numbers

A rational number is any number that can be written in the form of a ratio or fraction. Integers can be written as fractions with a denominator of 1 ($5 = \frac{5}{1}$; $-342 = \frac{-342}{1}$; etc.). Decimals that terminate and/or repeat can also be written as fractions ($47 = \frac{47}{100}$; $.\overline{33} = \frac{1}{3}$). For more on converting decimals to fractions, see the section *Converting Between Fractions, Decimals,* and *Percent.*

When adding or subtracting fractions, the numbers must have the same denominators. In these cases, numerators are added or subtracted and denominators are kept the same. For example, $\frac{2}{7} + \frac{3}{7} = \frac{5}{7}$ and $\frac{4}{5} - \frac{3}{5} = \frac{1}{5}$. If the fractions to be added or subtracted do not have the same denominator, a common denominator must be found. This is accomplished by changing one or both fractions to a different but equivalent fraction. Consider the example $\frac{1}{6} + \frac{4}{9}$. First, a common denominator must be found. One method is to find the least common multiple (LCM) of the denominators 6 and 9. This is the lowest number that both 6 and 9 will divide into evenly. In this case the LCM is 18. Both fractions should be changed to equivalent fractions with a denominator of 18. To obtain the numerator of the new fraction, the old numerator is multiplied by the same number by which the old denominator is multiplied. For the fraction $\frac{1}{6}$, 6 multiplied by 3 will produce a denominator of 18. Therefore, the numerator is multiplied by 3 to produce the new numerator $\left(\frac{1 \times 3}{6 \times 3} = \frac{3}{18}\right)$. For the fraction $\frac{4}{9}$, multiplying both the numerator and

denominator by 2 produces $\frac{8}{18}$. Since the two new fractions have common denominators, they can be added $\left(\frac{3}{18} + \frac{8}{18} = \frac{11}{18}\right)$.

When multiplying or dividing rational numbers, these numbers may be converted to fractions and multiplied or divided accordingly. When multiplying fractions, all numerators are multiplied by each other and all denominators are multiplied by each other. For example, $\frac{1}{3} \times \frac{6}{5} = \frac{1 \times 6}{3 \times 5} = \frac{6}{15}$ and $\frac{-1}{2} \times \frac{3}{1} \times \frac{11}{100} = \frac{-1 \times 3 \times 11}{2 \times 1 \times 100} = \frac{-33}{200}$. When dividing fractions, the problem is converted by multiplying by the reciprocal of the divisor. This is done by changing division to multiplication and "flipping" the second fraction, or divisor. For example, $\frac{1}{2} \div \frac{3}{5} \rightarrow \frac{1}{2} \times \frac{5}{3}$ and $\frac{5}{1} \div \frac{1}{3} \rightarrow \frac{5}{1} \times \frac{3}{1}$. To complete the problem, the rules for multiplying fractions should be followed.

Note that when adding, subtracting, multiplying, and dividing mixed numbers (ex. $4\frac{1}{2}$), it is easiest to convert these to improper fractions (larger numerator than denominator). To do so, the denominator is kept the same. To obtain the numerator, the whole number is multiplied by the denominator and added to the numerator. For example, $4\frac{1}{2} = \frac{9}{2}$ and $7\frac{2}{3} = \frac{23}{3}$. Also, note that answers involving fractions should be converted to the simplest form.

## Rational Numbers and Their Operations

### Irregular Products and Quotients

The following shows examples where multiplication does not result in a product greater than both factors, and where division does not result in a quotient smaller than the dividend.

If multiplying numbers where one or more has a value less than one, the product will not be greater than both factors. For example, $6 \times \frac{1}{2} = 3$ and $0.75 \times 0.2 = .15$. When dividing by a number less than one, the resulting quotient will be greater than the dividend. For example, $8 \div \frac{1}{2} = 16$, because division turns into a multiplication problem, $8 \div \frac{1}{2} \rightarrow 8 \times \frac{2}{1}$. Another example is $0.5 \div 0.2$, which results in 2.5. The problem can be stated by asking how many times 0.2 will go into 0.5. The number being divided is larger than the number that goes into it, so the result will be a number larger than both factors.

### Composing and Decomposing Fractions

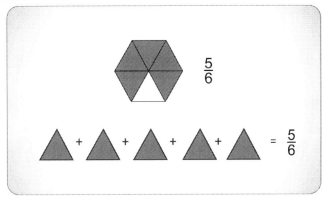

Fractions can be broken apart into sums of fractions with the same denominator. For example, the fraction $\frac{5}{6}$ can be decomposed into sums of fractions with all denominators equal to 6 and the numerators adding to 5. The fraction $\frac{5}{6}$ is decomposed as: $\frac{3}{6} + \frac{2}{6}$; or $\frac{2}{6} + \frac{2}{6} + \frac{1}{6}$; or $\frac{3}{6} + \frac{1}{6} + \frac{1}{6}$; or $\frac{1}{6} + \frac{1}{6} + \frac{1}{6} + \frac{2}{6}$; or $\frac{1}{6} + \frac{1}{6} + \frac{1}{6} + \frac{1}{6} + \frac{1}{6}$.

A unit fraction is a fraction in which the numerator is 1. If decomposing a fraction into unit fractions, the sum will consist of a unit fraction added the number of times equal to the numerator. For example, $\frac{3}{4} = \frac{1}{4} + \frac{1}{4} + \frac{1}{4}$ (unit fractions $\frac{1}{4}$ added 3 times). Composing fractions is simply the opposite of decomposing. It is the process of adding fractions with the same denominators to produce a single fraction. For example, $\frac{3}{7} + \frac{2}{7} = \frac{5}{7}$ and $\frac{1}{5} + \frac{1}{5} + \frac{1}{5} = \frac{3}{5}$.

## Decrease in Value of a Unit Fraction

A unit fraction is one in which the numerator is 1 ($\frac{1}{2}, \frac{1}{3}, \frac{1}{8}, \frac{1}{20}$, etc.). The denominator indicates the number of *equal pieces* that the whole is divided into. The greater the number of pieces, the smaller each piece will be. Therefore, the greater the denominator of a unit fraction, the smaller it is in value. Unit fractions can also be compared by converting them to decimals. For example, $\frac{1}{2} = 0.5$, $\frac{1}{3} = 0.\overline{3}$, $\frac{1}{8} = 0.125$, $\frac{1}{20} = 0.05$, etc.

## Use of the Same Whole when Comparing Fractions

Fractions all represent parts of the same whole. Fractions may have different denominators, but they represent parts of the same one whole, like a pizza. For example, the fractions $\frac{5}{7}$ and $\frac{2}{3}$ can be difficult to compare because they have different denominators. The first fraction may represent a whole divided into seven parts, where five parts are used. The second fraction represents the same whole divided into three parts, where two are used. It may be helpful to convert one or more of the fractions so that they have common denominators for converting to equivalent fractions by finding the LCM of the denominator. Comparing is much easier if fractions are converted to the equivalent fractions of $\frac{15}{21}$ and $\frac{14}{21}$. These fractions show a whole divided into 21 parts, where the numerators can be compared because the denominators are the same.

## Order of Operations

When reviewing calculations consisting of more than one operation, the order in which the operations are performed affects the resulting answer. Consider $5 \times 2 + 7$. Performing multiplication then addition results in an answer of 17 ($5 \times 2 = 10$; $10 + 7 = 17$). However, if the problem is written $5 \times (2 + 7)$, the order of operations dictates that the operation inside the parenthesis must be performed first. The resulting answer is 45 ($2 + 7 = 9$, then $5 \times 9 = 45$).

The order in which operations should be performed is remembered using the acronym PEMDAS. PEMDAS stands for parenthesis, exponents, multiplication/division, and addition/subtraction. Multiplication and division are performed in the same step, working from left to right with whichever comes first. Addition and subtraction are performed in the same step, working from left to right with whichever comes first.

Consider the following example: $8 \div 4 + 8(7 - 7)$. Performing the operation inside the parenthesis produces $8 \div 4 + 8(0)$ or $8 \div 4 + 8 \times 0$. There are no exponents, so multiplication and division are performed next from left to right resulting in: $2 + 8 \times 0$, then $2 + 0$. Finally, addition and subtraction are performed to obtain an answer of 2. Now consider the following example: $6x3 + 3^2 - 6$. Parentheses are not applicable. Exponents are evaluated first, $6 \times 3 + 9 - 6$. Then multiplication/division forms $18 + 9 - 6$. At last, addition/subtraction leads to the final answer of 21.

## Properties of Operations

Properties of operations exist that make calculations easier and solve problems for missing values. The following table summarizes commonly used properties of real numbers.

| Property | Addition | Multiplication |
|---|---|---|
| Commutative | $a + b = b + a$ | $a \times b = b \times a$ |
| Associative | $(a + b) + c = a + (b + c)$ | $(a \times b) \times c = a \times (bc)$ |
| Identity | $a + 0 = a;\ 0 + a = a$ | $a \times 1 = a;\ 1 \times a = a$ |
| Inverse | $a + (-a) = 0$ | $a \times \dfrac{1}{a} = 1;\ a \neq 0$ |
| Distributive | $a(b + c) = ab + ac$ | |

The cumulative property of addition states that the order in which numbers are added does not change the sum. Similarly, the commutative property of multiplication states that the order in which numbers are multiplied does not change the product. The associative property of addition and multiplication state that the grouping of numbers being added or multiplied does not change the sum or product, respectively. The commutative and associative properties are useful for performing calculations. For example, $(47 + 25) + 3$ is equivalent to $(47 + 3) + 25$, which is easier to calculate.

The identity property of addition states that adding zero to any number does not change its value. The identity property of multiplication states that multiplying a number by one does not change its value. The inverse property of addition states that the sum of a number and its opposite equals zero. Opposites are numbers that are the same with different signs (ex. 5 and -5; $-\frac{1}{2}$ and $\frac{1}{2}$). The inverse property of multiplication states that the product of a number (other than zero) and its reciprocal equals one. Reciprocal numbers have numerators and denominators that are inverted (ex. $\frac{2}{5}$ and $\frac{5}{2}$). Inverse properties are useful for canceling quantities to find missing values (see algebra content). For example, $a + 7 = 12$ is solved by adding the inverse of 7 (which is -7) to both sides in order to isolate $a$.

The distributive property states that multiplying a sum (or difference) by a number produces the same result as multiplying each value in the sum (or difference) by the number and adding (or subtracting) the products. Consider the following scenario: You are buying three tickets for a baseball game. Each ticket costs $18. You are also charged a fee of $2 per ticket for purchasing the tickets online. The cost is calculated: $3 \times 18 + 3 \times 2$. Using the distributive property, the cost can also be calculated $3(18 + 2)$.

## Representing Rational Numbers and Their Operations

### Concrete Models
Concrete objects are used to develop a tangible understanding of operations of rational numbers. Tools such as tiles, blocks, beads, and hundred charts are used to model problems. For example, a hundred chart ($10 \times 10$) and beads can be used to model multiplication. If multiplying 5 by 4, beads are placed

across 5 rows and down 4 columns producing a product of 20. Similarly, tiles can be used to model division by splitting the total into equal groups. If dividing 12 by 4, 12 tiles are placed one at a time into 4 groups. The result is 4 groups of 3. This is also an effective method for visualizing the concept of remainders.

Representations of objects can be used to expand on the concrete models of operations. Pictures, dots, and tallies can help model these concepts. Utilizing concrete models and representations creates a foundation upon which to build an abstract understanding of the operations.

## Rational Numbers on a Number Line

A number line typically consists of integers (...3,2,1,0,-1,-2,-3...), and is used to visually represent the value of a rational number. Each rational number has a distinct position on the line determined by comparing its value with the displayed values on the line. For example, if plotting -1.5 on the number line below, it is necessary to recognize that the value of -1.5 is .5 less than -1 and .5 greater than -2. Therefore, -1.5 is plotted halfway between -1 and -2.

Number lines can also be useful for visualizing sums and differences of rational numbers. Adding a value indicates moving to the right (values increase to the right), and subtracting a value indicates moving to the left (numbers decrease to the left). For example, $5 - 7$ is displayed by starting at 5 and moving to the left 7 spaces, if the number line is in increments of 1. This will result in an answer of -2.

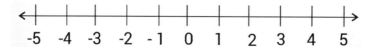

## Multiplication and Division Problems

Multiplication and division are inverse operations that can be represented by using rectangular arrays, area models, and equations. Rectangular arrays include an arrangement of rows and columns that correspond to the factors and display product totals.

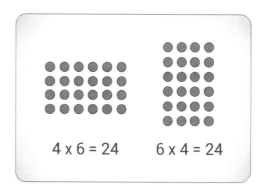

4 x 6 = 24       6 x 4 = 24

Another method of multiplication can be done with the use of an *area model*. An area model is a rectangle that is divided into rows and columns that match up to the number of place values within each number. For example, $29 \times 65 = 25 + 4$ and $66 = 60 + 5$. The products of those 4 numbers are found within the rectangle and then summed up to get the answer. The entire process is: $(60 \times 25) + (5 \times 25) + (60 \times 4) + (5 \times 4) = 1,500 + 240 + 125 + 20 = 1,885$.

Here is the actual area model:

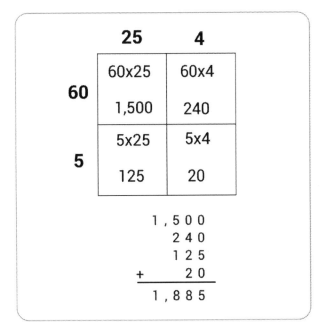

Dividing a number by a single digit or two digits can be turned into repeated subtraction problems. An area model can be used throughout the problem that represents multiples of the divisor. For example, the answer to $8580 \div 55$ can be found by subtracting 55 from 8580 one at a time and counting the total number of subtractions necessary.

However, a simpler process involves using larger multiples of 55. First, $100 \times 55 = 5,500$ is subtracted from 8,580, and 3,080 is leftover. Next, $50 \times 55 = 2,750$ is subtracted from 3,080 to obtain380. $5 \times 55 = 275$ is subtracted from 330 to obtain 55, and finally, $1 \times 55 = 55$ is subtracted from 55 to obtain zero. Therefore, there is no remainder, and the answer is $100 + 50 + 5 + 1 = 156$.

Here is a picture of the area model and the repeated subtraction process:

$$8580 \div 55$$

|      |      |
|------|------|
| 100  | 5500 |
| 50   | 2750 |
| 5    | 275  |
| 1    | 55   |

55 ) 8580
 -5500  (100 x 55)
  3080
 -2750  (50 x 55)
   330
  -275  (5 x 55)
    55
   -55  (1 x 55)
     0

## Comparing, Classifying, and Ordering Rational Numbers

A **rational number** is any number that can be written as a fraction or ratio. Within the set of rational numbers, several subsets exist that are referenced throughout the mathematics topics. Counting numbers are the first numbers learned as a child. Counting numbers consist of 1,2,3,4, and so on. Whole numbers include all counting numbers and zero (0,1,2,3,4,...). Integers include counting numbers, their opposites, and zero (...,-3,-2,-1,0,1,2,3,...). Rational numbers are inclusive of integers, fractions, and decimals that terminate, or end (1.7, 0.04213) or repeat (0.136$\overline{5}$).

When comparing or ordering numbers, the numbers should be written in the same format (decimal or fraction), if possible. For example, $\sqrt{49}$, 7.3, and $\frac{15}{2}$ are easier to order if each one is converted to a decimal, such as 7, 7.3, and 7.5 (converting fractions and decimals is covered in the following section). A number line is used to order and compare the numbers. Any number that is to the right of another number is greater than that number. Conversely, a number positioned to the left of a given number is less than that number.

## Converting Between Fractions, Decimals, and Percent

To convert a fraction to a decimal, the numerator is divided by the denominator. For example, $\frac{3}{8}$ can be converted to a decimal by dividing 3 by 8 ($\frac{3}{8} = 0.375$). To convert a decimal to a fraction, the decimal point is dropped, and the value is written as the numerator. The denominator is the place value farthest to the right with a digit other than zero. For example, to convert .48 to a fraction, the numerator is 48, and the denominator is 100 (the digit 8 is in the hundredths place). Therefore, .48 = $\frac{48}{100}$. Fractions should be written in the simplest form, or reduced. To reduce a fraction, the numerator and denominator are divided by the largest common factor. In the previous example, 48 and 100 are both divisible by 4. Dividing the numerator and denominator by 4 results in a reduced fraction of $\frac{12}{25}$.

To convert a decimal to a percent, the number is multiplied by 100. To convert .13 to a percent, .13 is multiplied by 100 to get 13 percent. To convert a fraction to a percent, the fraction is converted to a decimal and then multiplied by 100. For example, $\frac{1}{5} = .20$ and .20 multiplied by 100 produces 20 percent.

To convert a percent to a decimal, the value is divided by 100. For example, 125 percent is equal to 1.25 ($\frac{125}{100}$). To convert a percent to a fraction, the percent sign is dropped, and the value is written as the numerator with a denominator of 100. For example, 80% = $\frac{80}{100}$. This fraction can be reduced ($\frac{80}{100} = \frac{4}{5}$).

## Understanding Proportional Relationships and Percent

### Applying Ratios and Unit Rates

A ratio is a comparison of two quantities that represent separate groups. For example, if a recipe calls for 2 eggs for every 3 cups of milk, this is expressed as a ratio. Ratios can be written three ways:

- With the word "to"
- Using a colon
- As a fraction.

In the previous example, the ratio of eggs to cups of milk is written as 2 to 3, 2:3, or $\frac{2}{3}$. When writing ratios, the order is very important. The ratio of eggs to cups of milk is not the same as the ratio of cups of milk to eggs, 3:2.

In simplest form, both quantities of a ratio should be written as integers. These should also be reduced just as a fraction is reduced. For example, 5:10 is reduced to 1:2. Given a ratio where one or both quantities are expressed as a decimal or fraction, multiply both by the same number to produce integers. To write the ratio $\frac{1}{3}$ to 2 in simplest form, both quantities are multiplied by 3. The resulting ratio is 1 to 6.

A problem involving ratios may give a comparison between two groups. The problem may then provide a total and ask for a part, or provide a part and ask for a total. Consider the following: The ratio of boys to girls in the 11th grade class is 5:4. If there are a total of 270 11th grade students, how many are girls? The total number of *ratio pieces* should be determined first. The total number of 11th grade students is divided into 9 pieces. The ratio of boys to total students is 5:9, and the ratio of girls to total students is 4:9. Knowing the total number of students, the number of girls is determined by setting up a proportion: $\frac{4}{9} = \frac{x}{270}$.

A rate is a ratio comparing two quantities expressed in different units. A unit rate is a ratio in which the second quantity is one unit. Rates often include the word *per*. Examples include miles per hour, beats per minute, and price per pound. The word per is represented with a / symbol or abbreviated with the letter *p* and units abbreviated. For example, miles per hour is written as mi/h. When given a rate that is not in its simplest form (the second quantity is not one unit), both quantities are divided by the value of the second quantity. If 99 heartbeats were recorded in $1\frac{1}{2}$ minutes, both quantities are divided by $1\frac{1}{2}$ to determine the heart rate of 66 beats per minute.

## Percent

The word percent means per hundred. Similar to a unit rate in which the second quantity is always one unit, a percent is a rate where the second quantity is always 100 units. If the results of a poll state that 47 percent of people support a given policy, this indicates that 47 out of every 100 individuals polled were in support. In other words, 47 per 100 support the policy. If an upgraded model of a car costs 110 percent of the cost of the base model, for every $100 that is spent for the base model, $110 must be spent to purchase the upgraded model. In other words, the upgraded model costs $110 per $100 for the cost of the base model.

When dealing with percentages, the numbers can be evaluated as a value in hundredths. For example, 15 percent is expressed as fifteen hundredths and is written as $\frac{15}{100}$ or 0.15.

## Unit-Rate Problems

A rate is a ratio in which two terms are in different units. When rates are expressed as a quantity of one, they are considered unit rates. To determine a unit rate, the first quantity is divided by the second. Knowing a unit rate makes calculations easier than simply having a rate. For example, suppose a 3 pound bag of onions costs $1.77. To calculate the price of 5 pounds of onions, a proportion could show: $\frac{3}{1.77} = \frac{5}{x}$. However, by knowing the unit rate, the value of pounds of onions is multiplied by the unit price. The unit price is calculated: $\$1.77/3lb = \$0.59/lb$. Multiplying the weight of the onions by the unit price yields: $5lb \times \frac{\$0.59}{lb} = \$2.95$. The *lb.* units cancel out.

Similar to unit-rate problems, unit conversions appear in real-world scenarios including cooking, measurement, construction, and currency. Given the conversion rate, unit conversions are written as a fraction (ratio) and multiplied by a quantity in one unit to convert it to the corresponding unit. To determine how many minutes are in $3\frac{1}{2}$ hours, the conversion rate of 60 minutes to 1 hour is written as $\frac{60 \, min}{1h}$. Multiplying the quantity by the conversion rate results in $3\frac{1}{2}h \times \frac{60 \, min}{1h} = 210 \, min$. (The *h* unit is canceled.) To convert a quantity in minutes to hours, the fraction for the conversion rate is flipped to cancel the *min* unit. To convert 195 minutes to hours, $195min \times \frac{1h}{60 \, min}$ is multiplied. The result is $\frac{195h}{60}$ which reduces to $3\frac{1}{4}$h.

Converting units may require more than one multiplication. The key is to set up conversion rates so that units cancel each other out and the desired unit is left. To convert 3.25 yards to inches, given that 1yd = 3ft and 12in = 1ft, the calculation is performed by multiplying 3.25 yd $\times \frac{3ft}{1yd} \times \frac{12in}{1ft}$. The *yd* and *ft* units will cancel, resulting in 117in.

## Using Proportional Relationships

A proportion is a statement consisting of two equal ratios. Proportions will typically give three of four quantities and require solving for the missing value. The key to solving proportions is to set them up properly. Consider the following: 7 gallons of gas costs $14.70. How many gallons can you get for $20? The information is written as equal ratios with a variable representing the missing quantity $\left(\frac{gallons}{cost} = \frac{gallons}{cost}\right)$: $\frac{7}{14.70} = \frac{x}{20}$. To solve for $x$, the proportion is cross-multiplied. This means the numerator of the first ratio is multiplied by the denominator of the second, and vice versa. The resulting products are shown equal to each other. Cross-multiplying results in $(7)(20) = (14.7)(x)$. By solving

the equation for x (see the algebra content), the answer is that 9.5 gallons of gas may be purchased for $20.

Percent problems can also be solved by setting up proportions. Examples of common percent problems are:

 a. What is 15% of 25?
 b. What percent of 45 is 3?
 c. 5 is $\frac{1}{2}$% of what number?

Setting up the proper proportion is made easier by following the format: $\frac{is}{of} = \frac{percent}{100}$. A variable is used to represent the missing value. The proportions for each of the three examples are set up as follows:

 a. $\frac{x}{25} = \frac{15}{100}$
 b. $\frac{3}{45} = \frac{x}{100}$
 c. $\frac{5}{x} = \frac{\frac{1}{2}}{100}$

By cross-multiplying and solving the resulting equation for the variable, the missing values are determined to be:

 a. 3.75
 b. $6.\overline{6}$%
 c. 1,000

## Basic Concepts of Number Theory

### Prime and Composite Numbers

Whole numbers are classified as either prime or composite. A prime number can only be divided evenly by itself and one. For example, the number 11 can only be divided evenly by 11 and one; therefore, 11 is a prime number. A helpful way to visualize a prime number is to use concrete objects and try to divide them into equal piles. If dividing 11 coins, the only way to divide them into equal piles is to create 1 pile of 11 coins or to create 11 piles of 1 coin each. Other examples of prime numbers include 2, 3, 5, 7, 13, 17, and 19.

A composite number is any whole number that is not a prime number. A composite number is a number that can be divided evenly by one or more numbers other than itself and one. For example, the number 6 can be divided evenly by 2 and 3. Therefore, 6 is a composite number. If dividing 6 coins into equal piles, the possibilities are 1 pile of 6 coins, 2 piles of 3 coins, 3 piles of 2 coins, or 6 piles of 1 coin. Other examples of composite numbers include 4, 8, 9, 10, 12, 14, 15, 16, 18, and 20.

To determine if a number is a prime or composite number, the number is divided by every whole number greater than one and less than its own value. If it divides evenly by any of these numbers, then the number is composite. If it does not divide evenly by any of these numbers, then the number is prime. For example, when attempting to divide the number 5 by 2, 3, and 4, none of these numbers divide evenly. Therefore, 5 must be a prime number.

## Factors and Multiples of Numbers

The factors of a number are all integers that can be multiplied by another integer to produce the given number. For example, 2 is multiplied by 3 to produce 6. Therefore, 2 and 3 are both factors of 6. Similarly, $1 \times 6 = 6$ and $2 \times 3 = 6$, so 1, 2, 3, and 6 are all factors of 6. Another way to explain a factor is to say that a given number divides evenly by each of its factors to produce an integer. For example, 6 does not divide evenly by 5. Therefore, 5 is not a factor of 6.

Multiples of a given number are found by taking that number and multiplying it by any other whole number. For example, 3 is a factor of 6, 9, and 12. Therefore, 6, 9, and 12 are multiples of 3. The multiples of any number are an infinite list. For example, the multiples of 5 are 5, 10, 15, 20, and so on. This list continues without end. A list of multiples is used in finding the least common multiple, or LCM, for fractions when a common denominator is needed. The denominators are written down and their multiples listed until a common number is found in both lists. This common number is the LCM.

Prime factorization breaks down each factor of a whole number until only prime numbers remain. All composite numbers can be factored into prime numbers. For example, the prime factors of 12 are 2, 2, and 3 ($2 \times 2 \times 3 = 12$). To produce the prime factors of a number, the number is factored, and any composite numbers are continuously factored until the result is the product of prime factors only. A factor tree, such as the one below, is helpful when exploring this concept.

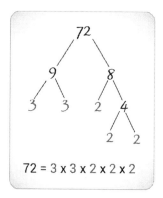

## Probabilities Relative to Likelihood of Occurrence

Probability is a measure of how likely an event is to occur. Probability is written as a fraction between zero and one. If an event has a probability of zero, the event will never occur. If an event has a probability of one, the event will definitely occur. If the probability of an event is closer to zero, the event is unlikely to occur. If the probability of an event is closer to one, the event is more likely to occur. For example, a probability of $\frac{1}{2}$ means that the event is equally as likely to occur as it is not to occur. An example of this is tossing a coin. To calculate the probability of an event, the number of favorable outcomes is divided by the number of total outcomes. For example, suppose you have 2 raffle tickets out of 20 total tickets sold. The probability that you win the raffle is calculated:

$$\frac{number\ of\ favorable\ outcomes}{total\ number of\ outcomes} = \frac{2}{20} = \frac{1}{10}$$

Therefore, the probability of winning the raffle is $\frac{1}{10}$ or 0.1.

Chance is the measure of how likely an event is to occur, written as a percent. If an event will never occur, the event has a 0% chance. If an event will certainly occur, the event has a 100% chance. If an event will sometimes occur, the event has a chance somewhere between 0% and 100%. To calculate chance, probability is calculated and the fraction is converted to a percent.

The probability of multiple events occurring can be determined by multiplying the probability of each event. For example, suppose you flip a coin with heads and tails, and roll a six-sided dice numbered one through six. To find the probability that you will flip heads AND roll a two, the probability of each event is determined and those fractions are multiplied. The probability of flipping heads is $\frac{1}{2} \left( \frac{1 \; side \; with \; heads}{2 \; sides \; total} \right)$ and the probability of rolling a two is $\frac{1}{6} \left( \frac{1 \; side \; with \; a \; 2}{6 \; total \; sides} \right)$. The probability of flipping heads AND rolling a 2 is: $\frac{1}{2} \times \frac{1}{6} = \frac{1}{12}$.

The above scenario with flipping a coin and rolling a dice is an example of independent events. Independent events are circumstances in which the outcome of one event does not affect the outcome of the other event. Conversely, dependent events are ones in which the outcome of one event affects the outcome of the second event. Consider the following scenario: a bag contains 5 black marbles and 5 white marbles. What is the probability of picking 2 black marbles without replacing the marble after the first pick?

The probability of picking a black marble on the first pick is $\frac{5}{10} \left( \frac{5 \; black \; marbles}{10 \; total \; marbles} \right)$. Assuming that a black marble was picked, there are now 4 black marbles and 5 white marbles for the second pick. Therefore, the probability of picking a black marble on the second pick is $\frac{4}{9} \left( \frac{4 \; black \; marbles}{9 \; total \; marbles} \right)$. To find the probability of picking two black marbles, the probability of each is multiplied: $\frac{5}{10} \times \frac{4}{9} = \frac{20}{90} = \frac{2}{9}$.

## Determining the Reasonableness of Results

When solving math word problems, the solution obtained should make sense within the given scenario. The step of checking the solution will reduce the possibility of a calculation error or a solution that may be *mathematically* correct but not applicable in the real world. Consider the following scenarios:

A problem states that Lisa got 24 out of 32 questions correct on a test and asks to find the percentage of correct answers. To solve the problem, a student divided 32 by 24 to get 1.33, and then multiplied by 100 to get 133 percent. By examining the solution within the context of the problem, the student should recognize that getting all 32 questions correct will produce a perfect score of 100 percent. Therefore, a score of 133 percent with 8 incorrect answers does not make sense, and the calculations should be checked.

A problem states that the maximum weight on a bridge cannot exceed 22,000 pounds. The problem asks to find the maximum number of cars that can be on the bridge at one time if each car weighs 4,000 pounds. To solve this problem, a student divided 22,000 by 4,000 to get an answer of 5.5. By examining the solution within the context of the problem, the student should recognize that although the calculations are mathematically correct, the solution does not make sense. Half of a car on a bridge is not possible, so the student should determine that a maximum of 5 cars can be on the bridge at the same time.

## Mental Math Estimation

Once a result is determined to be logical within the context of a given problem, the result should be evaluated by its nearness to the expected answer. This is performed by approximating given values to perform mental math. Numbers should be rounded to the nearest value possible to check the initial results.

Consider the following example: A problem states that a customer is buying a new sound system for their home. The customer purchases a stereo for $435, 2 speakers for $67 each, and the necessary cables for $12. The customer chooses an option that allows him to spread the costs over equal payments for 4 months. How much will the monthly payments be?

After making calculations for the problem, a student determines that the monthly payment will be $145.25. To check the accuracy of the results, the student rounds each cost to the nearest ten ($440 + 70 + 70 + 10$) and determines that the total is approximately $590. Dividing by 4 months gives an approximate monthly payment of $147.50. Therefore, the student can conclude that the solution of $145.25 is very close to what should be expected.

When rounding, the place-value that is used in rounding can make a difference. Suppose the student had rounded to the nearest hundred for the estimation. The result ($400 + 100 + 100 + 0 = 600$; $600 \div 4 = 150$) will show that the answer is reasonable but not as close to the actual value as rounding to the nearest ten.

# *Mathematical Reasoning and Data Analysis*

## Proofs

A proof is a deductive argument that supports a mathematical statement. Other previously established mathematical statements, such as theorems and axioms, are used within proofs. A proof shows that the concept is always true, and does not just give specific examples and cases. In direct proofs, the conclusion is found by combining the axioms, theorems, and possibly definitions in a specific and logical order. An indirect proof involves showing that the mathematical statement can never be false. However, it still involves a logical order of theorems, definitions, and axioms.

## Deductive Rand Inductive Reasoning

Deductive reasoning involves starting with stating a general rule, and then moving forward with logic to obtain a desired conclusion. If the original statements are true, then the conclusion is true. Most of mathematics involves deductive reasoning. For example, if $x = 2$ and $y = 4$ then $x + y = 6$. Also, if $x$ is an even number and $y$ is an odd number, then $x + y$ is an odd number.

Inductive reasoning involves starting with specific observations, but due to the nature of those observations, conclusions are classified as likely but not guaranteed. This process behaves similarly to probability in which nothing is completely certain. As opposed to deductive reasoning, a general conclusion can be drawn by observing specific examples. Note that inductive reasoning is not the same as proof by induction. Once a statement is found using inductive logic, specific examples can be found to be true or false using deductive reasoning. A counterexample is an example that shows a mathematical statement is false.

<u>Using Reasoning to Justify Mathematical Ideas</u>

A difference exists between formal and informal proofs. A formal proof involves the steps listed above, which include very structured deductive reasoning through the application of a specific order of theorems, axioms, and definitions. However, sometimes a formal proof is cumbersome and an informal proof might be used instead. These proofs are more applicable for everyday use and include high-level summaries that provide enough information to formulate the formal proof if given enough time.

## The Problem-Solving Process

Overall, the problem-solving process in mathematics involves a step-by-step procedure that one must follow when deciding what approach to take. First, one must understand the problem by deciding what is being sought, if enough information is given, and what units are necessary in the solution. Then, the plan of action must be determined. In some cases, there might be many options. Therefore, one should begin with one approach and if the strategy does not fit, he or she should move on to another. In some cases, a combination of approaches can be used. A beginning estimate is always useful for comparison once a solution is found. The answer must be reasonable and must fulfill all requirements of the problem.

## Mathematical Models to Represent Real-World Situations

A mathematical model is a representation in mathematical terms of a real-world situation, and is widely used in science and engineering. Formulas are derived that model phenomena such as population growth and decay. In any model, simplifications must be made to create such formulas, and parameters within the model usually do not represent the physical world exactly. Once the model is formulated, its output can be compared to real-world scenarios to judge how valid the model is. If a model is deemed to be inaccurate, original assumptions and restrictions can be lifted that initially simplified the model.

## Using Multiple Representations of a Mathematical Concept

There are many different areas of mathematics, and a single mathematical concept can have meaning in more than one area. Some of the main divisions of math include arithmetic, algebra, calculus, geometry, and statistics. A concept that spans across those divisions is *area*. Many different formulas in geometry involve calculating the area of different shapes. For example, area of a circle $A = \pi r^2$ is a quadratic function in r, the radius of the circle. In calculus, an area problem can involve calculating the area under a curve from two points on the $x$-axis, which is known as the definite integral. Also, the area between two curves is discussed. Finally, in statistics, the area under a density curve is defined to be probability.

## Using Math in Other Disciplines

As discussed previously, a mathematical model translates a real-world scenario into mathematical terms. Many disciplines involve the use of mathematical models. Usual disciplines that require the use of models are science and business, with their most widely-known models being population growth and compound interest. However, other disciplines such as art, music, and social science also can employ the use of mathematics. The keys are to first understand the problem needed to be solved, then to define variables, make assumptions and simplifications, and translate the concepts into mathematical formulas and equations. Once the model is built, different scenarios can be tested for accuracy and reasonableness.

## Translating Between Verbal and Symbolic Forms

Being able to translate verbal scenarios into symbolic forms is a critical skill in mathematics. This idea is seen mostly when solving word problems. First, the problem needs to be read carefully several times until one can state clearly what is being sought. Then, variables that represent the unknown quantities need to be defined. Equations can be defined using those variables that model the verbal conditions of the given problem. The equations then need to be solved to answer the problem's questions. The problem-solving skills learned in these types of problems is an invaluable skill, and is ultimately more important than finding the answer to each individual problem.

## Communicating Mathematical Ideas

Many different types of representations are useful in mathematics, and the most widely-used are written symbols, pictures or diagrams, models, spoken words, and real-world experiences. Real-world experiences and spoken words are both representations that can be expressed by written symbols that impart mathematical meaning to the situation being discussed. Pictures or diagrams, including graphs and geometric figures, allow for visual representations of mathematical concepts. These external representations are widely used and have been developed for centuries. Similarly, written representations, such as symbolic methods like equations and functions, are also widely used and are used the most in math classes.

### Using Visual Media

Students benefit from the use of visual media that represents mathematical information, and teachers should be able to go back and forth between each type. They should know which type of representation

is useful in given a scenario. For example, a function can be represented by a diagram, a table, a graph, and a set of numbers simultaneously. Here is such an example:

# Multiple Representations of a Function

## Mapping

Domain          Range
inputs          outputs

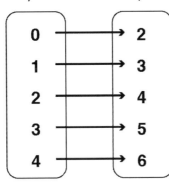

## Table

| x | y |
|---|---|
| 0 | 2 |
| 1 | 3 |
| 2 | 4 |
| 3 | 5 |
| 4 | 6 |

## Graph

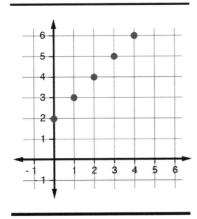

## Ordered Pairs

{(0,2),(1,3),(2,4),(3,5),(4,6)}

## Using Math Terminology

Using appropriate vocabulary that represents mathematical ideas is a critical skill in both being able to teach mathematics and use mathematical techniques to solve real-world situations. Each area in mathematics has its own set of definitions, and the translation of ideas onto paper requires a deep understanding of all the terminology. An important application of this idea is being able to translate word problems into equations that can be solved.

## Measures of Center and Range

The center of a set of data (statistical values) can be represented by its mean, median, or mode. These are sometimes referred to as measures of central tendency. The first property that can be defined for this set of data is the mean. This is the same as average. To find the mean, add up all the data points, then divide by the total number of data points. For example, suppose that in a class of 10 students, the scores on a test were 50, 60, 65, 65, 75, 80, 85, 85, 90, 100. Therefore, the average test score will be:

$$\frac{50 + 60 + 65 + 65 + 75 + 80 + 85 + 85 + 90 + 100}{10} = 75.5$$

The mean is a useful number if the distribution of data is normal (more on this later), which roughly means that the frequency of different outcomes has a single peak and is roughly equally distributed on both sides of that peak. However, it is less useful in some cases where the data might be split or where there are some *outliers*. Outliers are data points that are far from the rest of the data. For example, suppose there are 10 executives and 90 employees at a company. The executives make $1000 per hour, and the employees make $10 per hour.

Therefore, the average pay rate will be:

$$\frac{\$1000 \times 10 + \$10 \times 90}{100} = \$109 \text{ per hour}$$

In this case, this average is not very descriptive since it's not close to the actual pay of the executives or the employees.

## Median

Another useful measurement is the *median*. In a data set, the median is the point in the middle. The middle refers to the point where half the data comes before it and half comes after, when the data is recorded in numerical order. For instance, these are the speeds of the fastball of a pitcher during the last inning that he pitched (in order from least to greatest):

90, 92, 93, 93, 95, 96, 97, 97, 97

There are nine total numbers, so the middle or *median* number is the 5th one, which is 95.

In cases where the number of data points is an even number, then the average of the two middle points is taken. In the previous example of test scores, the two middle points are 75 and 80. Since there is no single point, the average of these two scores needs to be found. The average is:

$$\frac{75 + 80}{2} = 77.5$$

The median is generally a good value to use if there are a few outliers in the data. It prevents those outliers from affecting the "middle" value as much as when using the mean.

Since an outlier is a data point that is far from most of the other data points in a data set, this means an outlier also is any point that is far from the median of the data set. The outliers can have a substantial

effect on the mean of a data set, but they usually do not change the median or mode, or do not change them by a large quantity. For example, consider the data set (3, 5, 6, 6, 6, 8). This has a median of 6 and a mode of 6, with a mean of $\frac{34}{6} \approx 5.67$. Now, suppose a new data point of 1000 is added so that the data set is now (3, 5, 6, 6, 6, 8, 1000). This does not change the median or mode, which are both still 6. However, the average is now $\frac{1034}{7}$, which is approximately 147.7. In this case, the median and mode will be better descriptions for most of the data points.

The reason for outliers in a given data set is a complicated problem. It is sometimes the result of an error by the experimenter, but often they are perfectly valid data points that must be taken into consideration.

## Mode

One additional measure to define for X is the *mode*. This is the data point that appears most frequently. If two or more data points all tie for the most frequent appearance, then each of them is considered a mode. In the case of the test scores, where the numbers were 50, 60, 65, 65, 75, 80, 85, 85, 90, 100, there are two modes: 65 and 85.

The range of a data set is the difference between the highest and the lowest values in the set. The range can be considered the span of the data set. To determine the range, the smallest value in the set is subtracted from the largest value. The ranges for the data sets A, B, and C above are calculated as follows: A: $14 - 7 = 7$; B: $51 - 33 = 18$; C: $173 - 151 = 22$.

## Best Description of a Set of Data

Measures of central tendency, namely mean, median, and mode, describe characteristics of a set of data. Specifically, they are intended to represent a *typical* value in the set by identifying a central position of the set. Depending on the characteristics of a specific set of data, different measures of central tendency are more indicative of a typical value in the set.

When a data set is grouped closely together with a relatively small range and the data is spread out somewhat evenly, the mean is an effective indicator of a typical value in the set. Consider the following data set representing the height of sixth grade boys in inches: 61 inches, 54 inches, 58 inches, 63 inches, 58 inches. The mean of the set is 58.8 inches. The data set is grouped closely (the range is only 9 inches) and the values are spread relatively evenly (three values below the mean and two values above the mean). Therefore, the mean value of 58.8 inches is an effective measure of central tendency in this case.

When a data set contains a small number of values either extremely large or extremely small when compared to the other values, the mean is not an effective measure of central tendency. Consider the following data set representing annual incomes of homeowners on a given street: $71,000; $74,000; $75,000; $77,000; $340,000. The mean of this set is $127,400. This figure does not indicate a typical value in the set, which contains four out of five values between $71,000 and $77,000. The median is a much more effective measure of central tendency for data sets such as these. Finding the middle value diminishes the influence of outliers, or numbers that may appear out of place, like the $340,000 annual income. The median for this set is $75,000 which is much more typical of a value in the set.

The mode of a data set is a useful measure of central tendency for categorical data when each piece of data is an option from a category. Consider a survey of 31 commuters asking how they get to work with results summarized below.

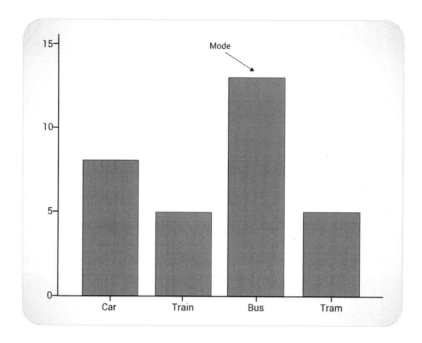

The mode for this set represents the value, or option, of the data that repeats most often. This indicates that the bus is the most popular method of transportation for the commuters.

## Effects of Changes in Data

Changing all values of a data set in a consistent way produces predictable changes in the measures of the center and range of the set. A linear transformation changes the original value into the new value by either adding a given number to each value, multiplying each value by a given number, or both. Adding (or subtracting) a given value to each data point will increase (or decrease) the mean, median, and any modes by the same value. However, the range will remain the same due to the way that range is calculated. Multiplying (or dividing) a given value by each data point will increase (or decrease) the mean, median, and any modes, and the range by the same factor.

Consider the following data set, call it set $P$, representing the price of different cases of soda at a grocery store: $4.25, $4.40, $4.75, $4.95, $4.95, $5.15. The mean of set $P$ is $4.74. The median is $4.85. The mode of the set is $4.95. The range is $0.90. Suppose the state passes a new tax of $0.25 on every case of soda sold. The new data set, set $T$, is calculated by adding $0.25 to each data point from set $P$. Therefore, set $T$ consists of the following values: $4.50, $4.65, $5.00, $5.20, $5.20, $5.40. The mean of set $T$ is $4.99. The median is $5.10. The mode of the set is $5.20. The range is $.90. The mean, median and mode of set $T$ is equal to $0.25 added to the mean, median, and mode of set $P$. The range stays the same.

Now suppose, due to inflation, the store raises the cost of every item by 10 percent. Raising costs by 10 percent is calculated by multiplying each value by 1.1. The new data set, set $I$, is calculated by multiplying each data point from set $T$ by 1.1. Therefore, set $I$ consists of the following values: $4.95, $5.12, $5.50, $5.72, $5.72, $5.94. The mean of set $I$ is $5.49. The median is $5.61. The mode of the set is

$5.72. The range is $0.99. The mean, median, mode, and range of set *I* is equal to 1.1 multiplied by the mean, median, mode, and range of set *T* because each increased by a factor of 10 percent.

## Describing a Set of Data

A set of data can be described in terms of its center, spread, shape and any unusual features. The center of a data set can be measured by its mean, median, or mode. Measures of central tendency are covered in the *Measures of Center and Range* section. The spread of a data set refers to how far the data points are from the center (mean or median). The spread can be measured by the range or the quartiles and interquartile range. A data set with data points clustered around the center will have a small spread. A data set covering a wide range will have a large spread.

When a data set is displayed as a histogram or frequency distribution plot, the shape indicates if a sample is normally distributed, symmetrical, or has measures of skewness or kurtosis. When graphed, a data set with a normal distribution will resemble a bell curve.

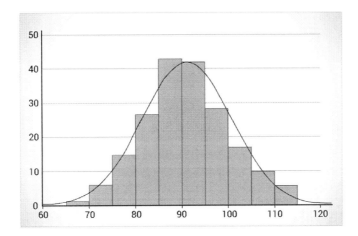

If the data set is symmetrical, each half of the graph when divided at the center is a mirror image of the other. If the graph has fewer data points to the right, the data is skewed right. If it has fewer data points to the left, the data is skewed left.

| Right-Skewed | Symmetric | Left-Skewed |

Kurtosis is a measure of whether the data is heavy-tailed with a high number of outliers, or light-tailed with a low number of outliers.

A description of a data set should include any unusual features such as gaps or outliers. A gap is a span within the range of the data set containing no data points. An outlier is a data point with a value either extremely large or extremely small when compared to the other values in the set.

## Interpreting Displays of Data

A set of data can be visually displayed in various forms allowing for quick identification of characteristics of the set. Histograms, such as the one shown below, display the number of data points (vertical axis) that fall into given intervals (horizontal axis) across the range of the set. The histogram below displays the heights of black cherry trees in a certain city park. Each rectangle represents the number of trees with heights between a given five-point span. For example, the furthest bar to the right indicates that two trees are between 85 and 90 feet. Histograms can describe the center, spread, shape, and any unusual characteristics of a data set.

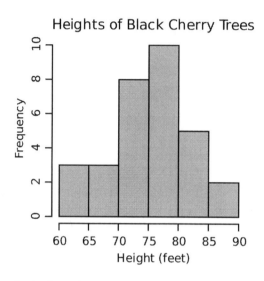

A box plot, also called a box-and-whisker plot, divides the data points into four groups and displays the five number summary for the set, as well as any outliers. The five number summary consists of:

- The lower extreme: the lowest value that is not an outlier
- The higher extreme: the highest value that is not an outlier
- The median of the set: also referred to as the second quartile or $Q_2$
- The first quartile or $Q_1$: the median of values below $Q_2$
- The third quartile or $Q_3$: the median of values above $Q_2$

Calculating each of these values is covered in the next section, *Graphical Representation of Data*.

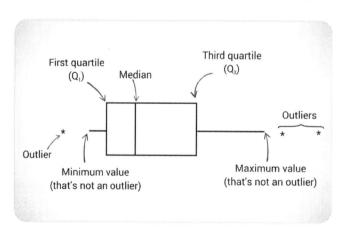

Suppose the box plot displays IQ scores for 12<sup>th</sup> grade students at a given school. The five number summary of the data consists of: lower extreme (67); upper extreme (127); $Q_2$ or median (100); $Q_1$ (91); $Q_3$ (108); and outliers (135 and 140). Although all data points are not known from the plot, the points are divided into four quartiles each, including 25% of the data points. Therefore, 25% of students scored between 67 and 91, 25% scored between 91 and 100, 25% scored between 100 and 108, and 25% scored between 108 and 127. These percentages include the normal values for the set and exclude the outliers. This information is useful when comparing a given score with the rest of the scores in the set.

A scatter plot is a mathematical diagram that visually displays the relationship or connection between two variables. The independent variable is placed on the $x$-axis, or horizontal axis, and the dependent variable is placed on the $y$-axis, or vertical axis. When visually examining the points on the graph, if the points model a linear relationship, or a line of best-fit can be drawn through the points with the points relatively close on either side, then a correlation exists. If the line of best-fit has a positive slope (rises from left to right), then the variables have a positive correlation. If the line of best-fit has a negative slope (falls from left to right), then the variables have a negative correlation. If a line of best-fit cannot be drawn, then no correlation exists. A positive or negative correlation can be categorized as strong or weak, depending on how closely the points are graphed around the line of best-fit.

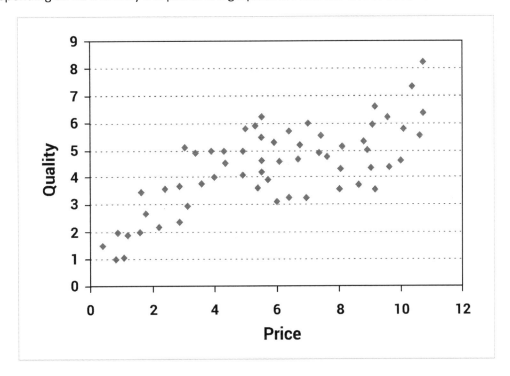

## Graphical Representation of Data

Various graphs can be used to visually represent a given set of data. Each type of graph requires a different method of arranging data points and different calculations of the data. Examples of histograms, box plots, and scatter plots are discussed in the previous section *Interpreting Displays of Data*. To construct a histogram, the range of the data points is divided into equal intervals. The frequency for each interval is then determined, which reveals how many points fall into each interval. A graph is constructed with the vertical axis representing the frequency and the horizontal axis representing the intervals. The lower value of each interval should be labeled along the horizontal axis. Finally, for each interval, a bar is drawn from the lower value of each interval to the lower value of the

next interval with a height equal to the frequency of the interval. Because of the intervals, histograms do not have any gaps between bars along the horizontal axis.

A scatter plot displays the relationship between two variables. Values for the independent variable, typically denoted by x, are paired with values for the dependent variable, typically denoted by y. Each set of corresponding values are written as an ordered pair (x, y). To construct the graph, a coordinate grid is labeled with the x-axis representing the independent variable and the y-axis representing the dependent variable. Each ordered pair is graphed.

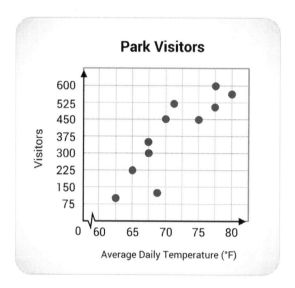

Like a scatter plot, a line graph compares variables that change continuously, typically over time. Paired data values (ordered pair) are plotted on a coordinate grid with the x- and y-axis representing the variables. A line is drawn from each point to the next, going from left to right. The line graph below displays cell phone use for given years (two variables) for men, women, and both sexes (three data sets).

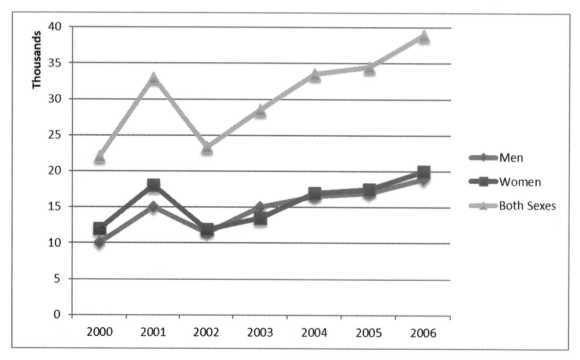

A line plot, also called dot plot, displays the frequency of data (numerical values) on a number line. To construct a line plot, a number line is used that includes all unique data values. It is marked with x's or dots above the value the number of times that the value occurs in the data set.

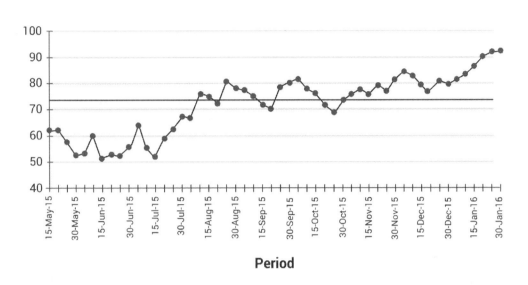

A bar graph looks similar to a histogram but displays categorical data. The horizontal axis represents each category and the vertical axis represents the frequency for the category. A bar is drawn for each category (often different colors) with a height extending to the frequency for that category within the data set. A double bar graph displays two sets of data that contain data points consisting of the same categories. The double bar graph below indicates that two girls and four boys like Pad Thai the most out of all the foods, two boys and five girls like pizza, and so on.

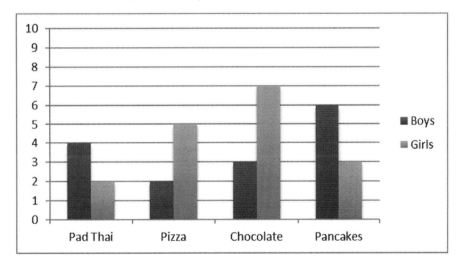

A circle graph, also called a pie chart, displays categorical data with each category representing a percentage of the whole data set. To construct a circle graph, the percent of the data set for each category must be determined. To do so, the frequency of the category is divided by the total number of data points and converted to a percent. For example, if 80 people were asked their favorite pizza topping and 20 responded cheese, then cheese constitutes 25% of the data ($\frac{20}{80} = .25 = 25\%$). Each category in a data set is represented by a *slice* of the circle proportionate to its percentage of the whole.

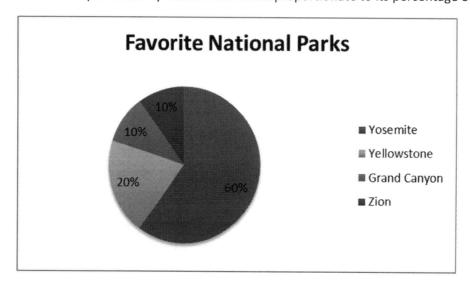

## Choice of Graphs to Display Data

Choosing the appropriate graph to display a data set depends on what type of data is included in the set and what information must be displayed. Histograms and box plots can be used for data sets consisting of individual values across a wide range. Examples include test scores and incomes. Histograms and box plots will indicate the center, spread, range, and outliers of a data set. A histogram will show the shape of the data set, while a box plot will divide the set into quartiles (25% increments), allowing for comparison between a given value and the entire set.

Scatter plots and line graphs can be used to display data consisting of two variables. Examples include height and weight, or distance and time. A correlation between the variables is determined by examining the points on the graph. Line graphs are used if each value for one variable pairs with a distinct value for the other variable. Line graphs show relationships between variables.

Line plots, bar graphs, and circle graphs are all used to display categorical data, such as surveys. Line plots and bar graphs both indicate the frequency of each category within the data set. A line plot is used when the categories consist of numerical values. For example, the number of hours of TV watched by individuals is displayed on a line plot. A bar graph is used when the categories consists of words. For example, the favorite ice cream of individuals is displayed with a bar graph. A circle graph can be used to display either type of categorical data. However, unlike line plots and bar graphs, a circle graph does not indicate the frequency of each category. Instead, the circle graph represents each category as its percentage of the whole data set.

# *Patterns, Algebra, and Functions*

## Number and Shape Patterns

Patterns within a sequence can come in 2 distinct forms: the items (shapes, numbers, etc.) either repeat in a constant order, or the items change from one step to another in some consistent way. The core is

the smallest unit, or number of items, that repeats in a repeating pattern. For example, the pattern oo▲oo▲o... has a core that is oo▲. Knowing only the core, the pattern can be extended. Knowing the number of steps in the core allows the identification of an item in each step without drawing/writing the entire pattern out. For example, suppose the tenth item in the previous pattern must be determined. Because the core consists of three items (oo▲), the core repeats in multiples of 3. In other words, steps 3, 6, 9, 12, etc. will be ▲ completing the core with the core starting over on the next step. For the above example, the 9th step will be ▲ and the 10th will be o.

The most common patterns in which each item changes from one step to the next are arithmetic and geometric sequences. An arithmetic sequence is one in which the items increase or decrease by a constant difference. In other words, the same thing is added or subtracted to each item or step to produce the next. To determine if a sequence is arithmetic, determine what must be added or subtracted to step one to produce step two. Then, check if the same thing is added/subtracted to step two to produce step three. The same thing must be added/subtracted to step three to produce step four, and so on. Consider the pattern 13, 10, 7, 4 . . . To get from step one (13) to step two (10) by adding or subtracting requires subtracting by 3. The next step is checking if subtracting 3 from step two (10) will produce step three (7), and subtracting 3 from step three (7) will produce step four (4). In this case, the pattern holds true. Therefore, this is an arithmetic sequence in which each step is produced by subtracting 3 from the previous step. To extend the sequence, 3 is subtracted from the last step to produce the next. The next three numbers in the sequence are 1, -2, -5.

A geometric sequence is one in which each step is produced by multiplying or dividing the previous step by the same number. To determine if a sequence is geometric, decide what step one must be multiplied or divided by to produce step two. Then check if multiplying or dividing step two by the same number produces step three, and so on. Consider the pattern 2, 8, 32, 128 . . . To get from step one (2) to step two (8) requires multiplication by 4. The next step determines if multiplying step two (8) by 4 produces step three (32), and multiplying step three (32) by 4 produces step four (128). In this case, the pattern holds true. Therefore, this is a geometric sequence in which each step is produced by multiplying the previous step by 4. To extend the sequence, the last step is multiplied by 4 and repeated. The next three numbers in the sequence are 512; 2,048; 8,192.

Although arithmetic and geometric sequences typically use numbers, these sequences can also be represented by shapes. For example, an arithmetic sequence could consist of shapes with three sides, four sides, and five sides (add one side to the previous step to produce the next). A geometric sequence could consist of eight blocks, four blocks, and two blocks (each step is produced by dividing the number of blocks in the previous step by 2).

## Corresponding Terms of Two Numerical Patterns

When given two numerical patterns, the corresponding terms should be examined to determine if a relationship exists between them. Corresponding terms between patterns are the pairs of numbers that appear in the same step of the two sequences. Consider the following patterns 1, 2, 3, 4 . . . and 3, 6, 9, 12 . . . The corresponding terms are: 1 and 3; 2 and 6; 3 and 9; and 4 and 12. To identify the relationship, each pair of corresponding terms is examined and the possibilities of performing an operation (+, −, ×, ÷) to the term from the first sequence to produce the corresponding term in the second sequence are determined. In this case:

$$1 + 2 = 3 \qquad \text{or} \qquad 1 \times 3 = 3$$

$$2 + 4 = 6 \qquad \text{or} \qquad 2 \times 3 = 6$$

$$3 + 6 = 9 \qquad \text{or} \qquad 3 \times 3 = 9$$

$$4 + 8 = 12 \qquad \text{or} \qquad 4 \times 3 = 12$$

The consistent pattern is that the number from the first sequence multiplied by 3 equals its corresponding term in the second sequence. By assigning each sequence a label (input and output) or variable (x and y), the relationship can be written as an equation. If the first sequence represents the inputs, or x, and the second sequence represents the outputs, or y, the relationship can be expressed as: $y = 3x$.

Consider the following sets of numbers:

| a | 2 | 4 | 6 | 8 |
|---|---|---|---|---|
| b | 6 | 8 | 10 | 12 |

To write a rule for the relationship between the values for a and the values for b, the corresponding terms (2 and 6; 4 and 8; 6 and 10; 8 and 12) are examined. The possibilities for producing b from a are:

$$2 + 4 = 6 \qquad \text{or} \qquad 2 \times 3 = 6$$

$$4 + 4 = 8 \qquad \text{or} \qquad 4 \times 2 = 8$$

$$6 + 4 = 10$$

$$8 + 4 = 12 \qquad \text{or} \qquad 8 \times 1.5 = 12$$

The consistent pattern is that adding 4 to the value of a produces the value of b. The relationship can be written as the equation $a + 4 = b$.

## Conjectures, Predictions, or Generalizations Based on Patterns

An arithmetic or geometric sequence can be written as a formula and used to determine unknown steps without writing out the entire sequence. (Note that a similar process for repeating patterns is covered in the previous section.) An arithmetic sequence progresses by a *common difference*. To determine the common difference, any step is subtracted by the step that precedes it. In the sequence 4, 9, 14, 19 . . . the common difference, or d, is 5. By expressing each step as $a_1$, $a_2$, $a_3$, etc., a formula can be written to represent the sequence. $a_1$ is the first step. To produce step two, step 1 ($a_1$) is added to the common difference (d): $a_2 = a_1 + d$. To produce step three, the common difference (d) is added twice to $a_1$: $a_3 = a_1 + 2d$. To produce step four, the common difference (d) is added three times to $a_1$: $a_4 = a_1 + 3d$. Following this pattern allows a general rule for arithmetic sequences to be written. For any term of the sequence ($a_n$), the first step ($a_1$) is added to the product of the common difference (d) and one less than the step of the term (n − 1): $a_n = a_1 + (n − 1)d$. Suppose the 8th term ($a_8$) is to be found in the previous sequence. By knowing the first step ($a_1$) is 4 and the common difference (d) is 5, the formula can be used: $a_n = a_1 + (n − 1)d \rightarrow a_8 = 4 + (7)5 \rightarrow a_8 = 39$.

In a geometric sequence, each step is produced by multiplying or dividing the previous step by the same number. The *common ratio*, or (r), can be determined by dividing any step by the previous step. In the sequence 1, 3, 9, 27 . . . the common ratio (r) is 3 ($\frac{3}{1} = 3$ or $\frac{9}{3} = 3$ or $\frac{27}{9} = 3$). Each successive step can be

expressed as a product of the first step $(a_1)$ and the common ratio $(r)$ to some power. For example, $a_2 = a_1 \times r$; $a_3 = a_1 \times r \times r$ or $a_3 = a_1 \times r^2$; $a_4 = a_1 \times r \times r \times r$ or $a_4 = a\_1 \times r^3$. Following this pattern, a general rule for geometric sequences can be written. For any term of the sequence $(a_n)$, the first step $(a_1)$ is multiplied by the common ratio $(r)$ raised to the power one less than the step of the term $(n - 1)$: $a_n = a_1 \times r^{(n-1)}$. Suppose for the previous sequence, the 7th term $(a_7)$ is to be found. Knowing the first step $(a_1)$ is one, and the common ratio $(r)$ is 3, the formula can be used: $a_n = a_1 \times r^{(n-1)} \rightarrow a_7 = (1) \times 3^6 \rightarrow a_7 = 729$.

## Algebraic Expressions and Equations

An algebraic expression is a statement about an unknown quantity expressed in mathematical symbols. A variable is used to represent the unknown quantity, usually denoted by a letter. An equation is a statement in which two expressions (at least one containing a variable) are equal to each other. An algebraic expression can be thought of as a mathematical phrase and an equation can be thought of as a mathematical sentence.

Algebraic expressions and equations both contain numbers, variables, and mathematical operations. The following are examples of algebraic expressions: $5x + 3$, $7xy - 8(x^2 + y)$, and $\sqrt{a^2 + b^2}$. An expression can be simplified or evaluated for given values of variables. The following are examples of equations: $2x + 3 = 7$, $a^2 + b^2 = c^2$, and $2x + 5 = 3x - 2$. An equation contains two sides separated by an equal sign. Equations can be solved to determine the value(s) of the variable for which the statement is true.

## Adding and Subtracting Linear Algebraic Expressions

An algebraic expression is simplified by combining like terms. A term is a number, variable, or product of a number and variables separated by addition and subtraction. For the algebraic expression $3x^2 - 4x + 5 - 5x^2 + x - 3$, the terms are $3x^2$, -4x, 5, -5x², x, and -3. Like terms have the same variables raised to the same powers (exponents). The like terms for the previous example are $3x^2$ and -5x², -4x and x, 5 and -3. To combine like terms, the coefficients (numerical factor of the term including sign) are added and the variables and their powers are kept the same. Note that if a coefficient is not written, it is an implied coefficient of 1 ($x = 1x$). The previous example will simplify to $-2x^2 - 3x + 2$.

When adding or subtracting algebraic expressions, each expression is written in parenthesis. The negative sign is distributed when necessary, and like terms are combined. Consider the following: add $2a + 5b - 2$ to $a - 2b + 8c - 4$. The sum is set as follows: $(a - 2b + 8c - 4) + (2a + 5b - 2)$. In front of each set of parentheses is an implied positive one, which, when distributed, does not change any of the terms. Therefore, the parentheses are dropped and like terms are combined:

$$a - 2b + 8c - 4 + 2a + 5b - 2 = 3a + 3b + 8c - 6$$

Consider the following problem: Subtract $2a + 5b - 2$ from $a - 2b + 8c - 4$. The difference is set as follows: $(a - 2b + 8c - 4) - (2a + 5b - 2)$. The implied one in front of the first set of parentheses will not change those four terms. However, distributing the implied -1 in front of the second set of parentheses will change the sign of each of those three terms: $a - 2b + 8c - 4 - 2a - 5b + 2$. Combining like terms yields the simplified expression $-a - 7b + 8c - 2$.

## Distributive Property

The distributive property states that multiplying a sum (or difference) by a number produces the same result as multiplying each value in the sum (or difference) by the number and adding (or subtracting) the products. Using mathematical symbols, the distributive property states $a(b + c) = ab + ac$. The expression $4(3 + 2)$ is simplified using the order of operations. Simplifying inside the parenthesis first produces $4 \times 5$, which equals 20. The expression $4(3 + 2)$ can also be simplified using the distributive property: $4(3 + 2) = 4 \times 3 + 4 \times 2 = 12 + 8 = 20$.

Consider the following example: $4(3x - 2)$. The expression cannot be simplified inside the parenthesis because $3x$ and -2 are not like terms and therefore cannot be combined. However, the expression can be simplified by using the distributive property and multiplying each term inside of the parenthesis by the term outside of the parenthesis: $12x - 8$. The resulting equivalent expression contains no like terms, so it cannot be further simplified.

Consider the expression $(3x + 2y + 1) - (5x - 3) + 2(3y + 4)$. Again, there are no like terms, but the distributive property is used to simplify the expression. Note there is an implied one in front of the first set of parentheses and an implied -1 in front of the second set of parentheses. Distributing the 1, -1, and 2 produces $1(3x) + 1(2y) + 1(1) - 1(5x) - 1(-3) + 2(3y) + 2(4) = 3x + 2y + 1 - 5x + 3 + 6y + 8$. This expression contains like terms that are combined to produce the simplified expression $-2x + 8y + 12$.

Algebraic expressions are tested to be equivalent by choosing values for the variables and evaluating both expressions (see 2.A.4). For example, $4(3x - 2)$ and $12x - 8$ are tested by substituting 3 for the variable $x$ and calculating to determine if equivalent values result.

## Simple Expressions for Given Values

An algebraic expression is a statement written in mathematical symbols, typically including one or more unknown values represented by variables. For example, the expression $2x + 3$ states that an unknown number ($x$) is multiplied by 2 and added to 3. If given a value for the unknown number, or variable, the value of the expression is determined. For example, if the value of the variable $x$ is 4, the value of the expression 4 is multiplied by 2, and 3 is added. This results in a value of 11 for the expression.

When given an algebraic expression and values for the variable(s), the expression is evaluated to determine its numerical value. To evaluate the expression, the given values for the variables are substituted (or replaced), and the expression is simplified using the order of operations. Parenthesis should be used when substituting. Consider the following: Evaluate $a - 2b + ab$ for $a = 3$ and $b = -1$. To evaluate, any variable $a$ is replaced with 3 and any variable $b$ with -1, producing (3)-2(-1)+(3)(-1). Next, the order of operations is used to calculate the value of the expression, which is 2.

## Parts of Expressions

Algebraic expressions consist of variables, numbers, and operations. A term of an expression is any combination of numbers and/or variables, and terms are separated by addition and subtraction. For example, the expression $5x^2 - 3xy + 4 - 2$ consists of 4 terms: $5x^2$, -3xy, 4y, and -2. Note that each term includes its given sign (+ or −). The variable part of a term is a letter that represents an unknown quantity. The coefficient of a term is the number by which the variable is multiplied. For the term 4y, the variable is y, and the coefficient is 4. Terms are identified by the power (or exponent) of its variable.

A number without a variable is referred to as a constant. If the variable is to the first power ($x^1$ or simply $x$), it is referred to as a linear term. A term with a variable to the second power ($x^2$) is quadratic, and a term to the third power ($x^3$) is cubic. Consider the expression $x^3 + 3x - 1$. The constant is -1. The linear term is $3x$. There is no quadratic term. The cubic term is $x^3$.

An algebraic expression can also be classified by how many terms exist in the expression. Any like terms should be combined before classifying. A monomial is an expression consisting of only one term. Examples of monomials are: 17, $2x$, and $-5ab^2$. A binomial is an expression consisting of two terms separated by addition or subtraction. Examples include $2x - 4$ and $-3y^2 + 2y$. A trinomial consists of 3 terms. For example, $5x^2 - 2x + 1$ is a trinomial.

## Use of Formulas

Formulas are mathematical expressions that define the value of one quantity, given the value of one or more different quantities. Formulas look like equations because they contain variables, numbers, operators, and an equal sign. All formulas are equations, but not all equations are formulas. A formula must have more than one variable. For example, $2x + 7 = y$ is an equation and a formula (it relates the unknown quantities $x$ and $y$). However, $2x + 7 = 3$ is an equation but not a formula (it only expresses the value of the unknown quantity $x$).

Formulas are typically written with one variable alone (or isolated) on one side of the equal sign. This variable can be thought of as the *subject* in that the formula is stating the value of the *subject* in terms of the relationship between the other variables. Consider the distance formula: $distance = rate \times time$ or $d = rt$. The value of the subject variable $d$ (distance) is the product of the variable $r$ and $t$ (rate and time). Given the rate and time, the distance traveled can easily be determined by substituting the values into the formula and evaluating.

The formula $P = 2l + 2w$ expresses how to calculate the perimeter of a rectangle ($P$) given its length ($l$) and width ($w$). To find the perimeter of a rectangle with a length of 3ft and a width of 2ft, these values are substituted into the formula for $l$ and $w$: $P = 2(3ft) + 2(2ft)$. Following the order of operations, the perimeter is determined to be 10ft. When working with formulas such as these, including units is an important step.

Given a formula expressed in terms of one variable, the formula can be manipulated to express the relationship in terms of any other variable. In other words, the formula can be rearranged to change which variable is the *subject*. To solve for a variable of interest by manipulating a formula, the equation may be solved as if all other variables were numbers. The same steps for solving are followed, leaving operations in terms of the variables instead of calculating numerical values. For the formula $P = 2l + 2w$, the perimeter is the subject expressed in terms of the length and width. To write a formula to calculate the width of a rectangle, given its length and perimeter, the previous formula relating the three variables is solved for the variable $w$. If $P$ and $l$ were numerical values, this is a two-step linear equation solved by subtraction and division. To solve the equation $P = 2l + 2w$ for $w$, $2l$ is first subtracted from both sides: $P - 2l = 2w$. Then both sides are divided by 2: $\frac{P-2l}{2} = w$.

## Dependent and Independent Variables

A variable represents an unknown quantity and, in the case of a formula, a specific relationship exists between the variables. Within a given scenario, variables are the quantities that are changing. If two variables exist, one is dependent and one is independent. The value of one variable depends on the other variable. If a scenario describes distance traveled and time traveled at a given speed, distance is dependent and time is independent. The distance traveled depends on the time spent traveling. If a scenario describes the cost of a cab ride and the distance traveled, the cost is dependent and the distance is independent. The cost of a cab ride depends on the distance travelled. Formulas often contain more than two variables and are typically written with the dependent variable alone on one side of the equation. This lone variable is the *subject* of the statement. If a formula contains three or more variables, one variable is dependent and the rest are independent. The values of all independent variables are needed to determine the value of the dependent variable.

The formula $P = 2l + 2w$ expresses the dependent variable $P$ in terms of the independent variables, $l$ and $w$. The perimeter of a rectangle depends on its length and width. The formula $d = rt$ ($distance = rate \times time$) expresses the dependent variable $d$ in terms of the independent variables, $r$ and $t$. The distance traveled depends on the rate (or speed) and the time traveled.

## Multistep One-Variable Linear Equations and Inequalities

Linear equations and linear inequalities are both comparisons of two algebraic expressions. However, unlike equations in which the expressions are equal, linear inequalities compare expressions that may be unequal. Linear equations typically have one value for the variable that makes the statement true. Linear inequalities generally have an infinite number of values that make the statement true.

When solving a linear equation, the desired result requires determining a numerical value for the unknown variable. If given a linear equation involving addition, subtraction, multiplication, or division, working backwards isolates the variable. Addition and subtraction are inverse operations, as are multiplication and division. Therefore, they can be used to cancel each other out.

The first steps to solving linear equations are distributing, if necessary, and combining any like terms on the same side of the equation. Sides of an equation are separated by an *equal* sign. Next, the equation is manipulated to show the variable on one side. Whatever is done to one side of the equation must be done to the other side of the equation to remain equal. Inverse operations are then used to isolate the variable and undo the order of operations backwards. Addition and subtraction are undone, then multiplication and division are undone.

For example, solve $4(t - 2) + 2t - 4 = 2(9 - 2t)$

Distributing: $4t - 8 + 2t - 4 = 18 - 4t$

Combining like terms: $6t - 12 = 18 - 4t$

Adding $4t$ to each side to move the variable: $10t - 12 = 18$

Adding 12 to each side to isolate the variable: $10t = 30$

Dividing each side by 10 to isolate the variable: $t = 3$

The answer can be checked by substituting the value for the variable into the original equation, ensuring that both sides calculate to be equal.

Linear inequalities express the relationship between unequal values. More specifically, they describe in what way the values are unequal. A value can be greater than (>), less than (<), greater than or equal to (≥), or less than or equal to (≤) another value. $5x + 40 > 65$ is read as *five times a number added to forty is greater than sixty-five.*

When solving a linear inequality, the solution is the set of all numbers that make the statement true. The inequality $x + 2 \geq 6$ has a solution set of 4 and every number greater than 4 (4.01; 5; 12; 107; etc.). Adding 2 to 4 or any number greater than 4 results in a value that is greater than or equal to 6. Therefore, $x \geq 4$ is the solution set.

To algebraically solve a linear inequality, follow the same steps as those for solving a linear equation. The inequality symbol stays the same for all operations *except* when multiplying or dividing by a negative number. If multiplying or dividing by a negative number while solving an inequality, the relationship reverses (the sign flips). In other words, > switches to < and vice versa. Multiplying or dividing by a positive number does not change the relationship, so the sign stays the same. An example is shown below.

Solve $-2x - 8 \leq 22$

Add 8 to both sides: $-2x \leq 30$

Divide both sides by -2: $x \geq -15$

Solutions of a linear equation or a linear inequality are the values of the variable that make a statement true. In the case of a linear equation, the solution set (list of all possible solutions) typically consists of a single numerical value. To find the solution, the equation is solved by isolating the variable. For example, solving the equation $3x - 7 = -13$ produces the solution $x = -2$. The only value for $x$ which produces a true statement is -2. This can be checked by substituting -2 into the original equation to check that both sides are equal. In this case, $3(-2) - 7 = -13 \rightarrow -13 = -13$; therefore, -2 is a solution.

Although linear equations generally have one solution, this is not always the case. If there is no value for the variable that makes the statement true, there is no solution to the equation. Consider the equation $x + 3 = x - 1$. There is no value for $x$ in which adding 3 to the value produces the same result as subtracting one from the value. Conversely, if any value for the variable makes a true statement, the equation has an infinite number of solutions. Consider the equation $3x + 6 = 3(x + 2)$. Any number substituted for $x$ will result in a true statement (both sides of the equation are equal).

By manipulating equations like the two above, the variable of the equation will cancel out completely. If the remaining constants express a true statement (ex. $6 = 6$), then all real numbers are solutions to the equation. If the constants left express a false statement (ex. $3 = -1$), then no solution exists for the equation.

Solving a linear inequality requires all values that make the statement true to be determined. For example, solving $3x - 7 \geq -13$ produces the solution $x \geq -2$. This means that -2 and any number greater than -2 produces a true statement. Solution sets for linear inequalities will often be displayed using a number line. If a value is included in the set ($\geq$ or $\leq$), a shaded dot is placed on that value and an arrow extending in the direction of the solutions. For a variable > or $\geq$ a number, the arrow will point right on a number line, the direction where the numbers increase. If a variable is < or $\leq$ a number, the arrow will point left on a number line, which is the direction where the numbers decrease. If the value is not included in the set (> or <), an open (unshaded) circle on that value is used with an arrow in the appropriate direction.

Like this:

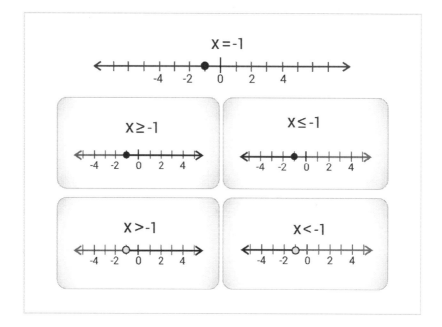

Similar to linear equations, a linear inequality may have a solution set consisting of all real numbers, or can contain no solution. When solved algebraically, a linear inequality in which the variable cancels out and results in a true statement (ex. $7 \geq 2$) has a solution set of all real numbers. A linear inequality in which the variable cancels out and results in a false statement (ex. $7 \leq 2$) has no solution.

## Functions

A *function* is defined as a relationship between inputs and outputs where there is only one output value for a given input. As an example, the following function is in function notation: $f(x) = 3x - 4$. The $f(x)$ represents the output value for an input of $x$. If $x = 2$, the equation becomes $f(2) = 3(2) - 4 = 6 - 4 = 2$. The input of 2 yields an output of 2, forming the ordered pair $(2, 2)$. The following set of ordered pairs corresponds to the given function: $(2, 2), (0, -4), (-2, -10)$. The set of all possible inputs of a function is its *domain*, and all possible outputs is called the *range*. By definition, each member of the domain is paired with only one member of the range.

Functions can also be defined recursively. In this form, they are not defined explicitly in terms of variables. Instead, they are defined using previously-evaluated function outputs, starting with either $f(0)$ or $f(1)$. An example of a recursively-defined function is $f(1) = 2, f(n) = 2f(n - 1) + 2n, n > 1$. The domain of this function is the set of all integers.

## Domain and Range

The domain and range of a function can be found visually by its plot on the coordinate plane. In the function $f(x) = x^2 - 3$, for example, the domain is all real numbers because the parabola stretches as far left and as far right as it can go, with no restrictions. This means that any input value from the real number system will yield an answer in the real number system. For the range, the inequality $y \geq -3$ would be used to describe the possible output values because the parabola has a minimum at $y = -3$. This means there will not be any real output values less than $-3$ because -3 is the lowest value it reaches on the y-axis.

These same answers for domain and range can be found by observing a table. The table below shows that from input values $x = -1$ to $x = 1$, the output results in a minimum of $-3$. On each side of $x = 0$, the numbers increase, showing that the range is all real numbers greater than or equal to $-3$.

| x (domain/input) | y (range/output) |
|------------------|------------------|
| -2 | 1 |
| -1 | -2 |
| 0 | -3 |
| -1 | -2 |
| 2 | 1 |

## Linear Relationships

Linear relationships describe the way two quantities change with respect to each other. The relationship is defined as linear because a line is produced if all the sets of corresponding values are graphed on a coordinate grid. When expressing the linear relationship as an equation, the equation is often written in the form $y = mx + b$ (slope-intercept form) where $m$ and $b$ are numerical values and $x$ and $y$ are variables (for example, $y = 5x + 10$). Given a linear equation and the value of either variable ($x$ or $y$), the value of the other variable can be determined.

Suppose a teacher is grading a test containing 20 questions with 5 points given for each correct answer, adding a curve of 10 points to each test. This linear relationship can be expressed as the equation $y = 5x + 10$ where $x$ represents the number of correct answers, and y represents the test score. To determine the score of a test with a given number of correct answers, the number of correct answers is substituted into the equation for $x$ and evaluated. For example, for 10 correct answers, 10 is substituted for $x$: $y = 5(10) + 10 \rightarrow y = 60$. Therefore, 10 correct answers will result in a score of 60. The number of correct answers needed to obtain a certain score can also be determined. To determine the number of correct answers needed to score a 90, 90 is substituted for $y$ in the equation ($y$ represents the test score) and solved: $90 = 5x + 10 \rightarrow 80 = 5x \rightarrow 16 = x$. Therefore, 16 correct answers are needed to score a 90.

Linear relationships may be represented by a table of 2 corresponding values. Certain tables may determine the relationship between the values and predict other corresponding sets. Consider the table below, which displays the money in a checking account that charges a monthly fee:

| Month | 0 | 1 | 2 | 3 | 4 |
|---------|-------|-------|-------|-------|-------|
| Balance | $210 | $195 | $180 | $165 | $150 |

An examination of the values reveals that the account loses $15 every month (the month increases by one and the balance decreases by 15). This information can be used to predict future values. To determine what the value will be in month 6, the pattern can be continued, and it can be concluded that the balance will be $120. To determine which month the balance will be $0, $210 is divided by $15 (since the balance decreases $15 every month), resulting in month 14.

Similar to a table, a graph can display corresponding values of a linear relationship.

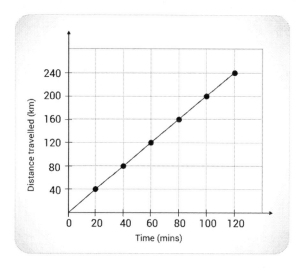

The graph above represents the relationship between distance traveled and time. To find the distance traveled in 80 minutes, the mark for 80 minutes is located at the bottom of the graph. By following this mark directly up on the graph, the corresponding point for 80 minutes is directly across from the 150 kilometer mark. This information indicates that the distance travelled in 80 minutes is 160 kilometers. To predict information not displayed on the graph, the way in which the variables change with respect to one another is determined. In this case, distance increases by 40 kilometers as time increases by 20 minutes. This information can be used to continue the data in the graph or convert the values to a table.

## Verbal Statements and Algebraic Expressions

An algebraic expression is a statement about unknown quantities expressed in mathematical symbols. The statement *five times a number added to forty* is expressed as $5x + 40$. An equation is a statement in which two expressions (with at least one containing a variable) are equal to one another. The statement *five times a number added to forty is equal to ten* is expressed as $5x + 40 = 10$.

Real world scenarios can also be expressed mathematically. Suppose a job pays its employees $300 per week and $40 for each sale made. The weekly pay is represented by the expression $40x + 300$ where $x$ is the number of sales made during the week.

Consider the following scenario: Bob had $20 and Tom had $4. After selling 4 ice cream cones to Bob, Tom has as much money as Bob. The cost of an ice cream cone is an unknown quantity and can be represented by a variable ($x$). The amount of money Bob has after his purchase is four times the cost of an ice cream cone subtracted from his original $20 → $20 - 4x$. The amount of money Tom has after his sale is four times the cost of an ice cream cone added to his original $4 → $4x + 4$. After the sale, the amount of money that Bob and Tom have are equal → $20 - 4x = 4x + 4$.

When expressing a verbal or written statement mathematically, it is vital to understand words or phrases that can be represented with symbols. The following are examples:

| Symbol | Phrase |
| --- | --- |
| + | Added to; increased by; sum of; more than |
| − | Decreased by; difference between; less than; take away |
| × | Multiplied by; 3(4,5...) times as large; product of |
| ÷ | Divided by; quotient of; half (third, etc.) of |
| = | Is; the same as; results in; as much as; equal to |
| x,t,n, etc. | A number; unknown quantity; value of; variable |

# Geometry and Measurement

## Lines, Rays, and Line Segments

The basic unit of geometry is a point. A point represents an exact location on a plane, or flat surface. The position of a point is indicated with a dot and usually named with a single uppercase letter, such as point *A* or point *T*. A point is a place, not a thing, and therefore has no dimensions or size. A set of points that lies on the same line is called collinear. A set of points that lies on the same plane is called coplanar.

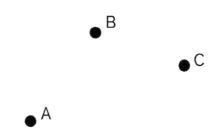

The image above displays point *A*, point *B*, and point *C*.

A line is as series of points that extends in both directions without ending. It consists of an infinite number of points and is drawn with arrows on both ends to indicate it extends infinitely. Lines can be named by two points on the line or with a single, cursive, lower case letter. The two lines below could be named line *AB* or line *BA* or $\overleftrightarrow{AB}$ or $\overleftrightarrow{BA}$; and line *m*.

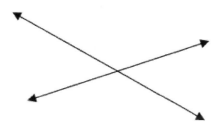

Two lines are considered parallel to each other if, while extending infinitely, they will never intersect (or meet). Parallel lines point in the same direction and are always the same distance apart. Two lines are considered perpendicular if they intersect to form right angles. Right angles are 90°. Typically, a small box is drawn at the intersection point to indicate the right angle.

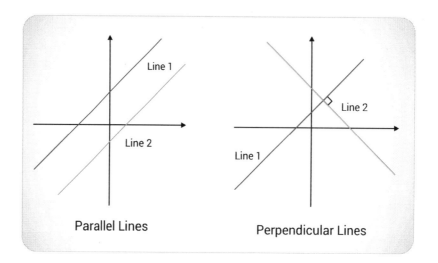

Line 1 is parallel to line 2 in the left image and is written as line 1 || line 2. Line 1 is perpendicular to line 2 in the right image and is written as line 1 ⊥ line 2.

A ray has a specific starting point and extends in one direction without ending. The endpoint of a ray is its starting point. Rays are named using the endpoint first, and any other point on the ray. The following ray can be named ray *AB* and written $\overrightarrow{AB}$.

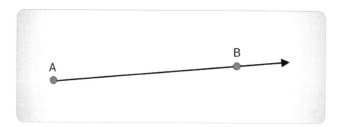

A line segment has specific starting and ending points. A line segment consists of two endpoints and all the points in between. Line segments are named by the two endpoints. The example below is named segment *KL* or segment *LK*, written $\overline{KL}$ or $\overline{LK}$.

## Classification of Angles

An angle consists of two rays that have a common endpoint. This common endpoint is called the vertex of the angle. The two rays can be called sides of the angle. The angle below has a vertex at point *B* and the sides consist of ray *BA* and ray *BC*. An angle can be named in three ways:

1. Using the vertex and a point from each side, with the vertex letter in the middle.
2. Using only the vertex. This can only be used if it is the only angle with that vertex.
3. Using a number that is written inside the angle.

The angle below can be written ∠*ABC* (read angle *ABC*), ∠*CBA*, ∠*B*, or ∠1.

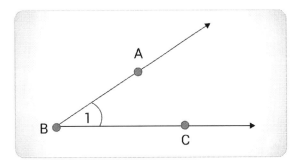

An angle divides a plane, or flat surface, into three parts: the angle itself, the interior (inside) of the angle, and the exterior (outside) of the angle. The figure below shows point *M* on the interior of the angle and point *N* on the exterior of the angle.

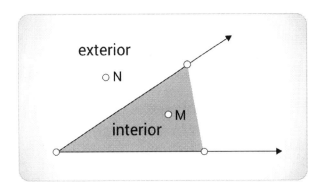

Angles can be measured in units called degrees, with the symbol °. The degree measure of an angle is between 0° and 180° and can be obtained by using a protractor.

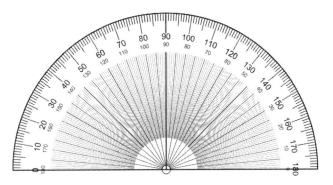

A straight angle (or simply a line) measures exactly 180°. A right angle's sides meet at the vertex to create a square corner. A right angle measures exactly 90° and is typically indicated by a box drawn in the interior of the angle. An acute angle has an interior that is narrower than a right angle. The measure of an acute angle is any value less than 90° and greater than 0. For example, 89.9°, 47°, 12°, and 1°. An obtuse angle has an interior that is wider than a right angle. The measure of an obtuse angle is any value greater than 90° but less than 180°. For example, 90.1°, 110°, 150°, and 179.9°.

- Acute angles: Less than 90°
- Obtuse angles: Greater than 90°
- Right angles: 90°
- Straight angles: 180°

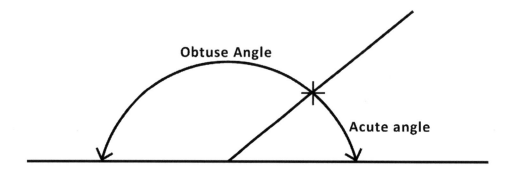

## Two- and Three-Dimensional Shapes

A polygon is a closed geometric figure in a plane (flat surface) consisting of at least 3 sides formed by line segments. These are often defined as two-dimensional shapes. Common two-dimensional shapes include circles, triangles, squares, rectangles, pentagons, and hexagons. Note that a circle is a two-dimensional shape without sides.

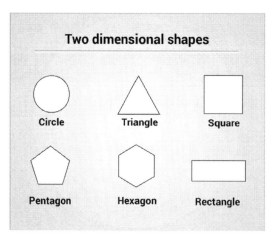

A solid figure, or simply solid, is a figure that encloses a part of space. Some solids consist of flat surfaces only while others include curved surfaces. Solid figures are often defined as three-dimensional shapes. Common three-dimensional shapes include spheres, prisms, cubes, pyramids, cylinders, and cones.

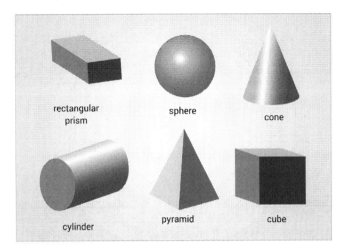

Composing two- or three-dimensional shapes involves putting together two or more shapes to create a new larger figure. For example, a semi-circle (half circle), rectangle, and two triangles can be used to compose the figure of the sailboat shown below.

Similarly, solid figures can be placed together to compose an endless number of three-dimensional objects.

Decomposing two- and three-dimensional figures involves breaking the shapes apart into smaller, simpler shapes. Consider the following two-dimensional representations of a house:

This complex figure can be decomposed into the following basic two-dimensional shapes: large rectangle (body of house); large triangle (roof); small rectangle and small triangle (chimney). Decomposing figures is often done more than one way. To illustrate, the figure of the house could also be decomposed into: two large triangles (body); two medium triangles (roof); two smaller triangles of unequal size (chimney).

## Polygons and Solids

A polygon is a closed two-dimensional figure consisting of three or more sides. Polygons can be either convex or concave. A polygon that has interior angles all measuring less than 180° is convex. A concave polygon has one or more interior angles measuring greater than 180°. Examples are shown below.

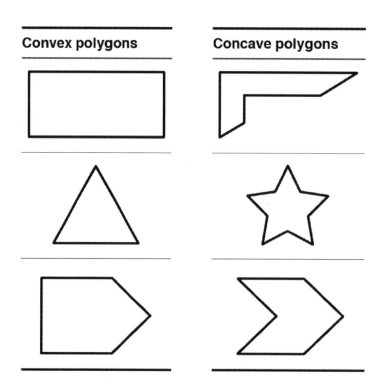

Polygons can be classified by the number of sides (also equal to the number of angles) they have. The following are the names of polygons with a given number of sides or angles:

| # of sides | 3 | 4 | 5 | 6 | 7 | 8 | 9 | 10 |
|---|---|---|---|---|---|---|---|---|
| Name of polygon | Triangle | Quadrilateral | Pentagon | Hexagon | Septagon (or heptagon) | Octagon | Nonagon | Decagon |

Equiangular polygons are polygons in which the measure of every interior angle is the same. The sides of equilateral polygons are always the same length. If a polygon is both equiangular and equilateral, the polygon is defined as a regular polygon. Examples are shown below.

Triangles can be further classified by their sides and angles. A triangle with its largest angle measuring 90° is a right triangle. A triangle with the largest angle less than 90° is an acute triangle. A triangle with the largest angle greater than 90° is an obtuse triangle. Below is an example of a right triangle.

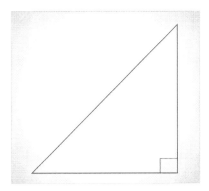

A triangle consisting of two equal sides and two equal angles is an isosceles triangle. A triangle with three equal sides and three equal angles is an equilateral triangle. A triangle with no equal sides or angles is a scalene triangle.

Isosceles triangle:

Equilateral triangle:

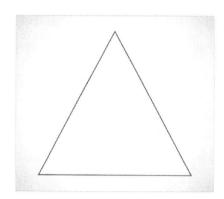

Scalene triangle:

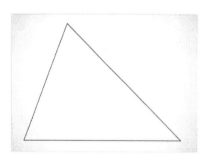

Quadrilaterals can be further classified according to their sides and angles. A quadrilateral with exactly one pair of parallel sides is called a trapezoid. A quadrilateral that shows both pairs of opposite sides parallel is a parallelogram. Parallelograms include rhombuses, rectangles, and squares. A rhombus has four equal sides. A rectangle has four equal angles (90° each). A square has four 90° angles and four equal sides. Therefore, a square is both a rhombus and a rectangle.

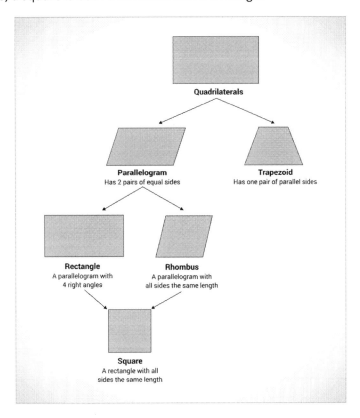

A solid is a three-dimensional figure that encloses a part of space. Solids consisting of all flat surfaces that are polygons are called polyhedrons. The two-dimensional surfaces that make up a polyhedron are called faces. Types of polyhedrons include prisms and pyramids. A prism consists of two parallel faces that are congruent (or the same shape and same size), and lateral faces going around (which are parallelograms). A prism is further classified by the shape of its base, as shown below:

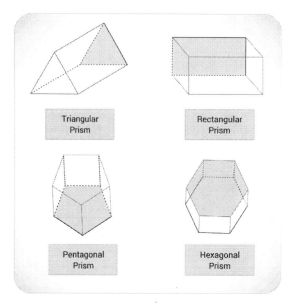

A pyramid consists of lateral faces (triangles) that meet at a common point called the vertex and one other face that is a polygon, called the base. A pyramid can be further classified by the shape of its base, as shown below.

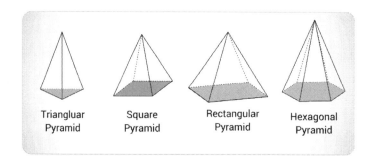

A tetrahedron is another name for a triangular pyramid. All the faces of a tetrahedron are triangles.

Solids that are not polyhedrons include spheres, cylinders, and cones. A sphere is the set of all points a given distance from a given center point. A sphere is commonly thought of as a three-dimensional circle. A cylinder consists of two parallel, congruent (same size) circles and a lateral curved surface. A cone consists of a circle as its base and a lateral curved surface that narrows to a point called the vertex.

Similar polygons are the same shape but different sizes. More specifically, their corresponding angle measures are congruent (or equal) and the length of their sides is proportional. For example, all sides of one polygon may be double the length of the sides of another. Likewise, similar solids are the same shape but different sizes. Any corresponding faces or bases of similar solids are the same polygons that are proportional by a consistent value.

## Three-Dimensional Figures with Nets

A net is a construction of two-dimensional figures that can be folded to form a given three-dimensional figure. More than one net may exist to fold and produce the same solid, or three-dimensional figure. The bases and faces of the solid figure are analyzed to determine the polygons (two-dimensional figures) needed to form the net.

Consider the following triangular prism:

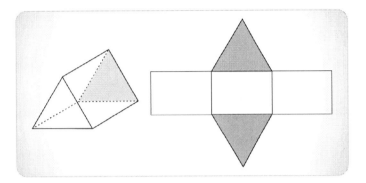

The surface of the prism consists of two triangular bases and three rectangular faces. The net beside it can be used to construct the triangular prism by first folding the triangles up to be parallel to each other, and then folding the two outside rectangles up and to the center with the outer edges touching.

Consider the following cylinder:

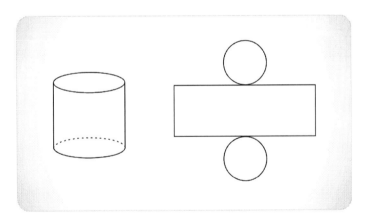

The surface consists of two circular bases and a curved lateral surface that can be opened and flattened into a rectangle. The net beside the cylinder can be used to construct the cylinder by first folding the circles up to be parallel to each other, and then curving the sides of the rectangle up to touch each other. The top and bottom of the folded rectangle should be touching the outside of both circles.

Consider the following square pyramid below on the left. The surface consists of one square base and four triangular faces. The net below on the right can be used to construct the square pyramid by folding each triangle towards the center of the square. The top points of the triangle meet at the vertex.

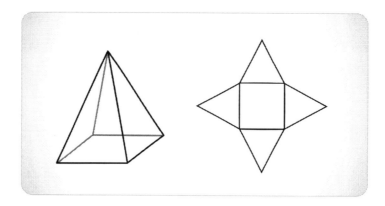

## Surface Area of Three-Dimensional Figures

The area of a two-dimensional figure refers to the number of square units needed to cover the interior region of the figure. This concept is similar to wallpaper covering the flat surface of a wall. For example, if a rectangle has an area of 10 square centimeters (written $10cm^2$), it will take 10 squares, each with sides one centimeter in length, to cover the interior region of the rectangle. Note that area is measured in square units such as: square centimeters or $cm^2$; square feet or $ft^2$; square yards or $yd^2$; square miles or $mi^2$.

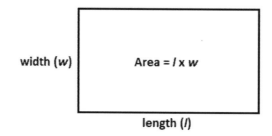

The surface area of a three-dimensional figure refers to the number of square units needed to cover the entire surface of the figure. This concept is similar to using wrapping paper to completely cover the outside of a box. For example, if a triangular pyramid has a surface area of 17 square inches (written $17in^2$), it will take 17 squares, each with sides one inch in length, to cover the entire surface of the pyramid. Surface area is also measured in square units.

Many three-dimensional figures (solid figures) can be represented by nets consisting of rectangles and triangles. The surface area of such solids can be determined by adding the areas of each of its faces and bases. Finding the surface area using this method requires calculating the areas of rectangles and triangles. To find the area ($A$) of a rectangle, the length ($l$) is multiplied by the width ($w$) $\rightarrow A = l \times w$. The area of a rectangle with a length of 8cm and a width of 4cm is calculated: $A = (8cm) \times (4cm) \rightarrow A = 32cm^2$.

To calculate the area ($A$) of a triangle, the product of $\frac{1}{2}$, the base ($b$), and the height ($h$) is found → $A =$ $\frac{1}{2} \times b \times h$. Note that the height of a triangle is measured from the base to the vertex opposite of it forming a right angle with the base.

The area of a triangle with a base of 11cm and a height of 6cm is calculated: $A = \frac{1}{2} \times (11cm) \times (6cm) \rightarrow A = 33cm^2$.

Consider the following triangular prism, which is represented by a net consisting of two triangles and three rectangles.

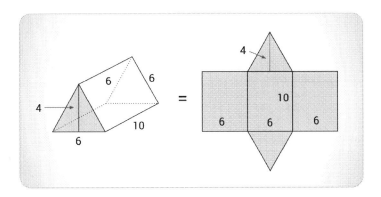

The surface area of the prism can be determined by adding the areas of each of its faces and bases. The surface area ($SA$) = area of triangle + area of triangle + area of rectangle + area of rectangle + area of rectangle.

$$SA = \left(\frac{1}{2} \times b \times h\right) + \left(\frac{1}{2} \times b \times h\right) + (l \times w) + (l \times w) + (l \times w)$$

$$SA = \left(\frac{1}{2} \times 6 \times 4\right) + \left(\frac{1}{2} \times 6 \times 4\right) + (6 \times 10) + (6 \times 10) + (6 \times 10)$$

$$SA = (12) + (12) + (60) + (60) + (60)$$

$$SA = 204 \; square \; units$$

## Area and Perimeter of Polygons

*Perimeter* is the measurement of a distance around something or the sum of all sides of a polygon. Think of perimeter as the length of the boundary, like a fence. In contrast, *area* is the space occupied by a defined enclosure, like a field enclosed by a fence.

When thinking about perimeter, think about walking around the outside of something. When thinking about area, think about the amount of space or *surface area* something takes up.

## Squares

The perimeter of a square is measured by adding together all of the sides. Since a square has four equal sides, its perimeter can be calculated by multiplying the length of one side by 4. Thus, the formula is $P = 4 \times s$, where $s$ equals one side. For example, the following square has side lengths of 5 meters:

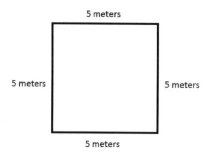

5 meters

5 meters      5 meters

5 meters

The perimeter is 20 meters because 4 times 5 is 20.

The area of a square is the length of a side squared. For example, if a side of a square is 7 centimeters, then the area is 49 square centimeters. The formula for this example is $A = s^2 = 7^2 = 49$ square centimeters. An example is if the rectangle has a length of 6 inches and a width of 7 inches, then the area is 42 square inches:

$$A = lw = 6(7) = 42 \text{ square inches}$$

## Rectangles

Like a square, a rectangle's perimeter is measured by adding together all of the sides. But as the sides are unequal, the formula is different. A rectangle has equal values for its lengths (long sides) and equal values for its widths (short sides), so the perimeter formula for a rectangle is:

$$P = l + l + w + w = 2l + 2w$$

$l$ equals length
$w$ equals width

The area is found by multiplying the length by the width, so the formula is $A = l \times w$.

For example, if the length of a rectangle is 10 inches and the width 8 inches, then the perimeter is 36 inches because:

$$P = 2l + 2w = 2(10) + 2(8) = 20 + 16 = 36 \text{ inches}$$

## Triangles

A triangle's perimeter is measured by adding together the three sides, so the formula is $P = a + b + c$, where $a, b,$ and $c$ are the values of the three sides. The area is the product of one-half the base and height so the formula is:

$$A = \frac{1}{2} \times b \times h$$

It can be simplified to:

$$A = \frac{bh}{2}$$

The base is the bottom of the triangle, and the height is the distance from the base to the peak. If a problem asks to calculate the area of a triangle, it will provide the base and height.

For example, if the base of the triangle is 2 feet and the height 4 feet, then the area is 4 square feet. The following equation shows the formula used to calculate the area of the triangle:

$$A = \frac{1}{2}bh = \frac{1}{2}(2)(4) = 4 \text{ square feet}$$

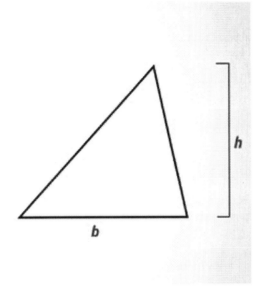

## Circles

A circle's perimeter—also known as its circumference—is measured by multiplying the diameter by $\pi$.

Diameter is the straight line measured from one end to the direct opposite end of the circle.

$\pi$ is referred to as pi and is equal to 3.14 (with rounding).

So the formula is $\pi \times d$.

This is sometimes expressed by the formula $C = 2 \times \pi \times r$, where $r$ is the radius of the circle. These formulas are equivalent, as the radius equals half of the diameter.

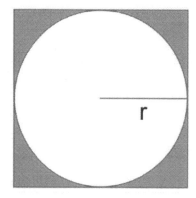

The area of a circle is calculated through the formula $A = \pi \times r^2$. The test will indicate either to leave the answer with $\pi$ attached or to calculate to the nearest decimal place, which means multiplying by 3.14 for $\pi$.

## Arc

The *arc of a circle* is the distance between two points on the circle. The length of the arc of a circle in terms of *degrees* is easily determined if the value of the central angle is known. The length of the arc is simply the value of the central angle. In this example, the length of the arc of the circle in degrees is 75°.

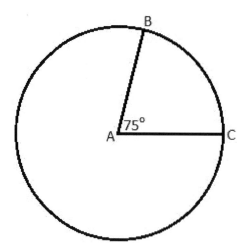

To determine the length of the arc of a circle in *distance*, the student will need to know the values for both the central angle and the radius. This formula is:

$$\frac{central\ angle}{360°} = \frac{arc\ length}{2\pi r}$$

The equation is simplified by cross-multiplying to solve for the arc length.

In the following example, the student should substitute the values of the central angle (75°) and the radius (10 inches) into the equation above to solve for the arc length.

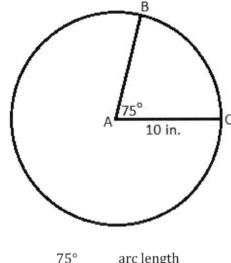

$$\frac{75°}{360°} = \frac{\text{arc length}}{2(3.14)(10\text{in.})}$$

To solve the equation, first cross-multiply: 4710 = 360(arc length). Next, divide each side of the equation by 360. The result of the formula is that the arc length is 13.1 (rounded).

## Parallelograms

Similar to triangles, the height of the parallelogram is measured from one base to the other at a 90° angle (or perpendicular).

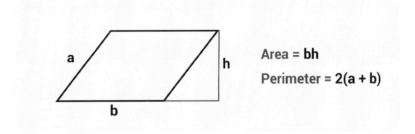

## Trapezoid

The area of a trapezoid can be calculated using the formula: $A = \frac{1}{2} \times h(b_1 + b_2)$, where $h$ is the height and $b_1$ and $b_2$ are the parallel bases of the trapezoid.

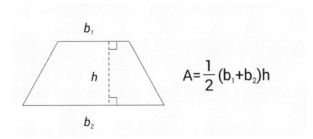

## Regular Polygon

The area of a regular polygon can be determined by using its perimeter and the length of the apothem. The apothem is a line from the center of the regular polygon to any of its sides at a right angle. (Note that the perimeter of a regular polygon can be determined given the length of only one side.) The formula for the area ($A$) of a regular polygon is $A = \frac{1}{2} \times a \times P$, where $a$ is the length of the apothem, and $P$ is the perimeter of the figure. Consider the following regular pentagon:

To find the area, the perimeter ($P$) is calculated first: $8cm \times 5 \rightarrow P = 40cm$. Then the perimeter and the apothem are used to find the area ($A$): $A = \frac{1}{2} \times a \times P \rightarrow A = \frac{1}{2} \times (6cm) \times (40cm) \rightarrow A = 120cm^2$. Note that the unit is $cm^2 \rightarrow cm \times cm = cm^2$.

## Irregular Shapes

The perimeter of an irregular polygon is found by adding the lengths of all of the sides. In cases where all of the sides are given, this will be very straightforward, as it will simply involve finding the sum of the provided lengths. Other times, a side length may be missing and must be determined before the perimeter can be calculated. Consider the example below:

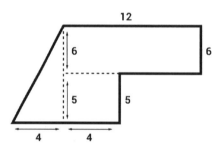

All of the side lengths are provided except for the angled side on the left. Test takers should notice that this is the hypotenuse of a right triangle. The other two sides of the triangle are provided (the base is 4 and the height is 6 + 5 = 11). The Pythagorean Theorem can be used to find the length of the hypotenuse, remembering that $a^2 + b^2 = c^2$.

Substituting the side values provided yields $(4)^2 + (11)^2 = c^2$.

Therefore, $c = \sqrt{16 + 121} = 11.7$

Finally, the perimeter can be found by adding this new side length with the other provided lengths to get the total length around the figure: 4+4+5+8+6+12+11.7=50.7. Although units are not provided in this figure, remember that reporting units with a measurement is important.

The area of irregular polygons is found by decomposing, or breaking apart, the figure into smaller shapes. When the area of the smaller shapes is determined, the area of the smaller shapes will produce the area of the original figure when added together. Consider the earlier example:

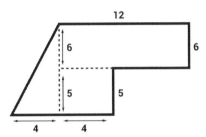

The irregular polygon is decomposed into two rectangles and a triangle. The area of the large rectangles ($A = l \times w \to A = 12 \times 6$) is 72 square units. The area of the small rectangle is 20 square units ($A = 4 \times 5$). The area of the triangle ($A = \frac{1}{2} \times b \times h \to A = \frac{1}{2} \times 4 \times 11$) is 22 square units. The sum of the areas of these figures produces the total area of the original polygon: $A = 72 + 20 + 22 \to A = 114$ square units.

Here's another example:

This irregular polygon is decomposed into two rectangles. The area of the large rectangle ($A = l \times w \to A = 8 \times 4$) is 32 square units. The area of the small rectangle is 20 square units ($A = 4 \times 5$). The sum of the areas of these figures produces the total area of the original polygon: $A = 32 + 20 \to A = 52$ square units.

## Right Rectangular Prisms

A right rectangular prism consists of:

- Two congruent (same size and shape) rectangles as the parallel *bases* (top and bottom).
- Two congruent rectangles as the *side* faces.
- Two congruent rectangles as the *front and back* faces.

It is called a right prism because the base and sides meet at right angles.

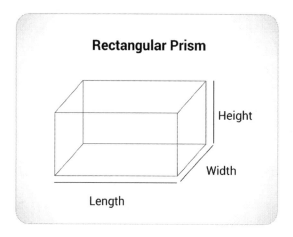

The length and width of the prism is the length and width of the rectangular base. The height of the prism is the measure from one base to the other.

The surface area of three-dimensional figures can be found by adding the areas of each of its bases and faces. The areas of a right rectangular prism are found as follows: two bases → $A = l \times w$; front and back faces → $A = l \times h$; two side faces → $A = w \times h$. The sum of these six areas will equal the surface area of the prism. (Surface area = area of 2 bases + area of front and back + area of 2 sides). This is true for all right rectangular prisms leading to the formula for surface area $SA = 2 \times l \times w + 2 \times l \times h + 2 \times w \times h$ or $SA = 2(l \times w + l \times h + w \times h)$. Given the right rectangular prism below, the surface area is calculated as follows:

$$SA = 2\left(3\frac{1}{2}\text{ft}\right)\left(2\frac{1}{2}\text{ft}\right) + 2\left(3\frac{1}{2}\text{ft}\right)\left(1\frac{1}{2}\text{ft}\right) + 2\left(2\frac{1}{2}\text{ft}\right)\left(1\frac{1}{2}\text{ft}\right) \rightarrow SA = 35.5\text{ft}^2$$

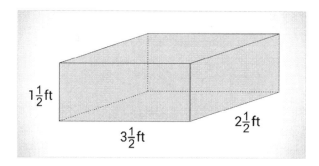

The volume of a solid (three-dimensional figure) is the number of cubic units needed to fill the space that the figure occupies. This concept is similar to filling a box with blocks. Volume is a three-dimensional measurement. Therefore, volume is expressed in cubic units such as cubic centimeters ($cm^3$), cubic feet ($ft^3$), and cubic yards ($yd^3$). If a rectangular prism has a volume of 30 cubic meters ($30m^3$), it will take 30 cubes, each with sides one meter in length, to fill the space occupied by the prism. A simple formula can be used to determine the volume of a right rectangular prism. The area of the base of the prism ($l \times w$) will indicate how many "blocks" are needed to cover the base. The height ($h$) of the prism will indicate how many "levels" of blocks are needed to construct the prism.

Therefore, to find the volume ($V$) of a right rectangular prism, the area of the base ($l \times w$) is multiplied by the height ($h$): $V = l \times w \times h$. The volume of the prism shown above is calculated:

$$V = \left(3\frac{1}{2}\text{ft}\right) \times \left(2\frac{1}{2}\text{ft}\right) \times \left(1\frac{1}{2}\text{ft}\right) \rightarrow V = 13.125\text{ft}^3$$

## Effects of Changes to Dimensions on Area and Volume

Similar polygons are figures that are the same shape but different sizes. Likewise, similar solids are different sizes but are the same shape. In both cases, corresponding angles in the same positions for both figures are congruent (equal), and corresponding sides are proportional in length. For example, the triangles below are similar. The following pairs of corresponding angles are congruent: $\angle A$ and $\angle D$; $\angle B$ and $\angle E$; $\angle C$ and $\angle F$. The corresponding sides are proportional:

$$\frac{AB}{DE} = \frac{6}{3} = 2$$

$$\frac{BC}{EF} = \frac{9}{4.5} = 2$$

$$\frac{CA}{FD} = \frac{10}{5} = 2$$

In other words, triangle $ABC$ is the same shape but twice as large as triangle $DEF$.

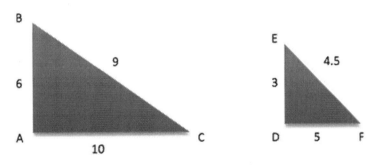

An example of similar triangular pyramids is shown below.

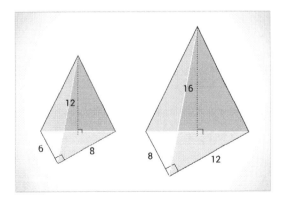

Given the nature of two- and three-dimensional measurements, changing dimensions by a given scale (multiplier) does not change the area of volume by the same scale. Consider a rectangle with a length of

**135**

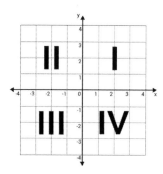Test Prep Books!!!

5 centimeters and a width of 4 centimeters. The area of the rectangle is $20cm^2$. Doubling the dimensions of the rectangle (multiplying by a scale factor of 2) to 10 centimeters and 8 centimeters *does not* double the area to $40cm^2$. Area is a two-dimensional measurement (measured in square units). Therefore, the dimensions are multiplied by a scale that is squared (raised to the second power) to determine the scale of the corresponding areas. For the previous example, the length and width are multiplied by 2. Therefore, the area is multiplied by $2^2$, or 4. The area of a 5cm × 4cm rectangle is $20cm^2$. The area of a 10cm × 8cm rectangle is $80cm^2$.

Volume is a three-dimensional measurement, which is measured in cubic units. Therefore, the scale between dimensions of similar solids is cubed (raised to the third power) to determine the scale between their volumes. Consider similar right rectangular prisms: one with a length of 8 inches, a width of 24 inches, and a height of 16 inches; the second with a length of 4 inches, a width of 12 inches, and a height of 8 inches. The first prism, multiplied by a scalar of $\frac{1}{2}$, produces the measurement of the second prism. The volume of the first prism, multiplied by $(\frac{1}{2})^3$, which equals $\frac{1}{8}$, produces the volume of the second prism. The volume of the first prism is 8in × 24in × 16in which equals $3,072in^3$. The volume of the second prism is 4in × 12in × 8in which equals $384in^3$ ($3,072in^3 \times \frac{1}{8} = 384in^3$).

The rules for squaring the scalar for area and cubing the scalar for volume only hold true for similar figures. In other words, if only one dimension is changed (changing the width of a rectangle but not the length) or dimensions are changed at different rates (the length of a prism is doubled and its height is tripled) the figures are not similar (same shape). Therefore, the rules above do not apply.

## X-Axis, *Y*-Axis, Origin, and Four Quadrants in the Coordinate Plane

The coordinate plane, sometimes referred to as the Cartesian plane, is a two-dimensional surface consisting of a horizontal and a vertical number line. The horizontal number line is referred to as the *x*-axis, and the vertical number line is referred to as the *y*-axis. The *x*-axis and *y*-axis intersect (or cross) at a point called the origin. At the origin, the value of the *x*-axis is zero, and the value of the *y*-axis is zero. The coordinate plane identifies the exact location of a point that is plotted on the two-dimensional surface. Like a map, the location of all points on the plane are in relation to the origin. Along the *x*-axis (horizontal line), numbers to the right of the origin are positive and increasing in value (1,2,3, . . .) and to the left of the origin numbers are negative and decreasing in value (-1,-2,-3, . . .). Along the *y*-axis (vertical line), numbers above the origin are positive and increasing in value and numbers below the origin are negative and decreasing in value.

The *x*- and *y*-axis divide the coordinate plane into four sections. These sections are referred to as quadrant one, quadrant two, quadrant three, and quadrant four, and are often written with Roman numerals I, II, III, and IV.

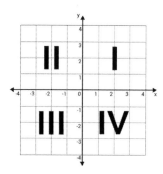

The upper right section is Quadrant I and consists of points with positive x-values and positive y-values. The upper left section is Quadrant II and consists of points with negative x-values and positive y-values. The bottom left section is Quadrant III and consists of points with negative x-values and negative y-values. The bottom right section is Quadrant IV and consists of points with positive x-values and negative y-values.

## Solving Problems in the Coordinate Plane

The location of a point on a coordinate grid is identified by writing it as an ordered pair. An ordered pair is a set of numbers indicating the x-and y-coordinates of the point. Ordered pairs are written in the form (x, y) where x and y are values which indicate their respective coordinates. For example, the point (3, -2) has an x-coordinate of 3 and a y-coordinate of -2.

Plotting a point on the coordinate plane with a given coordinate means starting from the origin (0, 0). To determine the value of the x-coordinate, move right (positive number) or left (negative number) along the x-axis. Next, move up (positive number) or down (negative number) to the value of the y-coordinate. Finally, plot and label the point. For example, plotting the point (1, -2) requires starting from the origin and moving right along the x-axis to positive one, then moving down until straight across from negative 2 on the y-axis. The point is plotted and labeled. This point, along with three other points, are plotted and labeled on the graph below.

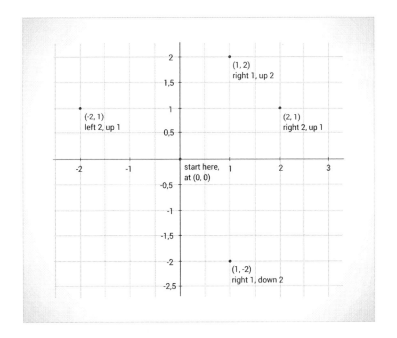

To write the coordinates of a point on the coordinate grid, a line should be traced directly above or below the point until reaching the x-axis (noting the value on the x-axis). Then, returning to the point, a line should be traced directly to the right or left of the point until reaching the y-axis (noting the value on the y-axis). The ordered pair (x, y) should be written with the values determined for the x- and y-coordinates.

Polygons can be drawn in the coordinate plane given the coordinates of their vertices. These coordinates can be used to determine the perimeter and area of the figure. Suppose triangle RQP has vertices located at the points: *R*(-4, 2), *Q*(1, 6), and *P*(1, 2). By plotting the points for the three vertices, the triangle can be constructed as follows:

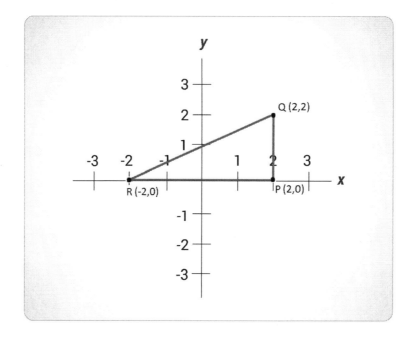

Because points *R* and *P* have the same *y*-coordinates (they are directly across from each other), the distance between them is determined by subtracting their *x*-coordinates (or simply counting units from one point to the other): 2 – (-2) = 4. Therefore, the length of side *RP* is 4 units. Because points *Q* and *P* have the same *x*-coordinate (they are directly above and below each other), the distance between them is determined by subtracting their *y*-coordinates (or counting units between them): 2 – 0 = 2. Therefore, the length of side *PQ* is 2 units. Knowing the length of side *RP*, which is the base of the triangle, and the length of side *PQ*, which is the height of the triangle, the area of the figure can be determined by using the formula $A = \frac{1}{2}bh$.

To determine the perimeter of the triangle, the lengths of all three sides are needed. Points *R* and *Q* are neither directly across nor directly above and below each other. Therefore, the distance formula must be used to find the length of side *RQ*.

The distance formula is as follows:

$$d = \sqrt{(x_2 - x_1)^2 + (y_2 - y_1)^2}$$

$$d = \sqrt{(2 - (-2))^2 + (2 - 0)^2}$$

$$d = \sqrt{(4)^2 + (2)^2}$$

$$d = \sqrt{16 + 4}$$

$$d = \sqrt{20}$$

The perimeter is determined by adding the lengths of the three sides of the triangle.

## Elapsed Time, Money, Length, Volume, and Mass

Word problems involving elapsed time, money, length, volume, and mass require determining which operations (addition, subtraction, multiplication, and division) should be performed, and using and/or converting the proper unit for the scenario.

The following table lists key words that can be used to indicate the proper operation:

| Addition | Sum, total, in all, combined, increase of, more than, added to |
|---|---|
| Subtraction | Difference, change, remaining, less than, decreased by |
| Multiplication | Product, times, twice, triple, each |
| Division | Quotient, goes into, per, evenly, divided by half, divided by third, split |

Identifying and utilizing the proper units for the scenario requires knowing how to apply the conversion rates for money, length, volume, and mass. For example, given a scenario that requires subtracting 8 inches from $2\frac{1}{2}$ feet, both values should first be expressed in the same unit (they could be expressed $\frac{2}{3}$ft & $2\frac{1}{2}$ft, or 8in and 30in). The desired unit for the answer may also require converting back to another unit.

Consider the following scenario: A parking area along the river is only wide enough to fit one row of cars and is $\frac{1}{2}$ kilometers long. The average space needed per car is 5 meters. How many cars can be parked along the river? First, all measurements should be converted to similar units: $\frac{1}{2}$km = 500m. The operation(s) needed should be identified. Because the problem asks for the number of cars, the total space should be divided by the space per car. 500 meters divided by 5 meters per car yields a total of 100 cars. Written as an expression, the meters unit cancels and the cars unit is left: $\frac{500m}{5m/car}$ the same as $500m \times \frac{1\ car}{5m}$ yields 100 cars.

When dealing with problems involving elapsed time, breaking the problem down into workable parts is helpful. For example, suppose the length of time between 1:15pm and 3:45pm must be determined. From 1:15pm to 2:00pm is 45 minutes (knowing there are 60 minutes in an hour). From 2:00pm to 3:00pm is 1 hour. From 3:00pm to 3:45pm is 45 minutes. The total elapsed time is 45 minutes plus 1 hour plus 45 minutes. This sum produces 1 hour and 90 minutes. 90 minutes is over an hour, so this is converted to 1 hour (60 minutes) and 30 minutes. The total elapsed time can now be expressed as 2 hours and 30 minutes.

## Measuring Lengths of Objects

The length of an object can be measured using standard tools such as rulers, yard sticks, meter sticks, and measuring tapes. The following image depicts a yardstick:

Choosing the right tool to perform the measurement requires determining whether United States customary units or metric units are desired, and having a grasp of the approximate length of each unit and the approximate length of each tool. The measurement can still be performed by trial and error without the knowledge of the approximate size of the tool.

For example, to determine the length of a room in feet, a United States customary unit, various tools can be used for this task. These include a ruler (typically 12 inches/1 foot long), a yardstick (3 feet/1 yard long), or a tape measure displaying feet (typically either 25 feet or 50 feet). Because the length of a room is much larger than the length of a ruler or a yardstick, a tape measure should be used to perform the measurement.

When the correct measuring tool is selected, the measurement is performed by first placing the tool directly above or below the object (if making a horizontal measurement) or directly next to the object (if making a vertical measurement). The next step is aligning the tool so that one end of the object is at the mark for zero units, then recording the unit of the mark at the other end of the object. To give the length of a paperclip in metric units, a ruler displaying centimeters is aligned with one end of the paper clip to the mark for zero centimeters.

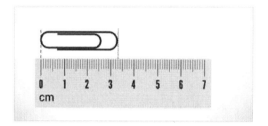

Directly down from the other end of the paperclip is the mark that measures its length. In this case, that mark is two small dashes past the 3 centimeter mark. Each small dash is 1 millimeter (or .1 centimeters). Therefore, the length of the paper clip is 3.2 centimeters.

To compare the lengths of objects, each length must be expressed in the same unit. If possible, the objects should be measured with the same tool or with tools utilizing the same units. For example, a ruler and a yardstick can both measure length in inches. If the lengths of the objects are expressed in different units, these different units must be converted to the same unit before comparing them. If two lengths are expressed in the same unit, the lengths may be compared by subtracting the smaller value from the larger value. For example, suppose the lengths of two gardens are to be compared. Garden A has a length of 4 feet, and garden B has a length of 2 yards. 2 yards is converted to 6 feet so that the measurements have similar units. Then, the smaller length (4 feet) is subtracted from the larger length (6ft): 6ft – 4ft = 2ft. Therefore, garden B is 2 feet larger than garden A.

## Relative Sizes of United States Customary Units and Metric Units

The United States customary system and the metric system each consist of distinct units to measure lengths and volume of liquids. The U.S. customary units for length, from smallest to largest, are: inch (in), foot (ft), yard (yd), and mile (mi). The metric units for length, from smallest to largest, are: millimeter (mm), centimeter (cm), decimeter (dm), meter (m), and kilometer (km). The relative size of each unit of length is shown below.

| U.S. Customary | Metric | Conversion |
|---|---|---|
| 12in = 1ft | 10mm = 1cm | 1in = 2.54cm |
| 36in = 3ft = 1yd | 10cm = 1dm(decimeter) | 1m ≈ 3.28ft ≈ 1.09yd |
| 5,280ft = 1,760yd = 1mi | 100cm = 10dm = 1m | 1mi ≈ 1.6km |
|  | 1000m = 1km |  |

The U.S. customary units for volume of liquids, from smallest to largest, are: fluid ounces (fl oz), cup (c), pint (pt), quart (qt), and gallon (gal). The metric units for volume of liquids, from smallest to largest, are: milliliter (mL), centiliter (cL), deciliter (dL), liter (L), and kiloliter (kL). The relative size of each unit of liquid volume is shown below.

| U.S. Customary | Metric | Conversion |
|---|---|---|
| 8fl oz = 1c | 10mL = 1cL | 1pt ≈ 0.473L |
| 2c = 1pt | 10cL = 1dL | 1L ≈ 1.057qt |
| 4c = 2pt = 1qt | 1,000mL = 100cL = 10dL = 1L | 1gal ≈ 3.785L |
| 4qt = 1gal | 1,000L = 1kL |  |

The U.S. customary system measures weight (how strongly Earth is pulling on an object) in the following units, from least to greatest: ounce (oz), pound (lb), and ton. The metric system measures mass (the quantity of matter within an object) in the following units, from least to greatest: milligram (mg), centigram (cg), gram (g), kilogram (kg), and metric ton (MT). The relative sizes of each unit of weight and mass are shown below.

| U.S. Measures of Weight | Metric Measures of Mass |
|---|---|
| 16oz = 1lb | 10mg = 1cg |
| 2,000lb = 1 ton | 100cg = 1g |
|  | 1,000g = 1kg |
|  | 1,000kg = 1MT |

Note that weight and mass DO NOT measure the same thing.

Time is measured in the following units, from shortest to longest: second (sec), minute (min), hour (h), day (d), week (wk), month (mo), year (yr), decade, century, millennium. The relative sizes of each unit of time is shown below.

- 60sec = 1min
- 60min = 1h
- 24hr = 1d
- 7d = 1wk

- 52wk = 1yr
- 12mo = 1yr
- 10yr = 1 decade
- 100yrs = 1 century
- 1,000yrs = 1 millennium

## Conversion of Units

When working with different systems of measurement, conversion from one unit to another may be necessary. The conversion rate must be known to convert units. One method for converting units is to write and solve a proportion. The arrangement of values in a proportion is extremely important. Suppose that a problem requires converting 20 fluid ounces to cups. To do so, a proportion can be written using the conversion rate of 8fl oz = 1c with $x$ representing the missing value. The proportion can be written in any of the following ways:

$$\frac{1}{8} = \frac{x}{20} \left( \frac{c\ for\ conversion}{fl\ oz\ for\ conversion} = \frac{unknown\ c}{fl\ oz\ given} \right); \frac{8}{1} = \frac{20}{x} \left( \frac{fl\ oz\ for\ conversion}{c\ for\ conversion} = \frac{fl\ oz\ given}{unknown\ c} \right);$$

$$\frac{1}{x} = \frac{8}{20} \left( \frac{c\ for\ conversion}{unknown\ c} = \frac{fl\ oz\ for\ conversion}{fl\ oz\ given} \right); \frac{x}{1} = \frac{20}{8} \left( \frac{unknown\ c}{c\ for\ conversion} = \frac{fl\ oz\ given}{fl\ oz\ for\ conversion} \right)$$

To solve a proportion, the ratios are cross-multiplied and the resulting equation is solved. When cross-multiplying, all four proportions above will produce the same equation: $(8)(x) = (20)(1) \rightarrow 8x = 20$. Dividing by 8 to isolate the variable $x$, the result is $x = 2.5$. The variable $x$ represented the unknown number of cups. Therefore, the conclusion is that 20 fluid ounces converts (is equal) to 2.5 cups.

Sometimes converting units requires writing and solving more than one proportion. Suppose an exam question asks to determine how many hours are in 2 weeks. Without knowing the conversion rate between hours and weeks, this can be determined knowing the conversion rates between weeks and days, and between days and hours. First, weeks are converted to days, then days are converted to hours. To convert from weeks to days, the following proportion can be written:

$$\frac{7}{1} = \frac{x}{2} \left( \frac{days\ conversion}{weeks\ conversion} = \frac{days\ unknown}{weeks\ given} \right)$$

Cross-multiplying produces: $(7)(2) = (x)(1) \rightarrow 14 = x$. Therefore, 2 weeks is equal to 14 days. Next, a proportion is written to convert 14 days to hours:

$$\frac{24}{1} = \frac{x}{14} \left( \frac{conversion\ hours}{conversion\ days} = \frac{unknown\ hours}{given\ days} \right)$$

Cross-multiplying produces: $(24)(14) = (x)(1) \rightarrow 336 = x$. Therefore, the answer is that there are 336 hours in 2 weeks.

# Practice Questions

1. Which of the following is equivalent to the value of the digit 3 in the number 792.134?

    a. $3 \times 10$

    b. $3 \times 100$

    c. $\frac{3}{10}$

    d. $\frac{3}{100}$

2. How will the following number be written in standard form: $(1 \times 10^4) + (3 \times 10^3) + (7 \times 10^1) + (8 \times 10^0)$

    a. 137

    b. 13,078

    c. 1,378

    d. 8,731

3. How will the number 847.89632 be written if rounded to the nearest hundredth?

    a. 847.90

    b. 900

    c. 847.89

    d. 847.896

4. What is the value of the sum of $\frac{1}{3}$ and $\frac{2}{5}$?

    a. $\frac{3}{8}$

    b. $\frac{11}{15}$

    c. $\frac{11}{30}$

    d. $\frac{4}{5}$

5. What is the value of the expression: $7^2 - 3 \times (4 + 2) + 15 \div 5$?

    a. 12.2

    b. 40.2

    c. 34

    d. 58.2

6. How will $\frac{4}{5}$ be written as a percent?

    a. 40%

    b. 125%

    c. 90%

    d. 80%

7. If Danny takes 48 minutes to walk 3 miles, how long should it take him to walk 5 miles maintaining the same speed?
    a. 32 min
    b. 64 min
    c. 80 min
    d. 96 min

8. What are all the factors of 12?
    a. 12, 24, 36
    b. 1, 2, 4, 6, 12
    c. 12, 24, 36, 48
    d. 1, 2, 3, 4, 6, 12

9. A construction company is building a new housing development with the property of each house measuring 30 feet wide. If the length of the street is zoned off at 345 feet, how many houses can be built on the street?
    a. 11
    b. 115
    c. 11.5
    d. 12

10. How will the following algebraic expression be simplified: $(5x^2 - 3x + 4) - (2x^2 - 7)$?
    a. $x^5$
    b. $3x^2 - 3x + 11$
    c. $3x^2 - 3x - 3$
    d. $x - 3$

11. Kassidy drove for 3 hours at a speed of 60 miles per hour. Using the distance formula, $d = r \times t$ ($distance = rate \times time$), how far did Kassidy travel?
    a. 20 miles
    b. 180 miles
    c. 65 miles
    d. 120 miles

12. If $-3(x + 4) \geq x + 8$, what is the value of $x$?
    a. $x = 4$
    b. $x \geq 2$
    c. $x \geq -5$
    d. $x \leq -5$

13. Karen gets paid a weekly salary and a commission for every sale that she makes. The table below shows the number of sales and her pay for different weeks.

| Sales | 2 | 7 | 4 | 8 |
|-------|------|------|------|------|
| Pay | $380 | $580 | $460 | $620 |

Which of the following equations represents Karen's weekly pay?
   a. $y = 90x + 200$
   b. $y = 90x - 200$
   c. $y = 40x + 300$
   d. $y = 40x - 300$

14. Which inequality represents the values displayed on the number line?

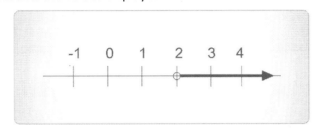

   a. $x < 2$
   b. $x \leq 2$
   c. $x > 2$
   d. $x \geq 2$

15. What is the 42$^{nd}$ item in the pattern: ▲○○□ ▲○○□ ▲ ...?
   a. ○
   b. ▲
   c. □
   d. None of the above

16. Which of the following statements is true about the two lines below?

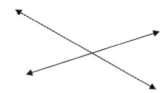

   a. The two lines are parallel but not perpendicular.
   b. The two lines are perpendicular but not parallel.
   c. The two lines are both parallel and perpendicular.
   d. The two lines are neither parallel nor perpendicular.

17. Which of the following figures is not a polygon?
   a. Decagon
   b. Cone
   c. Triangle
   d. Rhombus

18. What is the area of the regular hexagon shown below?

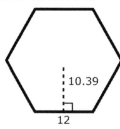

a. 72

b. 124.68

c. 374.04

d. 748.08

19. The area of a given rectangle is 24 square centimeters. If the measure of each side is multiplied by 3, what is the area of the new figure?

a. 48 cm$^2$

b. 72 cm$^2$

c. 216 cm$^2$

d. 13,824 cm$^2$

20. What are the coordinates of the point plotted on the grid?

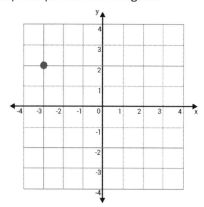

a. (-3, 2)

b. (2, -3)

c. (-3, -2)

d. (2, 3)

21. The perimeter of a 6-sided polygon is 56 cm. The length of three sides are 9 cm each. The length of two other sides are 8 cm each. What is the length of the missing side?

a. 11 cm

b. 12 cm

c. 13 cm

d. 10 cm

22. Katie works at a clothing company and sold 192 shirts over the weekend. $1/3$ of the shirts that were sold were patterned, and the rest were solid. Which mathematical expression would calculate the number of solid shirts Katie sold over the weekend?

    a. $192 \times \frac{1}{3}$

    b. $192 \div \frac{1}{3}$

    c. $192 \times (1 - \frac{1}{3})$

    d. $192 \div 3$

23. Which measure for the center of a small sample set is most affected by outliers?

    a. Mean
    b. Median
    c. Mode
    d. None of the above

24. Given the value of a given stock at monthly intervals, which graph should be used to best represent the trend of the stock?

    a. Box plot
    b. Line plot
    c. Line graph
    d. Circle graph

25. What is the probability of randomly picking the winner and runner-up from a race of 4 horses and distinguishing which is the winner?

    a. $\frac{1}{4}$

    b. $\frac{1}{2}$

    c. $\frac{1}{16}$

    d. $\frac{1}{12}$

# Answer Explanations

**1. D:** $\frac{3}{100}$. Each digit to the left of the decimal point represents a higher multiple of 10 and each digit to the right of the decimal point represents a quotient of a higher multiple of 10 for the divisor. The first digit to the right of the decimal point is equal to the value ÷ 10. The second digit to the right of the decimal point is equal to the value ÷ (10 × 10), or the value ÷ 100.

**2. B:** 13,078. The power of 10 by which a digit is multiplied corresponds with the number of zeros following the digit when expressing its value in standard form. Therefore, $(1 \times 10^4) + (3 \times 10^3) + (7 \times 10^1) + (8 \times 10^0) = 10,000 + 3,000 + 70 + 8 = 13,078$.

**3. A:** 847.90. The hundredths place value is located two digits to the right of the decimal point (the digit 9 in the original number). The digit to the right of the place value is examined to decide whether to round up or keep the digit. In this case, the digit 6 is 5 or greater so the hundredth place is rounded up. When rounding up, if the digit to be increased is a 9, the digit to its left is increased by one and the digit in the desired place value is made a zero. Therefore, the number is rounded to 847.90.

**4. B:** $\frac{11}{15}$. Fractions must have like denominators to be added. We are trying to add a fraction with a denominator of 3 to a fraction with a denominator of 5, so we have to convert both fractions to their respective equivalent fractions that have a common denominator. The common denominator is the least common multiple (LCM) of the two original denominators. In this case, the LCM is 15, so both fractions should be changed to equivalent fractions with a denominator of 15. To determine the numerator of the new fraction, the old numerator is multiplied by the same number by which the old denominator is multiplied to obtain the new denominator. For the fraction $\frac{2}{5}$, multiplying both the numerator and denominator by 3 produces $\frac{6}{15}$. When fractions have like denominators, they are added by adding the numerators and keeping the denominator the same: $\frac{5}{15} + \frac{6}{15} = \frac{11}{15}$.

**5. C:** 34. When performing calculations consisting of more than one operation, the order of operations should be followed: *Parenthesis, Exponents, Multiplication/Division, Addition/Subtraction.*

Parenthesis:

$$7^2 - 3 \times (4 + 2) + 15 \div 5 = 7^2 - 3 \times (6) + 15 \div 5$$

Exponents:

$$7^2 - 3 \times 6 + 15 \div 5 = 49 - 3 \times 6 + 15 \div 5$$

Multiplication/Division (from left to right):

$$49 - 3 \times 6 + 15 \div 5 = 49 - 18 + 3$$

Addition/Subtraction (from left to right):

$$49 - 18 + 3 = 34$$

**6. D:** 80%. To convert a fraction to a percent, the fraction is first converted to a decimal. To do so, the numerator is divided by the denominator: $4 \div 5 = 0.8$. To convert a decimal to a percent, the number is multiplied by 100: $0.8 \times 100 = 80\%$.

**7. C:** 80 min. To solve the problem, a proportion is written consisting of ratios comparing distance and time. One way to set up the proportion is: $\frac{3}{48} = \frac{5}{x}\left(\frac{distance}{time} = \frac{distance}{time}\right)$ where $x$ represents the unknown value of time. To solve a proportion, the ratios are cross-multiplied: $(3)(x) = (5)(48) \rightarrow 3x = 240$. The equation is solved by isolating the variable, or dividing by 3 on both sides, to produce $x = 80$.

**8. D:** 1, 2, 3, 4, 6, 12. A given number divides evenly by each of its factors to produce an integer (no decimals). The number 5, 7, 8, 9, 10, 11 (and their opposites) do not divide evenly into 12. Therefore, these numbers are not factors.

**9. A:** 11. To determine the number of houses that can fit on the street, the length of the street is divided by the width of each house: $345 \div 30 = 11.5$. Although the mathematical calculation of 11.5 is correct, this answer is not reasonable. Half of a house cannot be built, so the company will need to either build 11 or 12 houses. Since the width of 12 houses (360 feet) will extend past the length of the street, only 11 houses can be built.

**10. B:** $3x^2 - 3x + 11$. By distributing the implied one in front of the first set of parentheses and the $-1$ in front of the second set of parentheses, the parenthesis can be eliminated:

$$1(5x^2 - 3x + 4) - 1(2x^2 - 7) = 5x^2 - 3x + 4 - 2x^2 + 7$$

Next, like terms (same variables with same exponents) are combined by adding the coefficients and keeping the variables and their powers the same: $5x^2 - 3x + 4 - 2x^2 + 7 = 3x^2 - 3x + 11$.

**11. B:** 180 miles. The rate, 60 miles per hour, and time, 3 hours, are given for the scenario. To determine the distance traveled, the given values for the rate ($r$) and time ($t$) are substituted into the distance formula and evaluated: $d = r \times t \rightarrow d = (60mi/h) \times (3h) \rightarrow d = 180mi$.

**12. D:** $x \leq -5$. When solving a linear equation or inequality:

Distribution is performed if necessary: $-3(x + 4) \rightarrow -3x - 12 \geq x + 8$. This means that any like terms on the same side of the equation/inequality are combined.

The equation/inequality is manipulated to get the variable on one side. In this case, subtracting $x$ from both sides produces $-4x - 12 \geq 8$.

The variable is isolated using inverse operations to undo addition/subtraction. Adding 12 to both sides produces $-4x \geq 20$.

The variable is isolated using inverse operations to undo multiplication/division. Remember if dividing by a negative number, the relationship of the inequality reverses, so the sign is flipped. In this case, dividing by -4 on both sides produces $x \leq -5$.

**13. C:** $y = 40x + 300$. In this scenario, the variables are the number of sales and Karen's weekly pay. The weekly pay depends on the number of sales. Therefore, weekly pay is the dependent variable ($y$), and the number of sales is the independent variable ($x$). Each pair of values from the table can be written as an ordered pair ($x$, $y$): (2, 380), (7, 580), (4, 460), (8, 620). The ordered pairs can be substituted into the equations to see which creates true statements (both sides equal) for each pair. Even if one ordered pair produces equal values for a given equation, the other three ordered pairs must be checked.

The only equation which is true for all four ordered pairs is $y = 40x + 300$:

$$380 = 40(2) + 300 \rightarrow 380 = 380$$

$$580 = 40(7) + 300 \rightarrow 580 = 580$$

$$460 = 40(4) + 300 \rightarrow 460 = 460$$

$$620 = 40(8) + 300 \rightarrow 620 = 620$$

**14. D:** $x > 2$. The open dot on two indicates that the value is not included in the set. The arrow pointing right indicates that numbers greater than two (numbers get larger to the right) are included in the set. Therefore, the set includes numbers greater than two, which can be written as $x > 2$.

**15. A:** ○. The core of the pattern consists of 4 items: ▲○○□. Therefore, the core repeats in multiples of 4, with the pattern starting over on the next step. The closest multiple of 4 to 42 is 40. Step 40 is the end of the core (□), so step 41 will start the core over (▲) and step 42 is ○.

**16. D:** The two lines are neither parallel nor perpendicular. Parallel lines will never intersect or meet. Therefore, the lines are not parallel. Perpendicular lines intersect to form a right angle (90°). Although the lines intersect, they do not form a right angle, which is usually indicated with a box at the intersection point. Therefore, the lines are not perpendicular.

**17. B:** Cone. A polygon is a closed two-dimensional figure consisting of three or more sides. A decagon is a polygon with 10 sides. A triangle is a polygon with three sides. A rhombus is a polygon with 4 sides. A cone is a three-dimensional figure and is classified as a solid.

**18. C:** 374.04. The formula for finding the area of a regular polygon is $A = \frac{1}{2} \times a \times P$ where $a$ is the length of the apothem (from the center to any side at a right angle), and P is the perimeter of the figure. The apothem $a$ is given as 10.39, and the perimeter can be found by multiplying the length of one side by the number of sides (since the polygon is regular): $P = 12 \times 6 \rightarrow P = 72$. To find the area, substitute the values for $a$ and P into the formula $A = \frac{1}{2} \times a \times P \rightarrow A = \frac{1}{2} \times (10.39) \times (72) \rightarrow A = 374.04$.

**19. C:** 216cm. Because area is a two-dimensional measurement, the dimensions are multiplied by a scale that is squared to determine the scale of the corresponding areas. The dimensions of the rectangle are multiplied by a scale of 3. Therefore, the area is multiplied by a scale of $3^2$ (which is equal to 9): $24cm \times 9 = 216cm$.

**20. A:** (-3, 2). The coordinates of a point are written as an ordered pair (x, y). To determine the x-coordinate, a line is traced directly above or below the point until reaching the x-axis. This step notes the value on the x-axis. In this case, the x-coordinate is -3. To determine the y-coordinate, a line is traced directly to the right or left of the point until reaching the y-axis, which notes the value on the y-axis. In this case, the y-coordinate is 2. Therefore, the ordered pair is written (-3, 2).

**21. C:** Perimeter is found by calculating the sum of all sides of the polygon. $9 + 9 + 9 + 8 + 8 + s = 56$, where $s$ is the missing side length. Therefore, 43 plus the missing side length is equal to 56. The missing side length is 13 cm.

**22. C:** $\frac{1}{3}$ of the shirts sold were patterned. Therefore, $1 - \frac{1}{3} = \frac{2}{3}$ of the shirts sold were solid. Anytime "of" a quantity appears in a word problem, multiplication should be used.

Therefore:

$$192 \times \frac{2}{3} = \frac{192 \times 2}{3} = \frac{384}{3} = 128 \text{ solid shirts were sold}$$

The entire expression is $192 \times \left(1 - \frac{1}{3}\right)$.

**23. A:** Mean. An outlier is a data value that is either far above or far below the majority of values in a sample set. The mean is the average of all the values in the set. In a small sample set, a very high or very low number could drastically change the average of the data points. Outliers will have no more of an effect on the median (the middle value when arranged from lowest to highest) than any other value above or below the median. If the same outlier does not repeat, outliers will have no effect on the mode (value that repeats most often).

**24. C:** Line graph. The scenario involves data consisting of two variables, month and stock value. Box plots display data consisting of values for one variable. Therefore, a box plot is not an appropriate choice. Both line plots and circle graphs are used to display frequencies within categorical data. Neither can be used for the given scenario. Line graphs display two numerical variables on a coordinate grid and show trends among the variables.

**25. D:** $\frac{1}{12}$. The probability of picking the winner of the race is $\frac{1}{4}$, or $\left(\frac{number\ of\ favorable\ outcomes}{number\ of\ total\ outcomes}\right)$. Assuming the winner was picked on the first selection, three horses remain from which to choose the runner-up (these are dependent events). Therefore, the probability of picking the runner-up is $\frac{1}{3}$. To determine the probability of multiple events, the probability of each event is multiplied:

$$\frac{1}{4} \times \frac{1}{3} = \frac{1}{12}$$

# Social Studies

## *Government and Economics*

### Nature, Purpose, and Forms of Government

The United States of America's government, as outlined by the Constitution, is designed to prevent the mob rule or tyranny of the 51% of a direct democracy while at the same time protecting individual freedoms and rights from the iron fisted rule of Monarchs and aristocrats. The American Revolution brought independence from Britain and freedom from its aristocratic system of governance. On the other hand, the short-lived Articles of Confederation revealed the significant weaknesses of state-based governance with limited national control. By dividing power between local, state, and federal governments, the United States can uphold its value of individual liberties while, nevertheless, giving a sense of order to the country.

The federal government, which is in charge of laws that affect the entire nation, is split into three main branches: executive, judicial, and legislative. It is important to realize that the three segments of the federal government are intended to stand as equal counterparts to the others, and that none of them are "in charge." The executive branch centers on the president, the vice president, and the cabinet. The president and vice president are elected every four years. Also known as the commander-in-chief, the president is the official head of state and serves as the nation's head diplomat and military leader. The vice president acts as the president of the Senate in the legislative branch, while the president appoints members of the cabinet to lead agencies, including the Treasury and Department of Defense. However, the president can only sign and veto laws and cannot initiate them himself. As head of the executive branch it is the responsibility of the president to execute and enforce the laws passed by the legislative branch.

The *legislative branch*, specifically *Congress*, proposes and debates laws. Congress is *bicameral,* meaning it is divided into two separate legislative houses. Each state's representation in the House of Representatives is determined proportionally by population, with the total number of voting seats limited to 435. The Senate, in contrast, has only two members per state and a total of one hundred senators. Members of both houses are intended to represent the interests of the constituents in their home states and to bring their concerns to a national level. Ideas for laws, called bills, are proposed in either chamber and then are voted upon according to the body's rules; should the bill pass the first round of voting, the other legislative chamber must approve it before it can be sent to the president. Congress also has a variety of other powers, such as the rights to declare war, collect taxes, and impeach the president.

The *judicial branch*, though it cannot pass laws itself, serves to declare whether or not the laws passed by Congress are in conflict with the constitution. The *Supreme Court* consists of judges appointed by the president and approved by the Senate; these judges serve for life, unless they resign from their position or are removed by Congress for improper behavior. As the Constitution remains fundamental to the American legal system, the Supreme Court's rulings on how laws follow or fail to uphold the Constitution have powerful implications on future rulings.

While the federal government manages the nation as a whole, state governments address issues pertaining to their specific territory. In the past, states claimed the right, known as nullification, to

refuse to enforce federal laws that they considered unconstitutional. However, conflicts between state and federal authority, particularly in the South in regard to first, slavery, and later, discrimination, have led to increased federal power, and states cannot defy federal laws. Even so, the Tenth Amendment limits federal power to those specifically granted in the Constitution, and the rest of the powers are retained by the states and citizens. Therefore, individual state governments are left in charge of decisions with immediate effects on their citizens, such as state laws and taxes. Like the federal government, state governments consist of executive, judicial, and legislative branches, but the exact configuration of those branches varies between states. For instance, while most states follow the bicameral structure of Congress, Nebraska has only a single legislative chamber. State governments have considerable authority within their states, but they cannot impose their power on other states.

Local governments, which include town governments, county boards, library districts, and other agencies, are especially variable in their composition. They often reflect the overall views of their state governments but also have their own values, rules, and structures. Generally, local governments function in a democratic fashion, although the exact form of government depends on its role. Depending on the location within the state, local government may have considerable or minimal authority based on the population and prosperity of the area; some counties may have strong influence in the state, while others may have a limited impact.

Native American tribes are treated as dependent nations that answer to the federal government but may be immune to state jurisdiction. As with local governments, the exact form of governance is left up to the tribes, which ranges from small councils to complex systems of government. Other U.S. territories, including the District of Columbia (site of Washington, D.C.) and acquired islands, such as Guam and Puerto Rico, have representation within Congress, but their legislators cannot vote on bills.

As members of a Constitutional Republic with certain aspects of a *democracy*, U.S. citizens are empowered to elect most government leaders, but the process varies between branch and level of government. Presidential elections at the national level use the *Electoral College* system. Rather than electing the president directly, citizens cast their ballots to select *electors*, who generally vote for a specific candidate, that represent each state in the college. Legislative branches at the federal and state level are also determined by elections. In some areas, judges are elected, but in other states judges are appointed by elected officials. It should also be noted that the two-party system was not built into the Constitution but gradually emerged over time.

## Government and Good Citizenship

A *government* is a system put in place by a country, state, city, or region to institute rules and guidelines for its people to follow. It is typically made up of groups of people, offices, or departments and can be classified into several types, including democracy, republic, monarchy, aristocracy, dictatorship, theocracy, and totalitarian government. The United States is a *democracy*, which literally means *rule by the people*. This means that the people have the power to make changes and decisions. America's Founding Fathers realized that forming a democratic government would be difficult in the U.S. due to the country's sizeable and varied population spread over a vast area. Therefore, they established an *indirect* or *representative* democracy in which the people choose representatives to make decisions for the whole country. This is also referred to as a *democratic republic*.

Native-born and naturalized members of a society who pledge loyalty to its government and are thus protected by its laws are its *citizens*. The status of being a citizen is called *citizenship* and embodies the characteristics that a person is expected to uphold as a responsible member of a community. The term *citizen* originated from the Latin word for city and dates back to government's early days when people aligned with cities rather than countries. Under America's democratic form of government, citizens have the right to keep themselves informed about issues affecting the country, to have a say in government decisions by voting in elections, and to hold public office. They must also obey the law, pay taxes, serve on a jury if asked to do so, and defend the country if necessary (unless it is against their religious beliefs). In order to completely participate in society and understand what it means to be a citizen, it is crucial for students to develop an awareness of civic principles and systems.

## Rights and Responsibilities of Citizenship in a Democracy

Citizens living in a democracy have several rights and responsibilities to uphold. The first duty is that they uphold the established laws of the government. In a democracy, a system of nationwide laws is necessary to ensure that there is some degree of order. Therefore, citizens must try to obey the laws and also help enforce them because a law that is inadequately enforced, such as early civil rights laws in the South, is almost useless. Optimally, a democratic society's laws will be accepted and followed by the community as a whole.

However, conflict can occur when an unjust law is passed. For instance, much of the civil rights movement centered around Jim Crow laws in the South that supported segregation between black and whites. Yet these practices were encoded in state laws, which created a dilemma for African Americans who wanted equality but also wanted to respect the law. Fortunately, a democracy offers a degree of protection from such laws by creating a system in which government leaders and policies are constantly open to change in accordance with the will of citizens. Citizens can influence the laws that are passed by voting for and electing members of the legislative and executive branches to represent them at the local, state, and national levels.

This, however, requires citizens to be especially vigilant in protecting their liberties because they cannot depend solely on the existing government to meet their needs. To assert their role in a democracy, citizens should be active voters and speak out on issues that concern them. Even with these safeguards, it is possible for systems to be implemented that inhibit active participation. For instance, many southern states had laws that prevented blacks from voting. Under such circumstances, civil rights leaders felt that they had no choice but to resist the laws in order to defend their personal rights. Once voting became possible, civil rights groups strove to ensure that their votes counted by changing state and national policy.

An extension of citizens' voting rights is their ability to run as elected officials. By becoming leaders in the government, citizens can demonstrate their engagement and help determine government policy. The involvement of citizens as a whole in the selection of leaders is vital in a democracy because it helps to prevent the formation of an elite cadre that does not answer to the public. Without the engagement of citizens who run for office, voters are limited in their ability to select candidates that appeal to them. In this case, voting options would become stagnant, which inhibits the ability of the nation to grow and change over time. As long as citizens are willing to take a stand for their vision of America, America's government will remain dynamic and diverse.

These features of a democracy give it the potential to reshape itself continually in response to new developments in society. In order for a democracy to function, it is of the utmost importance that citizens care about the course of politics and be aware of current issues. Apathy among citizens is a constant problem that threatens the endurance of democracies. Citizens should have a desire to take part in the political process, or else they simply accept the status quo and fail to fulfill their role as

citizens. Moreover, they must have acute knowledge of the political processes and the issues that they can address as citizens. A fear among the Founding Fathers was the prevalence of mob rule, in which the common people did not take interest in politics except to vote for their patrons; this was the usual course of politics in the colonial era, as the common people left the decisions to the established elites. Without understanding the world around them, citizens may not fully grasp the significance of political actions and thereby fail to make wise decisions in that regard. Therefore, citizens must stay informed about current affairs, ranging from local to national or global matters, so that they can properly address them as voters or elected leaders.

Furthermore, knowledge of the nation's history is essential for healthy citizenship. History continues to have an influence on present political decisions. For instance, Supreme Court rulings often take into account previous legal precedents and verdicts, so it is important to know about those past events and how they affect the current processes. It is especially critical that citizens are aware of the context in which laws were established because it helps clarify the purpose of those laws. For instance, an understanding of the problems with the Articles of Confederation allows people to comprehend some of the reasons behind the framework of the Constitution. In addition, history as a whole shapes the course of societies and the world; therefore, citizens should draw on this knowledge of the past to realize the full consequences of current actions. Issues such as climate change, conflict in the Middle East, and civil rights struggles are rooted in events and cultural developments that reach back centuries and should be addressed.

Therefore, education is a high priority in democracies because it has the potential to instill generations of citizens with the right mind-set and knowledge required to do their part in shaping the nation. Optimally, education should cover a variety of different subjects, ranging from mathematics to biology, so that individuals can explore whatever paths they wish to take in life. Even so, social studies are especially important because students should understand how democracies function and understand the history of the nation and world. Historical studies should cover national and local events as well because they help provide the basis for the understanding of contemporary politics. Social studies courses should also address the histories of foreign nations because contemporary politics increasingly has global consequences. In addition, history lessons should remain open to multiple perspectives, even those that might criticize a nation's past actions, because citizens should be exposed to diverse perspectives that they can apply as voters and leaders.

## Basic Economic Concepts and their Effect on Historic Events

The term *economy* is used to describe and calculate the supply and demand of goods and services. *Economics* is the study of how people decide which resources to use in order to fulfill their needs and the outcome of these choices. It is a multi-tiered dynamic; people need to make personal choices about their own individual spending, while governments must make judgments that shape a whole society. There are two types of economics: micro and macro. *Microeconomics* looks at the interplay of consumers, households, and companies within individual markets and the relationships between them. *Macroeconomics* is the study of entire economies, such as a specific region (the U.S. Northeast, for example); an entire country (the U.S., for example); or a group of countries that share economic traits (the European Union, for example). It also includes the analysis of the influence economies have on each another.

Economic activity is cyclical with periods of booms and busts, which are typically prompted by extreme changes in the economy. *Booms* are cycles of increased activity resulting in new businesses, technologies, and jobs. However, these are often followed by periods of economic slowdowns, or *busts*,

which can lead to recessions and even depressions. For example, the Wall Street Crash of 1929 triggered the Great Depression of the 1930s. During the Great Depression, New York Stock Market share prices dropped dramatically, causing the world's economic output to decrease by one-third and prompting a spike in unemployment levels of 25 percent or greater among global economies.

## Types of Productive Resources and the Role of Money as a Resource

Productive resources are the means used by a society to succeed and survive. The four types are:

1. Natural resources—the raw materials taken from the land, such as corn, beef, lumber, water, oil, and iron.

2. Human resources—the human labor, both mental and physical, that are required to produce goods.

3. Capital resources—the man-made physical resources used to create products, such as machinery, tools, buildings, and equipment.

4. Entrepreneurship—the capability and motivation to cultivate, organize, and oversee the other three resources into a business venture.

Money functions as a method of exchange to obtain goods or services. It replaced the barter system, which was often considered inefficient and disorganized. Economists referred to the barter system as a double coincidence of wants since trades between parties were not always considered equal. Prices of goods are determined by supply and demand. *Inflation* occurs when people have money to spend, but not enough goods can be produced or imported to meet their demand for a product, which causes prices to rise. The amount of money issued by government-controlled central banks and the prices of leading commodities, such as oil, can also affect inflation. *Deflation* is when people save their money and spend less, leaving stores with surplus goods, which causes prices to drop.

## Major Sectors of the United States Economy and the Interactions Between Businesses and Consumers

Economies consist of the following four business sectors, or parts, that share similar products or services:

- *Primary sector*—gathers natural resources, including industries such as farming, fishing, and oil and gas drilling.

- *Secondary sector*—develops raw materials from the primary sector into finished goods through enhancement, manufacture, or construction, including industries such as car manufacturing, food processing, and steelworks.

- *Tertiary sector*—provides consumer or business services, including industries such as entertainment, travel and tourism, and banking.

- *Quaternary sector*—provides informational and knowledge services, including industries such as universities, consultancies, and research and development companies.

These sectors function like interconnected links in a chain, with each one passing its production along to the next sector. Service industries typically increase as a country develops and constitute the largest sector of both the U.S. and global economies. The U.S. is the leading global economy in terms of size and significance providing twenty percent of the world's total production of goods and services. About eighty percent of this output comes from its innovative, technically advanced services sector, and fifteen percent comes from manufacturing.

Economists often use the circular flow model to describe the movement of supply, demand, and payment between businesses and consumers (also referred to as sectors). Functioning as an interdependent continuous loop, consumers obtain income, goods, and services from business producers. These producers then receive profits and the ability to buy necessary supplies. Money flows one way, and the goods and productive resources flow in the opposite direction. Each sector relies on the other.

Here's an illustration of that:

## Circular Flow Model

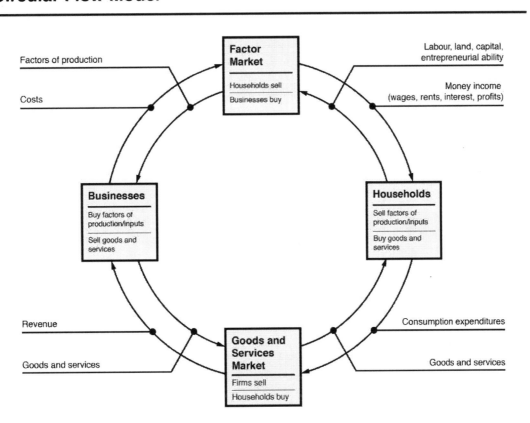

## Costs and Benefits of Personal Spending and Savings Choices

Individuals earn an income by trading their labor – both mental and physical – for pay. They then budget their money through spending or saving it. As consumers, every choice has an opportunity cost since they must choose which goods and services they want to buy with a limited income. By purchasing one good or service, they give up the chance to purchase another.

Additionally, consumers have the choice to save money when they don't have enough money to purchase what they want, or when they want to utilize a savings account to use during emergencies or periods of economic difficulty. People also choose to save for *retirement*, a time when they will no

longer be working and drawing a salary. Saving money by putting it in a bank is considered low-risk—the bank will pay the saver a low interest rate to keep it safe, but it will not increase much in value. A riskier path is investing money through the purchase of valuable items (or *assets*) in the hopes that they will increase in worth over time and yield returns (or *profits*). *Assets* can include shares in companies, real estate or land investments, or capital such as money, equipment, and structures used to create wealth.

## Government's Role in Economics and the Impact of Economics on Government

Governments have considerable influence over the flow of economies, which makes it important to understand the relationships between them. When a government has full control over the economic decisions of a nation, it is called a command system. This was the case in many absolute monarchies such as eighteenth-century France; King Louis XIV built his economy on the concept of mercantilism, which believed that the state should manage all resources, particularly by accumulating gold and silver. This system of economics discouraged exports and thereby limited trade.

In contrast, the market system is guided by the concept of capitalism, in which individuals and businesses have the freedom to manage their economic decisions. This allows for private property and increases the opportunities for entrepreneurship and trade. Early proponents of capitalism emphasized *laissez-faire* policies, which means "let it be," and argued that the government should not be involved with the economy at all. They believe the market is guided by the concept of self-interest and that individuals will optimally work for their personal success. However, individuals' interests do not necessarily correlate with the needs of the overall economy. For instance, during a financial recession, consumers may decide to save up their money rather than make purchases; doing so helps them in the short run but further reduces demand in a slumping economy. Therefore, most capitalist governments still assert a degree of control over their economies while still allowing for private business.

Likewise, many command system economies, such as monarchical France, still relied heavily on private businesses maintained by wealthy businessmen. With the end of most absolute monarchies, communism has been the primary form of command system economies in the modern era. Communism is a form of socialism that emphasizes communal ownership of property and government control over production. The high degree of government control gives more stability to the economy, but it also creates considerable flaws. The monopolization of the economy by the government limits its ability to respond to local economic conditions because certain regions often have unique resources and needs. With the collapse of the Soviet Union and other communist states, command systems have been largely replaced with market systems.

The U.S. government helps to manage the nation's economy through a market system in several ways. First and foremost, the federal government is responsible for the production of money for use within the economy; depending on how the government manages the monetary flow, it may lead to a stable economy, deflation, or inflation. Second, state and federal governments impose taxes on individuals, corporations, and goods. For instance, a tariff might be imposed on imports in order to stimulate demand for local goods in the economy. Third, the government can pass laws that require additional regulation or inspections. In addition, the government has passed antitrust laws to inhibit the growth of private monopolies, which could limit free growth in the market system. Debates continue over whether the government should take further action to manage private industries or reduce its control over the private sector.

Just as governments can affect the direction of the economy, the state of the economy can have significant implications on government policies. Financial stability is critical in maintaining a prosperous

state. A healthy economy will allow for new developments that contribute to the nation's growth and create jobs. On the other hand, an economic crisis, such as a recession or depression, can gravely damage a government's stability. Without a stable economy, business opportunities plummet, and people begin to lose income and employment. This, in turn, leads to frustration and discontent in the population, which can lead to criticism of the government. This could very well lead to demands for new leadership to resolve the economic crisis.

The dangers of a destabilized economy can be seen with the downfall of the French monarchy. The mercantilist approach to economics stifled French trade. Furthermore, regional aristocracies remained exempt from government taxes, which limited the government's revenues. This was compounded by expensive wars and poor harvests that led to criticism of King Louis XIV's government. The problems persisted for decades, and Louis XIV was forced to convene the Estates-General, a legislative body of representatives from across France, to address the crisis. The economic crises at the end of the eighteenth century were critical in the beginning of the French Revolution. Those financial issues, in turn, at least partially stemmed from both the government's control of the economy through mercantilism and its inability to impose economic authority over local regions.

# U.S. and World History

## Major Contributions of Classical Civilizations

There were a number of powerful civilizations during the classical period. Mesopotamia was home to one of the earliest civilizations between the Euphrates and the Tigris rivers in the Near East. The rivers provided water and vegetation for early humans, but they were surrounded by desert. This led to the beginning of irrigation efforts to expand water and agriculture across the region, which resulted in the area being known as the Fertile Crescent.

The organization necessary to initiate canals and other projects led to the formation of cities and hierarchies, which would have considerable influence on the structure of later civilizations. For instance, the new hierarchies established different classes within the societies, such as kings, priests, artisans, and workers. Over time, these city-states expanded to encompass outside territories, and the city of Akkad became the world's first empire in 2350 B.C. In addition, Mesopotamian scribes developed systemized drawings called pictograms, which were the first system of writing in the world; furthermore, the creation of wedge-shaped cuneiform tablets preserved written records for multiple generations.

Later, Mesopotamian kingdoms made further advancements. For instance, Babylon established a sophisticated mathematical system based on numbers from one to sixty; this not only influenced modern concepts, such as the number of minutes in each hour, but also created the framework for math equations and theories. In addition, the Babylonian king Hammurabi established a complex set of laws, known as the Code of Hammurabi, which would set a precedent for future legal systems.

Meanwhile, another major civilization began to form around the Nile River in Africa. The Nile's relatively predictable nature allowed farmers to use the river's water and the silt from floods to grow many crops along its banks, which led to further advancements in irrigation. Egyptian rulers mobilized the kingdom's population for incredible construction projects, including the famous pyramids. Egyptians also improved pictographic writing with their more complex system of hieroglyphs, which allowed for more diverse styles of writing. The advancements in writing can be seen through the Egyptians' complex system of religion, with documents such as the *Book of the Dead* outlining not only systems of worship and pantheons of deities but also a deeper, more philosophical concept of the afterlife.

While civilizations in Egypt and Mesopotamia helped to establish class systems and empires, other forms of government emerged in Greece. Despite common ties between different cities, such as the Olympic Games, each settlement, known as a polis, had its own unique culture. Many of the cities were oligarchies, in which a council of distinguished leaders monopolized the government; others were dictatorships ruled by tyrants. Athens was a notable exception by practicing an early form of democracy in which free, landholding men could participate, but it offered more freedom of thought than other systems.

Taking advantage of their proximity to the Mediterranean Sea, Greek cities sent expeditions to establish colonies abroad that developed their own local traditions. In the process, Greek merchants interacted with Phoenician traders, who had developed an alphabetic writing system built on sounds instead of pictures. This diverse network of exchanges made Greece a vibrant center of art, science, and philosophy. For example, the Greek doctor Hippocrates established a system of ethics for doctors called the Hippocratic Oath, which continues to guide the modern medical profession. Complex forms of literature were created, including the epic poem "The Iliad," and theatrical productions were also developed. Athens in particular sought to spread its vision of democratic freedom throughout the world, which led to the devastating Peloponnesian War between allies of Athens and those of oligarchic Sparta from 431 to 404 B.C.

Alexander the Great helped disseminate Greek culture to new regions. Alexander was in fact an heir to the throne of Macedon, which was a warrior kingdom to the north of Greece. After finishing his father's work of unifying Greece under Macedonian control, Alexander successfully conquered Mesopotamia, which had been part of the Persian Empire. The spread of Greek institutions throughout the Mediterranean and Near East led to a period of Hellenization, during which various civilizations assimilated Greek culture; this allowed Greek traditions, such as architecture and philosophy, to endure into the present day.

Greek ideas were later assimilated, along with many other concepts, into the Roman Empire. Located west of Greece on the Italian peninsula, the city of Rome gradually conquered its neighbors and expanded its territories abroad; by 44 B.C., Rome had conquered much of Western Europe, northern Africa, and the Near East. Romans were very creative, and they adapted new ideas and innovated new technologies to strengthen their power. For instance, Romans built on the engineering knowledge of Greeks to create arched pathways, known as aqueducts, to transport water for long distances and devise advanced plumbing systems.

One of Rome's greatest legacies was its system of government. Early Rome was a republic, a democratic system in which leaders are elected by the people. Although the process still heavily favored wealthy elites, the republican system was a key inspiration for later institutions such as the United States. Octavian "Augustus" Caesar later made Rome into an empire, and the senate had only a symbolic role in the government. The new imperial system built on the examples of earlier empires to establish a vibrant dynasty that used a sophisticated legal code and a well-trained military to enforce order across vast regions. Even after Rome itself fell to barbarian invaders in fifth century A.D., the eastern half of the empire survived as the Byzantine Empire until 1453 A.D. Furthermore, the Roman Empire's institutions continued to influence and inspire later medieval kingdoms, including the Holy Roman Empire; even rulers in the twentieth century called themselves Kaiser and Tsar, titles which stem from the word "Caesar."

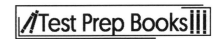

In addition, the Roman Empire was host to the spread of new religious ideas. In the region of Israel, the religion of Judaism presented a new approach to worship via monotheism, which is the belief in the existence of a single deity. An offshoot of Judaism called Christianity spread across the Roman Empire and gained popularity. While Rome initially suppressed the religion, it later backed Christianity and allowed the religious system to endure as a powerful force in medieval times.

## Twentieth-Century Development in World History

At the turn of the twentieth century, imperialism had led to powers, such as France, the United States, and Japan, to establish spheres of influence throughout the world. The combination of imperial competition and military rivalries led to the outbreak of World War I when Archduke Ferdinand of Austria was assassinated in 1914. The war pitted the Allies, including England, France, and Russia, against the Central Powers of Austria-Hungary, Germany, and the Ottoman Empire—a large Islamic realm that encompassed Turkey, Palestine, Saudi Arabia, and Iraq. The rapid advances in military technology turned the war into a prolonged bloodbath that took its toll on all sides. By the end of the war in 1918, the Ottoman Empire had collapsed, the Austrian-Hungarian Empire was split into multiple countries, and Russia had descended into a civil war that would lead to the rise of the Soviet Union and Communism.

The Treaty of Versailles ended the war, but the triumphant Allies also levied heavy fines on Germany, which led to resentment that would be accentuated by the Great Depression of the 1930s. The Great Depression destabilized the global economy and led to the rise of fascism, a militarized and dictatorial system of government, in nations such as Germany and Italy. The rapid expansion of the Axis Powers of Germany, Italy, and Japan led to the outbreak of World War II. The war was even more global than the previous conflicts, with battles occurring in Europe, Africa, and Asia. World War II encouraged the development of new technologies, such as advanced radar and nuclear weapons, that would continue to influence the course of future wars.

In the aftermath of World War II, the United Nations was formed as a step toward promoting international cooperation. Based on the preceding League of Nations, the United Nations included countries from around the world and gave them a voice in world policies. The formation of the United Nations coincided with the independence of formerly colonized states in Africa and Asia, and those countries joined the world body. A primary goal of the United Nations was to limit the extent of future wars and prevent a third world war; while the United Nations could not prevent the outbreak of wars, it nevertheless tried to peacefully resolve them. In addition to promoting world peace, the United Nations also helped protect human rights.

Even so, the primary leadership in the early United Nations was held by the United States and its allies, which contributed to tensions with the Soviet Union. The United States and the Soviet Union, while never declaring war on each other, fueled a number of proxy wars and coups across the world in what would be known as the Cold War. Cold War divisions were especially noticeable in Europe, where communist regimes ruled the eastern region and democratic governments controlled the western portion. These indirect struggles often involved interference with foreign politics, and sometimes local people began to resent Soviet or American attempts to influence their countries. For instance, American and Soviet interventions in Iran and Afghanistan contributed to fundamentalist Islamic movements. The Cold War ended when the Soviet Union collapsed in 1991, but the conflict affected nations across the globe and continues to influence current issues.

Another key development during the twentieth century, as noted earlier with the United Nations, was that most colonized nations broke free from imperial control and asserted their independence. Although these nations achieved autonomy and recognition in the United Nations, they still suffered from the legacies of imperialism. The borders of many countries in Africa and Asia were arbitrarily determined by colonists with little regard to the arrangement of native populations. Therefore, many former colonies have suffered conflicts between different ethnic groups; this was also the case with the British colony in India, which became independent in 1947. Violence occurred when it split into India and Pakistan because the borders were largely based on religious differences. In addition, former colonial powers continue to assert economic control that inhibits the growth of native economies. On the other hand, the end of direct imperialism has helped a number of nations, such as India and Iran, rise as world powers that have significant influence on the world as a whole.

Additionally, there were considerable environmental reforms worldwide during the twentieth century. In reaction to the growing effects of industrialization, organizations around the world protested policies that damaged the environment. Many of these movements were locally based, but others expanded to address various environmental threats across the globe. The United Nations helped carry these environmental reforms forward by making them part of international policies. For instance, in 1997, many members of the United Nations signed a treaty, known as the *Kyoto Protocol*, that tried to reduce global carbon dioxide emissions.

Most significantly, the twentieth century marked increasing globalization. The process had already been under way in the nineteenth century as technological improvements and imperial expansions connected different parts of the world, but the late twentieth century brought globalization to a new level. Trade became international, and local customs from different lands also gained prominence worldwide. Cultural exchanges occur on a frequent basis, and many people have begun to ponder the consequences of such rapid exchanges. One example of globalization was the 1993 establishment of the European Union—an economic and political alliance between several European nations.

## Cross-Cultural Comparisons in World History Instruction

Cross-cultural interactions are the very heart of world history and must be closely examined to understand the world's historical patterns. One of the main reasons why cross-cultural studies are so important is because cultures are not necessarily synonymous with political entities, such as states. Many countries, ranging from China to Greece, historically have many subcultures that should be considered individually. For example, a study of culture in the United States would need to consider multiple ethnic and regional groups. Even individual states and cities have their own traditions. On the other hand, these multiple cultures often coalesce into a larger, national culture that defines the overall society and politics of the nation. Therefore, cross-cultural studies of different subgroups in a larger body allow people to understand how the different parts of a culture interact and connect with each other.

Furthermore, cultures are not always restricted by the borders of nations, and cultural phenomena may extend through multiple countries. This can be seen in the spread of the Spanish language across Central and South America as well as other regions. The Spanish language and other various traditions tie the different countries together with a common culture. Even so, each nation changes the culture and gives it a unique style. A study of the culture in a single nation may be very insightful, but it would be incomplete if it failed to account for aspects of the culture beyond that country. In addition, this means that different cultures can overlap with each other and that the cultures of different countries may intersect in ways that their borders do not. By examining multiple cultures and how they are linked with

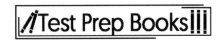

each other, larger cultural patterns become apparent, which makes these studies critical in world history.

Throughout history, cultures have not existed in isolation but rather have been affected by other traditions. A key influence in how different cultures develop is not only their setting and history but how they interact with neighboring cultures. For instance, the conflict from 499 to 449 B.C. between the Persian Empire and the Greek city-states helped to influence the course of Greek culture as a whole by creating a national sense of dichotomy between the Greek ideal of freedom and Persian autocracy. Aside from direct impacts such as wars, cultures can influence each other through interactions that spread some concepts while also adopting new ideas from their neighbors. Pasta became a phenomenon in Italy in part because the Silk Road linked Italy with China, which already had similar foods.

The pervasiveness of globalization in the present day has increased the importance of cross-cultural comparison and made it a topic of immediate relevance. The world now has a truly global market in which travel, communications, and trade function on an international scale. This means that people of different cultures can now interact with each other much more easily than in earlier centuries, which allows for a rapid exchange of ideas and goods between cultures. Furthermore, despite the international scope of modern trade, many globalized markets strive to build on the appeal of local cultures. Doing so gives the products a genuine and unique quality that resonates with consumers. Yet it is critical to realize how local cultures are transformed and combined with concepts from other cultures in the global market. For example, sushi is a traditional food in Japan, but its export to other nations has led chefs to create new culinary fusions, such as sushi tacos.

Cross-cultural comparisons also help to reveal common patterns in human society. Sometimes different cultures develop similar concepts without directly interacting with each other. For instance, both the Mayan culture in Central America and the ancient Egyptians independently developed pyramid structures. Although the similarities have sparked rumors that these civilizations were connected, it is most likely that each version originated independently. Close examination of the two types of pyramids and their respective cultures reveals significant differences amidst the similarities. These comparisons are important because they show how human cultures converge and diverge in their patterns of growth. A key function of historical study is to gain a better understanding and appreciation of how humanity develops. By examining the commonalities and differences between cultures, people can begin to theorize what factors influence the course of civilizations. However, such studies must account for the complex manners through which cultures interact with each other.

## Colonization and Expansion in U.S. History

When examining how Europeans explored what would become the United States of America, one must first examine why Europeans came to explore the New World as a whole. In the fifteenth century, tensions increased between the Eastern and Mediterranean nations of Europe and the expanding Ottoman Empire to the east. As war and piracy spread across the Mediterranean, the once-prosperous trade routes across Asia's Silk Road began to decline, and nations across Europe began to explore alternative routes for trade.

Italian explorer Christopher Columbus proposed a westward route. Contrary to popular lore, the main challenge that Columbus faced in finding backers was not proving that the world was round. Much of Europe's educated elite knew that the world was round; the real issue was that they rightly believed that a westward route to Asia, assuming a lack of obstacles, would be too long to be practical.

Nevertheless, Columbus set sail in 1492 after obtaining support from Spain and arrived in the West Indies three months later.

Spain launched further expeditions to the new continents and established *New Spain*. The colony consisted not only of Central America and Mexico, but also the American Southwest and Florida. France claimed much of what would become Canada, along with the Mississippi River region and the Midwest. In addition, the Dutch established colonies that covered New Jersey, New York, and Connecticut. Each nation managed its colonies differently, and thus influenced how they would assimilate into the United States. For instance, Spain strove to establish a system of Christian missions throughout its territory, while France focused on trading networks and had limited infrastructure in regions such as the Midwest.

Even in cases of limited colonial growth, the land of America was hardly vacant, because a diverse array of Native American nations and groups were already present. Throughout much of colonial history, European settlers commonly misperceived native peoples as a singular, static entity. In reality, Native Americans had a variety of traditions depending on their history and environment, and their culture continued to change through the course of interactions with European settlers; for instance, tribes such as the Cheyenne and Comanche used horses, which were introduced by white settlers, to become powerful warrior nations. However, a few generalizations can be made: many, but not all, tribes were matrilineal, which gave women a fair degree of power, and land was commonly seen as belonging to everyone. These differences, particularly European settlers' continual focus on land ownership, contributed to increasing prejudice and violence.

Situated on the Atlantic Coast, the Thirteen Colonies that would become the United States of America constituted only a small portion of North America. Even those colonies had significant differences that stemmed from their different origins. For instance, the Virginia colony under John Smith in 1607 started with male bachelors seeking gold, whereas families of Puritans settled Massachusetts. As a result, the Thirteen Colonies—Virginia, Massachusetts, Connecticut, Maryland, New York, New Jersey, Pennsylvania, Delaware, Rhode Island, New Hampshire, Georgia, North Carolina, and South Carolina—had different structures and customs that would each influence the United States.

Competition among several imperial powers in eastern areas of North America led to conflicts that would later bring about the independence of the United States. The French and Indian War from 1754 to 1763, which was a subsidiary war of the Seven Years' War, ended with Great Britain claiming France's Canadian territories as well as the Ohio Valley. The same war was costly for all the powers involved, which led to increased taxes on the Thirteen Colonies. In addition, the new lands to the west of the colonies attracted new settlers, and they came into conflict with Native Americans and British troops that were trying to maintain the traditional boundaries. These growing tensions with Great Britain, as well as other issues, eventually led to the American Revolution, which ended with Britain relinquishing its control of the colonies.

Britain continued to hold onto its other colonies, such as Canada and the West Indies, which reflects the continued power of multiple nations across North America, even as the United States began to expand across the continent. Many Americans advocated expansion regardless of the land's current inhabitants, but the results were often mixed. Still, events both abroad and within North America contributed to the growth of the United States. For instance, the rising tumult in France during the French Revolution and the rise of Napoleon led France to sell the Louisiana Purchase, a large chunk of land consisting not only of Louisiana but also much of the Midwest, to the United States in 1803. Meanwhile, as Spanish power declined, Mexico claimed independence in 1821, but the new nation became increasingly vulnerable to foreign pressure. In the Mexican-American War from 1846 to 1848, Mexico surrendered territory to the

United States that eventually became California, Nevada, Utah, and New Mexico, as well as parts of Arizona, Colorado, and Wyoming.

Even as the United States sought new inland territory, American interests were also expanding overseas via trade. As early as 1784, the ship *Empress of China* traveled to China to establish trading connections. American interests had international dimensions throughout the nation's history. For instance, during the presidency of Andrew Jackson, the ship *Potomac* was dispatched to the Pacific island of Sumatra in 1832 to avenge the deaths of American sailors. This incident exemplifies how U.S. foreign trade connected with imperial expansion.

This combination of continental and seaward growth adds a deeper layer to American development, because it was not purely focused on western expansion. For example, take the 1849 Gold Rush; a large number of Americans and other immigrants traveled to California by ship and settled western territories before more eastern areas, such as Nevada and Idaho. Therefore, the United States' early history of colonization and expansion is a complex network of diverse cultures.

## American Revolution and the Founding of the Nation

The American Revolution largely occurred as a result of changing values in the Thirteen Colonies that broke from their traditional relationship with England. Early on in the colonization of North America, the colonial social structure tried to mirror the stratified order of Great Britain. In England, the landed elites were seen as intellectually and morally superior to the common man, which led to a paternalistic relationship. This style of governance was similarly applied to the colonial system; government was left to the property-owning upper class, and the colonies as a whole could be seen as a child dutifully serving "Mother England."

However, the colonies' distance from England meant that actual, hereditary aristocrats from Britain only formed a small percentage of the overall population and did not even fill all the positions of power. By the mid-eighteenth century, much of the American upper class consisted of local families who acquired status through business rather than lineage. Despite this, representatives from Britain were appointed to govern the colonies. As a result, a rift began to form between the colonists and British officials.

Tensions began to rise in the aftermath of the French and Indian War of 1754 to 1763. To recover the financial costs of the long conflict, Great Britain drew upon its colonies to provide the desired resources. Since the American colonists did not fully subscribe to the paternal connection, taxation to increase British revenue, such as the Stamp Act of 1765, was met with increasing resistance. Britain sent soldiers to the colonies and enacted the 1765 Quartering Act to require colonists to house the troops. In 1773, the new Tea Act, which created a monopoly, led some colonists to raid a ship and destroy its contents in the Boston Tea Party.

Uncertain about whether they should remain loyal to Britain, representatives from twelve colonies formed the First Continental Congress in 1774 to discuss what they should do next. When Patriot militiamen at Lexington and Concord fought British soldiers in April 1775, the Revolutionary War began. While the rebel forces worked to present the struggle as a united, patriotic effort, the colonies remained divided throughout the war. Thousands of colonists, known as Loyalists or Tories, supported Britain. Even the revolutionaries proved to be significantly fragmented, and many militias only served in their home states. The Continental Congress was also divided over whether to reconcile with Britain or push for full separation. These issues hindered the ability of the revolutionary armies to resist the British, who had superior training and resources at their disposal.

Even so, the Continental Army, under General George Washington, gradually built up a force that utilized Prussian military training and backwoods guerrilla tactics to make up for their limited resources. Although the British forces continued to win significant battles, the Continental Army gradually reduced Britain's will to fight as the years passed. Furthermore, Americans appealed to the rivalry that other European nations had with the British Empire. The support was initially limited to indirect assistance, but aid gradually increased. After the American victory at the Battle of Saratoga in 1777, France and other nations began to actively support the American cause by providing much-needed troops and equipment.

In 1781, the primary British army under General Cornwallis was defeated by an American and French coalition at Virginia, which paved the way for negotiations. The Treaty of Paris in 1783 ended the war, recognized the former colonies' independence from Great Britain, and gave America control over territory between the Appalachian Mountains and Mississippi River. However, the state of the new nation was still uncertain. The new nation's government initially stemmed from the state-based structure of the Continental Congress and was incorporated into the Articles of Confederation in 1777.

The Articles of Confederation emphasized the ideals of the American Revolution, particularly the concept of freedom from unjust government. Unfortunately, the resulting limitations on the national government left most policies—even ones with national ramifications—up to individual states. For instance, states sometimes simply decided to not pay taxes. Many representatives did not see much value in the National Congress and simply did not attend the meetings. Some progress was still made during the period, such as the Northwest Ordinance of 1787, which organized the western territories into new states; nevertheless, the disjointed links in the state-oriented government inhibited significant progress.

Although many citizens felt satisfied with this decentralized system of government, key intellectuals and leaders in America became increasingly disturbed by the lack of unity. An especially potent fear among them was the potential that, despite achieving official independence, other powers could threaten America's autonomy. In 1786, poor farmers in Massachusetts launched an insurrection, known as Shays' Rebellion, which sparked fears of additional uprisings and led to the creation of the *Constitutional Convention* in 1787.

While the convention initially intended to correct issues within the Articles of Confederation, speakers, such as James Madison, compellingly argued for the delegates to devise a new system of government that was more centralized than its predecessor. The Constitution was not fully supported by all citizens, and there was much debate about whether or not to support the new government. Even so, in 1788, the Constitution was ratified. Later additions, such as the Bill of Rights, would help protect individual liberty by giving specific rights to citizens. In 1789, George Washington became the first president of the newly created executive branch of the government, and America entered a new stage of history.

## U.S. History from Founding to Present

One early development was the growth of political parties—something that Washington tried and failed to stop from forming. Federalists, such as Alexander Hamilton, wanted to expand the national government's power, while Democratic-Republicans, such as Thomas Jefferson, favored states' rights. The United States suffered multiple defeats by Britain in the War of 1812, but individual American victories, such as the Battle of New Orleans, still strengthened nationalistic pride.

In the aftermath of the war, the Federalists were absorbed into the Democratic-Republicans, which began the Era of Good Feelings. However, two new parties eventually emerged. The Democrats, whose leader Andrew Jackson became president in 1828, favored "Jacksonian" democracy, which emphasized mass participation in elections. However, Jackson's policies largely favored white male landowners and suppressed opposing views. The Whigs supported Federalist policies but also drew on democratic principles, particularly with marginalized groups such as African Americans and women.

At the same time, settlers continued to expand west in search of new land and fortune. The Louisiana Purchase of 1803 opened up large amounts of land west of the Mississippi River, and adventurers pushed past even those boundaries toward the western coast. The vision of westward growth into the frontier is a key part of American popular culture, but the expansion was often erratic and depended on a combination of incentives and assurances of relative security. Hence, some areas, such as California and Oregon, were settled more quickly than other areas to the east. Some historians have pointed to the growth of the frontier as a means through which American democracy expanded.

However, the matter of western lands became an increasingly volatile issue as the controversy over slavery heightened. Not all northerners supported abolition, but many saw the practice as outdated and did not want it to expand. Abolitionists formed the Republican Party, and their candidate, Abraham Lincoln, was elected as president in 1860. In response, southern states seceded and formed the Confederate States of America. The ensuing Civil War lasted from 1861 to 1865 and had significant consequences. Slavery was abolished in the United States, and the power of individual states was drastically curtailed. After being reunified, southern states worked to retain control over freed slaves, and the Reconstruction period was followed by Jim Crow segregation. As a result, blacks were barred from public education, unable to vote, and forced to accept their status as second-class citizens.

After the Civil War, the United States increasingly industrialized and became part of the larger Industrial Revolution, which took place throughout the western world. Steps toward industrialization had already begun as early as Jackson's presidency, but the full development of American industry took place in the second half of the nineteenth century. Railroads helped link cities like Chicago to locations across the West, which allowed for rapid transfer of materials. New technologies, such as electricity, allowed leisure time for those with enough wealth. Even so, the Gilded Age was also a period of disparities, and wealthy entrepreneurs rose while impoverished workers struggled to make their voices heard.

The late nineteenth and early twentieth century not only marked U.S. expansion within North America but also internationally. For instance, after the Spanish-American War in 1898, the United States claimed control over Guam, Puerto Rico, and the Philippines. Rivalries in Europe culminated in World War I, in which great powers ranging from France to Russia vied for control in a bloody struggle. Americans did not enter the war until 1917, but we had a critical role in the final phase of the war. During the peace treaty process, President Woodrow Wilson sought to establish a League of Nations in order to promote global harmony, but his efforts only achieved limited success.

After World War I, the United States largely stayed out of international politics for the next two decades. Still, American businesses continued overseas ventures and strengthened the economy in the 1920s. However, massive speculation in the stock market in 1929 triggered the Great Depression—a financial crisis that spread worldwide as nations withdrew from the global economy. The crisis shepherded in the presidency of Franklin D. Roosevelt, who reformed the Democratic Party and implemented new federal programs known as the New Deal.

The Great Depression had ramifications worldwide and encouraged the rise of fascist governments in Italy and Germany. Highly dictatorial, fascism emphasized nationalism and militarism. World War II began when the Axis powers of Germany, Italy, and Japan built up their military forces and launched invasions against neighboring nations in 1939. As part of the Allies, which also included Britain, France, and the Soviet Union, America defeated the Axis powers in 1945 and asserted itself as a global force.

The Union of Soviet Socialist Republics had emerged through the Bolshevik Revolution in 1917 in Russia and militantly supported Communism—a socialist system of government that called for the overthrow of capitalism. Although the Soviet Union formed an alliance with the United States during World War II, relations chilled, and the Cold War began in 1947. Although no true war was declared between the two nations, both the Union of Soviet Socialist Republics and the United States engaged in indirect conflict by supporting and overthrowing foreign governments.

Meanwhile, the Civil Rights Movement began to grow as marginalized groups objected to racial segregation and abuse by whites across the nation. Civil rights leaders, such as Martin Luther King Jr., argued for nonviolent resistance, but others, such as Malcolm X, advocated more radical approaches. Civil rights groups became increasingly discontented during the Vietnam War because they felt they were being drafted for a foreign war that ignored domestic problems. Even so, significant reforms, such as the Voting Rights Act of 1965, opened up new opportunities for freedom and equality in America.

In 1991, the Soviet Union collapsed, leaving the United States as the dominant global power. However, as the United States struggled to fill the void left by the Soviet Union, questions arose about America's role in the world. Terrorist acts, such as the 9/11 attack on the World Trade Center in 2001, have shed doubt on the United States' ability to enforce its authority on an international scale.

## Twentieth-Century Developments in the United States

Although the United States began industrializing in the second half of the nineteenth century, American technology continued to develop in new directions throughout the course of the twentieth century. A key example was the invention of the modern assembly line. Assembly lines and conveyor belts had already become a prominent part of industrial work, but Henry Ford combined conveyor belts with the system of assembly workers in 1913 in order to produce Model T automobiles. This streamlined production system, in which multiple parts were assembled by different teams along the conveyors, allowed industries in the United States to grow ever larger.

Ford's assembly lines also promoted the growth of the automobile as a means of transportation. Early cars were an expensive and impractical novelty and were primarily the toys of the rich. The Model T, on the other hand, was relatively affordable, which made the car available to a wider array of consumers. Many of the automobiles' early issues, such as radiator leaks and fragile tires, were gradually corrected, and this made the car more appealing than horses. With the support of President Eisenhower, the Federal Aid Highway Act of 1956 paved the way for a network of interstates and highways across the nation.

At the same time, a revolutionary approach to transportation was emerging: flight. Blimps and balloons were already gaining popularity by the turn of the twentieth century, but aviators struggled to create an airplane. The first critical success was by the Wright Brothers in 1903, and they demonstrated that aircrafts did not need to be lighter than air. In time, airplanes surpassed the popularity of balloons and blimps, which tended to be more volatile. Aircraft also added a new dimension to warfare, and aircraft carriers became an integral piece of the American navy during World War II.

Furthermore, by demonstrating that heavier-than-air vehicles could actually carry passengers upward, the stage was set for the space race in the second half of the twentieth century. In 1958, the U.S. government created the National Aeronautics and Space Administration (NASA) to head the budding initiative to extend American power into space. After the Soviet Union successfully launched the Sputnik satellite into Earth's orbit in 1957 and sent the first human in space in 1961, the United States intensified its own space program through the Apollo missions. Apollo 11 successfully landed on the moon in 1969 with Buzz Aldrin and Neil Armstrong. Later ventures into space would focus on space shuttles and satellites, and the latter significantly enhanced communications worldwide.

Indeed, the twentieth century also made considerable advancements in communications and media. Inventions such as the radio greatly boosted communication across the nation and world, such that news could be reported immediately rather than take days. Furthermore, motion pictures evolved from black-and-white movies at theaters to full-color television sets in households. From animation to live films, television matured into a compelling art form in popular culture. Live-action footage gave a new layer to news broadcasts and proved instrumental in the public's reaction to events, such as the Civil Rights Movement and the Vietnam War. With the success of the space program, satellites became a fundamental piece of Earth's communications network by transmitting signals across the planet instantaneously.

Further communications advancements resulted from the development of computer technology. The early computers in the twentieth century were enormous behemoths that were too bulky and expensive for anything but government institutions. However, computers gradually became smaller while still storing large amounts of data. A turning point came with the 1976 release of the Apple computer by entrepreneurs Steve Wozniak and Steve Jobs. The computer had a simplistic design that made it marketable for a mass consumer audience, and computers eventually became household items. Similarly, the networks that would become the Internet originated as government systems, but in time they were extended to commercial avenues that became a vibrant element of modern communications.

However, other advancements in American science during the twentieth century were aimed toward more lethal purposes. In response to the multiple wars throughout the century, the United States built up a powerful military force, and new technologies were devised for that purpose. One of the deadliest creations was the atomic bomb, which split molecular atoms to produce powerful explosions; in addition to the sheer force of the bombs, the aftereffects included toxic radiation and electronic shutdowns. Developed and used in the last days of World War II, the nuclear bomb was the United States' most powerful weapon during the Cold War.

On the other hand, the twentieth century also marked new approaches to the natural environments in America. In reaction to the depletion of natural habitats by industrialization and overhunting, President Theodore Roosevelt helped preserve areas for what would become the National Parks in 1916. Laws, such as the Clean Water Act of 1972, helped improve the health of ecosystems, which benefitted not only wildlife but people across the nation. This also led to the development of alternative energy sources such as wind and solar power.

America continues to change and grow into the twenty-first century by building on preexisting ideas but also pioneering new concepts. As globalization becomes an increasingly prominent phenomenon, American businesses strive to adapt their products to consumers worldwide while also funneling in new ideas from other nations. Yet many of the current developments in American enterprises stem in part from earlier events in American history. For instance, the environmental movement has expanded to address new issues such as global warming. NASA continues its space exploration endeavors, but

entrepreneurs hope one day to travel to Mars. Therefore, the history of technology within the United States remains an engaging and relevant subject in the present.

## Key Documents and Speeches in U.S. History

With more than two hundred years of history, American leaders have produced a number of important documents and speeches. One of the most essential is the Declaration of Independence, which the Second Continental Congress ratified on July 4, 1776. Although many historians and politicians have drawn upon the words of the Declaration to demonstrate the American ideal of freedom, most of them focus on the preamble, which focuses on the necessity of fair government and the right to overthrow tyrants. The main body of the document consists of a set of grievances against King George III. Still, this document was instrumental in American history because it asserted American independence from Great Britain. Even so, it is important to note that the Declaration did not immediately lead to the United States; the document does not outline the government of the soon-to-be independent colonies, and independence would not become reality until Britain agreed.

The colonies' first blueprint for government was the Articles of Confederation, which was ratified in 1777. The document declared that the confederacy would be called the United States of America and that the individual states would have "a firm league of friendship" with each other. The emphasis on friendship and cooperation highlights how the confederation was a voluntary effort that states could follow or ignore as they saw fit. Still, the document also revealed the importance of obeying decisions made by Congress as a whole; while this was not very effective during the confederation period, the framework would live on to a degree in the following Constitution.

Much like the Declaration of Independence, the 1787 Constitution of the United States is most remembered for the preamble, which takes a more philosophical approach. However, the body of the Constitution is highly complex, and it covers the framework and responsibilities of the different branches of the federal government and the limits to state power. These details are very important and help to define the key institutions within the government. To resolve later issues not addressed in the Constitution, the fifth article in the document establishes a process to modify the government, and the first ten amendments are known as the *Bill of Rights*. Under the Tenth Amendment, powers not specifically allotted to Congress by the Constitution are reserved for the people and to individual states.

George Washington was the first president of the United States, and his administration set many precedents for the nation, particularly with his Farewell Address. In it, he noted the rise of regional feelings, and he urged citizens to uphold their duty to the nation above sectionalism because he felt that America was strongest when united. The issue of regional conflicts and national identity would become increasingly important in years to come, especially during the Civil War. Washington also argued against intervention in European affairs, and this warning would become the cornerstone for advocates of American isolation. On the other hand, his advice that political parties are detrimental to democracy failed to halt the development of the party system.

Washington's fears about sectional conflict were confirmed at the start of the Civil War, when the southern states violently seceded from the Union. As the president during that tumultuous time, Abraham Lincoln was seen by many to embody the Union as a whole. This can be demonstrated through his Gettysburg Address in November of 1863. After the difficult and bloody Battle of Gettysburg ended in a Union victory, crowds gathered for the dedication of the Soldiers' National Cemetery. Although he was not the main speaker of the event, Lincoln's short yet eloquent speech proved to be the most significant. Drawing upon the Declaration of Independence's assertion that "all men are created equal,"

he argued that the current war was a test of that ideal. More than that, he emphasized the importance of the United States as a whole and argued that it must endure as a Union for the sake of the world.

Earlier that year in January, Lincoln had already indicated his opposition to slavery through the Emancipation Proclamation. Although it was an executive order instead of a law passed by Congress, this document was not challenged by the courts and helped determine the objectives of the Civil War. The proclamation asserted that all slaves in Confederate territories were free. One must note that some southern states remained in the Union, and therefore, were not affected by this proclamation. Even so, the order helped establish a basis for later laws and amendments that would end slavery in the United States.

Another presidential attempt to set a new precedent for American policy was Woodrow Wilson's Fourteen Points, which were outlined in a speech he gave to Congress in 1918 after the United States had entered World War I. Wilson saw the United States as a protector of democracy in the world and said that we could reform world policy by fighting in the war. For instance, Wilson called for an end to private negotiations, which had contributed to the secret alliances behind the war. Most of all, he argued for nations to come together in an international body to determine world policies. The negotiations after the war only partially fulfilled Wilson's ambitions by creating a weak League of Nations, but his vision of U.S. involvement in global affairs would become a key aspect of American foreign policy.

Even as the United States began playing a more active role on the international stage of politics, internal issues such as civil rights remained important, as shown in Martin Luther King Jr.'s "I Have a Dream" speech. A leader in the civil rights movement, King gave his speech as part of the 1963 March on Washington. Drawing on Lincoln's past speech at Gettysburg, King argued that America's journey to true equality was not over yet. His references to biblical passages gave the speech a spiritual tone, but he also mentioned specific locations across the nation to signify how local struggles were tied with national consequences. By emphasizing his optimism, King's speech reflects not only civil rights activism but also the American dream of freedom and progress.

## Connections between Causes and Effects

When examining the historical narratives of events, it is important to understand the relationship between causes and effects. A cause can be defined as something, whether an event, social change, or other factor, that contributes to the occurrence of certain events; the results of causes are called effects. Those terms may seem simple enough, but they have drastic implications on how one explores history. Events such as the American Revolution or the Civil Rights Movement may appear to occur spontaneously, but a closer examination will reveal that these events depended on earlier phenomena and patterns that influenced the course of history.

For example, although the battles at Concord and Lexington may seem to be instantaneous eruptions of violence during the American Revolution, they stemmed from a variety of factors. The most obvious influences behind those two battles were the assortment of taxes and policies imposed on the Thirteen Colonies following the French and Indian War from 1754 to 1763. Taxation without direct representation, combined with the deployment of British soldiers to enforce these policies, greatly increased American resistance. Earlier events, such as the Boston Massacre and the Boston Tea Party, similarly stemmed from conflicts between British soldiers and local colonists over perceived tyranny and rebelliousness. Therefore, the start of the American Revolution progressed from preceding developments.

Furthermore, there can be multiple causes and effects for any situation. The existence of multiple causes can be seen through the settling of the American West. Many historians have emphasized the role of manifest destiny—the national vision of expanding across the continent—as a driving force behind the growth of the United States. Yet there were many different influences behind the expansion westward. Northern abolitionists and southern planters saw the frontier as a way to either extend or limit slavery. Economic opportunities in the West also encouraged travel westward, as did the gradual pacification of Native American tribes.

Even an individual cause can be subdivided into smaller factors or stretched out in a gradual process. Although there were numerous issues that led to the Civil War, slavery was the primary cause. However, that topic stretched back to the very founding of the nation, and the existence of slavery was a controversial topic during the creation of the Declaration of Independence and the Constitution. The abolition movement as a whole did not start until the 1830s, but nevertheless, slavery is a cause that gradually grew more important over the following decades. In addition, opponents of slavery were divided by different motivations—some believed that it stifled the economy, while others focused on moral issues.

On the other end of the spectrum, a single event can have numerous results. The rise of the telegraph, for example, had several effects on American history. The telegraph allowed news to travel much quicker and turned events into immediate national news, such as the sinking of the USS Maine, which sparked the Spanish-American War. In addition, the telegraph helped make railroads run more efficiently by improving the links between stations. The faster speed of both travel and communications led to a shift in time itself, and localized times were replaced by standardized time zones across the nation.

The importance of grasping cause-and-effect relationships is critical in interpreting the growth and development of the Civil Rights Movement. Historical narratives of the movement often focus on charismatic individuals, such as Martin Luther King Jr., and they certainly played a key leadership role. Even so, elements of the movement had already emerged in previous decades through the growth of the National Association for the Advancement of Colored People (NAACP) and other organizations. Several factors proved critical to the formation of civil rights organizations during the 1950s. African American veterans returning from World War II, as well as those continuing to serve in the military, called for equal rights. Furthermore, the United States' role as a key member of the United Nations, which included African countries, required the federal government to take racial discrimination seriously.

A specific example in the Civil Rights Movement is the sit-ins during 1960, in which black and white students defied segregation policies in restaurants and other establishments. The wave is often thought to originate from spontaneous activism by students in Greensboro, North Carolina. However, there had already been other sit-ins, such as at Royal Ice Cream Parlor in Durham, North Carolina, in 1957. In fact, the sit-ins would not have spread as quickly without a preexisting network of activists across the nation, which in part stemmed from the growth of organizations through various local and national movements. By looking at such cases closely, it becomes clear that no event occurs without one—if not multiple—causes behind it, and that each historical event can have a variety of direct and indirect consequences.

One of the most critical elements of cause-and-effect relationships is how they are relevant not only in studying history but also in contemporary events. Much of the current political debate about social security and health care stems from FDR's New Deal in the 1930s, and at the time some people criticized the programs for being too extensive, while others argued that he did not go far enough with his vision.

Current environmental concerns have their origins in long-term issues that reach back centuries. The United States' mixed history of global isolation and foreign intervention continues to influence foreign policy approaches today. Most of all, people must realize that events and developments today will likely have a number of consequences later on. Therefore, the study of cause and effect remains vital in understanding the past, the present, and the future.

# *Geography and Social Studies Inquiry*

## World and Regional Geography

Geography is essential in understanding the world as a whole. This requires a study of spatial distribution, which examines how various locations and physical features are arranged in the world. The most common element in geography is the region, which refers to a specific area that is separate from surrounding ones. Regions can be defined based on a variety of factors, including environmental, economic, or political features, and these different kinds of regions can overlap with each other.

It is also important to know the difference between location and place. A location, defined either through its physical position or through its relation to other locations, determines where something is, and this characteristic is static. A place, on the other hand, describes a combination of physical and human elements in relation to each other; the determination of place is therefore changeable depending on the movement of individuals and groups.

Geography is visually conveyed using maps, and a collection of maps is called an atlas. To illustrate some key points about geography, please refer to the map below.

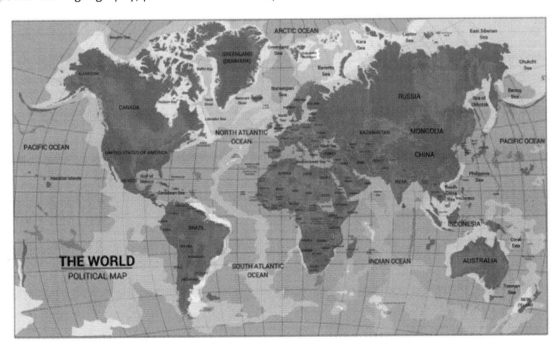

This is a traditional map of the world that displays all of the countries and six of the seven continents. Countries, the most common approach to political regions, can be identified by their labels. The continents are not identified on this map, with the exception of Australia, but they are larger landmasses that encompass most of the countries in their respective areas; the other five visible continents are North America, South America, Europe, Africa, and Asia. The seventh continent, Antarctica, is found at the South Pole and has been omitted from the map.

The absence of Antarctica leads into the issues of distortion, in which geographical features are altered on a map. Some degree of distortion is to be expected with a two-dimensional flat map of the world because the earth is a sphere. A map projection transforms a spherical map of the world into a flattened perspective, but the process generally alters the spatial appearance of landmasses. For instance, Greenland often appears, such as in the map above, larger than it really is.

Furthermore, Antarctica's exclusion from the map is, in fact, a different sort of distortion—that of the mapmakers' biases. Mapmakers determine which features are included on the map and which ones are not. Antarctica, for example, is often missing from maps because, unlike the other continents, it has a limited human population. Moreover, a study of the world reveals that many of the distinctions on maps are human constructions.

Even so, maps can still reveal key features about the world. For instance, the map above has areas that seem almost three-dimensional and jut out. They represent mountains and are an example of topography, which is a method used to display the differing elevations of the terrain. A more detailed topographical map can be viewed below.

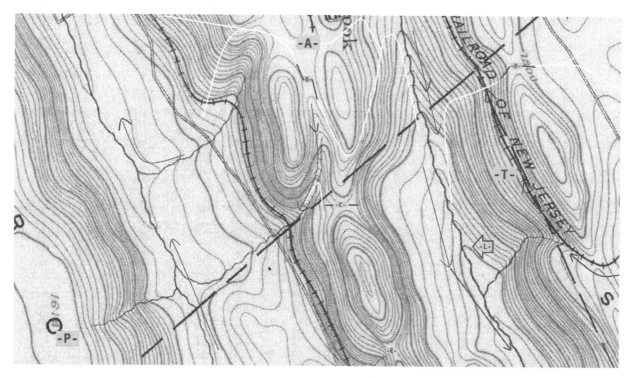

On some colored maps, the oceans, represented in blue between the continents, vary in coloration depending on depth. The differences demonstrate *bathymetry*, which is the study of the ocean floor's depth. Paler areas represent less depth, while darker spots reflect greater depth.

Please also note the many lines running horizontally and vertically along the map. The horizontal lines, known as *parallels*, mark the calculated latitude of those locations and reveal how far north or south these areas are from the equator, which bisects the map horizontally. Generally, with exceptions depending on specific environments, climates closer to the equator are warmer because this region

receives the most direct sunlight. The equator also serves to split the globe between the Northern and Southern hemispheres.

Longitude, as signified by the vertical lines, determines how far east or west different regions are from each other. The lines of longitude, known as meridians, are also the basis for time zones, which allocate different times to regions depending on their position eastward and westward of the prime meridian. As one travels west between time zones, the given time moves backward accordingly. Conversely, if one travels east, the time moves forward.

There are two particularly significant longitude-associated dividers in this regard. The prime [Greenwich] meridian, as displayed below, is defined as zero degrees in longitude, and thus determines the other lines. The line, in fact, circles the globe north and south, and it therefore divides the world into the Eastern and Western hemispheres. It is important to not confuse the Greenwich meridian with the International Date Line, which is an invisible line in the Pacific Ocean that was created to represent the change between calendar days. By traveling westward across the International Date Line, a traveler would essentially leap forward a day. For example, a person departing from the United States on Sunday would arrive in Japan on Monday. By traveling eastward across the line, a traveler would go backward a day. For example, a person departing from China on Monday would arrive in Canada on Sunday.

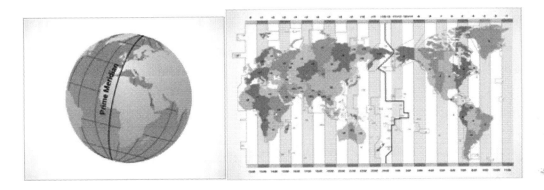

Although world maps are useful in showing the overall arrangement of continents and nations, it is also important at times to look more closely at individual countries because they have unique features that are only visible on more detailed maps.

For example, take the following map of the United States of America. It should be noted that the country is split into multiple states that have their own culture and localized governments. Other countries are often split into various divisions, such as provinces, and while these features are ignored for the sake of clarity on larger maps, they are important when studying specific nations. Individual

states can be further subdivided into counties and townships, and they may have their own maps that can be examined for closer analysis.

Finally, one of the first steps in examining any map should be to locate the map's key or legend, which will explain what features different symbols represent on the map. As these symbols can be arbitrary depending on the maker, a key will help to clarify the different meanings.

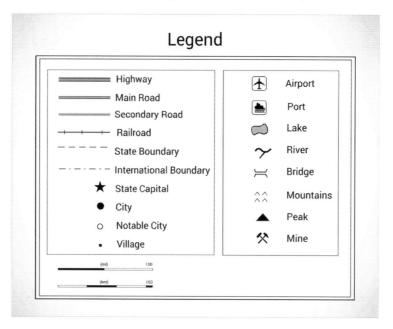

## Interaction of Physical and Human Systems

Humans have always interacted with nature, and humanity has been shaped by, and, in turn, reshaped environments. Using tools to accomplish things they cannot do on their own, humans have proven highly adaptable to different environments. However, the specific ecosystems have helped to shape human development as individuals and as groups. The earth is highly diverse and has many different

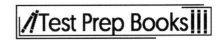

ecosystems, each with its own flora and fauna. The specific resources available in different places have, therefore, influenced how humans develop.

Water, in particular, has proved vital in determining the course of human civilizations. As humans require water daily to survive, even more than they do food, proximity to water has always been of utmost necessity. Many human settlements originated adjacent to sources, and only in time expanded to other areas. Water is also essential for the growth of plants, which form a considerable portion of the human diet. In the wild, edible plants grow in places where they can thrive but may not be conveniently located for harvesting by humans. Therefore, humans gradually learned to grow plants themselves in places of their own choice. Humans also diverted water sources to new areas for themselves and to irrigate crops, thus transforming ecosystems.

Another important factor in the relationships between humans and nature has been the role of other animals. From small pests, such as weevils and rodents, to predators, including crocodiles and bears, many species of animals have often posed threats to humans, and conflict increased as humans expanded into environments inhabited by other creatures. On the other hand, animals are invaluable to humans because they can provide sustenance and clothing. This led to hunting and domestication of animal species. Domestication of both plants and animals involves humans breeding species to fit their own needs, which leads to new qualities that would normally not appear in the wild.

However, despite the considerable role that humans can play in altering environments, these changes have remained limited to local levels for much of human history. This does not mean that humans did not affect their ecosystems; some Native American tribes, for instance, used regular fires or hunting methods to maintain environments suitable for their needs. Even so, for much of human existence, nature was seen not simply as an obstacle but rather a power of its own right that was above human interference. Natural phenomena such as severe weather, diseases, and famine all kept human populations in check. Many pantheons of deities center on the gods' roles as arbitrary powers in the natural world, which reflects the lack of influence that humans had in the larger course of environmental changes.

Therefore, natural resources such as water and food were often seen as forces to be respected. Natural environments were recognized as vital regions, and alterations to fully exploit the resources were limited so that the resources could remain adequately sustainable. Riparian customs meant that water was the right of those with immediate access to it, and ownership changed accordingly with who lived nearby. However, increasing industrialization meant that natural resources such as water and lumber became resources that could be commoditized. In addition, appropriation gave water rights to those individuals or businesses that had first used the resource instead of being based on physical proximity.

Another instrumental change in the relationship between humans and nature is the increasing global connections worldwide. In many cases, earlier changes to environments occurred at local levels, with travel between different regions requiring considerable time and effort. The ability to travel around the world quickly has sharply altered that dynamic. Many local ecosystems, and the human cultures that developed accordingly, originated in separate circumstances that created unique plants and animals. Now products from one part of the world can be transported to entirely different environments and create new exchanges of goods. In some cases, the transferred species escape into the wild, and they often have traits for which the local environments are not prepared. This can result in invasive species that quickly grow and overpower native species.

A key symbol of artificial environments created by humans since early civilization has been the city, which is a human center of habitation that exists separate from the countryside around it. The creation of cities usually requires significant changes to the environment in which it is located, and the city must provide for the needs of residents without being compromised by nature. Yet the city has always remained connected to the rest of the world and to nature. Because a city generally lacks the capacity for agriculture and few natural resources are located within its confines, urban populations rely on resources from outlying areas for nourishment. The city, in turn, acts as a processing center for nearby settlements and offers rural workers and farmers the opportunity to sell their goods to a larger market.

Furthermore, the city, while an artificial construct, is still an environment in its own right. Although many species of animals have perished with the creation of cities, others, such as coyotes and pigeons, have adapted to urban life, thereby creating new ecosystems within cities. Natural connections within cities used to be stronger and more common because people would raise livestock within the city and regularly reuse garbage for livestock feed. While less hygienic, this helped stimulate natural cycles within the city. Recent efforts in many cities to create natural pockets, such as parks and community gardens, have also strengthened the ties between cities and the natural world. In a sense, the city reflects humanity's mixed relationship with nature as a whole: while humans continue to reshape the environment, they also remain linked to nature.

## Uses of Geography

Geography helps people better understand the role that location plays in the past, present, and future. Historians make frequent use of maps in their studies to get a clearer picture of how history unfolded. Since the beginning of history, many different groups have fought conflicts that originated from struggles for land or other resources; therefore, knowing the location and borders of different empires and kingdoms helps reveal how they interacted with each other. In addition, environmental factors, such as access to water and the proximity of mountains, often help to shape the course of civilizations. Even single events and battles make more sense with maps that show how the warring sides met and maneuvered.

Furthermore, determining the geography of historical events, in particular geographical change over time, is essential due to the role that physical settings play in the present. Many important geographic landmarks continue to exist in the world, and they are often commemorated for their roles in history. Yet the physical geography has sometimes changed significantly. For instance, the Aswan Dam significantly reshaped the flow of the Nile River, which was the heart of ancient Egyptian society; without knowledge of the past geography, it is difficult to fully understand the civilization's context and how it differs from the present reality.

History also depends on archaeology, the study of human artifacts, for the evidence necessary to make conclusions about cultures. These items are generally buried, which helps preserve the artifacts yet makes it difficult to locate them. Historical geography helps in that regard by ascertaining key sites of human activity that could potentially retain artifacts. These insights help archaeologists discover new aspects of ancient cultures, which in turn strengthen historical arguments. Maps themselves sometimes serve as artifacts in their own right because they help reveal how humans of earlier periods viewed the world.

Along with the historical implications, knowledge of the world's geography remains important for people in the present day. The most immediate use of geography is in navigation. Tools such as Global Positioning Systems have helped improve navigation, but they too represent an approach to geography

that demonstrates how it continues to have a fundamental role in human society. Humans have even begun mapping the trajectories of planets and even their individual terrains.

However, beyond the direct uses for navigation, geography is invaluable in comprehending modern cultures and events. Whether through their proximity to other nations or their relation to environmental features, such as forests and deserts, societies remain deeply connected to their geographical settings. Therefore, to fully understand current affairs, such as wars and poverty, people must have a firm grasp on geographic settings. For instance, a study of nations in Africa, many of which continue to suffer from poverty, would require a close examination of geographic factors. The borders of many African countries were arbitrarily determined during the colonial period, and the conflicts of ethnic groups divided by these borders have influenced current struggles. On the environmental end, some nations have been significantly affected by desertification and deforestation, which makes studies of their ecological geography important as well.

Two recent key developments have made geography more important than ever before. The first change is the globalization of culture, economics, and politics. For much of human history, geography was most important at localized scales. Many people spent their entire lives in isolated communities, with intermittent trade between different centers. Geography was still important, but many people did not need to be familiar with anything other than their immediate locations. Today, on the other hand, places around the world are intricately connected to each other. Travel is relatively easy and quick and enables people to venture between different regions like never before. Areas that used to be geographically isolated from each other can now exchange ideas and products on an unprecedented scale.

In addition, due to the multinational relationship of politics, conflicts that would have been geographically isolated in the past can have international ramifications. Latin American revolutions, such as in Nicaragua during the Cold War, were seen as having larger implications in the struggle between American democracy and Soviet communism, which led to foreign interventions and wars that affected multiple countries. Therefore, geography is critical to not only addressing the current effects of globalization but also understanding how global interactions may influence international politics and economics in the future.

The second major factor in geography's role in modern events is the rising importance of environmental policies and climate change. Scientific developments have increasingly revealed how the planet as a whole can be considered a large ecosystem in its own right, with its own strengths and frailties. A change in one part of the environment, such as industrialization in India and China, can have larger consequences for neighboring regions and for the world as a whole. Geographical insights help to show how the world functions and how humans can work to improve their relationship with the natural world.

Moreover, as climate changes become more evident in the world, geography helps illustrate the effects of new environmental phenomena. For instance, scientists have studied the topography of nations to determine how rising sea levels will alter the land via flooding, and local and national governments are using these findings to prepare for the coming changes. Furthermore, the continued scrutiny of the state of the earth's geography reveals how climate change is transforming the planet at this very moment, as regional climates shift and islands vanish under the sea. As a result, geography will continue to have a role in future developments.

## Different Cultural Backgrounds

When studying different cultures, it is important to realize that cultures are always changing in response to individuals and groups within it. Therefore, one must avoid stereotyping members of a certain culture or overgeneralizing. For example, American culture is highly diverse with multiple ethnic groups. Many ethnic communities have resided in the United States for generations, so it is incorrect to label them as a foreign culture, yet each group must be closely examined to understand American culture as a whole.

This diversity within larger classifications of cultures can be seen with Native Americans. There are many different tribes of Native Americans, and each has its own unique history and characteristics. Nevertheless, a few general qualities describe most Native American groups. First of all, Native Americans continue to struggle to escape the poverty that they were historically forced into during white settlement of the United States. Many, but not all, tribes have been traditionally matrilineal—with ancestry defined through female lineage—and emphasized communal sharing and a sustainable relationship with nature, but the American government often suppressed these customs. This has led many Native Americans to begin protecting their surviving heritage, including their rights to traditional religious practices and access to historical artifacts.

South of the United States, Mexico has a vibrant yet troubled culture. Mexico was one of the principal colonies of Spain, and the culture is therefore a diverse blend of Spanish and native customs. One enduring legacy of Spain's rule is the prominence of Roman Catholicism, albeit mixed with pre-Spanish concepts; for instance, the traditional Day of the Dead embodies both pre-Columbian and Christian ideals. On the other hand, the Spanish system of large estates created significant class disparities. Furthermore, Mexico's war for independence and conflicts with other nations drastically destabilized its government, and the nation continues to struggle with corruption and violence. Still, Mexico retains a rich culture that celebrates its complex history. Mexican families are generally large and cooperate to help each other.

French national identity is relatively new because regional ties were prevalent until the French Revolution in the 1790s. A rising sense of nationalism unites French culture today, but various regions maintain their own local traditions. Much of France has been traditionally agricultural, but the globalization of the food trade has disrupted local markets and led to mass migration to cities. Reflecting Catholic values, most of France's families follow a nuclear model of a two-parent household with children.

South Africa is culturally and ethnically diverse, but historically white settlers used apartheid to oppress and isolate other groups. However, previously marginalized ethnic groups are now actively working to assert their own identity within South Africa. Rural communities tend to be more traditional, while people within cities have adopted new values. South Africa is largely patriarchal with defined gender roles that give men dominance over women. Efforts to strengthen South Africa's industries have depleted many of its natural resources and created a growing environmental crisis that is particularly devastating to rural populations.

Laying claim to the legacies of ancient Persia, Iran's culture was at the crossroads of trade routes between multiple continents for centuries, which gave it a long and diverse background. Iran is primarily Islamic, with the majority of Muslims belonging to the Shi'a faith. They believe that their religious leaders, imams, are divinely appointed as the religious successors, known as caliphs, to the prophet Muhammad; even so, other religions such as Judaism and Zoroastrianism are also practiced in the

country. Iran's patriarchal culture generally restricts the role of women, but women have nevertheless become more involved in the civil service, sciences, and other fields.

Russia's culture is built on a rich history but has been especially influenced by the dominance of communism until the Soviet Union's dissolution in 1991. The use of state police and other agents to enforce government policies led to a sense of paranoia and distrust of anyone outside the family. On the other hand, this situation created strong support networks within families that led to strong relationships with relatives. The Soviet Union's drive to industrialize also led to numerous current environmental issues across Russia.

As with Russia, the People's Republic of China's modern culture is deeply influenced by decades of Communist rule. Under the leadership of Mao, China enacted massive efforts to strengthen Chinese industry and agriculture at the cost of environmental damage; China continues to undergo intense industrial operations in the present, which has caused pollution in the cities. On the other hand, China takes great pride in its long traditions and history that date back thousands of years. China has been traditionally patriarchal, and children have been expected to respect and care for their elders. Chinese culture is not monolithic, and there are many different ethnic groups within the country, including the Han, Manchu, and Uyghur. However, the one-child policy from 1978 to 2015 has destabilized long-term family dynamics by putting considerable pressure on single children to look after their parents.

Japan's family structure has also been disrupted in the modern era. Japanese culture is built on a sense of interdependence within families and the community as a whole, but a low birthrate has led to a rising number of elderly relatives and few children, which has unsettled the traditional foundation. Even so, Japan embraces a blend of modern advancements and traditional customs. Japanese culture is built on multiple layers of social status, and people use different forms of language depending on their relationship with others. As a result, traditional Japanese society is highly formal, but recent generations have become more open to new ideas. As Japan's islands have limited space and resources, it has been at the forefront of many natural conservation efforts, although some controversial traditions, such as whaling, still persist.

## Helping Students Locate, Analyze, and Synthesize Information Related to Social Studies Topics

Social studies curriculum should offer content that is comprehensive and thematic, introducing a variety of viewpoints on historical events and highlighting the relevance of connecting the past with the present. Teachers must know how to guide students in obtaining, evaluating, and processing the information associated with these topics. Although the school's textbook is a ready resource, teachers should suggest and encourage alternate sources of information, such as the library, field trips, maps, and other visual material, interviews, and discussions of current events. These opportunities allow students to analyze information and increase their societal understanding. Classroom activities can help students apply previously acquired learning through problem solving, such as performing their own mock election in order to gain a better grasp of the election process. Encouraging students to investigate social studies topics that interest them and involve real-world projects helps them to become objective observers and develop a sense of public duty. When students can interpret, organize, and present what they have learned through a variety of methods, it promotes a deeper understanding and application of wider social studies themes.

# Practice Questions

1. Which of the following correctly lists the Thirteen Colonies?
    a. Connecticut, Delaware, Georgia, Maryland, Massachusetts, New Hampshire, New Jersey, New York, North Carolina, Pennsylvania, Rhode Island, South Carolina, Virginia
    b. Carolina, Connecticut, Delaware, Maryland, Massachusetts, New Hampshire, New Jersey, New York, Ohio, Pennsylvania, Rhode Island, Virginia, West Virginia
    c. Connecticut, Delaware, Georgia, Maine, Massachusetts, New Hampshire, New Jersey, New York, North Carolina, South Carolina, Pennsylvania, Vermont, Virginia
    d. Canada, Connecticut, Delaware, Georgia, Florida, Maryland, Massachusetts, New Hampshire, New York, North Carolina, Rhode Island, South Carolina, Virginia

2. Which of the following was NOT an issue contributing to the American Revolution?
    a. Increased taxes on the colonies
    b. Britain's defeat in the French and Indian War
    c. The stationing of British soldiers in colonists' homes
    d. Changes in class relations

3. The election of a presidential candidate from which party led to the Civil War?
    a. Democrat
    b. Whig
    c. Republican
    d. Federalist

4. Which of the following was NOT an important invention in the twentieth century?
    a. Airplanes
    b. Telegraph
    c. Television
    d. Computers

5. Which of the following sets comprises a primary cause and effect of the American Revolution?
    a. A cause was the taxation of the colonies, and an effect was the civil rights movement.
    b. A cause was the Declaration of Independence, and an effect was the Constitution.
    c. A cause was the French and Indian War, and an effect was the Bill of Rights.
    d. A cause was the debate over slavery, and an effect was the Seven Years' War.

6. What are the two main parts of the federal legislative branch?
    a. President and vice president
    b. Federal and state
    c. District court and court of appeals
    d. Senate and House of Representatives

7. What was a concern that George Washington warned of in his Farewell Address?
    a. The danger of political parties
    b. To be prepared to intervene in Europe's affairs
    c. The abolition of slavery
    d. To protect states' rights through sectionalism

8. What is NOT a responsibility for citizens of democracy?
   a. To stay aware of current issues and history
   b. To avoid political action
   c. To actively vote in elections
   d. To understand and obey laws

9. Which of the following statements is true?
   a. Times zones are defined by their latitude.
   b. Eastern and Western hemispheres are defined by the prime meridian.
   c. A place is constant, while a location is changeable with the movement of people.
   d. A continent is one of six especially large landmasses in the world.

10. Which of the following statements is true?
    a. Water usage has largely shifted from appropriation to riparian.
    b. Native Americans lived in harmony with nature by never disrupting it.
    c. Cities are fully isolated environments.
    d. Invasive species can have catastrophic impacts on ecosystems.

11. Which of the following are reasons that geography is important to the examination of history?
    I. Historians make use of maps in their studies to get a clear picture of how history unfolded.
    II. Knowing the borders of different lands helps historians learn different cultures' interactions.
    III. Geography is closely linked with the flow of resources, technology, and population in societies.
    IV. Environmental factors, such as access to water and proximity of mountains, help shape the course of civilization.

    a. I, II, and III only
    b. II, III, and IV only
    c. I, II, and IV only
    d. I, III, and IV only

12. Which of the following statements is true?
    a. All Native American tribes are matrilineal.
    b. Japan is struggling to manage its high birthrate.
    c. Shi'a Muslims traditionally follow imams.
    d. Mexico's culture is deeply tied to its Protestant roots.

13. Which of the following advancements was NOT invented by Greek culture?
    a. The alphabet
    b. The Hippocratic Oath
    c. Democratic government
    d. Theater

14. Which of the following was an important development in the twentieth century?
    a. The United States and the Soviet Union officially declared war on each other in the Cold War.
    b. The League of Nations signed the Kyoto Protocol.
    c. World War I ended when the United States defeated Japan.
    d. India violently partitioned into India and Pakistan after the end of colonialism.

15. Which of the following is NOT an example of cross-cultural interactions?
    a. Egyptian and Mayan pyramids
    b. The Spanish language
    c. Styles of sushi
    d. Study of Chinese culture

16. Which of the following is true?
    a. The barter system no longer exists.
    b. Economic resources can be divided into four categories: natural, capital, manufactured, and nonrenewable.
    c. Individuals help to determine the scarcity of items through their choices.
    d. According to the law of supply, as the price of a product increases, the supply of the product will decrease.

17. What is NOT an effect of monopolies?
    a. Promote a diverse variety of independent businesses
    b. Inhibit developments that would be problematic for business
    c. Control the supply of resources
    d. Limit the degree of choice for consumers

18. Which method is NOT a way that governments manage economies in a market system?
    a. Laissez-faire
    b. Absolute Monarchy
    c. Capitalism
    d. Self-interest

19. Which of the following nations did NOT establish colonies in what would become the United States?
    a. Italy
    b. England
    c. France
    d. Spain

20. Which of the following statements about the U.S. Constitution is true?
    a. It was signed on July 4, 1776.
    b. It was enacted at the end of the Revolutionary War.
    c. New York failed to ratify it, but it still passed by majority.
    d. It replaced the Articles of Confederation.

21. Which of the following locations was NOT subjected to American imperialism?
    a. Philippines
    b. Puerto Rico
    c. Canada
    d. Guam

22. What is a power that Congress has?
    a. To appoint the cabinet
    b. Right of nullification
    c. To impeach the president
    d. To interpret laws through courts

23. Which of the following is true?
   a. The Emancipation Proclamation ended slavery in the United States.
   b. President Wilson called for the foundation of the United Nations in his Fourteen Points.
   c. The Constitution of 1787 and the Bill of Rights were ratified simultaneously.
   d. The Declaration of Independence was primarily concerned with the colonists' complaints against King George III.

24. *The entire Roman Empire was destroyed in the fifth century A.D.* Is this statement true or false?
   a. True; it was conquered by barbarians in that era.
   b. True; it was destroyed by a civil war during that time period.
   c. False; the western half survived as the Holy Roman Empire.
   d. False; the eastern half, known as the Byzantine Empire, survived until 1453 A.D.

25. Which of the statements about the United Nations is false?
   a. It ensured the continuance of an alliance between the United States and Soviet Union.
   b. It was based on the idea for the League of Nations.
   c. It helps to promote human rights.
   d. It includes many former colonies from around the world.

# Answer Explanations

**1. A:** Carolina is divided into two separate states—North and South. Maine was part of Nova Scotia and did not become an American territory until the War of 1812. Likewise, Vermont was not one of the original Thirteen Colonies. Canada remained a separate British colony. Finally, Florida was a Spanish territory. Therefore, by process of elimination, *A* is the correct list.

**2. B:** Britain was not defeated in the French and Indian War, and, in fact, disputes with the colonies over the new territories it won contributed to the growing tensions. All of the other options were key motivations behind the Revolutionary War.

**3. C:** Abraham Lincoln was elected president as part of the new Republican Party, and his plans to limit and potentially abolish slavery led the southern states to secede from the Union.

**4. B:** Out of the four inventions mentioned, the first telegraphs were invented in the 1830s, not in the twentieth century. In contrast, the other inventions had considerable influence over the course of the twentieth century.

**5. C:** The Declaration of Independence occurred during the American Revolution, so it should therefore be considered an effect, not a cause. Similarly, slavery was a cause for the later Civil War, but it was not a primary instigator for the Revolutionary War. Although a single event can have many effects long into the future, it is also important to not overstate the influence of these individual causes; the civil rights movement was only tangentially connected to the War of Independence among many other factors, and therefore it should not be considered a primary effect of it. The French and Indian War (which was part of the Seven Years' War) and the Bill of Rights, on the other hand, were respectively a cause and effect from the American Revolution, making Choice *C* the correct answer.

**6. D:** The president and vice president are part of the executive branch, not the legislative branch. The question focuses specifically on the federal level, so state government should be excluded from consideration. As for the district court and the court of appeals, they are part of the judicial branch. The legislative branch is made up of Congress, which consists of the House of Representatives and the Senate.

**7. A:** George Washington was a slave owner himself in life, so he did not make abolition a theme in his Farewell Address. On the other hand, he was concerned that sectionalism could potentially destroy the United States, and he warned against it. Furthermore, he believed that Americans should avoid getting involved in European affairs. However, one issue that he felt was especially problematic was the formation of political parties, and he urged against it in his farewell.

**8. B:** To avoid involvement in political processes such as voting is antithetical to the principles of a democracy. Therefore, the principal responsibility of citizens is the opposite, and they should be steadily engaged in the political processes that determine the course of government.

**9. B:** Time zones are determined by longitude, not latitude. Locations are defined in absolute terms, while places are in part defined by the population, which is subject to movement. There are seven continents in the world, not six. On the other hand, it is true that the prime meridian determines the border for the Eastern and Western hemispheres.

**10. D:** Riparian water usage was common in the past, but modern usage has shifted to appropriation. While often practicing sustainable methods, Native Americans used fire, agriculture, and other tools to shape the landscape for their own ends. Due to the importance of trade in providing essential resources to cities, a city is never truly separated from the outside world. However, invasive species are a formidable threat to native environments, making *D* the correct answer.

**11. C:** I, II, and IV only. Historians make use of maps in their studies to get a clear picture of how history unfolded, knowing the borders of different lands helps historians learn different cultures' interactions, and environmental factors, such as access to water and the proximity of mountains, help determine the course of civilization. The phrase "Geography is closely linked with the flow of resources, technology, and population in societies" is a characteristic of economics.

**12. C:** While many Native American tribes are matrilineal, not all of them are. Japan is currently coping with an especially low birthrate, not a high one. Mexico's religion, like that of Spain, is primarily Roman Catholic rather than Protestant. On the other hand, Shi'a Islam is based on the view that imams should be honored as Muhammad's chosen heirs to the Caliphate, making *C* correct.

**13. A:** Although Greeks used the alphabet as the basis for their written language, leading to a diverse array of literature, they learned about the alphabet from Phoenician traders. All the other options, in contrast, were invented in Greece.

**14. D:** It is important to realize that the Cold War was never an official war and that the United States and the Soviet Union instead funded proxy conflicts. The Kyoto Protocol was signed by members of the United Nations, as the League of Nations was long since defunct. While Japan was a minor participant in World War I, it was not defeated by America until World War II. The correct answer is *D*: India's partition between Hindu India and Islamic Pakistan led to large outbreaks of religious violence.

**15. A:** Although Egyptian and Mayan civilizations are an interesting subject for comparisons, the two cultures never interacted. The other answers are all examples of interactions between different cultures; a study of Chinese culture, for instance, would require examination of the multiple ethnic groups throughout China.

**16. C:** Although monetary systems were invented to solve problems with barter systems, it is wrong to assume that barter systems have ceased to exist; bartering remains a common practice throughout the world, albeit less common than money. The four main categories for economic resources are land, labor, capital, and entrepreneurship. The law of supply says that supplies will increase, not decrease, as prices increase. The correct answer is *C,* as scarcity is determined by human choice.

**17. A:** Rather than competition, a monopoly prevents other businesses from offering a certain product or service to consumers.

**18. B:** Absolute monarchies often use command system economies, but they do not represent a way that governments manage economies. Laissez-faire, capitalism, and self-interest, in contrast, are all fundamental concepts behind the market system.

**19. A:** England, France, and Spain all established North American colonies that would later be absorbed into the United States, but Italy, despite Christopher Columbus' role as an explorer, never established a colony in America.

**20. D:** The Constitution was signed in 1787; the Declaration of Independence was signed in 1776. It was successfully ratified by all the current states, including New York. Finally, the Articles of Confederation was established at the end of the American Revolution; the Constitution would replace the articles years later due to issues with the government's structure.

**21. C:** Although American forces made several early attempts to take Canada from Britain, the United States was never able to successfully seize this territory. On the other hand, the United States did control the Philippines, Puerto Rico, and Guam.

**22. C:** The executive branch determines the cabinet, while the judicial branch has the responsibility of interpreting the Constitution and laws. Even so, the legislative branch can check the president's power by impeaching him.

**23. D:** The Emancipation Proclamation only freed slaves in Confederate-held territories; southern states still loyal to the Union kept their slaves for the time being. Although Wilson succeeded in instituting the League of Nations, the United Nations would not emerge until decades later. The Bill of Rights was ratified after the Constitution to provide additional protection for individual liberties. However, it is true that the main body of the Declaration of Independence consisted of grievances that the colonies had against British rule.

**24. D:** While it is true that Rome fell to barbarians in the fifth century A.D., it would be inaccurate to say the Roman Empire had been completely destroyed. The Byzantine Empire considered itself the heir of the Roman Empire. The western sections, on the other hand, certainly collapsed; the later Holy Roman Empire tried to draw on Rome's past glory but was not a true successor.

**25. A:** Based on the prior League of Nations, the United Nations included many nations in postcolonial Africa and Asia and worked to support human rights. However, it failed to maintain the World War II alliance between the United States and the Soviet Union, leading to the unofficial Cold War.

# Science

## *Life Science*

### Prokaryotes, Viruses, and Eukaryotes

Every living organism is made up of cells, and these cells come in various shapes and sizes, depending on the organism. There are two types of cells: prokaryotes and eukaryotes. The big difference between them is that eukaryotes have a nucleus and prokaryotes do not. The structures that will be focused on for this section will be:

| Bacteria | Protist, Fungus, Plant, Animal |
|---|---|
| DNA<br>Ribosomes<br>Cytoplasm<br>Cell Membrane<br>Cell Wall | DNA<br>Ribosomes<br>Cytoplasm<br>Cell Membrane<br>Cell Wall (except animal cells)<br>Unique structures<br>Nucleus<br>Mitochondria<br>Chloroplasts (only autotrophs, or organisms that can produce their own food. Only protists and plants are producers). |

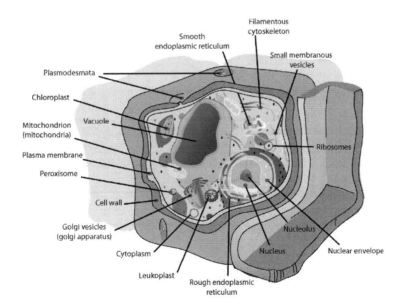

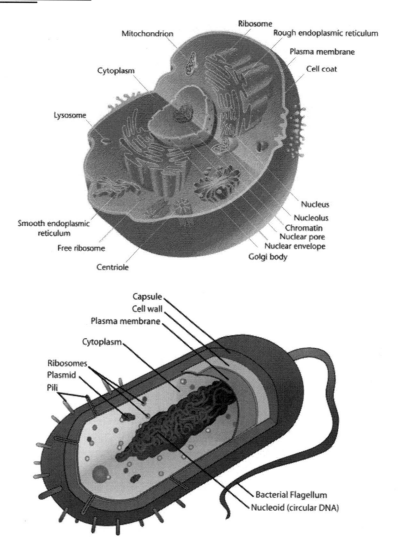

Like all cells, bacterial cells contain DNA, the genetic material that gives instructions for every single structure and process that the cell undergoes. DNA is a code made up of four letters: A (adenine), T (thymine), G (guanine), and C (cytosine). There are billions of these letters in DNA, and the order of these letters tells a cell exactly what to do and how to do it (just like reading a book of instructions).

Because DNA doesn't do anything on its own, all cells must have a means of decoding DNA and turning it into the structure, which is the function of ribosomes—they are protein-makers. If DNA is like a recipe, then the ribosomes are like the chef.

DNA and ribosomes sit in a fluid called cytoplasm, which contains a cytoskeleton (a network of proteins) that holds them in place. All cells need a covering to contain everything inside—these are called cell membranes in animals or cell walls for plant cells.

Bacteria can also have a capsule and a flagellum, which are all external structures. A capsule is sticky and causes bacteria to cluster with other cells or on food. Only about 50 percent of bacteria can move, and those that do often have a flagellum, which is a whip-like structure like a tadpole's tail.

Viruses are commonly thought of as living organisms, but many scientists argue they aren't for two reasons: (1) they are not cells, and (2) they cannot reproduce by themselves. Both qualities are required

for an organism to be considered alive. Viruses are unique in that they require a host in order to make proteins and reproduce, because viruses don't have all of the complex tools of a living cell. When a virus has infected a host, it acts like a living organism—it moves and reproduces—but outside of a host, it does nothing. A virus can survive outside of a host, but it cannot reproduce. Scientists are still trying to properly define a virus, so we can currently say that viruses are not like bacteria or any other living thing.

Eukaryotic cells are more complex than prokaryotic cells. They make up all the organisms in the kingdoms protist, fungus, plant, and animal. Eukaryotic cells are also larger than prokaryotes and contain a nucleus and other organelles.

Eukaryotic cells hold their DNA inside a nucleus in pieces called chromosomes. Chromosomes are a cell's way of organizing long strands of DNA in twisted-up bundles. Imagine a room filled with rolls of toilet paper compared to a room that has all of those rolls unraveled and thrown everywhere; it would be a mess!

Other important organelles include chloroplasts and mitochondria. Chloroplasts can be found in cells called autotrophs, which can convert sunlight into energy. Plants are autotrophs. Mitochondria are little energy factories found in almost every type of cell. They use chemical reactions to make little packets of energy that can be used by other parts of the cell.

## Energy

Energy is everywhere and is one of the few things in the universe believed to be constant. That means that in the whole universe, if all the energy could be measured (energy in all the stars, atoms, etc.), the amount of energy that was present at the beginning of time is exactly the same as it is now. The only difference is that energy has been converted into different forms. For example, a plant gets its energy from the Sun, using it to grow bigger and stronger; therefore, the Sun's energy is converted and stored inside the plant. Then a person eats the plant, using its stored energy. In this example, energy exists in the form of light, growth, and movement (picking the plant and chewing it).

Only with the energy food provides can organisms exist. Think of a construction team and a pile of bricks and mortar. The bricks are not going to just arrange themselves into a building. However, if a construction team uses their muscles and energy, the complex building can be built. If the construction team runs out of food, though, they will become exhausted and will be unable to construct the building.

The human body is the same way. Organs (heart, brain, stomach, etc.) are like the bricks. The chemical reactions in the body are like the workers. Energy is the food that the workers need to build the organism. The food of life is sugar, specifically glucose. A candy bar, soda, or a slice of birthday cake can provide a boost of energy because of all the sugar they contain. There are many bonds between the molecules of sugar, holding them in place (like the mortar holding the bricks in a building). When the bonds are broken in digestion, all that energy is released so that living things can invest that energy into chemical reactions.

Two chemical reactions are critical for living things: photosynthesis and respiration.

## Photosynthesis in the Chloroplast Provides Energy

Any producer must have a chloroplast in order to convert light energy into food, usually in the form of a carbohydrate. Chloroplasts are organelles that look like little green beans because they contain the pigment chlorophyll, which is able to absorb the sunlight's energy in the form of photons, or light rays. Some prokaryotes are also photosynthetic, and although they don't have a chloroplast because they're too simple and don't contain organelles, they have a pigment in order to make their own food.

Plants need water and sunlight to live. Plants suck up water from their roots. The sunlight they need is absorbed by the chlorophyll in chloroplasts, which are clustered and concentrated in their leaves. Interestingly, the chlorophyll actually is able to absorb every color of light except for green, which is why leaves look green: they reflect green light. If the roots take in water and the leaves take in carbon dioxide and sunlight energy, why are stems important? The stems in plants are an example of how structure helps function. The stem is like a skeleton for plants; it holds the leaves high so they can be closer to the sun.

Plants are critical for life on earth because they absorb the energy from the sun and invest it in the bonds that make sugar. Sugar passes through the food chain to provide energy for all living organisms. Plants and other autotrophs can make their own energy, while heterotrophs (which cannot make their own energy) consume the sugar, break it down, and convert it into usable energy with their mitochondria.

## Cellular Respiration in the Mitochondria

The glucose that provides energy does nothing by itself; it is the bonds between atoms holding these complex glucose molecules together that hold the energy. When the molecule is intact, the bonds between them hold energy in the form of potential energy. When the bonds are broken, that potential energy is released and becomes available to the workers in the cell to perform chemical reactions.

The process of cellular respiration breaks the bonds in an organelle called the mitochondria in eukaryotes (protists, fungi, plants, animals).

Note that the equation for cellular respiration is the almost exact opposite of photosynthesis:

$$C_6H_{12}O_6 + 6O_2 \rightarrow 6CO_2 + 6H_2O + 36ATP$$

The only difference between the above equation and photosynthesis is the new product: ATP. ATP is a conversion of light energy into usable pockets of energy that provide energy to all the workers in cells that do the chemical reactions. While glucose is like a $100 bill with lots of energy in its bonds, ATP is like one hundred $1 bills that can be invested here and there as needed.

Bacteria do not have mitochondria, so they perform different reactions in their cytoplasm that produce much less energy (2ATP).

## Organisms Need Food for More than Just Energy

When we eat a hamburger, we're eating more than carbohydrates; we're also eating proteins and fats. Plants provide more than just carbohydrates when we eat them; they also are able to use the light energy to make proteins, fats, and, of course, their DNA, because if they didn't have DNA, they'd have no instructions to grow.

The following organic compounds and their atoms don't magically appear in organisms—life has to either grab the nutrients from soil or seeds or eat them.

- Carbohydrates, proteins, fats, and DNA/RNA have carbon, hydrogen, and oxygen
- DNA, proteins, and fats also have phosphorous
- DNA and proteins also have nitrogen
- Proteins also can have sulfur

Plants need all of these elements to make food. Where do they get them? Remember that earth's atmosphere is a conglomerate of different gases, including nitrogen. Bacteria in the soil are able to convert that nitrogen into a usable form, and the roots of plants absorb the critical nitrogen. Carbon and oxygen get into the plant via photosynthesis (carbon dioxide), as does the element hydrogen, because plants take in water, which contains hydrogen. Phosphorous and sulfur are absorbed in plants through soil. Since heterotrophs cannot make their own food, they have to eat an autotroph (or eat something that ate an autotroph) in order to obtain these critical elements.

Cycles are a recurring pattern in science, and making food is no exception. When living things die, fungi and bacteria act as decomposers and break down the material. That's actually why dead things and rotten meat smell bad; the decomposers have broken them down so much that gases containing carbon, oxygen, phosphorous, nitrogen, and even smelly sulfur are released. Remember that sulfur is heavy in protein, and eggs are protein-rich. It makes sense that rotten eggs have an unpleasant smell as they release sulfur because they're mostly protein. Once living things decompose, all the elements eventually recycle back to the atmosphere or to the soil, and the atoms are available to construct molecules once again.

## Diversity of Life

Due to the speciation that has occurred, the variety of organisms is astronomical. Scientists have identified about 2 million species, and they suspect that there are at least 8 million others out there.

A man named Carolus Linnaeus developed a naming system to try to create some order in classifying all species. For example, the classification of humans through the seven levels, from all-inclusive to the most specific, looks like this:

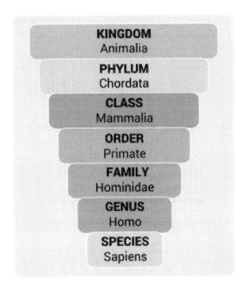

One benefit of this universal naming system is that because some organisms have different common names, like the roly-poly and doodlebug, or the cougar and panther, it allows scientists to have a common language. Due to the sheer magnitude of species, scientists need the seven levels, but when referring to organisms, their official names are just the last two: genus and species. Humans are simply referred to as *Homo sapiens*. This two-name system is called binomial nomenclature.

There are currently six kingdoms, although the prokaryotes (simpler cells) used to be lumped together into one kingdom called Monera. Currently, there are two prokaryotic kingdoms, Archaebacteria and Eubacteria.

## Archaebacteria
Prokaryotes that have a cell membrane made of fats. They live in harsh places including extremely hot areas (volcanic vents or hot springs) and extremely salty locations (Utah's Salt Lake). These are the rarest prokaryotes.

## Eubacteria
Common bacteria that have a cell membrane made of a protein-carbohydrate blend. They make up the vast majority of existing prokaryotes. An example is staphylococcus.

## Protista
This kingdom consists of eukaryotes. Most are unicellular. This kingdom is the most diverse and can be divided into three types: fungus-like (including slime-molds), plant-like (including algae), and animal-like (including amoeba). Some scientists believe that there is so much diversity within the kingdom that they should be split into separate kingdoms, but so far they remain in one group.

Animal-like protists are heterotrophs (they do not make their own food), and plant-like protists are autotrophs (they make their own food). Fungus-like protists are heterotrophs. Like actual fungi, these organisms externally digest their food by acting as parasites and decomposers. Animal-like protists ingest their food via phagocytosis (cell eating) or by absorbing it.

Depending on the particular protists, some produce asexually via mitosis and others reproduce sexually.

## Fungi
Fungi are eukaryotic heterotrophs that digest their food externally. Many of them, including common mushrooms and toadstools, act as decomposers by breaking down dead organisms then absorbing the broken down nutrients. Other fungi accomplish ingestion as parasites feeding off of living organisms, as in the case of a yeast infection. All fungi are multicellular with one exception—yeast. Fungi have cell walls made of a complex carbohydrate called chitin. Most fungi reproduce sexually and asexually.

## Plantae
Plants are multicellular autotrophs like daisies, roses, and pine trees. They are closely related to the aquatic producer, algae, but different in that algae don't contain true roots, stems, or leaves. Plants are photosynthesizers, and their cells have surrounding cell walls made of the starch cellulose.

## Animalia
Animals are multicellular heterotrophs, like fungi, except that animals move and internally ingest their food by consuming it. Animals are the only kingdom to not have cells with cell walls due to their flexibility and ability to move. The animal kingdom is very diverse and includes humans, jellyfish, and spiders, as well as all sorts of other organisms.

## Cellular Organization

Prokaryotes contain ribosomes, DNA, cytoplasm, a cell membrane, a cytoskeleton, and a cell wall. Eukaryotes vary between kingdoms but contain all of these structures except a cell wall because animal cells require so much mobility. Large, land-dwelling animals typically compensate with an exoskeleton (like insects) or an endoskeleton (like humans and other mammals, reptiles, and birds) for structure.

All bacterial cells are unicellular (existing as just one cell). Almost all types of protist and some species in fungi kingdom are unicellular, but they still have the complicated organelles of eukaryotes. A few protists, almost all fungi, and all plants and animals are multicellular. Multicellularity leads to development of structures that are perfectly designed for their function.

Cells combine to form tissue. Tissue combines to form organs. Organs combine to form organ systems, and organ systems combine to form one organism. The structures of all of these combinations allow for the maximum functionality of an organism, as demonstrated by the nervous system.

A neuron is a cell in the nervous system designed to send and receive electrical impulses. Neurons have dendrites, which are sensors waiting to receive a message. Neurons also have an axon, a long arm that sends the message to the neighboring neuron. The axon also has insulation known as myelin that speeds the message along. Many neurons combine to form a nerve, the tissue of the nervous system, which is like a long wire. The structure of this nerve is perfect—it is a long cable whose function is to send signals to the brain so the brain can process the information and respond. Nerve tissue combines with other tissue to form the brain, a complex structure of many parts.

The brain also has glands (epithelial tissue) that release hormones to control processes in our body. The brain and spinal cord together form the central nervous system that controls the stimulus/response signaling in our body. The nervous system coordinates with the circulatory system to make our heart beat, the digestive system to control food digestion, the muscular system to move an arm, the respiratory system to facilitate breathing, and all other body systems to make the entire organism functional. Cells are the basic building block in our bodies, and their structure is critical for their function and the function of the tissues, organs, and systems that they comprise.

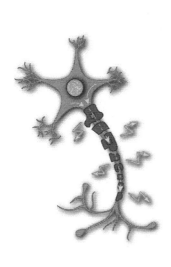
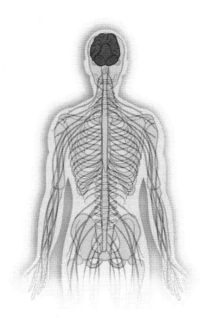

In the graphic above, the left depicts a neuron, and the right depicts the nervous system. A neuron is a nerve cell, and it is the basic building block of the nervous system. Cell, tissue, organ, and organ system structure are critical for function.

The following table lists organ systems in the human body:

| Name | Function | Main organs |
|------|----------|-------------|
| Nervous | Detect stimuli and direct response | Brain and spinal cord |
| Circulatory | Pump blood to deliver oxygen to cells so they can perform cellular respiration | Heart |
| Respiratory | Breathe in oxygen (reactant for cellular respiration) and release carbon dioxide waste | Lungs |
| Muscular | Movement | Heart and muscles |
| Digestive | Break down food so that glucose can be delivered to cells for energy | Stomach, small intestine, lots of others |
| Skeletal | Support and organ protection | All sorts of joints, skull, ribcage |

## Cellular Reproduction

Unlike viruses, all living organisms can independently reproduce, but reproduction occurs differently between bacteria and the more complex kingdoms. Bacteria reproduce via binary fission, which is a simpler process than eukaryotic division because it doesn't involve splitting a nucleus and doesn't have a web of proteins to pull chromosomes apart. Prokaryotes have simpler DNA compared to cells that have

a much larger number of individual chromosomes (humans have two sets of 23 chromosomes—one set from mom and one set from dad, for a total of 46 chromosomes). Think of going from class to class with two identical binders (like bacteria) versus going from class to class with 23 identical pairs of binders (humans); it would be much more difficult to organize the large set of binders than the smaller one.

Binary fission in bacteria is therefore relatively easy. Bacteria copy their DNA in a process called DNA replication, grow, and then the replicated DNA moves to either side, and two new cells are made.

Eukaryotic cell division is part of a well-defined cycle with the following phases:

- G1 phase: The cell is growing and working.

- S phase: The cell is getting too large, so it copies its DNA because it wants to make sure the two new cells have the full instruction manual that is DNA.

- G2 phase: The cell uses its workers to get ready for cell division.

- M phase: Chromosomes condense and line up in the middle of the cell. The copies are sent to either side.

- Cytokinesis: The moment when the cytoplasm is officially split in two, and then two identical daughter cells are produced and enter G1 phase.

The M phase has subdivisions because it quickly goes through a series of events. Each sub-phase of events is described and illustrated below.

| PHASE | PHASE EVENTS | ANIMAL CELL DIAGRAM | PLANT CELL DIAGRAM |
|---|---|---|---|
| **Interphase (G1, S, and G2)** | DNA is loose and spread out and contained in nucleus. This is important because it is actively growing and needs access to its instructions to do chemical reactions correctly. Chromosomes are replicated (copied) in S phase so that they look like an X. Each side of the X has identical DNA. | | |
| **Prophase** | Nucleus disappears and DNA condenses into chromosomes | | |
| **Metaphase** | Chromosomes line up in center and proteins from either side of cell attach to them | | |
| **Anaphase** | Proteins shorten and pull chromosomes apart so that one half (either left side of X or right side of X) of DNA goes to each new cell | | |
| **Telophase and Cytokinesis** | Nuclei reform and chromosomes start to spread out<br>**Animal cells**: cytoplasm to split in half<br>**Plant cells**: cell plate (new cell wall) forms between daughter cells and extends (animal cells don't have a cell wall) | | |

## Organism Reproduction

For bacteria, cell reproduction is the same as organism reproduction; binary fission is an asexual process that produces two new cells that are clones of each other because they have identical DNA.

Eukaryotes are more complex than prokaryotes and can go through sexual reproduction. They produce gametes (sex cells). Females make eggs and males make sperm. The process of making gametes is called meiosis, which is similar to mitosis except for the following differences:

- There are two cellular divisions instead of one.

- Four genetically different haploid daughter cells (one set of chromosomes instead of two) are produced instead of two genetically identical diploid daughter cells.

- A process called crossing over (recombination) occurs, which makes the daughter cells genetically different. If chromosomes didn't cross over and rearrange genes, siblings could be identical clones. There would be no genetic variation, which is a critical factor in the theory of evolution of organisms.

In sexual reproduction, a sperm fertilizes an egg and creates the first cell of a new organism, called the zygote. The zygote will go through countless mitotic divisions over time to create the adult organism.

## Biological Molecules

Repeating units of monomers (small molecules that bond with identical small molecules) that are linked together are called *polymers*. The most important polymers found in all living things can be divided into five categories: nucleic acids (such as DNA), carbohydrates, proteins, lipids, and enzymes. Carbon (C), hydrogen (H), oxygen (O), nitrogen (N), sulfur (S), and phosphorus (P) are the major elements of most biological molecules. Carbon is a common backbone of large molecules because of its ability to bond to four different atoms.

### DNA and RNA

*Nucleotides* consist of a five-carbon sugar, a nitrogen-containing base, and one or more phosphate groups. *Deoxyribonucleic acid (DNA)* is made up of two strands of nucleotides coiled together in a double-helix structure. It plays a major role in enabling living organisms to pass their genetic information and complex components on to subsequent generations. There are four nitrogenous bases that make up DNA: adenine, thymine, guanine, and cytosine. Adenine always pairs with thymine, and guanine always

pairs with cytosine. *Ribonucleic acid (RNA)* is often made up of only one strand of nucleotides folded in on itself. Like DNA, RNA has four nitrogenous bases; however, in RNA, thymine is replaced by uracil.

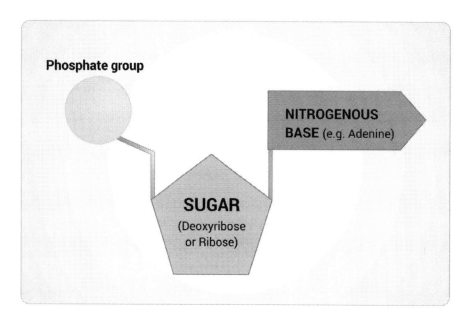

## Carbohydrates

*Carbohydrates* consist of sugars and polymers of sugars, such as starches, which make up the cell walls of plants. The simplest sugar is called a *monosaccharide* and has the molecular formula of $CH_2O$, or a multiple of that formula. Monosaccharides are important molecules for cellular respiration. Their carbon skeleton can also be used to rebuild new small molecules. *Polysaccharides* are made up of a few hundred to a few thousand monosaccharides linked together.

## Proteins

*Proteins* are essential for almost all functions in living beings. All proteins are made from a set of twenty *amino acids* that are linked in *unbranched polymers*. The amino acids are linked by *peptide bonds*, and polymers of amino acids are called *polypeptides*. These polypeptides, either individually or in linked combination with each other, fold up and form coils of biologically functional molecules.

There are four levels of protein structure: primary, secondary, tertiary, and quaternary. The *primary structure* is the sequence of amino acids, similar to the letters in a long word. The *secondary structure* comprises the folds and coils that are formed by hydrogen bonding between the slightly charged atoms of the polypeptide backbone. *Tertiary structure* is the overall shape of the molecule that results from the interactions between the side chains that are linked to the polypeptide backbone. *Quaternary structure*

is the overall protein structure that occurs when a protein is made up of two or more polypeptide chains.

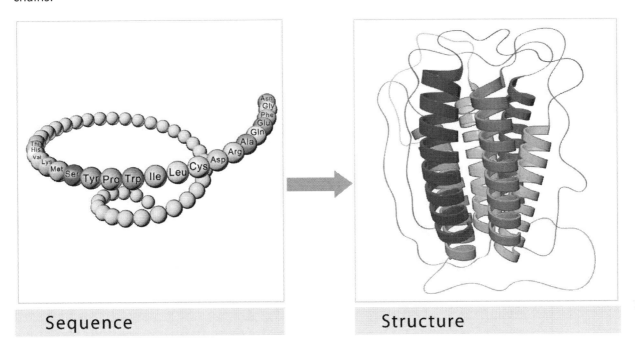

## Lipids

*Lipids* are a class of biological molecules that are *hydrophobic*, which means that they do not mix well with water. They are mostly made up of large chains of carbon and hydrogen atoms, termed *hydrocarbon chains*. The three most important types of lipids are fats, phospholipids, and steroids.

*Fats* are made up of two types of smaller molecules: three fatty acids and one glycerol molecule. Saturated fats do not have double bonds between the carbons in the fatty acid chain, such as glycerol, pictured below. They are fairly straight molecules and can pack together closely, so they form solids at room temperature. Unsaturated fats have one or more double bonds between carbons in the fatty acid chain. Since they cannot pack together as tightly as saturated fats, they take up more space and are called oils. They remain liquid at room temperature.

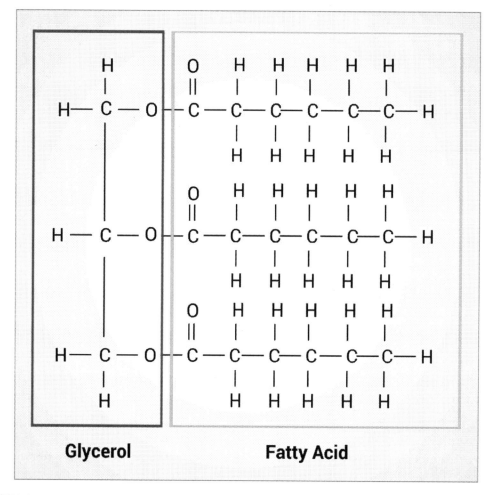

**Glycerol**  **Fatty Acid**

*Phospholipids* are made up of two fatty acid molecules linked to one glycerol molecule. When phospholipids are mixed with water, they inherently create double-layered structures, called *bilayers*, which shield their hydrophobic regions from the water molecules.

*Steroids* are lipids that consist of four fused carbon rings. They can mix in between the phospholipid bilayer cell membrane and help maintain its structure, as well as aid in cell signaling.

## Enzymes

*Enzymes* are biological molecules that accelerate the rate of chemical reactions by lowering the activation energy needed to make the reaction proceed. Although most enzymes can be classified as proteins, some are ribonucleic acid (RNA) molecules. Enzymes function by interacting with a specific substrate in order to create a different molecule, or product. Most reactions in cells need enzymes to make them occur at rates fast enough to sustain life.

## Structure and Function of DNA and RNA

DNA and RNA are made up of *nucleotides*, which are formed from a five-carbon sugar, a nitrogenous base, and one or more phosphate group. While DNA is made up of the sugar deoxyribose, RNA is made up of the sugar ribose. Deoxyribose has one fewer oxygen atom than ribose. DNA and RNA each

comprise four nitrogenous bases, three of which they have in common: adenine, guanine, and cytosine. Thymine is found only in DNA and uracil is found only in RNA. Each base has a specific pairing formed by hydrogen bonds, and is known as a *base pair*. Adenine interacts with thymine or uracil, and guanine interacts only with cytosine. While RNA is found in a single strand, DNA is a double-stranded molecule that coils up to form a *double helix* structure.

The specific pairing of the nitrogenous bases allows for the hereditary information stored in DNA to be passed down accurately from parent cells to daughter cells. When chromosomes are *replicated* during cell division, the double-helix DNA is first uncoiled, each strand is replicated, and then two new identical DNA molecules are generated. DNA can also be used as a template for generating proteins. A *single-stranded* RNA is generated from the DNA during a process called *transcription*; proteins are then generated from this RNA in a process called *translation*.

## Chromosomes, Genes, Alleles

*Chromosomes* are found inside the nucleus of cells and contain the hereditary information of the cell in the form of *genes*. Each gene has a specific sequence of DNA that eventually encodes proteins and results in inherited traits. *Alleles* are variations of a specific gene that occur at the same location on the chromosome. For example, blue and brown are two different alleles of the gene that encodes for eye color.

## Dominant and Recessive Traits

In genetics, *dominant alleles* are mostly noted in capital letters (A) and *recessive alleles* are mostly noted in lower case letters (a). There are three possible combinations of alleles among dominant and recessive alleles: AA, Aa (known as a heterozygote), and aa. Dominant traits are phenotypes that appear when at least one dominant allele is present in the gene. Dominant alleles are considered to have stronger phenotypes and, when mixed with recessive alleles, will mask the recessive trait. The recessive trait would only appear as the phenotype when the allele combination is "aa" because a dominant allele is not present to mask it.

## Mendelian Inheritance

A monk named Gregor Mendel is referred to as the father of genetics. He was responsible for coming up with one of the first models of inheritance in the 1860s. His model included two laws to determine which traits are inherited. These laws still apply today, even after genetics has been studied much more in depth.

- *The Law of Segregation*: Each characteristic has two versions that can be inherited. When two parent cells form daughter cells, the two alleles of the gene segregate and each daughter cell can inherit only one of the alleles from each parent.

- *The Law of Independent Assortment*: The alleles for different traits are inherited independent of one another. In other words, the biological selection of one allele by a daughter cell is not linked to the biological selection of an allele for a different trait by the same daughter cell. The genotype that is inherited is the alleles that are encoded on the gene, and the phenotype is the outward appearance of the physical trait for that gene. For example, "A" is the dominant allele for brown eyes and "a" is the recessive allele for blue eyes; the phenotype of brown eyes would occur for two different genotypes: both "AA" and "Aa."

## Punnett Squares

For simple genetic combinations, a *Punnett square* can be used to assess the phenotypic ratios of subsequent generations. In a 2 x 2 cell square, one parent's alleles are set up in columns and the other parent's alleles are set up in rows. The resulting allele combinations are shown in the four internal cells.

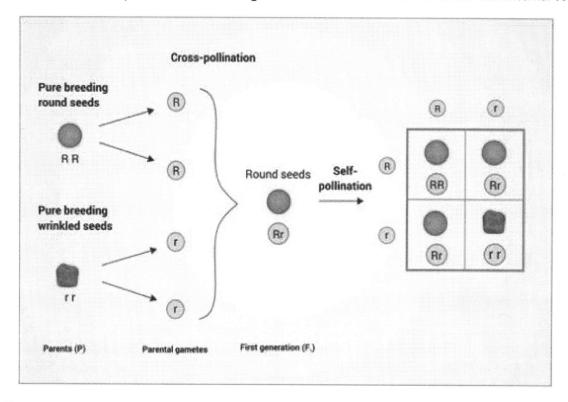

## Pedigree

For existing populations where genetic crosses cannot be controlled, phenotype information can be collected over several generations and a *pedigree analysis* can be done to investigate the dominant and recessive characteristics of specific traits. There are several rules to follow when determining the pedigree of a trait. For dominant alleles:

- Affected individuals have at least one affected parent;
- The phenotype appears in every generation; and
- If both parents are unaffected, their offspring will always be unaffected.

For recessive alleles:

- Unaffected parents can have affected offspring; and
- Affected offspring are male and female.

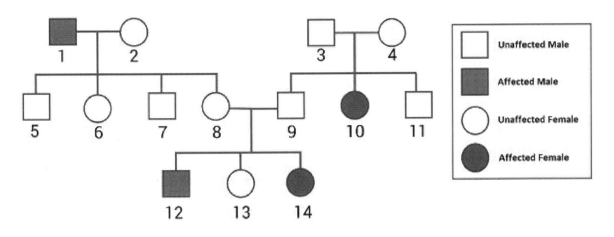

## Mutations, Chromosomal Abnormalities, and Common Genetic Disorders

### Mutations

Genetic *mutations* occur when there is a permanent alteration in the DNA sequence that codes for a specific gene. They can be small, affecting only one base pair, or large, affecting many genes on a chromosome. Mutations are classified as either hereditary, which means they were also present in the parent gene, or acquired, which means that they occurred after the genes were passed down from the parents. Although mutations are not common, they are an important aspect of genetics and variation in the general population.

### Chromosomal Abnormalities and Common Genetic Disorders

*Structural chromosomal abnormalities* are mutations that affect a large chromosomal segment of more than one gene. This often occurs due to an error in cell division. Acute myelogenous leukemia is caused by a *translocation error*, which is when a segment of one chromosome is moved to another chromosome.

There can also be an abnormal number of chromosomes, which is referred to as *aneuploidy*. Down syndrome is an example of an aneuploidy in which there are three copies of chromosome 21 instead of two copies. Turner syndrome is another example of aneuploidy, in which a female is completely or partially missing an X chromosome. Without the second X chromosome, these females do not develop all of the typical female physical characteristics and are unable to bear children.

## Mechanisms of Evolution

*Evolution* is the concept that there is one common ancestor for all living organisms, and, over time, genetic variation and mutations cause the development of different species. Charles Darwin came up with a scientific model of evolution based on the idea that individuals within a population can have longer lives (better survival) and higher reproduction rates based on certain specific traits that they have inherited, called *natural selection*. The variation of a trait that enhances survival and reproduction in the environment is the one that gets passed on. The survival and inheritance of these traits through many subsequent generations causes a change in the overall population. The traits that are more advantageous for survival and reproduction become more common in subsequent generations and increase the diversity of the population. For example, when there was a drought in the Galapagos Islands, the finches with large beaks became more populous because they were able to survive on the larger, rougher seeds that were remaining.

## Speciation and Isolation Methods

*Speciation* is the method by which one species splits into two or more species due to either geographic separation, called allopatric speciation, or a reduction in gene flow between varying members of the population, called sympatric speciation. In *allopatric speciation*, one population is divided into two subpopulations. For example, if a drought occurs and a large lake becomes divided into two smaller lakes, each lake is left with its own population that cannot intermingle with the population of the other lake. When the genes of these two subpopulations are no longer mixing with each other, new mutations can arise and natural selection can take place.

In *sympatric speciation*, gene flow in the population is reduced by polyploidy, sexual selection, and habitat differentiation. *Polyploidy* is more common in plants than animals and results when cell division during reproduction creates an extra set of chromosomes. In *sexual selection*, organisms of one sex choose their mate of the opposite sex based on certain traits. If there is high selection for two extreme variations of a trait, sympatric speciation may occur. *Habitat differentiation* occurs when a subpopulation exploits a resource that is not used by the parent population. Both allopatric and sympatric speciation can occur quickly or slowly, and may involve just a few gene changes or many gene changes between the new species.

One important distinguishing factor in the formation of two species is their *reproductive isolation*. Species are characterized by their members' ability to breed and produce viable offspring. When speciation occurs and new species are formed, there must have been a biological barrier that prevented the two species from producing viable offspring.

Following speciation, there are two types of *reproductive barriers* that keep the two populations from mating with each other. These are classified as either prezygotic barriers or postzygotic barriers. *Prezygotic barriers* prevent fertilization via habitat isolation, temporal isolation, and behavioral isolation. Through habitat isolation, two species may inhabit the same area but don't often encounter each other. *Temporal isolation* is when species breed at different times of the day, during different seasons, or during different years, so their mating patterns never coincide. *Behavioral isolation* refers to mating rituals that prevent an organism from recognizing a different species as potential mate.

Other prezygotic barriers block fertilization after a mating attempt. *Mechanical isolation* occurs when anatomical differences prevent fertilization. *Gametic isolation* occurs when the gametes of two species are incompatible.

## Supporting Evidence

### The Fossil Record
*Fossils* are the preserved remains of animals and organisms from the distant past. They provide evidence of evolution and can elucidate the homology of both living and extinct species. Looking at the *fossil*

*record* over time can help identify how quickly or slowly evolutionary changes occurred, and can also help match those changes to environmental changes that were occurring concurrently.

## Comparative Genetics

In *comparative genetics*, different organisms are compared at a genetic level to look for similarities and differences. DNA sequence, genes, gene order, and other structural features are among the features that may be analyzed in order to look for evolutionary relationships and common ancestors between the organisms. Comparative genetics was useful in elucidating the similarities between humans and chimpanzees and linking their evolutionary history.

## Homology

Organisms that developed from a common ancestor often have similar characteristics that function differently. This similarity is known as *homology*. For example, humans, cats, whales, and bats all have bones arranged in the same manner from their shoulders to their digits. However, the bones form arms in humans, forelegs in cats, flippers in whales, and wings in bats, and these forelimbs are used for lifting, walking, swimming, and flying, respectively. The similarity of the bone structure shows a common ancestry, but the functional differences are the product of evolution.

## Homologous Structures

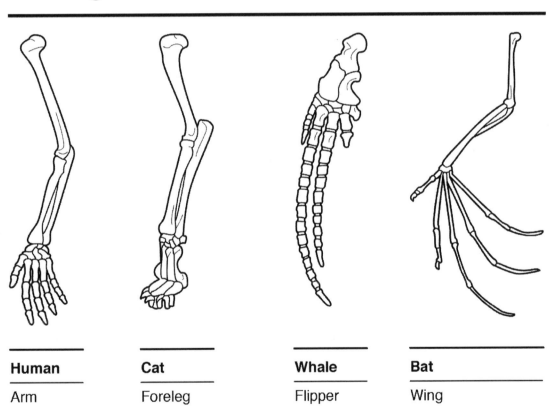

| Human | Cat | Whale | Bat |
| Arm | Foreleg | Flipper | Wing |

## Interdependence of Organisms

The biosphere has layers and layers of complexity:

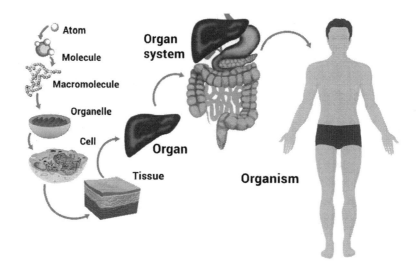

All organisms work together so that life can exist. An organism represents one of a species, like the fish below, and all organisms serve a particular function. The fish's niche is to eat aquatic producers and excrete waste that acts as fertilizer.

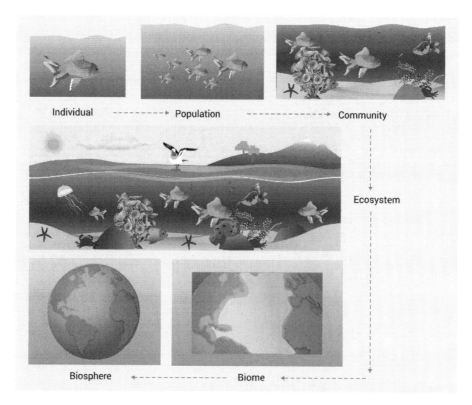

This fish is just one organism within a population. A population represents multiple individuals living in the same habitat. The community includes every biotic factor (living organism) within an ecosystem, in this case, the fish, jellyfish, algae, crab, bacteria, etc. An ecosystem includes all the biotic factors as well as the abiotic, which includes anything non-living—for the fish, that's a rock, a shipwreck, and a nearby

glacier. For biomes, add weather and climate into the mix. The biosphere is all of Earth, which is the combination of all biomes.

We already discussed that producers (plants, protists, and even some bacteria) photosynthesize and make the food that provides energy required for all chemical reactions to occur and therefore all life to exist. A non-photosynthesizer must find and eat food, and this feeding relationship can be visualized in food chains. Consider this food chain:

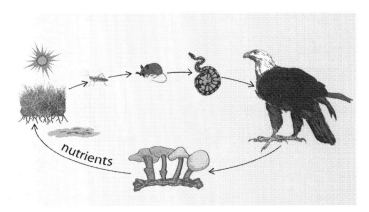

The true source of the energy for every living organism is the sun. Plants absorb the sun's energy to make glucose and are on the first trophic level (feeding level). The grasshopper on the second trophic level is an example of an herbivore and is a primary consumer, as he is the first eater in the food chain. Unfortunately, he receives only 10 percent of the energy that the plant absorbed (this is known as the 10 percent rule) because the other 90 percent of energy was either used by the plant to grow or will be lost as heat. The mouse on the third trophic level is the secondary consumer, or second eater. Food chains are not as inclusive as food webs, which show all feeding relationships in an ecosystem. Looking at this food chain suggests that mice are carnivores (eaters of animals), but mice also eat berries and plants, so they are actually considered omnivores (eaters of both plants and animals). The mouse only gets 10 percent of the energy from the grasshopper, which is actually only 1 percent of the original energy provided by the Sun. The snake on the fourth trophic level is a carnivore, as is the hawk on the highest trophic level.

The arrows in the food chain show the transfer of energy, and fungi as well as bacteria act as decomposers, which break down organic material. Decomposers act at every trophic level because they

feed on all organisms; they are non-discriminating omnivores. Decomposers are critical for life, as they recycle the atoms and building blocks of organisms.

Feeding relationships and predator-prey relationships (hunter-hunted, like the hawk and the rabbit in the food web above) are not the only relationships in an ecosystem. There also can be competition within and between species. For example, in the food chain above, the rabbit and snail both eat grass, showing a relationship called competition, when two organisms want the same thing. Other relationships include symbiotic relationships, which represent two species living together. Symbiosis comes in three varieties:

- Mutualism: an arrangement where both organisms help each other. An example is the relationship between birds and flowers. When birds consume the nectar that the flower produces, pollen rubs on the bird's body so that when it travels to a neighboring plant, it helps with fertilization. The plant helps the bird by providing food, and the bird helps the plant by helping it reproduce. This is a win-win.

- Parasitism: when one organism is hurt while the other is helped. Fleas and dogs are a prime example. Fleas suck the dog's blood, and dogs are itchy and lose blood. This is a win-lose.

- Commensalism: when one organism is helped and the other is neither harmed nor helped. For example, barnacles are crusty little creatures that attach themselves to whales. They don't feed on the whale like a parasite. Instead, they use the whale to give them a free ride so they have access to food. The whales don't care about the barnacles. This is a win-do not care.

## Change Over Time

The theory of natural selection is one of the fundamental tenets of evolution. It affects the phenotype, or visible characteristics, of individuals in a species, which ultimately affects the genotype, or genetic makeup, of those same individuals. Charles Darwin was the first to explain the theory of natural selection, and it is described by Herbert Spencer as favoring survival of the fittest.

Natural selection encompasses three assumptions:

- A species has heritable traits: All traits have some likelihood of being propagated to offspring.

- The traits of a species vary: Some traits are more advantageous than others.

- Individuals of a species are subject to differing rates of reproduction: Some individuals of a species may not get the opportunity to reproduce while others reproduce frequently.

Over time, certain variations in traits may increase both the survival and reproduction of certain individuals within a species. The desirable heritable traits are passed on from generation to generation. Eventually, the desirable traits will become more common and permeate the entire species.

## Adaptation

The theory of *adaptation* is defined as an alteration in a species that causes it to become more well-suited to its environment. It increases the probability of survival, thus increasing the rate of successful reproduction. As a result, an adaptation becomes more common within the population of that species.

For examples, bats use reflected sound waves (echolocation) to prey on insects, and chameleons change colors to blend in with their surroundings to evade detection by its prey and predators. These adaptations are believed to be brought about by natural selection.

*Adaptive radiation* refers to the idea of rapid diversification within a species into an array of unique forms. It's thought to happen as a result of changes in a habitat creating new challenges, ecological niches, or natural resources.

Darwin's finches are often thought of as an example of the theory of adaptive radiation. Charles Darwin documented 13 varieties of finches on the Galapagos Islands. Each island in the chain presented a unique and changing environment, which was believed to cause rapid adaptive radiation among the finches. There was also diversity among finches inhabiting the same island. Darwin believed that as a result of natural selection, each variety of finch developed adaptations to fit into its native environment.

A major difference in Darwin's finches had to do with the size and shapes of beaks. The variation in beaks allowed the finches to access different foods and natural resources, which decreased competition and preserved resources. As a result, various finches of the same species were allowed to coexist, thrive, and diversify. Finches had:

- Short beaks, which were suited for foraging for seeds
- Thin, sharp beaks, which were suited for preying on insects
- Long beaks, which were suited for probing for food inside plants

Darwin believed that the finches on the Galapagos Islands resulted from chance mutations in genes transmitted from generation to generation.

## Life Cycle

Here's a look at the life cycles of many animals.

| | |
|---|---|
| **Chicken** | Hens are female chickens, and they lay about one egg per day. If there is no rooster (male chicken) around to fertilize the egg, the egg never turns into a chick and instead becomes an egg that we can eat.<br><br>If a rooster is around, he mates with the female chicken and fertilizes the egg. Once the egg is fertilized, the tiny little embryo (future chicken) will start as a white dot adjacent to the yolk and albumen (egg white) and will develop for 21 days.<br><br>The mother hen sits on her clutch of eggs (several fertilized eggs) to incubate them and keep them warm. She will turn the eggs to make sure the embryo doesn't stick to one side of the shell. The embryo continues to develop, using the egg white and yolk nutrients, and eventually develops an "egg tooth" on its beak that it uses to crack open the egg and hatch. Before it hatches, it even chirps to let the mom know of its imminent arrival! |
| **Frog** | Frogs mate similar to the way chickens do, and then lay eggs in a very wet area. Sometimes, the parents abandon the eggs and let them develop on their own. The eggs, like chickens', will hatch around 21 days later. Just like chickens, a frog develops from a yolk, but when it hatches, it continues to use the yolk for nutrients.<br><br>A chicken hatches and looks like a cute little chick, but a baby frog is actually a tadpole that is barely developed. It can't even swim around right away, although eventually it will develop gills, a mouth, and a tail.<br><br>After more time, it will develop teeth and tiny legs and continue to change into a fully grown frog! This type of development is called *metamorphosis*. |
| **Fish** | Most fish also lay eggs in the water, but unlike frogs, their swimming sperm externally fertilize the eggs. Like frogs, when fish hatch, they feed on a yolk sac and are called *larvae*. Once the larvae no longer feed on their yolk and can find their own nutrients, they are called fry, which are basically baby fish that grow into adulthood. |
| **Butterfly** | Like frogs, butterflies go through a process called *metamorphosis*, where they completely change into a different looking organism. After the process of mating and internal fertilization, the female finds the perfect spot to lay her eggs, usually a spot with lots of leaves.<br><br>When the babies hatch from the eggs, they are in the larva form, which for butterflies is called a *caterpillar*. The larvae eat and eat and then go through a process like hibernation and form into a *pupa*, or a *cocoon*. When they hatch from the cocoon, the butterflies are in their adult form. |
| **Bugs** | After fertilization, other bugs go through incomplete metamorphosis, which involves three states: eggs that hatch, nymphs that look like little adults without wings and molt their exoskeleton over time, and adults. |

All of these organisms depend on a proper environment for development, and that environment depends on their form. Frogs need water, caterpillars need leaves, and baby chicks need warmth in order to be born.

## Population Dynamics

*Population dynamics* is the study of the composition of populations, including size, age, and the biological and environmental processes that cause changes. These can include immigration, emigration, births, and deaths.

### Growth Curves and Carrying Capacity

Population dynamics can be characterized by *growth curves*. Growth can either be *unrestricted*, which is modeled by an exponential curve, or *restricted*, which is modeled by a logistic curve. Population growth can be restricted by environmental factors such as the availability of food and water sources, habitat, and other necessities. The *carrying capacity* of a population is the maximum population size that an environment can sustain indefinitely, given all of the above factors.

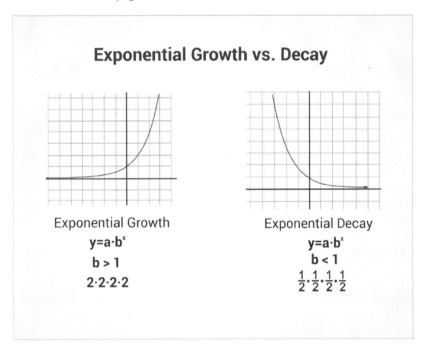

### Behavior

Different species within a population can act differently regarding their environment. Some species display *territoriality*, which is a specific type of competition that excludes other species from a given area. It can be shown through specific animal calls, intimidating behavior, or marking an area with scents, and is often a display of defense.

### Intraspecific Relationships

*Intraspecific relationships* is a term that describes the competition and cooperation between organisms that belong to the same species. They may compete for the same food sources, or for mates that are necessary for their personal survival and reproduction. Stronger organisms may display dominance that allows them to reside at the top of a social hierarchy and obtain better food and higher quality mates.

However, organisms may also cooperate with each other in order to benefit the larger group; for instance, they may divide laborious activities among themselves.

## Community Ecology

An *ecological community* is a group of species that interact and live in the same location. Because of their shared environment, they tend to have a large influence on each other.

### Niche
An *ecological niche* is the role that a species plays in its environment, including how it finds its food and shelter. It could be a predator of a different species, or prey for a larger species.

### Species Diversity
*Species diversity* is the number of different species that cohabitate in an ecological community. It has two different facets: *species richness*, which is the general number of species, and *species evenness*, which accounts for the population size of each species.

### Interspecific Relationships
*Interspecific relationships* include the interactions between organisms of different species. The following list defines the common relationships that can occur:

- *Commensalism*: One organism benefits while the other is neither benefited nor harmed

- *Mutualism*: Both organisms benefit

- *Parasitism*: One organism benefits and the other is harmed

- *Competition*: Two or more species compete for limited resources that are necessary for their survival

*Predation (Predator-Prey)*: One species is a food source for another species

# *Physical, Earth, and Space Sciences*

## Physical and Chemical Properties

In the physical sciences, it is important to break things down to their simplest components in order to truly understand why they act and react the way they do. It may seem burdensome to separate out each part of an object or to diagram each movement made by an object, but these methods provide a solid basis for understanding how to accurately depict the motion of objects and then correctly predict their future movements.

Everything around us is composed of different materials. To properly understand and sort objects, we must classify what types of materials they comprise. This includes identifying the foundational properties of each object such as its reaction to chemicals, heat, water, or other materials. Some objects might not react at all and this is an important property to note. Other properties include the physical appearance of the object or whether it has any magnetic properties. The importance of being able to sort and classify objects is the first step to understanding them.

- Matter: anything that has mass and takes up space

- Substance: a type of matter that cannot be separated out into new material through a physical reaction

- Elements: substances that cannot be broken down by either physical or chemical reactions. Elements are in the most basic form and are grouped by identified properties using the Periodic Table. The periodic table groups elements based on similar properties. Metallic elements, inert elements, and transition elements are a few categories used to organize elements on the periodic table. New elements are added as they are discovered or created, and these newer elements tend to be heavier, fall into the metal section of the periodic table, and are often unstable. Examples of elements include carbon, gold, and helium.

- Atoms: the building blocks of all elements. Atoms are the smallest particles of matter that retain their identities during chemical reactions. Atoms have a central nucleus that includes positively charged protons, and neutrons, which carry no charge. Atoms are also surrounded by electrons that carry a negative charge. The amount of each component determines what type of atom is formed when the components come together. For example, two hydrogen atoms and one oxygen atom can bond together to form water, but the hydrogen and oxygen atoms still remain true to their original identities.

- Mass: the measure of how much of a substance exists in an object. The measure of mass is not the same as weight, area, or volume.

## Physical Properties vs. Chemical Properties

Both physical and chemical properties are used to sort and classify objects:

- Physical properties: refers to the appearance, mass, temperature, state, size, or color of an object or fluid; a physical change indicates a change in the appearance, mass, temperature, state, size or color of an object or fluid.

- Chemical properties: refers to the chemical makeup of an object or fluid; a chemical change refers to an alteration in the makeup of an object or fluid and forms a new solution or compound.

## Reversible Change vs. Non-Reversible Change

Reversible change (physical change) is the changing of the size or shape of an object without altering its chemical makeup. Examples include the heating or cooling of water, change of state (solid, liquid, gas), the freezing of water into ice, or cutting a piece of wood in half.

When two or more materials are combined, it is called a mixture. Generally, a mixture can be separated out into the original components. When one type of matter is dissolved into another type of matter (a solid into a liquid or a liquid into another liquid), and cannot easily be separated back into its original components, it is called a solution.

States of matter refers to the form substances take such as solid, liquid, gas, or plasma. Solid refers to a rigid form of matter with a flexed shape and a fixed volume. Liquid refers to the fluid form of matter with no fixed shape and a fixed volume. Gas refers to an easily compressible fluid form of matter with no fixed shape that expands to fill any space available. Finally, plasma refers to an ionized gas where electrons flow freely from atom to atom.

Examples: A rock is a solid because it has a fixed shape and volume. Water is considered to be a liquid because it has a set volume, but not a set shape; therefore, you could pour it into different containers of different shapes, as long as they were large enough to contain the existing volume of the water. Oxygen is considered to be a gas. Oxygen does not have a set volume or a set shape; therefore, it could expand or contract to fill a container or even a room. Gases in fluorescent lamps become plasma when electric current is applied to them.

Matter can change from one state to another in many ways, including through heating, cooling, or a change in pressure.

Changes of state are identified as:

- Melting: solid to liquid
- Sublimation: solid to gas
- Evaporation: liquid to gas
- Freezing: liquid to solid
- Condensation: gas to liquid
- Non-reversible change (chemical change): When one or more types of matter change and it results in the production of new materials. Examples include burning, rusting, and combining solutions. If a piece of paper is burned it cannot be turned back into its original state. It has forever been altered by a chemical change.

## Forces and Motion

People have been studying the movement of objects since ancient times, sometimes prompted by curiosity, and sometimes by necessity. On earth, items move according to specific guidelines and have motion that is fairly predictable. In order to understand why an object moves along its path, it is important to understand what role forces have on influencing an object's movements. The term force describes an outside influence on an object. Force does not have to refer to something imparted by another object. Forces can act upon objects by touching them with a push or a pull, by friction, or without touch like a magnetic force or even gravity. Forces can affect the motion of an object.

In order to study an object's motion, the object must be locatable and describable. When locating an object's position, it can help to locate it relative to another known object, or put it into a frame of reference. This phrase means that if the placement of one object is known, it is easier to locate another object with respect to the position of the original object.

The measurement of an object's movement or change in position (x), over a change in time (t) is an object's speed. The measurement of speed with direction is velocity. A "change in position" refers to the difference in location of an object's starting point and an object's ending point. In science, the Greek letter Delta, Δ, represents a change.

Equation: $$\boldsymbol{velocity}\ (v) = \frac{\Delta x}{\Delta t}$$

Position is measured in meters, and time is measured in seconds. The standard measurement for velocity is meters/second (m/s).

$$\frac{meters}{second} = \frac{m}{s}$$

The measurement of an object's change in velocity over time is an object's acceleration. Gravity is considered to be a form of acceleration.

Equation: $$acceleration\ (a) = \frac{\Delta v}{\Delta t}$$

Velocity is measured in meters/second and time is measured in seconds. The standard measurement for acceleration is meters/second$^2$ (m/s$^2$).

$$\frac{\frac{meters}{second}}{second} = \frac{meters}{second^2} = \frac{m}{s^2}$$

For example, consider a car traveling down the road. The speed can be measured by calculating how far the car is traveling over a certain period of time. However, since the car is traveling in a direction (north, east, south, west), the distance over time is actually the car's velocity. It can be confusing, as many people will often interchange the words speed and velocity. But if something is traveling a certain distance, during a certain time period, in a direction, this is the object's velocity. Velocity is speed with direction.

The change in an object's velocity over a certain amount of time is the object's acceleration. If the driver of that car keeps pressing on the gas pedal and increasing the velocity, the car would have a change in velocity over the change in time and would be accelerating. The reverse could be said if the driver were depressing the brake and the car was slowing down; it would have a negative acceleration, or be decelerating. Since acceleration also has a direction component, it is possible for a car to accelerate without changing speed. If an object changes direction, it is accelerating.

Motion creates something called momentum. This is a calculation of an object's mass multiplied by its velocity. Momentum can be described as the amount an object wants to continue moving along its current course. Momentum in a straight line is called linear momentum. Just as energy can be transferred and conserved, so can momentum.

For example, a car and a truck moving at the same velocity down a highway will not have the same momentum, because they do not have the same mass. The mass of the truck is greater than that of the car, therefore the truck will have more momentum. In a head-on collision, the vehicles would be expected to slide in the same direction of the truck's original motion because the truck has a greater momentum.

The amount of force during a length of time creates an impulse. This means that if a force acts on an object during a given amount of time, it will have a determined impulse. However, if the length of time can be extended, the force will be less, due to the conservation of momentum.

Consider another example: when catching a fast baseball, it helps soften the blow of the ball to follow through, or cradle the catch. This technique is simply extending the time of the application of the force of the ball, so the impact of the ball does not hurt the hand. As a final example, if a martial arts expert wants to break a board by executing a chop from their hand, they need to exert a force on a small point on the boards, extremely quickly. If they slow down the time of the impact from the force of their hand, they will probably injure their hand and not break the board.

## Newton's Three Laws of Motion

Sir Isaac Newton spent a great deal of time studying objects, forces, and how an object's motion responds to forces. Newton made great advancements by using mathematics to describe the motion of objects and to predict future motions of objects by applying his mathematical models to situations. Through his extensive research, Newton is credited for summarizing the basic laws of motion for objects here on Earth. These laws are as follows:

### First Law

The first law is the law of inertia. An object in motion remains in motion, unless acted upon by an outside force. An object at rest remains at rest, unless acted upon by an outside force. Simply put, inertia is the natural tendency of an object to continue along with what it is already doing; an outside force would have to act upon the object to make it change its course. This includes an object that is sitting still. The inertia of an object is relative to its momentum.

> Example: If a car is driving at a constant speed in a constant direction (also called a constant velocity), it would take a force in a different direction to change the path of the car. Conversely, if the car is sitting still, it would take a force greater than that of friction from any direction to make that stationary car move.

### Second Law

The force (F) on an object is equal to the mass (m) multiplied by the acceleration (a) on that object. Mass (m) refers to the amount of a substance and acceleration (a) refers to a rate of velocity over time. In the case of an object falling on Earth, the value of gravity will be placed in for acceleration ($a$). In the case of an object at rest on Earth, gravity is placed in for acceleration ($a$), and the force calculated by $F = ma$ is called Weight (W). It is important to discern that an object's mass (measured in kilograms, kg) is not the same as an object's weight (measured in Newtons, N). Weight is the mass times the gravity.

> Example: The gravity on the earth's moon is considerably less than the gravity on earth. Therefore, the weight of an object on the earth's moon would be considerably less than the weight of the object on earth. In each case, a different value for acceleration/gravity would be used in the equation $F = ma$. Mass is used to calculate weight, and they are not the same.

> Example: If a raisin is dropped into a bowl of pudding, it would make a small indentation and stick in the pudding a bit, but if a grapefruit is dropped into the same bowl of pudding, it would splatter the pudding out of the bowl and most likely hit the bottom of the bowl. Even though both items are accelerating at the same rate (gravity), the mass of the grapefruit is larger than that of the raisin; therefore, the force with which the grapefruit hits the bowl of pudding is considerably larger than the force from the raisin hitting the bowl of pudding.

### Third Law

The third law of motion states that for every action there is an equal and opposite reaction. If someone pounds a fist on a table, the reactionary force from the table causes the person to feel a sharp force on the fist. The magnitude of the force felt on the fist increases the harder that they pound on the table. It should be noted that action/reaction pairs occur simultaneously. As the fist applies a force on the table, the table instantaneously applies an equal and opposite force on the fist.

> Example: Imagine a person is wearing ice skates on ice and attempts to push on a heavy sled sitting in front of them. They will be pushed in the direction opposite of their push on the sled;

the push the skater is experiencing is equal and opposite to the force they are exerting on the sled. This is a good example of how the icy surface helps to lessen the effects of friction and allows the reactionary force to be more easily observed.

Forces are anything acting upon an object either in motion or at rest; this includes friction and gravity. These forces are often depicted by using a force diagram or free body diagram. A force diagram shows an object as the focal point, with arrows denoting all the forces acting upon the object. The direction of the head of the arrow indicates the direction of the force. The object at the center can also be exerting forces on things in its surroundings.

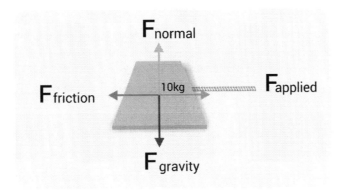

## Equilibrium

If an object is in constant motion or at rest (its acceleration equals zero), the object is said to be in equilibrium. It does not imply that there are no forces acting upon the object, but that all of the forces are balanced in order for the situation to continue in its current state. This can be thought of as a "balanced"' situation.

Note that if an object is resting on top of a mountain peak or traveling at a constant velocity down the side of that mountain, both situations describe a state of equilibrium.

## Falling Objects

Objects falling within the earth's atmosphere are all affected by gravity. Their rate of acceleration will be that of gravity. If two objects were dropped from a great height at the exact same time, regardless of mass, theoretically, they should hit the ground at the same time. This is due to gravity acting upon them at the same rate. In actuality, if this were attempted, the shape of the objects and external factors such as air resistance would affect their rates of fall and cause a discrepancy in when each lands. Consider the traditional illustration of this principle: a feather and a rock are released at the same time in regular air versus being released at the same time in a vacuum. In the open atmosphere, the feather would slowly loft down to the ground, due to the effects of air resistance, while the rock would quickly drop to the ground. If the feather and the rock were both released at the same time in a vacuum, they would both hit the bottom at the same time. The rate of fall is not dependent upon the mass of the item or any external factors in a vacuum (there is no air resistance in a vacuum); therefore, all that would be affecting the rate of fall would be gravity. Gravity affects every object on the earth with the same rate of acceleration.

## Circular Motion

An axis is an invisible line on which an object can rotate. This is most easily observed with a toy top. There is actually a point (or rod) through the center of the top on which the top can be observed to be spinning. This is called the axis.

When objects move in a circle by spinning on their own axis, or because they are tethered around a central point (also an axis), they exhibit circular motion. Circular motion is similar in many ways to linear (straight line) motion; however, there are a few additional points to note. A spinning object is always accelerating because it is always changing direction. The force causing this constant acceleration on or around an axis is called centripetal force and is often associated with centripetal acceleration. Centripetal force always pulls toward the axis of rotation. An imaginary reactionary force, called centrifugal force, is the outward force felt when an object is undergoing circular motion. This reactionary force is not the real force; it just feels like it is there. This has also been referred to as a "fictional force." The true force is the one pulling inward, or the centripetal force.

The terms centripetal and centrifugal are often mistakenly interchanged. If the centripetal force acting on an object moving with circular motion is removed, the object will continue moving in a straight line tangent to the point on the circle where the object last experienced the centripetal force. For example, when a traditional style washing machine spins a load of clothes in order to expunge the water from the load, it spins the machine barrel in a circle at a high rate of speed. A force is pulling in toward the center of the circle (centripetal force). At the same time, the wet clothes, which are attempting to move in a straight line, are colliding with the outer wall of the barrel that is moving in a circle. The interaction between the wet clothes and barrel wall cause a reactionary force to the centripetal force and expel the water out of the small holes that line the outer wall of the barrel.

## Conservation of Angular Momentum

An object moving in a circular motion also has momentum; for circular motion it is called angular momentum. This is determined by rotational inertia and rotational velocity and the distance of the mass from the axis of rotation or center of rotation. When objects are exhibiting circular motion, they also demonstrate the conservation of angular momentum, meaning that the angular momentum of a system is always constant, regardless of the placement of the mass. Rotational inertia can be affected by how far the mass of the object is placed with respect to the center of rotation (axis of rotation). The larger the distance between the mass and the center of rotation, the slower the rotational velocity. Conversely, if the mass is closer to the center of rotation, the rotational velocity increases. A change in one affects the other, thus conserving the angular momentum. This holds true as long as no external forces act upon the system.

For example, an ice skater spinning on one ice skate extends their arms out for a slower rotational velocity. When the skater brings their arms in close to their body (or lessens the distance between the mass and the center of rotation), their rotational velocity increases and they spin much faster. Some skaters extend their arms straight up above their head, which causes an extension of the axis of rotation, thus removing any distance between the mass and the center of rotation and maximizing their rotational velocity.

Another example is when a person selects a horse on a merry-go-round: the placement of their horse can affect their ride experience. All of the horses are traveling with the same rotational speed, but in order to travel along the same plane as the merry-go-round turns, a horse on the outside will have a

220

greater linear speed, due to it being farther away from the axis of rotation. Another way to think of it is that an outside horse has to cover a lot more ground than a horse on the inside, in order to keep up with the rotational speed of the merry-go-round platform. Thrill seekers should always select an outer horse.

## Energy

The term *energy* typically refers to an object's ability to perform work. This can include a transfer of heat from one object to another, or from an object to its surroundings. Energy is usually measured in Joules. There are two main categories of energy: renewable and non-renewable.

- Renewable: energy produced from the exhaustion of a resource that can be replenished. Burning wood to produce heat, then replanting trees to replenish the resource is an instance of using renewable energy.

- Non-renewable: energy produced from the exhaustion of a resource that cannot be replenished. Burning coal to produce heat would be an example of a non-renewable energy. Although coal is a natural resource found in/on the earth that is mined or harvested from the earth, it cannot be regrown or replenished. Other examples include oil and natural gas (fossil fuels).

Temperature is measured in degrees Celsius (C) or Kelvin (K). Temperature should not be confused with heat. Heat is a form of energy: a change in temperature or a transfer of heat can also be a measure of energy. The amount of energy measured by the change in temperature (or a transfer) is the measure of heat.

Heat energy (thermal energy) can be transferred through the following ways:

## Conduction
Conduction is the heating of one object by another through the actual touching of molecules, in order to transfer heat across the objects involved. A spiral burner on an electric stovetop heats from one molecule touching another to transfer the heat via conduction.

## Convection
Heat transfer due to the movement/flow of molecules from areas of high concentration to ones of low concentration. Warmer molecules tend to rise, while colder molecules tend to sink. The heat in a house will rise from the vents in the floor to the upper levels of the structure and circulate in that manner, rising and falling with the movement of the molecules. This molecular movement helps to heat or cool a house and is often called convection current.

## Radiation
The sun warms the earth through radiation or radiant energy. Radiation does not need any medium for the heat to travel; therefore, the heat from the sun can radiate to the earth across space.

## Greenhouse Effect
The sun transfers heat into the earth's atmosphere through radiation traveling in waves. The atmosphere helps protect the earth from extreme exposure to the sun, while reflecting some of the waves continuously within the atmosphere, creating habitable temperatures. The rest of the waves are meant to dissipate out through the atmosphere and back into space. However, humans have created pollutants and released an overabundance of certain gasses into the earth's atmosphere, causing a layer of blockage. So, the waves that should be leaving the atmosphere continue to bounce back upon the

earth repeatedly, thus contributing to global warming. This is a negative effect from the extra re-radiation of the sun's energy and causes planetary overheating.

This additional warming is not something easily or quickly reversed. Because the rate of reflection within the atmosphere only multiplies the more a light wave is bounced around, it will take a concerted effort to undue past reflectance and stop future reflectance of the light waves in the earth's atmosphere. Once the re-reflectance occurs, it duplicates exponentially, along with the additional compounding of more waves. Each degree the atmospheric temperature increases has a profound effect on the delicate balance of our planet, including the melting of polar ice caps, the rise of tidal currents—which cause strong weather systems—and the depletion of specific ecosystems necessary to sustain certain species of animals or insects, to name a few.

Energy can be harnessed to operate objects, and this energy is obtained from various sources such as electricity, food, gasoline, batteries, wind, and sun. For example, wind turbines out in a field are turned by the natural power of the wind. The turbines then store that energy internally in power cells; that stored energy can be used to power the lights on a farm or run machinery.

## Potential Energy vs. Kinetic Energy

Potential energy (gravitational potential energy, or PE) is stored energy, or energy due to an object's height above the ground. Kinetic energy (KE) is the energy of motion. If an object is moving, it has some amount of kinetic energy.

Consider a rollercoaster car sitting still on the tracks at the top of a hill. The rollercoaster has all potential energy and no kinetic energy. As it travels down the hill, the energy transfers from potential energy into kinetic energy. At the bottom of the hill, where the car is going the fastest, it has all kinetic energy, but no potential energy. If energy losses to the environment (friction, heat, sound) are ignored, the amount of potential energy at the top of the hill equals the amount of kinetic energy at the bottom of the hill.

## Mechanical Energy

Mechanical energy is the sum of the potential energy plus the kinetic energy in a system, minus energy lost to non-conservative forces. Often, the effects of non-conservative forces are small enough that they can be ignored. The total mechanical energy of a system is conserved or always the same. The amount of potential energy and the amount of kinetic energy can vary to add up to this total, but the total mechanical energy in the situation remains the same.

$$ME = PE + KE$$

$$Mechanical\ Energy = Potential\ Energy + Kinetic\ Energy$$

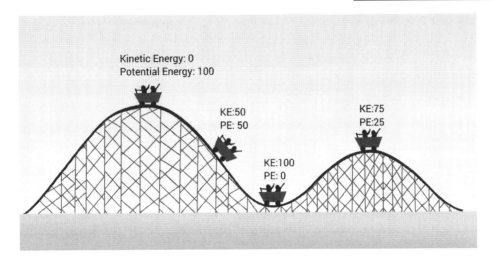

An illustration of a rollercoaster going down a hill demonstrates this point. At the top of the hill a label of $ME = PE$ describes the rollercoaster, halfway down the hill the label $ME = \frac{1}{2}PE + \frac{1}{2}KE$ describes the rollercoaster, and at the bottom of the hill, $ME = KE$ describes the rollercoaster.

Remember, energy can transfer or change forms, but it cannot be created or destroyed. This transfer can take place through waves (including light waves and sound waves), heat, impact, etc.

## Simple Machines

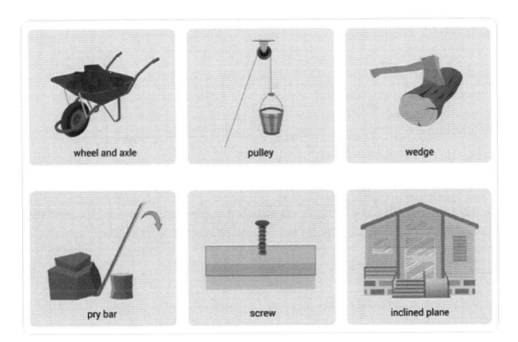

The use of simple machines can help by requiring less force to perform a task with the same result. This is also referred to as mechanical advantage.

Trying to lift a child into the air to pick an apple from a tree would require less force if the child was placed on the end of a teeter-totter and the adult pushed the other end of the teeter-totter down, in

order to elevate the child to the same height to pick the apple. In this instance, the teeter-totter is a lever and provides a mechanical advantage to make the job easier.

## Interactions of Energy

There is a fundamental law of thermodynamics (the study of heat and movement) called Conservation of Energy. This law states that energy cannot be created or destroyed, but rather energy is transferred to different forms involved in a process. For instance, a car pushed beginning at one end of a street will not continue down that street forever; it will gradually come to a stop some distance away from where it was originally pushed. This does not mean the energy has disappeared or has been exhausted; it means the energy has been transferred to different mediums surrounding the car. The frictional force from the road on the tires dissipates some of the energy, the air resistance from the movement of the car dissipates some of the energy, the sound from the tires on the road dissipates some of the energy, and the force of gravity pulling on the car dissipates some of the energy. Each value can be calculated in a number of ways including measuring the sound waves from the tires, measuring the temperature change in the tires, measuring the distance moved by the car from start to finish, etc. It is important to understand that many processes factor into such a small situation, but all situations follow the conservation of energy.

As in the earlier example, the rollercoaster at the top of a hill has a measurable amount of potential energy, and when it rolls down the hill, it converts most of that energy into kinetic energy. There are still additional factors like friction and air resistance working on the rollercoaster and dissipating some of the energy, but energy transfers in every situation.

## Electrostatics

Electrostatics is the study of electric charges at rest. A charge comes from an atom having more or fewer electrons than protons. If an atom has more electrons than protons, it has a negative charge. If an atom has fewer electrons than protons, it has a positive charge. It is important to remember that opposite charges attract each other, while like charges repel each other. So, a negative attracts a positive, a negative repels a negative, and similarly, a positive repels a positive. Just as energy cannot be created or destroyed, neither can charge; charge is transferred. This transfer can be done through touch.

If a person wears socks and scuffs their feet across carpeting, they are transferring electrons to the carpeting through friction. If that person then goes to touch a light switch, they will receive a small shock, which is the electrons transferring from the switch to their hand. The person lost electrons to the carpet, which left them with a positive charge; therefore, the electrons from the switch attract to the person for the transfer. The shock is the electrons jumping from the switch to the person's finger.

Another method of charging an object is through induction. Induction is when a charged object is brought near, but not touched to, a neutral conducting object. The charged object will cause the electrons within the conductor to move. If the charged object is negative, the electrons will be induced away from the charged object and vice versa.

Yet another way to charge an object is through polarization. Polarization can be achieved by simply reconfiguring the electrons on an object. If a person were to rub a balloon on their hair, the balloon would then stick to a wall. This is because rubbing the balloon causes it to become negatively charged and when the balloon is held against a neutral wall, the negatively charged balloon repels all of the

wall's electrons, causing a positively charged surface on the wall. This type of charge would be temporary, due to the massive size of the wall, and the charges would quickly redistribute.

## Electric Current

Electrical current is the process by which electrons carry charge. In order to make the electrons move so that they can carry a charge, a change in voltage must be present. On a small scale, this is demonstrated through the electrons travelling from the light switch to a person's finger in the example where the person scuffed their socks on a carpet. The difference between the switch and the finger caused the electrons to move. On a larger and more sustained scale, this movement would need to be more controlled. This can be achieved through batteries/cells and generators. Batteries or cells have a chemical reaction that takes place inside, causing energy to be released and a charge to be able to move freely. Generators convert mechanical energy into electric energy.

If a wire is run from touching the end of a battery to the end of a light bulb, and then another is run from touching the base of the light bulb to the opposite end of the original battery, the light bulb will light up. This is due to a complete circuit being formed with the battery and the electrons being carried across the voltage drop (the two ends of the battery). The appearance of the light from the bulb is the visible heat caused by the friction of the electrons moving through the filament.

## Electric Energy

Electric energy can be derived from a number of sources including coal, wind, sun, and nuclear reactions. Electricity has numerous applications, including being able to transfer into light, sound, heat, or magnetic forces.

## Magnetic Forces

Magnetic forces can occur naturally in certain types of materials. If two straight rods are made from iron, they will naturally have a negative end (pole) and a positive end (pole). These charged poles react just like any charged item: opposite charges attract and like charges repel. They will attract each other when set up positive to negative, but if one rod is turned around, the two rods will repel each other due to the alignment of negative to negative and positive to positive.

These types of forces can also be created and amplified by using an electric current.

The relationship between magnetic forces and electrical forces can be explored by sending an electric current through a stretch of wire, which creates an electromagnetic force around the wire from the charge of the current, as long as the flow of electricity is sustained. This magnetic force can also attract and repel other items with magnetic properties. Depending upon the strength of the current in the wire, a smaller or larger magnetic force can be generated around this wire. As soon as the current is cut off, the magnetic force also stops.

## Magnetic Energy

Magnetic energy can be harnessed, or controlled, from natural sources or from a generated source (a wire carrying electric current). Magnetic forces are used in many modern applications, including the creation of super-speed transportation. Super-magnets are used in rail systems and supply a cleaner form of energy than coal or gasoline.

**Optics and Waves**

## Electromagnetic Spectrum

The movement of light is described like the movement of waves. Light travels with a wave front, has an amplitude (height from the neutral), a cycle or wavelength, a period, and energy. Light travels at approximately $3.00 \times 10^8$ m/s and is faster than anything created by humans thus far.

Light is commonly referred to by its measured wavelengths, or the distance between two successive crests or troughs in a wave. Types of light with the longest wavelengths include radio, TV, and micro, and infrared waves. The next set of wavelengths are detectable by the human eye and create the *visible spectrum*. The visible spectrum has wavelengths of $10^{-7}$ m, and the colors seen are red, orange, yellow, green, blue, indigo, and violet. Beyond the visible spectrum are shorter wavelengths (also called the *electromagnetic spectrum*) containing ultraviolet light, X-rays, and gamma rays. The wavelengths outside of the visible light range can be harmful to humans if they are directly exposed or are exposed for long periods of time.

## Basic Characteristics and Types of Waves

A *mechanical wave* is a type of wave that passes through a medium (solid, liquid, or gas). There are two basic types of mechanical waves: longitudinal and transverse.

A *longitudinal wave* has motion that is parallel to the direction of the wave's travel. This can best be visualized by compressing one side of a tethered spring and then releasing that end. The movement travels in a bunching/un-bunching motion across the length of the spring and back.

A *transverse wave* has motion that is perpendicular to the direction of the wave's travel. The particles on a transverse wave do not move across the length of the wave; instead, they oscillate up and down, creating peaks and troughs.

A wave with a combination of both longitudinal and transverse motion can be seen through the motion of a wave on the ocean—with peaks and troughs, and particles oscillating up and down.

Mechanical waves can carry energy, sound, and light, but they need a medium through which transport can occur. An electromagnetic wave can transmit energy without a medium, or in a vacuum.

A more recent addition in the study of waves is the *gravitational wave*. Its existence has been proven and verified, yet the details surrounding its capabilities are still somewhat under inquiry. Gravitational waves are purported to be ripples that propagate as waves outward from their source and travel in the curvature of space/time. They are thought to carry energy in a form of radiant energy called *gravitational radiation*.

## Basic Wave Phenomena

When a wave crosses a boundary or travels from one medium to another, certain things occur. If the wave can travel through one medium into another medium, it experiences *refraction*. This is the bending of the wave from one medium to another due to a change in density of the mediums, and thus, the speed of the wave changes. For example, when a pencil is sitting in half of a glass of water, a side view of the glass makes the pencil appear to be bent at the water level. What the viewer is seeing is the

refraction of light waves traveling from the air into the water. Since the wave speed is slowed in water, the change makes the pencil appear bent.

When a wave hits a medium that it cannot penetrate, it is bounced back in an action called *reflection*. For example, when light waves hit a mirror, they are reflected, or bounced, off the mirror. This can cause it to seem like there is more light in the room, since there is a "doubling back" of the initial wave. This same phenomenon also causes people to be able to see their reflection in a mirror.

When a wave travels through a slit or around an obstacle, it is known as *diffraction*. A light wave will bend around an obstacle or through a slit and cause what is called a *diffraction pattern*. When the waves bend around an obstacle, it causes the addition of waves and the spreading of light on the other side of the opening.

*Dispersion* is used to describe the splitting of a single wave by refracting its components into separate parts. For example, if a wave of white light is sent through a dispersion prism, the light appears as its separate rainbow-colored components, due to each colored wavelength being refracted in the prism.

When wavelengths hit boundaries, different things occur. Objects will absorb certain wavelengths of light and reflect others, depending on the boundaries. This becomes important when an object appears to be a certain color. The color of an object is not actually within that object, but rather, in the wavelengths being transmitted by that object. For example, if a table appears to be red, that means the table is absorbing all other wavelengths of visible light except those of the red wavelength. The table is reflecting, or transmitting, the wavelengths associated with red back to the human eye, and so it appears red.

*Interference* describes when an object affects the path of a wave, or another wave interacts with a wave. Waves interacting with each other can result in either *constructive interference* or *destructive interference*, based on their positions. With constructive interference, the waves are in sync with each other and combine to reinforce each other. In the case of deconstructive interference, the waves are out of sync and reduce the effect of each other to some degree. In *scattering*, the boundary can change the direction or energy of a wave, thus altering the entire wave. *Polarization* changes the oscillations of a wave and can alter its appearance in light waves. For example, polarized sunglasses remove the "glare" from sunlight by altering the oscillation pattern observed by the wearer.

When a wave hits a boundary and is completely reflected, or if it cannot escape from one medium to another, it is called *total internal reflection*. This effect can be seen in the diamonds with a brilliant cut. The angle cut on the sides of the diamond causes the light hitting the diamond to be completely reflected back inside the gem, making it appear brighter and more colorful than a diamond with different angles cut into its surface.

The *Doppler effect* applies to situations with both light and sound waves. The premise of the Doppler effect is that, based upon the relative position or movement of a source and an observer, waves can seem shorter or longer than they actually are. When the Doppler effect is noted with sound, it warps the noise being heard by the observer. This makes the pitch or frequency seem shorter or higher as the source is approaching, and then longer or lower as the source is getting farther away. The frequency/pitch of the source never actually changes, but the sound in respect to the observer makes it seem like the sound has changed. This can be observed when a siren passes by an observer on the road. The siren sounds much higher in pitch as it approaches the observer and then lower after it passes and is getting farther away.

The Doppler effect also applies to situations involving light waves. An observer in space would see light approaching as being shorter wavelengths than the light actually is, causing it to look blue. When the light wave gets farther away, the light would appear red because of the apparent elongation of the wavelength. This is called the *red-blue shift*.

## Basic Optics

When reflecting light, a mirror can be used to observe a virtual (not real) image. A *plane mirror* is a piece of glass with a coating in the background to create a reflective surface. An image is what the human eye sees when light is reflected off the mirror in an unmagnified manner. If a *curved mirror* is used for reflection, the image seen will not be a true reflection. Instead, the image will either be enlarged or miniaturized compared to its actual size. Curved mirrors can also make the object appear closer or farther away than the actual distance the object is from the mirror.

*Lenses* can be used to refract or bend light to form images. Examples of lenses are the human eye, microscopes, and telescopes. The human eye interprets the refraction of light into images that humans understand to be actual size. *Microscopes* allow objects that are too small for the unaided human eye to be enlarged enough to be seen. *Telescopes* allow objects to be viewed that are too far away to be seen with the unaided eye. *Prisms* are pieces of glass that can have a wavelength of light enter one side and appear to be divided into its component wavelengths on the other side. This is due to the ability of the prism to slow certain wavelengths more than others.

## Sound/Acoustic Energy

Just like light, sound travels in waves and both are forms of energy. The transmittance of a sound wave produced when plucking a guitar string sends vibrations at a specific frequency through the air, resulting in one's ear hearing a specific note or sets of notes that form a chord. If the same guitar is plugged into an electric amplifier, the strength of the wave is increased, producing what is perceived as a "louder" note. If a glass of water is set on the amplifier, the production of the sound wave can also be visually observed in the vibrations in the water. If the guitar were being plucked loudly enough and in great

succession, the force created by the vibrations of the sound waves could even knock the glass off of the amplifier.

Waves can travel through different mediums. When they reach a different material (i.e., light traveling from air to water), they can bend around and through the new material. This is called refraction.

If one observes a straw in half a glass of water from above, the straw appears to be bent at the height of the water. The straw is still straight, but the observation of light passing from air to water (different materials) makes the straw seem as though it bends at the water line. This illusion occurs because the human eye can perceive the light travels differently through the two materials. The light might slow down in one material, or refract or reflect off of the material, causing differences in an object's appearance.

In another example, imagine a car driving straight along a paved road. If one or two of the tires hit the gravel along the side of the road, the entire car will pull in that direction, due to the tires in the gravel now traveling slower than the tires on the paved road. This is what happens when light travels from one medium to another: its path becomes warped, like the path of the car, rather than traveling in a straight line. This is why a straw appears to be bent when the light travels from water to air; the path is warped.

When waves encounter a barrier, like a closed door, parts of the wave may travel through tiny openings. Once a wave has moved through a narrow opening, the wave begins to spread out and may cause interference. This process is called diffraction.

## Structure of Earth System

Earth is a complex system of the atmosphere (air), hydrosphere (water), as well as continental land (land). All work together to support the biosphere (life).

The atmosphere is divided into several layers: the troposphere, stratosphere, mesosphere, and thermosphere. The troposphere is at the bottom and is about seven and a half miles thick. Above the troposphere is the 30-mile-thick stratosphere. Above the stratosphere is the mesosphere, a 20-mile layer, followed by the thermosphere, which is more than 300 miles thick.

The troposphere is closest to Earth and has the greatest pressure due to the pull of gravity on its gas particles as well as pressure from the layers above. 78 percent of the atmosphere is made of nitrogen. Surprisingly, the oxygen that we breathe only makes up 21 percent of the gases, and the carbon dioxide critical to insulating Earth makes up less than 1 percent of the atmosphere. There are other trace gases present in the atmosphere, including water vapor.

Although the stratosphere has minimal wind activity, it is critical for supporting the biosphere because it contains the ozone layer, which absorbs the sun's damaging ultra-violet rays and protects living organisms. Due to its low level of air movement, airplanes travel in the stratosphere. The mesosphere contains few gas particles, and the gas levels are so insignificant in the thermosphere that it is considered space.

Visible light is colors reflecting off particles. If all colors reflect, we see white; if no colors reflect, we see black. This means a colored object is reflecting only that color—a red ball reflects red light and absorbs other colors.

Because the thermosphere has so few particles to reflect light rays (photons), it appears black. The troposphere appears blue in the day, and various shades of yellow and orange at sunset due to the angle of the sun hitting particles that refract, or bend, the light. In certain instances, the entire visible spectrum can be seen in the form of rainbows. Rainbows occur when sunlight passes through water droplets and is refracted in many different directions by the water particles.

The hydrosphere, or water-containing portion of the Earth's surface, plays a major role in supporting the biosphere. In the picture below, a single water molecule (molecular formula $H_2O$) looks like a mouse head. The small ears of the mouse are the two hydrogen atoms connected to the larger oxygen atom in the middle.

Each hydrogen atom has one proton (positively charged, like the plus end of a magnet) in its nucleus (center), while oxygen has eight protons in its center. Hydrogen also has only one electron (negatively charged, like the minus end of a magnet) orbiting around the nucleus. Because hydrogen has only one proton, its electron is pulled more toward the oxygen nucleus (more powerful magnet). This makes hydrogen exist without an electron most of the time, so it is positively charged. On the other hand, oxygen often has two extra electrons (one from each hydrogen), so it is negatively charged. These bonds between the oxygen and hydrogen are called covalent bonds.

This charged situation is what makes water such a versatile substance; it also causes different molecules of water to interact with each other.

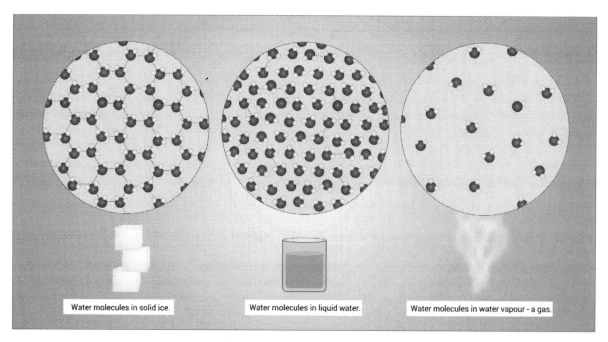

Water molecules in solid ice.    Water molecules in liquid water.    Water molecules in water vapour - a gas.

In a solid form (ice), water lines up in a crystal structure because the positive hydrogen atoms prefer to be next to the negative oxygen atoms that belong to other water molecules. These attractions are represented by the blue lines in the molecular picture of ice above. As heat is added and the ice melts, the water molecules have more kinetic energy and move faster; therefore, they are unable to perfectly arrange in the lattice structure of ice and turn into liquid. If enough heat is added, the water molecules will have so much kinetic energy they vaporize into gas. At this point, there are no bonds holding the water together because the molecules aren't close enough.

Notice how ice in its intricate arrangement has more space between the particles than liquid water, which shows that the ice is less dense than water. This contradicts the scientific fact that solids are denser than liquids. In water's case only, the solid will float due to a lower density! This is significant for the hydrosphere, because if temperatures drop to lower than freezing, frozen water will float to the surface of lakes or oceans and insulate the water underneath so that life can continue in liquid water. If ice was not less dense than liquid water, bodies of water would freeze from the bottom up and aquatic ecosystems would be trapped in a block of ice.

The hydrosphere has two components: seawater and freshwater (less than 5 percent of the hydrosphere). Water covers more than 70 percent of the Earth's surface.

The final piece of the biosphere is the lithosphere, the rocky portion of earth. Geology is the study of solid earth. Earth's surface is composed of elemental chunks called minerals, which are simply crystallized groups of bonded atoms. Minerals that have the same composition but different arrangements are called polymorphs, like graphite and diamonds. All minerals contain physical properties such as luster (shine), color, hardness, density, and boiling point. Their chemical properties, or how they react with other compounds, are also different. Minerals combine to form the rocks that make up Earth.

Earth has distinct layers—a thin, solid outer surface, a dense, solid core, and the majority of its matter between them. It is kind of like an egg: the thin crust is the shell, the inner core is the yolk, and the mantle and outer core that compose the space in between are like the egg white.

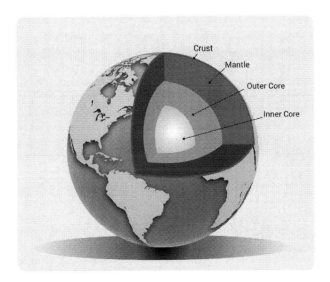

The outer crust of Earth consists of igneous or sedimentary rocks over metamorphic rocks (dense compacted rock underneath). The crust, combined with the upper portion of the mantle, forms the lithosphere, which is broken into several different plates, like puzzle pieces.

## Major plates of the lithosphere

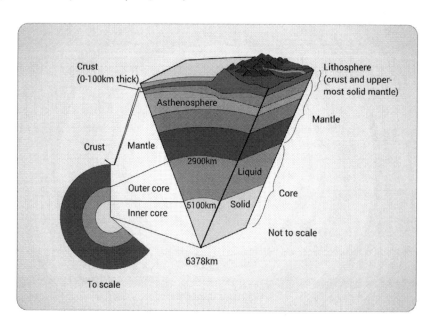

## Major Plates of the Lithosphere

The mantle is divided in three zones. The thin zone adjacent to the crust is solid rock (the lower part of the lithosphere). Below that is the asthenosphere, which contains liquid magma (molten rock). The lower mantle is completely solid rock. Underneath the mantle is the outer core, a molten layer rich with iron and nickel, followed by the compact, solid, inner core.

The inner and outer cores contain the densest elements (mostly iron with some nickel), which explains why they are at the center of earth: dense elements sink. Moving from outside in, Earth gets hotter and

hotter, with inner core temperatures as hot as the surface of the sun. One source of this immense heat is nuclear fission, which occurs when a heavy element's nucleus breaks into smaller and smaller pieces and in the process produces huge amounts of energy. Some power plants that run on fission energy are used to produce electricity. The problem with fission is that it releases huge amounts of radiation. In Chernobyl, Ukraine in 1986, a power plant explosion killed thirty-one people and exposed hundreds to radiation, a known source of mutation and cancer.

Nuclear fusion is the opposite reaction, combining small elements into a larger atom. This process produces three to four times as much energy as fission. Nuclear fusion releases energy hotter than the sun, so some believe that finding a way to use it as an energy source may be a meaningful endeavor. Scientists haven't been able to construct a facility that can harness such high temperatures, but research is currently underway.

Even though the inner and outer cores contain the same elements, the inner core is solid while the outer core is liquid, indicating that they have different melting points. How can this be? This is because tremendous pressure (the weight of the world, literally) on the inner core is so forceful that the particles remain close together and stay in their solid form, making it harder to melt.

## Processes of Earth

The water cycle is the cycling of water between its three physical states: solid, liquid, and gas. The sun is a critical component of the water cycle because its thermal energy heats up surface liquid water so much that parts of it evaporate. Transpiration is a similar process that occurs when the sun evaporates water from plant pores called stomata. As water vapor rises into the atmosphere through evaporation and transpiration, it eventually condenses and forms clouds heavy with liquid water droplets. The liquid (or solid ice or snow) will precipitate back to Earth, collect on land, and either be absorbed by soil or run-off to the oceans and lakes where it will accumulate, circulate, and evaporate once again.

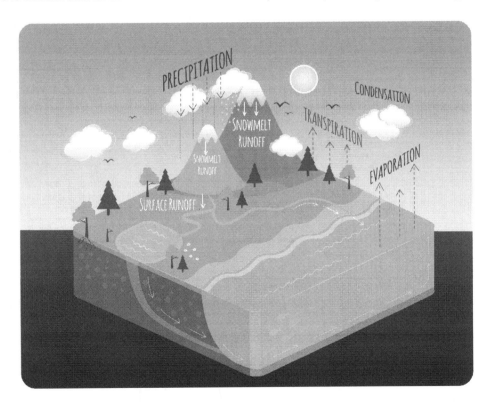

Clouds are condensed water vapor, which is water that has cooled from a gas to liquid, like the droplets on the outside of a glass of lemonade on a hot summer day. That water on the glass is water vapor that cooled enough to slow down the moving particles so that they become denser, forming a liquid. In the sky, water vapor combines in different ways so clouds appear in different forms. Cloud height, shape, and behavior results in a variety of different types:

- High-Clouds
  - Cirrus: wispy and thread-like
  - Cirrostratus: like cirrus clouds, but wider and thicker sheets. They have a halo effect where sunlight and moonlight refract through.
  - Cirrocumulus: a cross between cirrus and cirrostratus clouds. These have rows of round puffs like a cotton-ball stretched out.
  - Contrails: clouds made by jets
- Mid-Clouds
  - Altostratus: thick, stretched clouds that block sunlight and are blue-grayish in color
  - Nimbostratus: a thick altostratus cloud accompanied by rain
  - Altocumulus: layered rolls of clouds
- Low-Clouds
  - Cumulus: white, round, puffy clouds
  - Stratus: wide, thick, stretched-out, gray clouds that may cause drizzle
  - Fog: lazy stratus clouds that have drooped so low that they reach Earth's surface
  - Cumulonimbus: the angry cloud that brings thunderstorms, hail, and tornadoes. It looks like a thick mountain.
  - Stratocumulus: stretched-out, grayish, puffy, cumulus clouds

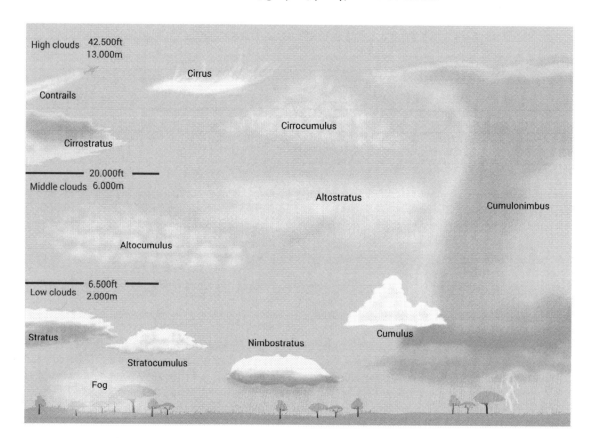

Precipitation comes in many different forms:

- *Rain* occurs due to water vapor condensing on dust particles in the troposphere. As more and more water condenses, the drops will eventually enlarge and accumulate mass, becoming so heavy that they fall to Earth.

- If the temperature is above the freezing point, the water falls as rain. Rain can freeze on the ground if the temperature on Earth's surface is colder than that of the troposphere. Freezing rain causes extremely dangerous driving conditions due to the slickness of the ice.

- *Sleet* freezes on its way down as opposed to freezing upon impact. Sleet starts as ice that melts as it falls through the atmosphere due to hitting spots of warmer temperature, and then it freezes again before hitting the ground.

- *Hail* is precipitation of balls of ice. Hail begins as ice at very cold temperatures in the atmosphere. Instead of precipitating sheets of ice like sleet storms, hailstorms precipitate ice that looks like rocks because hail is formed during thunderstorms. The massive winds throw hail up and down so more and more water vapor condenses and freezes on the original ice. Layer upon layer of ice combine, creating hail sometimes as large as golf balls.

- *Snow* forms as loosely packed ice crystals. Snow is less dangerous than the other frozen forms of precipitation and can produce beautiful snowflakes.

Even though seasons have predictable temperatures, there can be significant differences day to day. In the troposphere, the Sun's heat is trapped by the blanket of greenhouse gases and creates warm, low-pressure air. Because warm gas particles move faster and have less space between them, they are less dense than colder air, and they rise. Cool air moves below the warm air. This atmospheric movement is called general circulation and is the source of wind. Earth's spinning motion also causes wind.

Weather depends in a large part on temperature. Earth's equator is closest to the sun and receives more heat, so this area of earth is significantly warmer than the poles (Arctic and Antarctic). This warm air can form huge bubbles, as can the colder air at the poles. When warm air and cold air meet, the boundary is called a front. Fronts can be the site of extreme weather like thunderstorms, which are caused by water particles in clouds quickly rubbing against each other and transferring electrons, creating positive and negative regions. Lightning occurs when there is a massive electric spark due to the electrical current within a cloud, between two clouds, and even between a cloud and the ground.

While seasons are predictable trends in temperatures over a few months, climate describes the average weather and temperature patterns for a particular area over a long period of time, upwards of thirty years. While *fall* describes a season and *rain* describes weather, *rainforest* describes a climate. The climate of a rainforest, due to its proximity to the equator and oceans, consists of warm temperatures with humid air.

Even more extreme weather includes tornadoes and hurricanes. Tornadoes are spinning winds that can exceed 300 miles per hour and are caused by changing air pressure and quick winds. Hurricanes, typhoons, and tropical cyclones (the same phenomenon with different regional names) are storms with spinning winds that form over the ocean. Hurricanes are caused by warm ocean water quickly evaporating and rising to a colder, lower-pressure portion of the atmosphere. The fast movement of the warm air starts a cyclone around a central origination point (the eye of the storm). Blizzards are also caused by the clash of warm air and cold air. They occur when the cold Arctic air moves toward warmer air and involve massive amounts of snow.

Precipitation and run-off are constantly affecting the surface of Earth, as the run-off weathers rocks or breaks them down from the original bedrock into pieces called regolith. Regolith sizes range from microscopic to large and quickly form either soil or sediment. *Weathering* is the process of breaking rock while *erosion* is the process of moving rock. Weathering can be caused by both physical and chemical changes. Mechanical forces such as roots growing, animal contact, wind, and extreme weather cause weathering. Another cause is the water cycle, which includes flowing water, moving glaciers, and liquid ice seeping into rocks and cracking them as water freezes and expands. Chemical weathering actually transforms the regolith into clay and soft minerals. One consequence of chemical weathering is corrosive acid rain.

Rocks cover the surface of Earth. Igneous rock comes from the molten, hot, liquid magma circulating beneath Earth's surface in the upper mantle. Through vents called volcanoes, magma explodes or seeps onto the Earth's surface. Magma is not uniform; it varies in its elemental composition, gas composition, and thickness or viscosity. There are three main types of volcanoes: shield, cinder, and composite.

*Shield volcanoes* are the widest because their thin magma flows out of a central crater calmly and quietly, like a gentle fountain. This flowing magma results in layers of solid lava. The slow flow results in a convex hill that spans a wide area.

Like shield volcanoes, *cinder volcanoes* typically have a central crater and thin lava. In contrast to shield volcanoes, they are small, cone-shaped hills with steep sides. They are made of volcanic debris, or cinders. They are often found as secondary volcanoes near shield and composite volcanoes. In cinder volcanoes, the central vent spews lava that shatters into rock and debris and settles around it, resulting in its characteristic cone shape. Cinder volcanoes are surrounded by ashy, loose, magma dust.

*Composite volcanoes* (also called stratovolcanoes) are the most common and the tallest type of volcano. Their thick magma gets stuck at the vent, and as more and more builds up, the volcano eventually explodes and removes the clog. These eruptions generate loose debris, and once the plug has been violently expelled, the thick lava oozes out like a fountain. These volcanoes are the most dangerous with their extremely violent behavior and huge height. Most volcanoes are located around cracks in Earth's lithosphere.

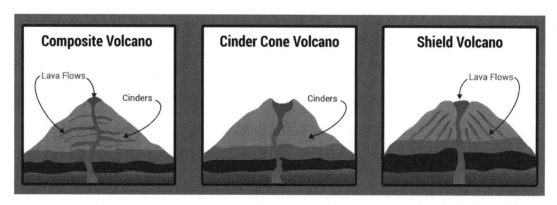

Once magma makes it to the surface, it is called lava. Once it cools, it solidifies into igneous rock. Common examples of igneous rock are obsidian, pumice, and granite. Weathering and erosion result in these rocks becoming soil or sediment and accumulating in layers mostly found in the ocean. These

loose sediments settle over time and compress to become a uniform rock in a process called lithification. Examples of sedimentary rock include shale, limestone, and sandstone. As layers are piled atop each other, the bottom rock experiences an intense amount of pressure and transforms into metamorphic rock. Examples of metamorphic rocks are marble and slate. After long periods of time, the metamorphic rock moves closer to the asthenosphere and becomes liquid hot magma

Magma's eventual fate is lava and igneous rock, and the cycle starts anew:

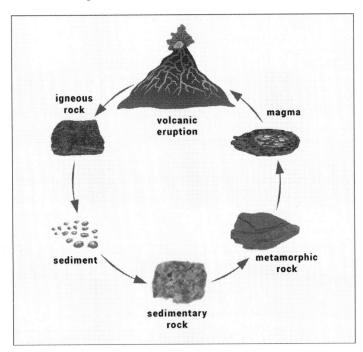

How does magma return to the surface if the lithosphere presses it down? Intense heat from the Earth's core travels to the upper mantle via convection. Convection involves thermal energy (heat) that converts into kinetic energy (movement), resulting in rapidly circulating molecules. Convection moves heat energy through fluids. In a pot of boiling water, the water closest to the burner becomes hot, causing its particles to move faster. Faster-moving molecules have more space between them and become less dense, so they rise. Some will vaporize, and some hit the cool air and slow down, becoming dense and sinking. Likewise, Earth's interior particles undergo convection (the heat source being the nuclear fission from the core), and the rock in the upper mantle will acquire so much kinetic energy that magma will be expelled from underneath Earth to the surface.

There are seven or eight major plates in the lithosphere and several minor plates. These tectonic plates explain the changing topography, or shape, of earth.

There are three types of boundaries between plates: divergent, convergent, and transform. All boundaries can be sites of volcanic activity. A *divergent boundary* occurs when plates separate. Lava fills in the space the plates create and hardens into rock, which creates oceanic crust. In a *convergent boundary*, if one of the plates is in the ocean, that plate is denser due to the weight of water. The dense ocean plate will slip under the land plate, causing a subduction zone where the plate moves underneath. Where plates converge on land, the continental crusts are both lighter with a similar density, and as a result they will buckle together and create mountains.

In *transform boundaries*, adjacent plates sliding past each other create friction and pressure that destroy the edges of the boundary and cause earthquakes. Transform boundaries don't produce magma, as they involve lateral movement.

Just as plates pushing together cause mountains, *canyons* are deep trenches caused by plates moving apart. Weather and erosion from rivers and precipitation run-off also create canyons. *Deltas* form when rivers dump their sediments and water into oceans. They are triangular flat stretches of land that are kind of like a triangular spatula; the handle represents the river and the triangle represents the mouth of a delta.

*Sand dunes* are another landform caused by wind or waves in combination with the absence of plants to hold sand in place. These are found in sandy areas like the desert or the ocean.

## Earth and the Universe

Earth is part of a solar system that rotates around a star. Our solar system is a miniscule portion of the universe; the Sun is just one star, and there are more stars in the universe than there are grains of sands on Earth. Almost every existing star belongs to a galaxy, clusters of stars, rocks, ice, and space dust. Between galaxies there is nothing, just darkness. There could be as many as a hundred billion galaxies. There are three main types of galaxies: spiral, elliptical, and irregular.

The majority of galaxies are spiral galaxies, with a large, central galactic bulge, which is a cluster of older stars. They look like a disk with arms circulating stars and gas. Elliptical galaxies have no particular rotation pattern. They can be spherical or extremely elongated and do not have circulating arms.

Irregular galaxies have no pattern and can vary significantly in size and shape:

Earth's galaxy, the Milky Way, is a spiral galaxy and contains hundreds of billions of stars.

Pre-stars form from nebulas, clouds of gas and dust that can combine to form two types of small stars: brown and red dwarves. Stars produce enormous amounts energy by combining hydrogen atoms to form helium via nuclear fusion. Brown dwarves don't have enough hydrogen to undergo much fusion and fizzle out. Red dwarves have plenty of gas (hydrogen) to undergo nuclear fusion and mature into white dwarves. When they use all of their fuel (hydrogen), a burst of energy expands the star into a red giant. Red giants eventually condense into a white dwarf, which is a star approaching the end of its life.

Stars that undergo nuclear fusion will run out of gas quickly and burst in violent explosions called supernovas. This burst releases as much energy in a few seconds as the Sun will release in its entire lifetime. The particles from the explosion will condense into the smallest type of star, a neutron star; this will eventually condense into a black hole, which has such a high amount of gravity that not even light energy can escape.

Earth's sun is currently a red dwarf; it is early in its life cycle. As the center of Earth's solar system, the Sun has planets and space debris (rocks and ice) orbiting around it. The various forms of space debris include:

- Comet: made of rock and ice with a tail due to the melting ice

- Asteroid: a large rock orbiting a star. The asteroid belt lies between Mars and Jupiter and separates the smaller rocky planets (Mercury, Venus, Earth, and Mars) from the larger, gassy planets (Jupiter, Saturn, Uranus, and Neptune). Pluto is not considered a planet anymore due to its small size and distance from the Sun.

- Meteoroid: a mini-asteroid with no specific orbiting pattern

- Meteor: a meteoroid that has entered Earth's atmosphere and starts melting due to the warmth provided by our insulating greenhouse gases. These are commonly known as "falling stars."

- Meteorite: a meteor that hasn't completely burned away and lands on Earth. One is believed to have caused the Cretaceous mass extinction.

Each planet travels around the Sun in an elliptic orbit. The time it takes for one complete orbit is considered a year. The gravity of the massive Sun keeps the planets rotating, and the farther the planets are from the Sun, the slower they move and the longer their orbits. Earth's journey is little bit over 365 days a year. Because Mercury is so close to the Sun, one year for Mercury is actually only 88 Earth days. The farthest planet, Neptune, has a year that is about 60,255 Earth days long. Planets not only rotate around the Sun, but they also spin like a top. The time it takes for a planet to complete one spin is considered one day. On Earth, one day is about 24 hours. On Jupiter, one day is about nine Earth hours, while a day on Venus is 241 Earth days.

Planets may have natural satellites that rotate around them called moons. Some planets have no moons and some have dozens. In 1969, astronaut Neil Armstrong became the first man to set foot on Earth's only moon.

## Earth Patterns

The temperature on the sun varies from its core to its atmosphere. Its atmospheric temperature is predicted at over 1 million °F. The sun accounts for two types of energy reaching earth: light energy and thermal (heat) energy.

Plants absorb the light energy and they use it to perform photosynthesis.

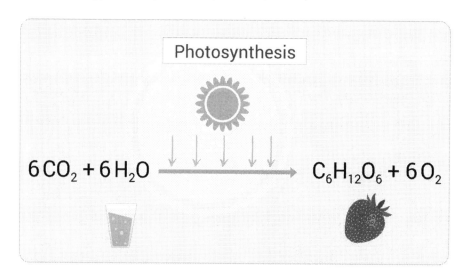

The thermal energy is transferred to earth's atmosphere through radiation. Unlike the transfer of heat through convection, radiation is a direct transfer—there are no particles in space to transfer the sun's heat. Once thermal energy reaches earth, the carbon dioxide in the atmosphere acts as a blanket to trap the heat.

The heat from the sun as well as the orbit and position of earth cause seasons. As discussed, earth rotates around the sun and spins on an axis. Earth is slightly tilted on its side. An imaginary line around the middle called the equator splits the earth into the northern and southern hemispheres.

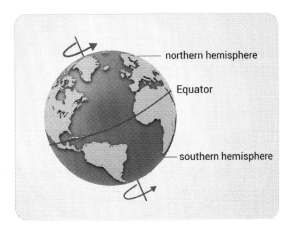

To understand seasons and the heating of the planet, refer to this picture:

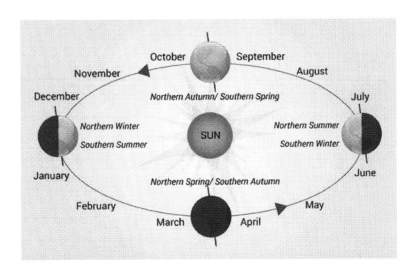

Observing July, these facts are apparent:

- Earth is tilted so that the northern hemisphere is pointing towards the sun. The southern hemisphere is pointed away.

- Because the north is tilted toward the sun, it gets more daylight in July than the southern hemisphere.

These observations explain why in July, the northern hemisphere experiences summer while the southern hemisphere experiences winter.

Notice in December that the opposite is true: the southern hemisphere gets more daylight compared to the northern hemisphere.

In spring and fall, both the north and the south get around the same sun exposure; therefore, those seasons have milder temperatures.

As the earth rotates, the distribution of light slowly changes, which explains why seasons gradually change. In June, the northern hemisphere experiences the summer solstice, the day with the most daylight. As the earth continues to orbit, its days will get shorter and shorter until the winter solstice, the shortest day of the year. Equinoxes occur in the fall and the spring and represent the days when the amount of daylight and darkness are relatively equal.

Just as the earth orbits the sun, the moon orbits the earth. The moon is much closer to earth than the sun. And even though the moon is so close to the earth, the moon contains no life because it lacks water and an atmosphere. Without greenhouse gases to blanket the sun's heat, temperatures on the moon are very low at night.

The moon is visible from the earth because it reflects sunlight at certain points in its orbit. The moon's orbit has a predictable pattern. It has two main phases, waxing and waning. When the moon is waxing, it goes from a new moon to a full moon. Notice that only the left side of the moon is dark during the waxing phase. The waning phase goes from full moon to new moon. Only the right side of the moon is dark when it is waning.

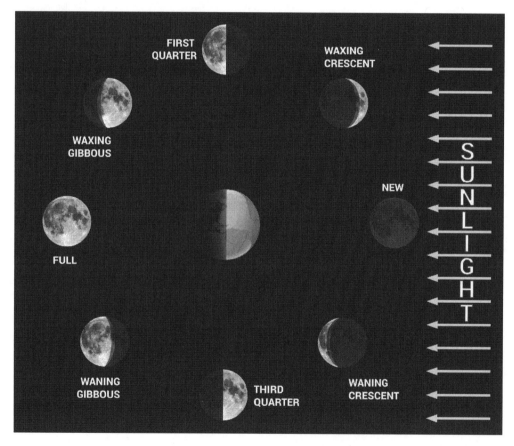

This picture shows that when the moon is behind the earth, then the moon's entire surface is reflected and we see a full moon. When the moon is between the earth and the sun, it is invisible at night, which is called a *new moon*.

Half-moons are visible when the moon and the earth are in a line that is perpendicular to the direction of sunlight. Only half of the moon reflects light to the earth at night, as seen in the figure above.

A moon that looks larger than a half moon is called a *gibbous moon*, and a moon that looks smaller is called a *crescent moon*.

Eclipses occur when the earth, the sun, and the moon are all aligned—the earth blocks the others from seeing each other. If they are perfectly lined up, a total eclipse happens, and if they are only a little lined up, there is a partial eclipse.

There are two types of eclipses: lunar and solar. A lunar eclipse occurs when the earth interrupts the sun's light reflecting off of the full moon. Earth will then cast a shadow on the moon, and particles in earth's atmosphere refract the light so some reaches the surface of the moon, causing the moon to look yellow, brown, or red.

During a new moon, when the moon is between the earth and the sun, the moon will interrupt the sunlight, casting a shadow on earth. This is called a solar eclipse.

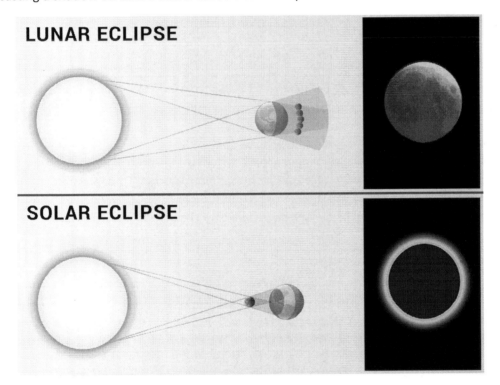

The moon also affects ocean tide due to gravity. Earth is much larger than the moon and has a very significant gravitational force that keeps us on the ground even though it is spinning very quickly. The moon is much smaller than earth, but because it is so close, it has a pulling effect on earth's oceans. When it is closest to earth, it pulls the water more, resulting in high tide. When the moon is farthest from earth, it pulls the ocean less and is called low tide.

## Energy Production and the Management of Natural Resources

As the Earth's human population grows, more energy and natural resources are required to sustain communities. This need is increasing at a rate of approximately two-to-three percent annually. The growth in human population and related energy needs presents energy production and management issues that need to be addressed.

## Renewable and Non-Renewable Energy Sources

*Renewable energy sources* are those that cannot be depleted; they are able to replenish themselves (or humans are able to replenish what they use) after consumption. These include sources such as solar energy, wind energy, hydro energy from the ocean, and geothermal heat. To be considered a viable resource, these energy sources should be able to translate into usable electricity, heat, cooling, or transportation fuel. Some biomass sources, such as waste, can also technically be considered "renewable" due to the amount of waste that humans produce. This would allow humans to recycle materials, and become less dependent on foreign fossil fuels. Scientists are also examining ways to make energy out of more plentiful biomass sources such as algae. Out of all human energy consumption in 2016, approximately one-fifth was from renewable resources. Out of all human energy production in 2016, approximately one-fourth was from renewable resources. Most large developed nations are investing heavily in renewable energy resources.

Traditionally, energy has come from *non-renewable energy sources* such as *fossil fuels* (common fossil fuels include carbon, coal, petroleum, oil, and natural gas) and other non-renewable biomass sources, such as wood. Fossil fuel consumption makes up almost three-fourths of all global energy consumption, with the United States responsible for almost twenty-five percent of that consumption. Fossil fuels take a long time to form, and supplies are quickly dwindling. Additionally, the methods of extracting fossil fuels are considered to be environmentally detrimental as is the exceedingly high production of greenhouse gases that results from their use. Fossil fuels are also concentrated in certain geographic locations around the globe, which has led to extensive geopolitical tension and conflict. These reasons have all led to the increased global interest in developing and utilizing renewable energy resources. However, barriers to developing renewable energy sources include those that are similar to any new start-up venture. Permitting, regulating, marketing to consumers, training employees, examining long-term implications, and costs are all barriers that are still being examined and managed.

## Recycling and Conservation

Recycling and conservation are two important tools for protecting the Earth's resources, but as relatively newer practices, they are not without issues. In general, the practice of *recycling* allows for the *conservation* of Earth's resources by reusing manufactured products, which limits the production and use of raw materials. This reduces landfill use, minimizes waste elimination practices that release greenhouse gas emissions, and is often more cost-effective for manufacturers. However, introducing new recycling centers to an area is often costly in the beginning, as it requires constructing and developing the facility and hiring and training workers. Recycling facilities are often dirty, due to the nature of the items that are recycled, which may have once contained food items, human waste, and other organic materials. These materials quickly rot, may attract vermin, and/or create an overall biological hazard. If the waste from recycled materials is improperly handled, it can cause a pollution problem. Additionally, recycled materials used to create new goods may not be high quality, which can be problematic for the consumer. Finally, recycling is a newer trend that has not yet been adopted on a global scale. Some researchers worry that the amount of recycling that occurs is on a scale that is too small to have a lasting impact, and therefore may be a cost-prohibitive practice.

## Pros and Cons of Power Generation

All presently available energy resources have pros and cons to their utilization. Fossil fuels are a non-renewable resource created from organic sources (such as coal). Two pros for using fossil fuels include the existence of systems that are already in place to use this form of energy, and that a fairly large

resource of fossil fuel material still exists. However, burning this resource for energy is a primary contributor to greenhouse gas production and disrupts many ecosystems. Sources are concentrated in certain areas around the globe, which has led to geopolitical conflict and tension. Additionally, the current rate of expenditure is faster than the rate of replenishment. This fact has led to research and development in the alternative energy industry.

*Alternative energy sources* include any source of energy that protects the environment and can be used as an alternative to fossil fuels. The term usually refers to solar, wind, water, and biomass power, but additional options also exist. In general, alternative energy sources are considered to be sustainable and conserving measures. However, a major con is that the industry is relatively new, and research is ongoing to utilize these sources in the most productive, efficient, and wide-reaching ways. Specific pros and cons of different types of alternative energy sources are listed below.

*Nuclear fuel* is a renewable resource created by the splitting of uranium atoms. This source greatly limits air pollution, as greenhouse gas emissions are low. Nuclear fuel also enjoys a relatively low production cost. However, upfront costs to build safe facilities are high. Nuclear accidents are also likely to be catastrophic to life, and adequate and safe storage of radioactive waste is another issue yet to resolve.

*Hydropower* refers to a renewable resource created from fast-flowing water sources that may be natural or man-made. This source is cheap, helps with global irrigation, and can provide drinking water. Disadvantages to hydropower include its inevitable disruption to many ecosystems; facilities are costly and may displace residents; and finally, while the risk of flooding is moderate, the risk of pollution is high.

*Wind power* refers to a renewable resource created by harnessing air flow. This source is abundant, cheap, clean, and does not require water or large facilities to use. However, wind has to be moving swiftly in order to be harnessed, and it cannot be stored. Commercializing a resource that easily crosses man-made borders can become complicated from legal and business standpoints.

*Solar power* is a renewable resource that uses the sun's rays for energy. This source is abundant, easily accessible, receives capital funding from both government and private sources, and requires minimal maintenance. However, even with subsidizing, initial production can be costly. It requires land or roof space for cell panels, and utilizes large-scale batteries. These can be a major contributor to waste and pollution.

Finally, *geothermal power* is a renewable resource that uses the Earth's core temperature to generate energy. This resource does not involve combustion (therefore no greenhouse gas emission), yet is three-to-five times more efficient than other sources. It can be used to heat or cool any residential or commercial space. However, utilizing this resource has a high upfront cost. It also requires a large amount of water, and can cause underground and well water damage. Additionally, emergency events, such as geyser eruptions and landslides, have a high risk of being catastrophic to life.

## The Use and Extraction of Earth's Resources

Extracting resources from the Earth is inherently damaging in its process. *Mining* for minerals and fossil fuels has vast environmental impacts. Surface damage, unnatural erosion, increases in sinkholes, disruption to ecosystems, unnatural animal migration, and pollution are all side effects of mining. *Deforesting* lands to use the land for commercial or residential use or to use the trees for raw materials significantly disrupts ecosystems, contributes to global warming from reduced carbon dioxide consumption, affects water levels, reduces biodiversity, and endangers wildlife. Many rainforests, such

as the Amazon rainforest, are believed to have "tipping points" of damage, where the land will be unable to replenish itself and the overall climate will have changed so drastically that it will set off other climate feedback responses. For example, cutting down trees leads to increased atmospheric carbon dioxide in the area, which leads to higher temperatures, which decreases plant water availability, resulting in less vegetation (and the loop continues). *Land reclamation* often focuses on correcting negative impacts to natural resources (i.e., restoring deforested lands by planting indigenous vegetation, replacing sands near beaches that have eroded, and so forth).

# *Scientific Inquiry and the Process of Science*

## Science as an Endeavor, Process, and Career

People of all cultures around the world utilize science in order to explore questions and find solutions to problems. The systematic process of designing, conducting, and analyzing experiments is universally known and respected. These processes are time-consuming and require specific knowledge and skills. Therefore, the pursuit of science is its own career path, with many smaller paths for each respective area of study (i.e., life sciences, chemical sciences, physical sciences). Of course, each of those paths splits into even more refined areas and requires much study and dedication. Men and women alike pursue scientific questions; some are driven by pure curiosity and others are compelled by finding a faster, or even a more economical way, of performing a task or producing an object.

Not all ideas, methods, or results are popular or accepted by society. Thus, the pursuit of science is often riddled with controversy. This has been an underlying theme since the early days of astronomical discovery. Copernicus was excommunicated from his religious establishment when he announced the belief that the sun, not the Earth, was the controlling body of the heavens known to humans at the time. Despite his having documented observations and calculations, those opposed to his theory could not be convinced. Copernicus experienced great ridicule and suffering due to his scientific research and assertions. In addition, other scientists have faced adverse scrutiny for their assertions including Galileo, Albert Einstein, and Stephen Hawking. In each case, logical thought, observations, and calculations have been used to demonstrate their ideas, yet opposition to their scientific beliefs still exists.

The possibilities for careers involving science range from conducting research, to the application of science and research (engineering), to academia (teaching). All of these avenues require intensive study and a thorough understanding of the respective branch of science and its components. An important factor of studying and applying science is being able to concisely and accurately communicate knowledge to other people. Many times this is done utilizing mathematics or even through demonstration. The necessity of communicating ideas, research, and results brings people from all nationalities together. This often lends to different cultures finding common ground for research and investigation, and opens lines of communication and cooperation.

## Science as Inquiry

Scientific questions can be derived from a multitude of sources including observation, experience, or even just wondering how something is made or works. In order to answer these questions, experiments should be designed and conducted to try to achieve a solution. At the end of an experiment, there often is no clear solution and a new experiment must be designed to test the same question. If a sound, logical solution is reached through experimentation, then it must be repeatable, by the experimenter and any other person wishing to test this solution. This entire process is commonly referred to as the scientific method.

A question or situation exists, a hypothesis (or a well-educated guess) is formulated, an experiment is designed to test this guess, a prediction is made as to what the outcome might be based upon research, and a conclusion is formed (either the guess was correct or not). This simple method is repeated over and over, as much as necessary for each question, idea, or proposed investigation.

An experiment must be carefully designed to include concerns for safety, use of proper instrumentation for measurement, systematic methods of documentation or data collection, appropriate mathematics for analysis of data and for the interpretation to draw valid conclusions. These conclusions must be explainable and verifiable by an outside source.

The importance of having an independent party test a solution is one of the critical parts of scientific inquiry. This ensures an experiment is free from bias, truly repeatable, and documentable to multiple sources. Without this confirmation, people could make erroneous claims and cause disastrous results. There would be no order to the inquiry of science.

In scientific experimentation, safety, respect for living things, and the effect on an environment must be acknowledged and protected, as necessary. There exist universal rules for research in order to preserve these underlying tenets. Most researchers or facilities that demonstrate an adherence to these rules garner the most support from others in the scientific community when accepting ideas.

## Unifying Process of Science

Following the scientific method, and keeping to the standards of proper research and reporting, lends to easier communication of data and results. When information can be conveyed to multiple audiences in a manner of common understanding (i.e., mathematics), it increases the possibilities for the use of such information. Having other scientists understand an idea can also lead to further experimentation and discovery in that area. This leads to the further organization of information and a deeper understanding of our universe.

It is more systematic to group, sort, and organize information for commonalities in order to increase understanding. The organization of groups can also serve as a reference point when attempting to identify other members of that group. For instance, a newly discovered type of rock can be compared to known rocks and then better categorized as to its uses or properties, based upon how it appears and responds in experiments, when measured against known rocks. This occurs regularly when varying crystal rock structures are developed for use in super-cooled or super-conductive experiments because certain properties are more useful with regard to conduction and strength. In order to have knowledge and access to this type of variation of information, societies are formed and people from all over the world find ways to communicate and share in the scientific endeavor.

The communication of research can further questions and explorations across the world. This common goal of reaching new discoveries or uses for the application of science can bring people together. Oftentimes, the quest for scientific discovery is spawned by competition or the race to create something before another society or country. Examples of this include the race to explore space, the race for nuclear armaments, and the race to create and cure strains of deadly bacteria. In these situations, the urge to push scientific discovery ahead may not be for the most humanitarian motives; however, oftentimes these research prompts result in accidental discoveries that can solve other problems. The discoveries of vaccinations, stronger materials such as plastics, and cleaner forms of energy through superconducting crystals have all been accidental discoveries along the way of competitive scientific

research. Whatever the motive for scientific discovery, it can be seen as a common thread across many nations with a potential to create unity through its demand for structure and organization.

## Process of Science

Theories are well-supported ideas that evolve from hypotheses and experimentation. A hypothesis is an educated guess about a scientific process or object. Once every angle of investigation has been examined and all evidence supports a hypothesis, only then can it be called a theory. It is important to know that theory development is a process. As technology advances and more aspects of science can be explored, evidence might no longer support a theory. With non-supportive data, either the theory can be modified or completely thrown out while new investigations are developed to examine other explanations.

For example, plate tectonic theory didn't appear until the early 20th century. People thought the earth was static and immobile. Only after many years of investigation and evidence did skeptics finally concede that the earth's surface was broken into plates. This theory wasn't universally accepted until the late 1960s and was considered revolutionary.

Early evidence that supported plate tectonics was publicized in the 1910s by Alfred Wegener, who observed that the South American and African borders to the Atlantic Ocean seemed like they could fit together like puzzle pieces. He proposed the idea of Pangaea, a massive supercontinent that existed long ago and must have broken into pieces due to a process called continental drift. Other evidence supporting plate tectonics were similar fossils found in Africa and South America, suggesting that they were once connected. But skeptics continued to scoff at the theory. Then, in the 1960s it was discovered, with the help of early computers, that a continental shelf (an underwater boundary between plates) between the two continents had a remarkable fit that was very unlikely to be due to chance.

## Research

Part of the process of scientific inquiry is researching a problem or question. Before an experiment can be designed, proper research should be conducted into the question. The initial question needs to be well formed and based in logical reasoning. A literature review should be conducted on existing material pertaining to the subject in question, and confirmation of any experimentation on the question that has been conducted prior should be made. If prior experimentation exists, what were the results obtained and were any conclusions drawn from those results? In addition, research should be done on all possible information regarding the initial question, the experiment, how to investigate the question, and what tools will be necessary to draw conclusions and explain any findings. Just as an experiment must be unbiased, so should any research regarding the experiment. All sources of information need to be proven reliable and accredited. For instance, a person's account of their opinion on a situation does not constitute as a valid source for research. Sources should be free of opinion or speculation.

During experimentation, research should be conducted with appropriate mechanisms for observation and measurement. Knowing the proper tools and units for accurately measuring a volume or a mass is a fundamental skill of research. Researchers also need to be held to standards of ethics and honesty. The independent repetition of an experiment helps to ensure this level of accountability. Often, the most reliable resources are those of accredited experimenters, universities, and other research laboratories. In order for such sources to publish information, they should demonstrate strict adherence to scientific methods, precise measurements for observations, and specific mathematical reporting.

It is often common for different scientists in the same place, or even separate countries, to be conducting experiments to test the same hypothesis. This does not always lead to a race to see who finishes first, but it can lead to cooperative research and shared accolades if the results prove successful. Awards for research, discoveries, and scientific application are often used by the scientific community to show appreciation for advancements in science.

# Practice Questions

1. At what point in its swing does a pendulum have the most mechanical energy?
    a. At the top of its swing, just before going into motion
    b. At the bottom of its swing, in full motion
    c. Halfway between the top of its swing and the bottom of its swing
    d. It has the same amount of mechanical energy throughout its path

2. What does the scientific method describe?
    a. How to review a scientific paper
    b. How to organize a science laboratory
    c. The steps utilized to conduct an inquiry into a scientific question
    d. How to use science to earn money in society

3. The energy of motion is also referred to as what?
    a. Potential energy
    b. Kinetic energy
    c. Solar energy
    d. Heat energy

4. Burning a piece of paper is what type of change?
    a. Chemical change
    b. Physical change
    c. Sedimentary change
    d. Potential change

5. A ramp leading up to a loading dock would be considered which type of simple machine?
    a. Screw
    b. Lever
    c. Inclined plane
    d. Pulley

6. Who is credited for simplifying the laws of motion?
    a. Einstein
    b. Hawking
    c. Copernicus
    d. Newton

7. The heat transfer due to the movement of gas molecules from an area of higher concentration to one of lower concentration is known as what?
    a. Conduction
    b. Convection
    c. Solarization
    d. Radiation

8. Which of the following is true of an object at rest on earth?
   a. It has no forces acting upon it.
   b. It has no gravity acting upon it.
   c. It is in transition.
   d. It is in equilibrium.

9. When researching a problem in science, what are the best sources to use?
   a. People you have seen on television
   b. Anyone with a Ph.D.
   c. Accredited laboratories and universities
   d. Any source with an internet webpage

10. What is a change in state from a solid to a gas called?
    a. Evaporation
    b. Melting
    c. Condensation
    d. Sublimation

11. The forces acting upon an object can be illustrated using what?
    a. A Venn diagram
    b. A periodic table
    c. A force diagram
    d. A stress-strain diagram

12. Which is not a form of Energy?
    a. Light
    b. Sound
    c. Heat
    d. Mass

13. A projectile at a point along its path has 30 Joules of potential energy and 20 Joules of kinetic energy. What is the total mechanical energy for the projectile?
    a. 50 Joules
    b. 30 Joules
    c. 20 Joules
    d. 10 Joules

14. What factors can prompt scientific inquiry and progress?
    a. Curiosity
    b. Competition
    c. Greed
    d. All of the above

15. Which of the following is considered a force?
    a. Weight
    b. Mass
    c. Acceleration
    d. Gravity

16. Why would a pencil appear to bend at the water line in a glass of water?
    a. The wood of the pencil becomes warped from being in the water.
    b. It appears to bend because of the refraction of light traveling from air to water.
    c. The pencil temporarily bends because of its immersion into separate mediums.
    d. The reflection of the light from water to a human's pupil creates the illusion of a warping object.

17. Which of the following is NOT one of Newton's three laws of motion?
    a. Inertia: an object at rest tends to stay at rest, and an object in motion tends to stay in motion
    b. $E = mc^2$
    c. For every action there is an equal and opposite reaction
    d. $F = ma$

18. The law of the conservation of energy states which of the following?
    a. Energy should be stored in power cells for future use.
    b. Energy will replenish itself once exhausted.
    c. Energy cannot be created or destroyed.
    d. Energy should be saved because it can run out.

19. Which of the following is true regarding magnets?
    a. Opposite charges attract
    b. Like charges attract
    c. Opposite charges repel
    d. Like charges do not repel or attract

20. Running electricity through a wire generates which of the following?
    a. A gravitational field
    b. A frictional field
    c. An acoustic field
    d. A magnetic field

21. When an ice skater spins on one skate in a circle, what happens if they extend their arms out like the letter "T"?
    a. They spin faster.
    b. They spin slower.
    c. They stop spinning.
    d. Nothing changes.

22. For circular motion, what is the name of the actual force pulling toward the axis of rotation?
    a. Centrifugal force
    b. Gravity
    c. Centripetal force
    d. No force is acting.

23. Which is not a method for transferring electrostatic charge?
    a. Polarization
    b. Touch
    c. Election
    d. Induction

24. What does the re-radiation of solar waves trapped in the earth's atmosphere contribute to?
    a. Global warming
    b. Greenhouse effect
    c. Climate change
    d. All of the above

25. Velocity is a measure of which of the following?
    a. Speed with direction
    b. The change in position over the change in time
    c. Meters covered over seconds elapsed
    d. All of the above

26. Which of the following sources of energy are non-renewable?
    a. Wind energy
    b. Solar energy
    c. Fossil fuel energy
    d. Geothermal energy

*Use the following image to answer question 27.*

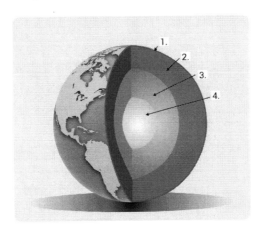

27. Which choice describes layer 4?
    a. Inner core: solid
    b. Inner core: liquid
    c. Outer core: solid
    d. Outer core: liquid

28. Which type of rock accumulates in layers at the bottom of the ocean due to run-off?
    a. Igneous
    b. Sedimentary
    c. Metamorphic
    d. Minerals

29. The water cycle involves phase changes. Which example below is evaporation?
    a. Clouds forming in the sky
    b. Rain, snow, or ice storms
    c. River water flowing to the ocean
    d. Sunlight's effect on morning dew

30. Which of the following is NOT directly caused by tectonic plate movement?
    a. Spreading of the ocean floor
    b. Earthquakes
    c. Mountain formation
    d. Precipitation

31. Which of the following statements is false?
    a. Magma circulates in the upper mantle.
    b. All volcanoes have explosive eruptions.
    b. Igneous rocks are formed by crystallized lava.
    c. Igneous rocks recycle and form magma.

*Use the following image to answer questions 32 and 33.*

32. Which fossil is the oldest?
    a. Dinosaur head
    b. Seashell
    c. Skeleton
    d. Grass

33. The fossils in the figure are embedded in which type of rock?
    a. Metamorphic
    b. Igneous
    c. Sedimentary
    d. Magma

*Use the following image to answer question 34.*

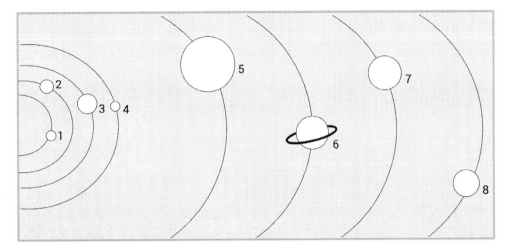

34. Where is the asteroid belt located in the figure above?
    a. Between structures #2 and #3
    b. Between structures #3 and #4
    c. Between structures #4 and #5
    d. Between each planet

35. Why is a year on Mars shorter than a year on Jupiter?
    a. Mars is much smaller than Jupiter.
    b. Mars is a rocky planet, while Jupiter is made of gas.
    c. Mars has a smaller orbit around the Sun.
    d. Mars is inside the asteroid belt.

*Use the following image to answer question 36.*

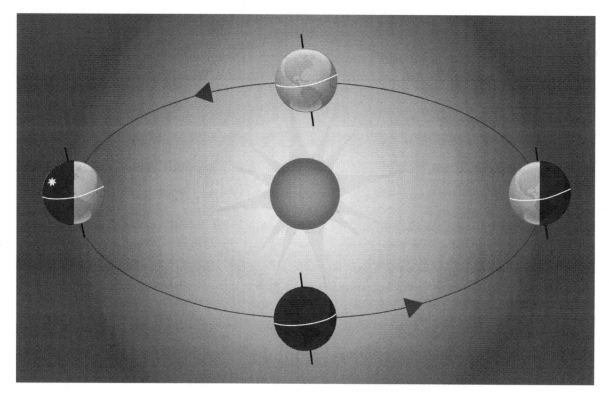

36. The figure above illustrates earth's orbit around the sun. What season is it where the dot is located?
    a. Summer
    b. Winter
    c. Fall
    d. Spring

37. Which statement(s) are true about the phases of the moon?
    a. Full moons are farther away from the sun than new moons.
    b. Crescent moons are smaller than half moons.
    c. Gibbous moons are larger than half moons.
    d. All of the above are true.

38. Why are greenhouse gases important?
    a. They allow UV rays to penetrate the troposphere.
    b. They insulate earth and keep it warm.
    c. They reflect light so that the sky looks blue.
    d. They form clouds and directly participate in the water cycle.

39. How is a theory different from a hypothesis?
    a. Theories are predictions based on previous research, and hypotheses are proven.
    b. Hypotheses can change, while theories cannot.
    c. Theories are accepted by scientists, while hypotheses remain to be proven.
    d. Hypotheses are always wrong, while theories are always true.

40. Which scientist is correctly paired with what he or she studies?
    a. Paleontologist: earth's crust
    b. Meteorologist: fossils
    c. Seismologist: earthquakes
    d. Geologist: weather

41. What part of most plants performs photosynthesis?
    a. Root
    b. Stem
    c. Leaf
    d. Flower

42. Which definition describes an ecosystem?
    a. One individual organism
    b. Rocks, soil, and atmosphere within an area
    c. All the organisms in a food web
    d. All living and nonliving things in an area

*Use the following image to answer questions 43 and 44.*

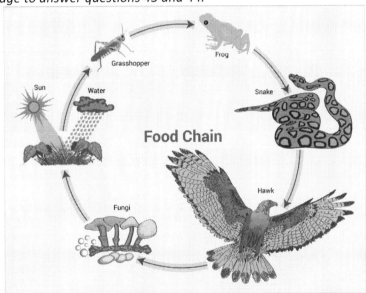

43. Which is the decomposer in the food chain above?
    a. Sun
    b. Grass
    c. Frog
    d. Fungi

44. Which is the herbivore in the food chain above?
    a. Grass
    b. Grasshopper
    c. Frog
    d. Fungi

45. What is a product of photosynthesis?
    a. Water
    b. Sunlight
    c. Oxygen
    d. Carbon Dioxide

46. What is cellular respiration?
    a. Making high-energy sugars
    b. Breathing
    c. Breaking down food to release energy
    d. Sweating

47. Which is true regarding DNA?
    a. It is the genetic code.
    b. It provides energy.
    c. It is single-stranded.
    d. All of the above.

48. Which one of the following can perform photosynthesis?
    a. Mold
    b. Ant
    c. Mushroom
    d. Algae

49. What happens at stomata?
    a. Carbon dioxide enters.
    b. Water exits due to transpiration.
    c. Oxygen exits.
    d. Glucose exits.

50. Which of the following represents a helpful inherited adaptation?
    a. A male elephant defending his territory by chasing another elephant away.
    b. A female dog that has a permanent strong odor that other male dogs tend to avoid.
    c. A male moose born with bigger horns that enable him to reduce competition for mating.
    d. A monkey learning to peel a banana after several tries.

51. Esther is left-handed. Hand dominance is a genetic factor. If being right-handed is a dominant trait over being left-handed, which of the following cannot be true about Esther's parents?
    a. Her parents are both right-handed.
    b. Her parents are both left-handed.
    c. Only one parent is right-handed.
    d. All of the above can be true.

52. What structures are made by the body's white blood cells that fight bacterial infections?
    a. Antibodies
    b. Antibiotics
    c. Vaccines
    d. Red blood cells

53. Cell -> ___1___ -> ___2___ -> organ system -> organism
Fill in blank #2 with the correct structure and a possible example in the circulatory system.
   a. Organ: heart
   b. Organ: blood vessel
   c. Tissue: heart
   d. Tissue: blood vessel

*Use the following image to answer question 54.*

54. Ants and aphids are organisms commonly found in nature. The ant doesn't eat the aphid, nor does the aphid eat the ant, so they have a different type of relationship than predator-prey. When aphids feed on plants, they simultaneously secrete a sugary substance that ants like to snack on. Ants in return protect the aphids from predators. What kind of relationship do the ant and the aphid demonstrate?
   a. Competition
   b. Parasitism
   c. Mutualism
   d. Commensalism

55. Jackson wants to open a dog-training business. He wants to see which dog treat is most effective in training dogs to sit. If he wants to design an experiment testing twenty dogs to figure out which treats to use, what would be a good dependent variable?
   a. Type of food
   b. Time in seconds the dogs sit
   c. How many times the dog wags its tail
   d. Shape of food

# Answer Explanations

**1. D:** It has the same amount of mechanical energy throughout its path. Mechanical energy is the total amount of energy in the situation; it is the sum of the potential energy and the kinetic energy. The amount of potential and kinetic energy both vary by the position of an object, but the mechanical energy remains constant.

**2. C:** The scientific method refers to how to conduct a proper scientific inquiry, including recognizing a question/problem, formulating a hypothesis, making a prediction of what will happen based on research, experimenting, and deciding whether the outcome confirmed or denied the hypothesis.

**3. B:** Kinetic energy is energy an object has while moving. Potential energy is energy an object has based on its position or height. Solar energy is energy that comes from the sun. Heat energy is the energy produced from moving atoms, molecules, or ions, and can transfer between substances.

**4. A:** A chemical change alters the chemical makeup of the original object. When a piece of paper burns it cannot be returned to its original chemical makeup because it has formed new materials. Physical change refers to changing a substance's form, but not the composition of that substance. In physical science, "sedimentary change" and "potential change" are not terms used to describe any particular process.

**5. C:** An inclined plane is a simple machine that can make it easier to raise or lower an object in height. Simple machines offer a mechanical advantage to performing tasks. While a screw, a level, and a pulley are also simple machines, they would be used to offer a mechanical advantage in other situations.

**6. D:** Sir Isaac Newton simplified the laws of motion into three basic rules, based upon his observations in experimentation and advanced mathematical calculations. Albert Einstein was known for his theories involving electricity and magnetism, relativity, energy, light, and gravitational waves. Stephen Hawking is known for his theories and studies of space, dark matter, black holes, and relativity. Copernicus was known for his observations and theories regarding the movements of the planets in our universe; specifically, that the sun was the center of our solar system, not earth.

**7. B:** Convection is the transfer of heat due to the movement of molecules from an area of higher concentration to that of lower concentration; this is also how heat can travel throughout a house to warm each room. Conduction is the transfer of energy from one molecule to another molecule through actually touching or making contact with each other. Radiation is how the sun warms the earth; no medium is needed for this type of transfer.

**8. D:** An object at rest has forces acting upon it, including gravitational, normal, and frictional forces. All of these forces are in balance with each other and cause no movement in the object's position. This is equilibrium. An object in constant motion is also considered to be in equilibrium or a state of balanced forces.

**9. C:** When conducting scientific research, it is best to rely on sources that are known for honest, ethical, and unbiased research and experimentation. Most laboratories and universities must have their work validated through independent means in order to publish or claim results. Anyone can publish things on the Internet—it does not mean their work has been validated, and therefore, their work may not be correct.

**10. D:** Sublimation is a change in state from a solid to a gas. Evaporation is a change in state from a liquid to a gas, melting is a change in state from a solid to a liquid, and condensation is a change in state from a gas to a liquid.

**11. C:** A force diagram shows all of the forces acting upon an object in a situation. The direction of arrows pointing around the object shows the direction of each force. A Venn diagram is used to show mathematical sets, a periodic table shows how the elements are categorized, and a stress-strain diagram is used in engineering.

**12. D:** Mass refers to the amount or quantity there is of an object. Light, sound, and heat are all forms of energy that can travel in waves.

**13. A:** The mechanical energy is the total (or sum) of the potential energy and the kinetic energy at any given point in a system.

$ME = PE + KE; 50\ Joules = 30\ Joules + 20\ Joules$

**14. D:** Scientific inquiry can be prompted by simple curiosity as to how or why something works. As seen in the race to enter outer space, scientific progress can be driven by competition. Many inventors are motivated by the idea of finding a better, faster, or more economical way of doing or producing something so that they can prosper from their discovery.

**15. A:** Using Newton's equation for motion, $F = ma$, and substituting gravity in for acceleration (a), the weight, or force could be calculated for an object having mass (m). Weight is a force, mass is the amount of a substance, and acceleration and gravity are rate of speed over time.

**16. B:** It appears to bend because of the refraction of light traveling from air to water. When light travels from one material to another it can reflect, refract, and go through different materials. Choice *A* is incorrect, as the pencil does not actually become warped but only *appears* to be warped. Choice *C* is incorrect; although the pencil appears to bend because of its immersion into separate mediums where speed is different, the pencil does not become temporarily warped—it only appears to be warped. Choice *D* is incorrect; it is the refraction of light, not reflection. The latter happens within the same medium, which makes the answer choice incorrect.

**17. B:** While this is Einstein's application of Newton's theory to that of light, it is not one of Newton's original three laws of motion. Newton's three laws are $F = ma$, the law of inertia, and for every action there is an equal and opposite reaction.

**18. C:** This is a fundamental law of thermodynamics. Energy can only transfer, transform, or travel. The amount of energy in a system is always the same.

**19. A:** The ends (or poles) of a straight magnet are different charges. One end is positive and one end is negative. Therefore, the positive end of magnet #1 would attract the negative end of magnet #2 and repel magnet #2's positive end.

**20. D:** When electricity is run through a wire, it is carrying current and current has a charge. Therefore, there is a charge running down the wire, which creates a magnetic field that can attract and repel just like any magnet.

**21. B:** The ice skater is demonstrating the conservation of angular momentum. This means that the amount of momentum for the situation will remain the same. If the skater is redistributing the mass (their arms), then the angular speed will compensate for that alteration. In this case, the mass is extended out away from the axis of rotation, so the rate of rotation is slowed down. If their arms were brought back in near their body, then the rate of rotation would increase, making the skater spin faster.

**22. C:** This is the actual force recognized in a rotational situation. The reactive force acting opposite of the centripetal force is named the centrifugal force, but it is not an actual force on its own. A common mistake is to interchange the two terms. But, the real force acting in a rotational situation is pulling in toward the axis of rotation and is called the centripetal force.

**23. C:** Electric charge can be transferred through touch of one physical object to another, induction by bringing a charged object near another object, and polarization, or the forcing of one charge to the end of an object in a centralized area.

**24. D:** The solar waves from the sun warm the earth. Many of the waves are meant to reflect back off of the atmosphere to keep the earth warm, and the rest of the waves are meant to reflect back out into space through the atmosphere. This is known as the greenhouse effect. However, when the atmosphere has become too dense (polluted by gases), the waves meant to escape are trapped and re-radiate in the earth's atmosphere, causing an overall warming of the climate, known as global warming.

**25. D:** Velocity is a measure of speed with direction. To calculate velocity, find the distance covered and the time it took to cover that distance; change in position over the change in time. A standard measurement for velocity is in meters per second (m/s).

**26. C:** Fossil fuel energy. Wind energy from turbines, solar energy from sun panels, and geothermal energy are all considered renewable and preferable alternatives to fossil fuel, of which there is a limited supply.

*The following image is the answer to question 27.*

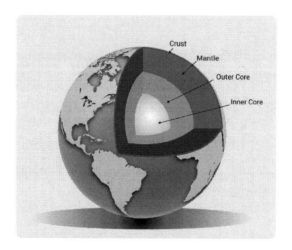

**27. A:** Inner core: solid. Layer 4 is the inner core; therefore, Choices *C* and *D* are incorrect. The inner core is solid due to the intense pressure upon it, making Choice *B* incorrect.

**28. B:** Sedimentary. Choice *A* (igneous) is incorrect, because that is crystallized magma found on land. Choice *C* (metamorphic) is incorrect, because that is unified, solid rock close to earth's mantle. Choice *D* (minerals) isn't a type of rock, but what composes rock.

**29. D:** Sunlight evaporates dew from plants. Choice *A* is incorrect because cloud formation is condensation. Choice *B* is incorrect because rain, snow, and ice storms are different forms of precipitation. Choice *C* is incorrect because rivers flowing into the oceans are examples of run-off.

**30. D:** Precipitation. Precipitation has nothing to do with plate tectonic theory. Plate movement causes ocean floor spreading, mountain formation, and earthquakes; therefore, all other answer choices are correct.

**31. B:** All volcanoes have explosive eruptions. This isn't true; shield volcanoes have thin magma that oozes out gently. Choice *A* is correct because magma circulates in the upper mantle. Choice *C* is correct because igneous rock is cooled lava. Choice *D* is correct because igneous rock goes through the rock cycle and will eventually become magma again.

*The following image is for questions 32 and 33.*

**32. B:** Seashells. The oldest rock layer is on the bottom. Choice *D* doesn't show a fossil—the grass is a living organism. Choices *A* and *C* show fossils in higher layers, so these are not the correct answers.

**33. C:** Sedimentary rock. Fossils are only found in sedimentary rock. Igneous rock, metamorphic rock, and liquid magma don't contain fossils, so Choices *A*, *B*, and *D* are incorrect.

*The following image is for question 34.*

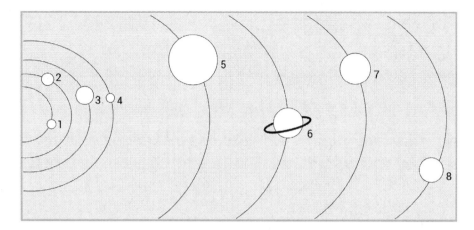

**34. C:** Between structures #4 and #5. The asteroid belt is rock orbiting between the inner, solid planets and the outer, gassy planets. More precisely, it is between Mars (planet #4) and Jupiter (planet #5). It is not Choice *A* (between Venus and Earth), nor is it Choice *B* (between Earth and Mars). Choice *D* is incorrect since it is not between every planet.

**35. C:** Mars has a smaller orbit around the Sun. This question requires critical thinking because every answer choice is true, but only one of them has to do with orbiting time. A year is the time it takes a planet to orbit the Sun, and because Mars is closer to the Sun and has a smaller orbit, its year is significantly shorter than a year on Jupiter.

*The following image is for question 36.*

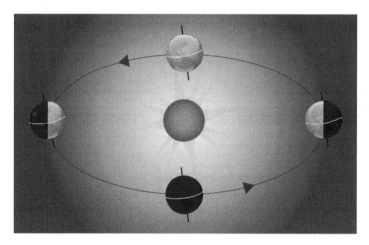

**36. B:** Winter. Students must identify the lateral equator and know the difference between North and South. They should recognize that because the top hemisphere is tilted away from the Sun; it would be winter at that time. Spring and fall (Choices *D* and *C*) are incorrect because both hemispheres have the same exposure to the sun, and summer (Choice *A*) is incorrect since the top hemisphere is tilted toward the sun.

**37. D:** All of the above. All choices are correct. New moons are closest to the sun and full moons are farthest (Choice *A*). Crescent moons are smaller than half-moons (Choice *B*), and gibbous moons are larger than half-moons (Choice *C*).

**38. B:** They insulate earth and keep it warm. Greenhouse gases serve as a blanket and allow earth to exist at livable temperatures. Choice *D* is incorrect because greenhouse gases do not form clouds; clouds are formed by condensed water vapor. Choice *C* is incorrect because while it is true that particles in the atmosphere reflect light so that the sky appears blue, this isn't an important function of the particles in the troposphere. The blue appearance is just cosmetic. Choice *A* is incorrect because ozone in the stratosphere actually prevents UV rays from passing.

**39. C:** Theories are accepted by scientists, while hypotheses remain to be proven. Choice *A* is incorrect because theories are far more than predictions; they are actually highly supported and accepted as truth. Choice *B* is incorrect because theories can change with new technology and understanding. Choice *D* is also incorrect because theories may not always be true and can change. Also, hypotheses can be and often are supported.

**40. C:** Seismologist: earthquakes. All other choices have been mixed up. Paleontologists study fossils, meteorologists study weather, and geologists study the earth's crust.

**41. C:** Leaf. Leaves are the part of the plant that contain chloroplast (due to their green appearance), thus they are the parts that perform photosynthesis. Roots (Choice *A*) suck up water. Seeds and flowers are reproductive structures (Choices *B* and *D*).

**42. D:** All living and nonliving things in an area. Choice *C* (all the organisms in a food web) describes feeding relationships and not symbiosis. Choice *B* (rocks, soil, and atmosphere in an area) includes nonliving factors in an ecosystem. Choice *A*, one organism, is too small to be considered an ecosystem.

*The following image is for questions 43 and 44.*

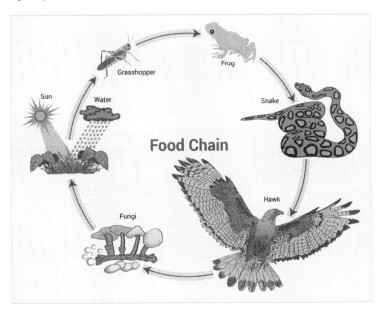

**43. D:** Fungi. Choice *A* (the sun) is not even a living thing. Grass (*B*) is a producer, and the frog (*C*) is a consumer. The fungi break down dead organisms and are the only decomposer shown.

**44. B:** Grasshopper. An herbivore is an organism that eats only plants, and that's the grasshopper's niche in this particular food chain. Grass (*A*) is a producer, the frog (*C*) is a consumer, and the fungi (*D*) is a decomposer.

**45. C:** Oxygen. Water (*A*) is a reactant that gets sucked up by the roots. Carbon dioxide (*D*) is a reactant that goes into the stomata, and sunlight (*B*) inputs energy into the reaction in order to create the high-energy sugar.

**46. C:** Breaking down food to release energy. Breathing (*B*) is not cellular respiration; breathing is an action that takes place at the organism level with the respiratory system. Making high-energy sugars (*A*) is photosynthesis, not cellular respiration. Perspiration (*D*) is sweating, and has nothing to do with cellular respiration.

**47. A:** It is the genetic code. Choice *B* is incorrect because DNA does not provide energy—that's the job of carbohydrates and glucose. Choice *C* is incorrect because DNA is double-stranded. Because Choices *B* and *C* are incorrect, Choice *D*, all of the above, is incorrect.

**48. D:** Algae can perform photosynthesis. One indicator that a plant is able to perform photosynthesis is the color green. Plants with the pigment chlorophyll are able to absorb the warmer colors of the light spectrum, but are unable to absorb green. That's why they appear green. Choices *A* and *C* are types of fungi, and are therefore not able to perform photosynthesis. Fungi obtain energy from food in their environment. Choice *B*, ant, is also unable to perform photosynthesis, since it is an animal.

**49. D:** Glucose exits. The stomata are pores at the bottom of the leaf, and carbon dioxide enters (it is a reactant for photosynthesis) and oxygen exits (it is a product for photosynthesis), so Choices *A* and *C* are correct. Water exits through the stomata in the process of transpiration, so Choice *B* is correct as well. Glucose is the sugar that is either broken down by the plant for its own energy usage or eaten by other organisms for energy.

**50. C:** A male moose with horns that enable him to reduce competition for mating. Choices *A* and *D* (elephant and monkey) are not caused by genes. These are learned behaviors from other animals. Choice *B* (smelly dog) is actually a detriment because the dog will be less likely to mate, so she will not pass on her smelly genes.

**51. D:** All of the above. Let's label *R* as the right-handed allele and *r* as the left-handed allele. Esther has to have the combination rr since she's left-handed. She had to get at least one recessive allele from each parent. So, mom could either be Rr or rr (right-handed or left-handed), and dad can also be Rr or rr. As long as each parent carries one recessive allele, it is possible that Esther is left-handed. Therefore, all answer choices are possible.

**52. A:** Antibodies. Antibiotics (*B*) fight bacteria, but the body does not make them naturally. White blood cells, not red blood cells (*D*) are the blood cells produced that fight the bacteria. Vaccines (*C*) are given to create antibodies and prevent future illness.

**53. A:** Organ: Heart. Blank #1 is tissue and blank #2 is organ, so Choices *C* and *D* are automatically incorrect. Blood vessels (*B*) are a type of smooth muscle tissue. The heart is an organ.

*The following image is for question 54.*

**54. C:** Mutualism. In the ant-aphid case, both organisms benefit, as the ants are getting food and the aphids are getting protection. Competition (*A*) is when organisms want the same thing (food, water, shelter, space), which is clearly not the case here. Parasitism (*B*) involves one organism getting hurt in the relationship at the expense of the other, while commensalism (*D*) involves an organism that is benefited connected to an indifferent party.

**55. B:** Time in seconds the dogs sit. This is a better choice than Choice *C* (tail wagging) because it is a measurable, meaningful, and relevant dependent variable. Tail wagging, although quantitative, is not a valid measure of anything. Choices *A* and *D* could be independent variables in the experiment.

**Photo Credits**

The following photo is licensed under CC BY 2.5 (creativecommons.org/licenses/by/2.5/)

"Black cherry tree histogram" by Mwtoews (https://commons.wikimedia.org/wiki/Histogram#/media/File:Black_cherry_tree_histogram.svg)

The following photo is licensed under CC BY 3.0 (creativecommons.org/licenses/by/3.0/)

"Eukaryotic Cell (animal)" by Mediran (https://commons.wikimedia.org/wiki/File:Eukaryotic_Cell_(animal).jpg)

# The Arts, Health, and Fitness

## Foundations of Art Education

The four general categories of arts are visual arts, dance, music, and theater arts. As children progress through elementary school, they should be exposed to the basic foundations, creative expression and production of each type of art, and the ability to critically analyze a work of art and make connections within a cultural and historical context. Art education should build progressively during childhood so that older children are able to eventually take on these more sophisticated and advanced applications.

There are a wide variety of visual and performing arts that can enhance a child's creativity and learning experience. It is optimal to expose young children to many different types of art – both as a creator and observer – for well-rounded cultural, creative, and comprehensive learning. Depending on the child's age, early childhood educators can tailor art assignments and activities to meet the child's interests, motor skills, attention, and needs.

## Visual Arts

Visual arts include things like drawing, painting, sketching, collage, sculpture, etc. Before the age of three, most artwork is produced less in an artistic way and more in a scientific and sensory way. Children at these youngest ages are more interested in the textures, colors, and shapes of what they create rather than expressing any sort of emotion or symbol. There are a variety of crafting activities that young children enjoy and can benefit from including finger painting, pasting, modeling with Play-Doh and clay, folding paper for origami, tracing and making models, and using a variety of craft supplies in creative ways including pom-poms, googly eyes, glitter, pipe cleaners, felt, and yarn. Craft activities help small children develop fine motor skills as they use instruments such as scissors and try to make precise movements like stringing beads and coloring within boundaries. As children develop, they can focus for longer periods of time and can handle more precise movements with smaller materials and areas. For example, a three- to four-year-old child may make simple Play-Doh snakes or snowmen, while a six- to eight-year-old child can add spots, a tongue, and facial features to the snowman with smaller bits of material laid in more exact locations. Through arts and crafts, young children can learn about colors and observe colors in the world around them, recognizing things such as green grass and blue sky. Working on arts and crafts projects helps children develop skills in planning, attention and focusing, problem-solving, and originality. It also helps them learn how to observe the world around them, be appreciative

of other people's interpretations and ideas, deal with frustrations when things do not go as planned, and develop hand-eye coordination.

Early childhood educators should strive to expose children to a vast array of arts and craft materials and different types of arts. Activities should be age-appropriate. For example, four- to five-year-old children are likely unable to use small beads and fine pencils and markers, and do better with wider drawing utensils and larger beads that are easier to grasp and manipulate. Children who are ten to twelve are able to work with more intricate objects and may be bored with crayons and coloring books. There are a variety of other art forms that students may view or try to create such as jewelry, pottery, stained glass, wire art, sewing, quilting, knitting, and decoupage.

## Music

Studies show that learning an instrument, especially at a young age, improves thinking, mathematical skills, attention, and brain activity. Children benefit from being exposed to a variety of instruments and musical genres including woodwinds, strings, brass, piano, vocals, jazz, blues, classical, folk, etc. Older children can learn basic music theory and how to read music, and may be able to take on more advanced instrument lessons and play or sing collaboratively in groups. As children mature, their attention spans, fine motor skills, ability to understand and maintain rhythm and pitch, and musical fluency improve. Activities and expectations should be age-appropriate. Smaller versions of some instruments are also manufactured and available to very young children to fit their small bodies and fingers.

For young children, learning to identify and maintain rhythm and beat is an important early skill and can be practiced by listening to music accompanied by physical movements such as clapping, stomping, dancing, or following the beat with percussive instruments like tambourines or small drums. They can learn to recognize musical notes and the position of the notes on a staff as well as the various characteristics of basic note types such as eighth notes, quarter notes, half notes, and whole notes. Singing and learning basic traditional and folk songs are simple ways to expose children to music as an easy, low-cost group activity. As children get older and more experienced, the group can be divided into sections to create harmonies and maintain separate singing roles within a varied group, which is a more advanced skill requiring concentration, attention, and group coordination.

## Dance

Dance incorporates not only music, creativity, and arts, but also physical activity, which is very important to young children. Dance can help improve kinesthetic sense or awareness of one's body in space, rhythm and mathematical thinking, fluidity of motion, and coordination and balance. There are many varieties of dance, and educators should pick age-appropriate music and dances. The youngest children tend to do best with free movement to music or simple choreographed dances such as the hokey pokey, which are accompanied by easy sing-along songs.

## Theater

Educators can expose young children to theater, both as participants and audience members. Young children may enjoy puppets, and older children can begin to take on roles and learn and memorize short lines. Memorization and recitation skills are transferable to educational activities in other subjects such as spelling words, learning history dates, and memorizing state capitals. Theater activities provide opportunities for imaginative play for children who enjoy dressing up, pretending to be various

characters, imagining and acting out scenes, improvising lines, and mimicking jobs, characters, and roles in society. This is healthy and developmentally-appropriate.

## Fundamental Concepts Related to the Arts

Artists, regardless of medium, typically rely on the following six main principles in art: emphasis, rhythm, balance, contrast, harmony, and movement.

### Emphasis
Artists often want to make one part of their work stand out from the rest and guide viewers to pay attention to specific components of their piece. For example, lines and textures in paintings and sculptures may direct viewers to specific details or target features, and altering the texture of one area may make it stand out in contrast to the rest of the work.

### Rhythm
Rhythm involves repeating elements within a work such as colors, shapes, lines, notes, or steps to create a pattern of visual or auditory motion.

### Balance
Balance is positioning objects or using size, color, shape and lighting in the artwork so that all of the elements are equally present with no particular component overpowering the rest. Symmetrical balance is when two halves of an image create a mirror image, so that if the work is folded in half, each half is the same. Balance can also be asymmetrical, wherein the composition is balanced but the two halves are not the same. For example, a large central object is balanced by a smaller figure on one edge.

### Contrast
Contrast exemplifies differences between two unlike things such as loud and soft music, major and minor tones, fast and slow dancing movements, and light and dark colors.

### Harmony
Somewhat opposite of contrast, harmony highlights the similarities in separate but related parts of a composition. Rather than emphasizing their dissimilarities, harmony shows that different things can actually be related to each other and blend together.

### Movement
Artwork that contains a sense of motion or action has movement. Even stationary art, like painting and sculpture, can imply movement based on the positioning of objects or the artist's use of lines, which draw the viewer's eye to different areas of the artwork.

## Art Terminology

Each of the four forms of art have a vast list of terminology unique to that art form. Educators should be familiar with such terms to help effectively communicate with and educate students and, more importantly, to empower students to have intelligent and meaningful conversations about artwork with peers, artists, and community members. Listed below are some examples of common terms to introduce at age-appropriate levels with each of the various forms of art:

## Visual Arts

Early learners can focus on the basic vocabulary of visual art like identifying colors and shapes. Older students can be exposed to more nuanced terms in the world of visual art. Some visual art is *representational* and depicts objects as they appear in the real world. One visual tool that heightens the realistic accuracy of visual art is *perspective*, an artistic technique that creates the illusion of depth through the use of line (for example, lines in the foreground converge in the background), size and placement of objects (objects that are supposed to be closer to the viewer appear larger than objects that are further away), or color (for example, a hill that is close to the viewer is depicted in a vibrant green, while a distant mountain appears with a more muted, hazy color).

In contrast to representational art, other visual art is *abstract*. When artists use abstraction, they use line, color, and other elements to communicate the presence of objects and emotions rather than realistically portraying the objects. For example, a swirl of warm colors like red and orange might represent anger or anxiety; cool colors like blue and gray could communicate sadness or passivity. In this way, the artist's *palette*, or range of colors used in their work, can communicate a mood or emotion to the viewer. Some works are *monochromatic*, meaning that they only use one color (although the artist might use different shades of the same color—for example, dark blue and light blue). Different shades of color can also create the illusion of shape or represent different lighting.

Other tools of both abstract and representational visual art include *contrast* (the pairing of dissimilar elements to make each other stand out), *positive* and *negative space* (positive space refers to the areas of the artwork occupied by its subject, whereas negative space includes all the areas that do not contain any subject), *balance*, and *symmetry*. Some artistic techniques to introduce to students might include caricature, collage, painting, sculpture, portraiture, landscape, and still life. If educators are able to take students on museum field trips, students should know museum-related vocabulary terms like *gallery*, *exhibit*, and *curator*.

## Music

Students should be familiar with terms related to *meter*, which is the repeating pattern of stressed and unstressed sounds in a piece of music. While meter is a somewhat complex concept, students can easily understand the idea of a musical beat, which is the audible result of meter. In written music, meter is noted by a time signature, which looks like a fraction with one number on the top and one number on the bottom, like ¾. The bottom number expresses the beat as a division of a whole note (for example, the number four means that it is a quarter note), while the top number shows how many beats make up a bar (so ¾ means that three quarter note beats make up one bar).

In addition to patterns of stress, music also contains an arrangement of sounds, known as its melody. *Melody* refers to the development of a single tone; when many tones are combined simultaneously in a way that sounds pleasing to the listener, it is referred to as *harmony*. Other sound elements related to tone include *chords* (the combination of musical tones), *keys* (the principal tone in a piece of music), and *scales* (a series of tones at fixed intervals, either ascending or descending, usually beginning at a certain note). These elements can be described as either major or minor.

Words to describe the *tempo*, or the speed of a piece of music, include, from slowest to fastest: *largo, adagio, andante, allegro, vivace,* and *presto.* In terms of the intensity of the sound, *piano* refers to music that is played softly whereas *forte* means played with force. Students should also be familiar with vocabulary terms that describe different instruments, different genres of music, and different musical periods.

## Dance

In dance, a *step* is one isolated movement, and *choreography* refers to the arrangement of a series of steps. Even young students can learn simple choreography that they rehearse with an instructor and perform with classmates as a group. Older students can learn about different styles of dance such as the waltz, tap, jazz, and ballet, as well as more contemporary styles like *lyrical dance* (combining ballet and jazz) or *fusion dance* (a highly rhythmical dance form). Students of ballet should be familiar with terms like *pirouette* (spinning on one foot or on the points of the toes), *arabesque* (standing on one leg while extending one arm in front and the other arm and leg behind), *plié* (bending at the knees while holding the back straight), *elevé* (rising up from flat foot to pointed feet), and *pivot* (turning the body without traveling to a new location; a pirouette is a type of pivot). Students can also learn about folk dances, partner dances, and line dances.

## Theater Arts

Students can become familiar with a host of terms related to theater productions. In terms of people working in theater, there is the *director* leading the production and *actors* performing it. The *cast* is comprised of a group of actors, and an organization of actors and other theater workers is known as a *company*. During the casting process, actors usually need to *audition* for parts in a play, and they may get a *callback* if their audition goes well! In addition to a main performer, leading roles in a production might also have an *understudy*, an actor who can step into the role when the main performer is unable to appear in the show.

On the technical side, students can learn about *props, sets, costumes* and *wardrobe, effects,* and *staging*. Theater arts education also presents an opportunity to teach students about the literary aspects of a play, such as the *narrator*, *act* and *scene* divisions, and stage directions contained in the script. Students can also become familiar with different dramatic modes like *comedy* and *tragedy*. They can learn about the structure of classic drama as well as more open ended structures like *ad lib* and *improvisation*.

## Basic Techniques, Tools, and Materials for Producing Art

Art has personal (self-expression, gratification, narrative functions), social (collective meaning for a group of people, such as symbolic art honoring a god or political art), and physical (such as a pottery mug for tea) functions that often overlap within a single piece of work. As children go through elementary school, they become familiar with an increasing variety and complexity of visual art forms beginning with things like drawing, painting, and sculpting, then adding printmaking, sponge painting, film animation, and graphics in third and fourth grades, and dabbling in environmental design and art based on personal experience and observation by the fifth grade. They may also try computer-generated art, photography, metalworking, textile arts, and ceramics. Materials include scissors, brushes, papers, glue, beads, clay, film, and computers.

Instruments used in the early education classroom typically fall into one of the following categories: melodic instruments (melody bells, xylophones, flutes, and recorders), rhythmic instruments (drums, triangles, tambourines, and blocks), or harmonic instruments (chording instruments such as the autoharp). The key elements of music include rhythm, melody, harmony, form (the structure or design of the music, usually referring to the music's different sections and their repetition, such as binary (AB), ternary (ABA), theme and variation and rondo (ABACA), and the musical phrases), and expression [dynamics (volumes) and timbre].

The main skills of the theatrical arts are literary, technical, and performance elements. For theater, teachers can use a variety of techniques to incorporate dramatic arts into the classroom, including the following:

## Theater-in-Education (TIE)

This is performed by teachers and students using curriculum material or social issues. Participants take on roles that enable them to explore and problem-solve in a flexible structure that is also educational. TIE productions are conducted with clear educational objectives, such as teaching facts or communicating a lesson to the audience.

## Puppetry

Puppetry can be used for creative drama with either simple puppets and stages made of bags, cardboard, socks, or more elaborate, artistic materials. Using puppets in theater allows students to tell stories about a wide variety of characters and settings without requiring large and complex costumes, props, or sets. Telling stories with puppets also allows children to develop their motor skills.

More formal theater works for children are typically product-oriented and audience-centered, and children can be either participants or audience members. Such forms may include the following:

### *Traditional Theater*

Actors use characters and storylines to communicate and the audience laughs, applauds, or provides other feedback. The performers and audience are separate entities and the acting takes place on a stage, supported by technical workers.

### *Participation Theater*

Students can engage their voices or bodies in the work by contributing ideas, joining the actors, or contributing in other ways. This is more interactive than traditional theater.

### *Story Theater*

Often told with simple sets, story theater can take place easily in the classroom with minimal scenery and costumes. Due to the sparse use of sets, props, and costumes, story theater often incorporates improvisational strategies to communicate character and setting to the audience. The actors function as characters and narrators and play multiple parts, often commenting on their own actions in their roles.

### *Readers' Theater*

Readers perform a dramatic presentation while reading lines (typically from children's literature), enabling performance opportunities in the absence of elaborate staging or script memorization. This

allows students to focus on emotional expression and speaking skills while reading their lines. The students can sit or stand but no movement is needed.

**Readers' Theater**

Dance simultaneously incorporates a variety of elements, including the following:

*Body:* refers to *who* – the dancer – and may describe the whole body or its parts, the shape of the body (such as angular, twisted, symmetrical), the systems of the body and its anatomy, or inner aspects of the body such as emotions, intention, and identity.

*Action:* refers to *what* – the movement created in the dance such as the steps, facial changes, or actions with the body – and can occur in short bouts or long, continuous actions.

*Time:* refers to *when*, and may be metered or free. Time may also refer to clock time or relationships of time such as before, after, in unison with, or faster than something else.

*Space:* refers to *where* through space, and how the dancer fills the space and interacts with it. For example, it can refer to whether the dancer's body is low to the ground or up high; moving or in place; going forward, backwards, or sideways; in a curved or random pattern; in front or behind others; or in a group or alone.

*Energy:* refers to *how*. It is with energy that a force or action causes movement. Dancers may play with flow, tension, and weight. Their energy may be powerful or it may be gentle and light.

## Self-Expression and Communication through Art

One of the fundamental benefits of the arts is their ability to be used as forms of self-expression, creativity, and self-identity, and a means to communicate emotions, culture, and personal and societal narratives. While the youngest students may not fully grasp the ability to express themselves through art, even fairly young children can use art to communicate ideas, stories, and feelings. Early childhood educators can encourage students to use all forms of art for self-expression and should engage children in active critical thinking and analysis to uncover the meanings and emotions behind artwork generated by others. For example, educators can play a variety of music clips with different tempos, moods, tones, and keys and ask students to explain how the music makes them feel and what they think the composer

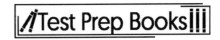

was trying to express. Compositions in minor keys, at slower largo and adagio tempos, and music with harmonic dissonance may evoke feelings of sadness, trepidation, anxiety, or fear, whereas lively, spirited songs in major keys at faster allegro tempos are likely expressing happier feelings. Students can begin to contrast different moods and types of music and talk about how the moods are conveyed by differences in the music.

Similarly, the students can look at visual artwork and analyze the artist's use of different colors, textures, brushstrokes, etc. to express the feelings behind the artwork. Students can also try to discern the narrative within art, particularly in theater, music, and dance. They can try to understand how stories can be told abstractly and recognize that not every story is told through concrete narrative writing. For example, operatic works and ballets often tell elaborate stories with few or no words. Yet, even when they are presented in foreign languages, operas and ballets can be universally understood by varying audiences due to the emotions and movements present on stage. While these abstract concepts are likely too complex for young children, as students mature and develop, they will gradually become more aware of the nuances and arts' function as a vehicle of expression. Young children are able to understand how their pictorial drawings or paintings convey a narrative in their mind; from there, they can begin to understand how artwork generated by another person conveys his or her storyline. Educators can also encourage students to use art as a cathartic release when they are feeling sad, angry, frustrated, or nervous. Dance, visual arts, and music are constructive, safe, and appropriate ways to temper difficult emotions. Children can use dance choreography and improvisation to express feelings and ideas as well.

## Arts in Various Cultures and Throughout History

It is imperative that early childhood educators focus on the fact that artwork has been used throughout history and in every culture as a means of expression and storytelling. Even seemingly new forms of art were not created out of nowhere, but rather, they have evolved from other previously existing forms of art. One of the best ways to discuss art is actually through embedding it in discussions of history and culture. The evolution of music can easily be discussed through various time periods. For example, the assassination of President John F. Kennedy, the Hippie movement, the Vietnam War, and the Beatles coexisted in the same time period, so students can find similarities and differences among these social and artistic ideals within their historical context.

Students can also study different time periods of art and architecture. In the Classical period, Greek artists focused on physical beauty and the human form, paying particular attention to Olympian gods and their idealized proportions in their works. The Medieval period that occurred in Europe from 500-1400 CE saw a flourish of Romanesque style art that shifted the emphasis from portraying realism to conveying a message, particularly symbolic Christian ideals. Students should also learn about the history of art in other countries such as China, with its jade, pottery, bronze, porcelain, and calligraphy. Educators should focus on how various influences over time affected the predominant artwork each period. For example, Buddhism in the early first century BCE increased calligraphy on silks, the Song dynasty created landscape paintings that were popular, and the Ming and Qing dynasties developed color painting and printing with an evolution towards individualism. As China became increasingly influenced by Western society in the nineteenth and early twentieth centuries, social realism predominated. In addition to covering other Asian nations, educators should expose students to traditional African art, which generally demonstrates moral values, focuses on human subjects, and seeks to please the viewer. Educators can also introduce art from the American Indians such as woodcarving, weaving, stitchery, and beading. Art in American Indian populations varies widely from tribe to tribe but tends to beautify everyday objects and create items of spiritual significance. Students

should be exposed to music and theater from other cultures and observe the costumes, movements, instruments, and themes in performing arts from places like the Caribbean islands, Japan, Mexico, Australia, Africa, Italy, and Russia.

## Basic Structures of Bones, Skeletal Muscle, and Connective Tissue Bone

The skeleton is divided into the axial (skull, vertebrae, ribs, and sternum) and appendicular (shoulder girdles, arms, hips, legs) skeletons. There are two types of bone or osseous tissue. Compact (cortical) bone comprises 80 percent of bone mass and is made of dense, organized Haversian systems, which are arrangements of minerals, living bone cells, nerves, blood, and lymph vessels. Cancellous (spongy) bone, the other 20 percent of bone mass, lacks Haversian systems, is porous with trabeculae (lattice, branching arrangement), and has marrow and fat storage.

## Skeletal Muscle

This muscle is voluntarily controlled by the nervous system and is elastic, extensible, and able to contract. It is striated, and cells have multiple nuclei.

## Connective Tissue

The three major structures are tendons (attaching muscle to bone), ligaments (connecting bone to bone), and fascia (attaches, stabilizes, encloses, and separates muscles and other internal organs).

## Basic Anatomy of Cardiovascular and Respiratory Systems

The heart has the smaller right and left atria on top of the larger right and left ventricles. A series of valves keeps blood flowing in the correct direction and prevents backflow to optimize cardiac efficiency: the bicuspid, tricuspid, pulmonary semilunar, and aortic semilunar valves.

The aorta is the main blood vessel branching off the top of the heart and sends blood to circulate through the body. The blood vessels, in order of decreasing size away from the heart, are arteries, arterioles, and capillaries. Towards the heart, from smallest to largest, are capillaries, venules, and veins.

Blood enters the (1) right atrium. When it contracts, blood passes through the (2) tricuspid valve into the (3) right ventricle. After filling, the right ventricle contracts, and the tricuspid valve closes, pushing blood through the (4) pulmonary semilunar valve into the (5) pulmonary arteries. These arteries, unlike all other arteries in the body, carry deoxygenated blood to the lungs, where blood travels through the (6) alveolar capillaries. Here, oxygen is absorbed, and carbon dioxide is removed.

The newly-oxygenated blood is carried by the (7) pulmonary veins back to the (8) left atrium. Contraction of the left atrium moves blood through the (9) bicuspid valve into the (10) left ventricle (the largest heart chamber). When the bicuspid valve closes and the left ventricle contracts, blood is forced into the (11) aortic valve through the aorta and on to systemic circulation.

## Major Muscles

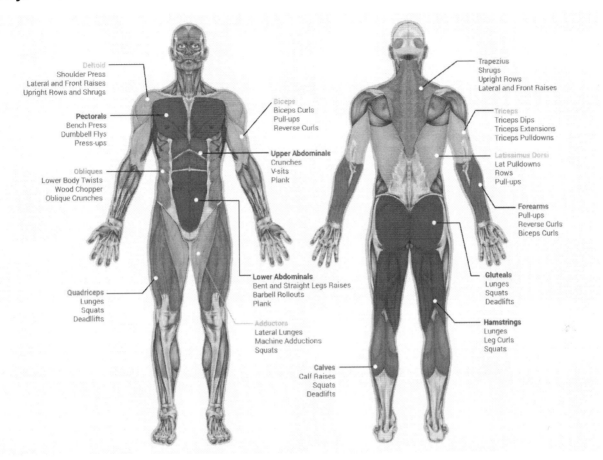

Teachers should not only be aware of muscle names, but also their origins, insertions, primary action, and nerve innervation. An understanding of these criteria can help in identifying injuries. It can also help ensure that exercises are targeting all muscles to maximize strength, strengthen stabilizing muscles, and provide proximal stability for functional distal mobility.

- Upper body muscles: trapezius, pectoralis major, deltoids, serratus anterior, latissimus dorsi, biceps, triceps, rectus abdominis, internal and external obliques, erector spinae, rhomboids, flexor carpi radialis

- Lower body muscles: iliopsoas, gluteus maximus, quadriceps, piriformis, hamstrings, adductors, abductors, soleus, gastrocnemius

## Major Bones

Knowledge of bone anatomy enables the physical education instructor to understand the bones involved in joint motions and the bones that may be implicated in certain orthopedic injuries, which is important when communicating with physicians. There are different types of bones. Flat bones, like the cranial bones of the skull and the sternum, protect internal organs. Long bones, like the femur and tibia, support weight and facilitate movement. Short bones, like the carpal bones in the wrist, provide stability and some movement. Irregular bones also protect structures like the vertebrae over the spinal cord. Lastly, sesamoid bones, like the patella, protect tendons from stress.

- Upper body bones: clavicle, scapula, sternum, humerus, carpals, ulna, radius, metacarpals, vertebrae, ribs

- Lower body bones: ilium, ischium, pubis, femur, fibula, tibia, metatarsals, tarsals

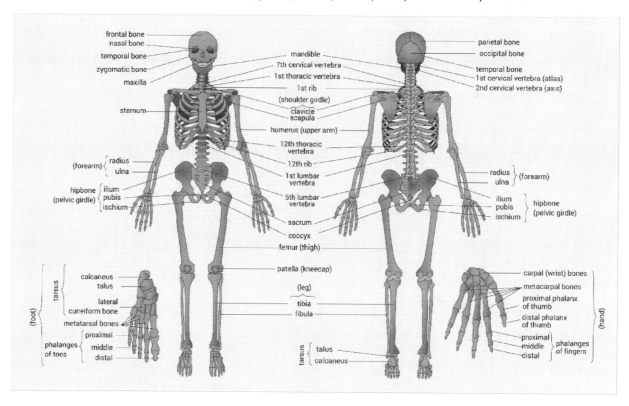

## Joint Classifications

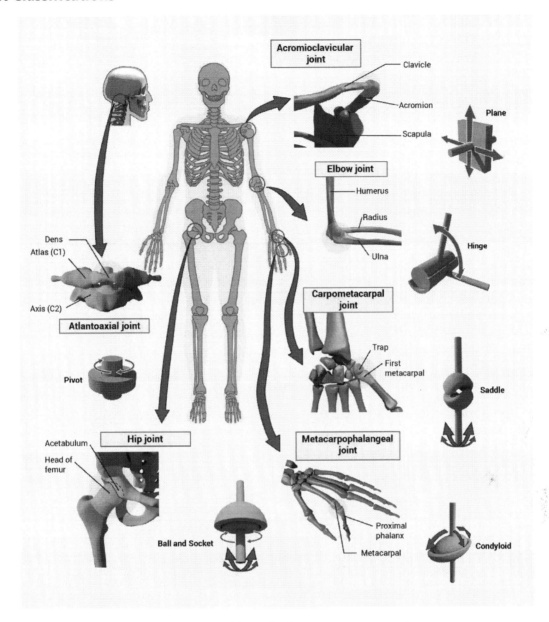

Joints can be classified based on structure of how the bones are connected:

- Fibrous joints: bones joined by fibrous tissue and that lack a joint cavity, e.g., sutures of the skull

- Cartilaginous joints: bones joined by cartilage and lack a joint cavity, e.g., the pubic symphysis

- Synovial joints: bones separated by a fluid-containing joint cavity with articular cartilage covering the ends of the bone and forming a capsule

- Plane joints: flat surfaces that allow gliding and transitional movements, e.g., intercarpal joints

- Hinge joints: cylindrical projection that nests in a trough-shaped structure, single plane of movement (e.g. the elbow)

- Pivot joints: rounded structure that sits into a ring-like shape, allowing uniaxial rotation of the bone around the long axis (e.g. radius head on ulna)

- Condyloid joints: oval articular surface that nests in a complementary depression, allowing all angular movements (e.g. the wrist)

- Saddle joints: articular surfaces that both have complementary concave and convex areas, allowing more movement than condyloid joints (e.g. the thumb)

- Ball-and-socket joints: spherical structure that fits in a cuplike structure, allowing multiaxial movements (e.g. the shoulder)

## Primary Action and Joint Range of Motion

Each type of joint permits different movements, controlled by the shape of the joint and the muscles surrounding it. Educators should be aware of these movements and the normal ROM to ensure that students are performing exercises safely, are within a healthy range, and are utilizing a variety of motions to optimize health and muscular balance. Ball-and-socket joints, like the shoulder and hip, are the most mobile and allow flexion, extension, abduction, adduction, internal and external rotation, and circumduction. The elbow is a hinge joint and allows flexion and extension. Intervertebral joints are cartilaginous and allow flexion, extension, lateral flexion, and rotation. The ankle has a hinge joint (dorsiflexion, plantarflexion) and a gliding joint (inversion, eversion).

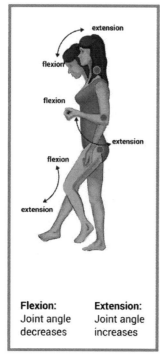

**Flexion:** Joint angle decreases **Extension:** Joint angle increases

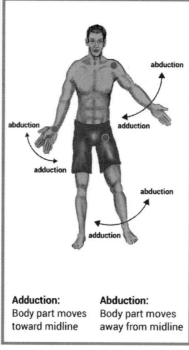

**Adduction:** Body part moves toward midline **Abduction:** Body part moves away from midline

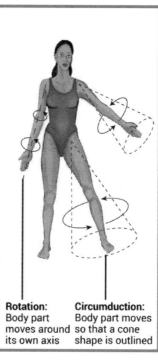

**Rotation:** Body part moves around its own axis **Circumduction:** Body part moves so that a cone shape is outlined

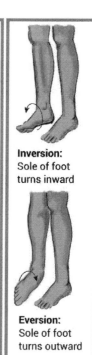

**Inversion:** Sole of foot turns inward

**Eversion:** Sole of foot turns outward

## Components of Physical Fitness

A well-rounded program addresses all five components of health-related physical fitness:

- Cardiovascular fitness: capacity of circulatory and respiratory systems to supply oxygen during continued activity

- Muscular strength: force capability of a muscle
- Muscular endurance: ability to maintain level of muscular work without fatigue
- Body composition: relative amounts of body fat, muscle, bone, and other tissues
- Flexibility: permitted joint range of motion

## Prevention of Common Injuries and Health Problems

One critically important component of health and safety education is the prevention of common injuries and illnesses. By practicing safety and exercising caution, many common injuries and illnesses can be avoided. For example, wearing helmets and seat belts can reduce the risk of injury during automobile or bicycle accidents. Washing hands thoroughly and frequently with antibacterial soap can help prevent the spread of germs, and thus safeguard against viral and bacterial infections. Even very young children should be encouraged to wash hands thoroughly before and after eating, after using the bathroom, after coming in from outdoor play, and when transitioning to a new activity. It is sometimes helpful to demonstrate how to wash in between each finger, under the fingernails, and up to the wrists, modeling not only how to wash hands but for how long. The common song "Row, Row, Row Your Boat" repeated three times is sometimes used to measure the appropriate length of time for hand washing.

By instilling an attitude of mindfulness and awareness, educators can help children to develop practices of safety, which will ultimately keep them healthy. Other longer-term behavioral and lifestyle principles – such as keeping a healthy weight through caloric balance and a healthy diet – will help prevent disease risk factors such as obesity, high triglycerides, hypercholesterolemia, and high blood sugar. Children should be informed about the dangers of smoking and the detrimental health consequences of tobacco products, including ingestion of secondhand smoke. Other simple safety practices include wearing proper footwear, practicing good hygiene, remaining alert when out in traffic, using sidewalks and pedestrian walkways, and wearing sunscreen.

### Wearing Seat Belts and Helmets

Children should be informed that they should always wear a seat belt in the car. Children under eighty pounds should be in an appropriate car seat as well to maximize safety in moving vehicles. Many unfortunate traffic injuries and fatalities could have been prevented had the victim appropriately worn a seat belt. Riding bicycles, skateboarding, using scooters, and rollerblading are examples of excellent exercise and recreational pursuits; however, helmets and appropriate padding and protection on elbows and knees should always be worn. Children or their supervisors often neglect to fasten on a helmet when the child is simply trying out a skateboard or scooter around the driveway or park. This is quite dangerous because falls are inevitable in the learning process and even minor head bumps can be damaging. Helmets should fit snugly with the band clipped securely under the chin and the dome of the helmet should cover the entire forehead. Helmets should not move freely on the head and should be snug enough to stay in place. They should be sized appropriately to the child's head with use of additional padding if necessary. Kneepads and shoulder pads are great adjuncts to safety gear for rollerblading, skateboarding, and scooters. Children riding in bicycle trailers should also wear helmets, and children should never ride on the handlebars of a bicycle. Although more stable, tricycles and bicycles with training wheels still require helmets with their use.

### Drugs, Alcohol, and Tobacco

Drugs, alcohol, and tobacco are unhealthy substances that early childhood educators should begin informing young children about. Exposure to drugs, cigarettes, and alcohol happens at increasingly younger ages, particularly when children have older siblings. By educating children about the risks and

consequences of such substances at young ages, teachers can begin to thwart the risks of unhealthy behaviors. The Drug Abuse Resistance Education (D.A.R.E.) program is often helpful at introducing such substances, their health consequences, and how to navigate social situations involving peer pressure. The difference between alcohol abuse and alcohol in moderation should also be discussed.

## Routine Preventative Medical and Dental Care

By practicing routine medical and dental care and adhering to recommended guidelines regarding the frequency of preventative healthcare, certain risks for various diseases and dental issues (such as cavities and gingivitis) can be reduced. It is typically recommended the children see their pediatrician and get dental cleanings at least once every six months. In between these appointments, healthy habits continue to safeguard against health issues. Examples include thoroughly brushing teeth at least twice a day and flossing daily, getting at least sixty minutes of moderate to vigorous exercise a day, meeting healthy sleep requirements (the National Sleep Foundation recommends ten to thirteen hours for preschoolers and nine to eleven hours for elementary school children), consuming an adequate amount of water, and following nutritional guidelines. By keeping children on a routine schedule of preventive care with consistency in providers of that care, the health and wellbeing of each child can be tracked during their growth to ensure health issues do not slip through the cracks.

## Food Preparation Choices

Early childhood educators should devote instructional attention to the methods of food preparation and how various choices in preparation affect the nutritive value of the food. For example, baking and steaming are healthier than pan frying, deep frying, and sautéing. Eating whole foods is healthier than eating their processed counterparts because the whole foods retain a greater percentage of the inherent nutrients. For example, apples are healthier than applesauce because applesauce strips away much of the fiber and the vitamins in the apple skin. Similarly, whole grain bread is healthier than refined white breads, which remove the bran from the grain, thereby reducing the fiber, protein, and B vitamin content. Foods that are organic do not have the pesticides and chemicals used with certain conventional foods. This is an important consideration for thin-skinned fruits and vegetables such as spinach, tomatoes, and berries, which can absorb harmful chemicals.

## Health Promotion and Disease Prevention

Early childhood educators should be able to incorporate health and physical education concepts into the classroom for the overall health, wellness, and growth of their students. Physical activity is especially important at young ages, and children need at least sixty minutes of moderate to vigorous physical activity daily according to the U.S. Surgeon General's Recommendations. There are five components of health-related physical fitness: cardiovascular fitness, muscular strength, muscular endurance, flexibility, and body composition. All five areas should be addressed in physical education classes. With cardiovascular training, as the heart enlarges, the volume of the chambers increase, allowing for a greater stroke volume and cardiac output. This also enables the heart to be more efficient, with a resultant lowering of the resting and submaximal exercise heart rate and blood pressure, which increases the body's exercise duration and intensity tolerance. Blood volume—both in terms of plasma and hemoglobin—increases oxygen-carrying capacity and lactic acid metabolism improves, which allows the aerobic system to more effectively metabolize substrates for usable energy. Muscle glycogen

storage, another important form of energy storage in the body, also increases. Vasculature increases as well, improving the blood perfusion of muscles.

Other positive results of physical fitness include increased bone mineral density, improvements in body composition, and neural adaptations. Resistance training, even with body weight alone (such as squats and push-ups), affords strength, power, and coordination improvements and leads to greater efficiency of the anaerobic metabolic systems. Nervous system adaptations occur quickly with training as motor units (connections between the spine and other muscles throughout the body) become conditioned to activate more quickly and more often. As a greater number of motor units activate together and coordinate with each other, a higher percentage of fibers in a muscle contract simultaneously, increasing strength. Over time, muscle fibers increase in size and bone mineral density increases in load-bearing bones. Flexibility training increases elasticity and resting length of muscle and connective tissues and joint range of motion (ROM) before the stretch reflex is initiated (muscle spindle adaptation), reducing injury risk.

Health education – even beginning at preschool ages – has been shown to have a significant positive impact on an individual for maintaining healthy behaviors as an adolescent and adult. Preschool children who receive high-quality physical and health education may have improved nutrition and exercise habits and are more likely to receive routine medical and dental care as adults. Early childhood educators can start laying the groundwork for a lifetime of healthier behaviors and attitudes by fostering an environment of enjoyment of physical activity, an understanding of nutrition and hydration, and methods of disease and injury prevention.

Educators can talk with older children about the types, causes, and characteristics of chronic, degenerative, communicable, and non-communicable diseases, as well as ways to detect and prevent them. Students can learn about modifiable risk factors for various diseases and conditions such as diabetes, coronary artery disease, cardiovascular disease, and obesity.

## The Relation Between Healthy Behaviors and a Healthy Person

Early childhood educators can introduce young children to a wide variety of healthy behaviors that will help improve overall health. An important concept to begin teaching students is that optimal health is brought about through routine practice of daily healthy behaviors and an overall commitment to a healthy lifestyle. For example, educators can discuss the importance of establishing regular physical activity and daily healthy eating habits and that, through these habits, students can control their body weight and help avoid obesity. Obesity is a modifiable risk factor for many diseases including insulin-resistant Type 2 diabetes mellitus and cardiovascular disease. It is important and empowering for children to start to understand their roles and responsibilities in healthy habits and disease prevention. By giving them the necessary knowledge and tools to put the information into practice in their lives, educators can increase the self-efficacy and behaviors of even young children. In this way, early childhood educators can be instrumental in bringing about a healthier generation of young children who have an awareness of their health and an understanding of their own influence on risk factors for certain diseases. The following are healthy behaviors that can lead to a healthy body and mind:

## Nutrition

Children should be taught how to identify foods and the importance of consuming a daily variety of food within each healthy food group. The benefits of trying new foods, especially those from other cultures, can help students understand diversity and challenge their preconceived notions about different cultures and flavors. Older children can learn how to prepare simple foods, recognize the USDA recommended daily allowances of each food group in order to keep the body healthy, and classify foods based on their group and health benefits. Older students can also learn about the role of various nutrients in the body such as fat, fiber, and protein, and how to select nutrient-dense foods from a given list. Children benefit from understanding what makes a food healthy and knowing options for healthy meals and snacks. By the third grade, students can start learning how to read nutrition labels, how to compare foods based on nutrition labels, and how to modify food choices to improve healthfulness, such as replacing low-fiber foods with higher fiber choices, like opting for apples instead of applesauce. When students are in the fourth grade, educators can start talking about portion sizes and the relationship between food consumption and physical activity on energy balance and weight control. In the context of introducing the basics about calories, prevention of obesity and the ramifications of an unhealthy diet can also be discussed. Children in the fifth and sixth grades can learn about the differences in types of fats, examples of common vitamins and minerals and food sources of these nutrients, the disadvantages of "empty-calories," and how to recognize misleading nutrition information.

## Physical Activity

In childhood, regular physical activity improves strength and endurance, helps build healthy bones and muscles, controls weight, reduces anxiety and stress, increases self-esteem, and may improve blood pressure and cholesterol. Children should get at least sixty minutes of physical activity daily. Typically, young children are less concerned about their physical fitness and more concerned about having fun; therefore, physical education should center on fun and play as a means to engage the body in activity. Play-centered physical education programs are an effective means to promote children's movement development and meet their requisite activity needs for health. Early childhood educators should develop physical education programs that focus on the enjoyment of movement rather than sport-specific skill mastery for two reasons. Firstly, play-centered activity will help the child be more engaged and likely to adopt a positive attitude towards exercise; and secondly, in early childhood, basic general fitness and movement skills are more important than mastery of highly specialized skills unique to certain sports. Young children also tend to lack the gross and fine motor skills and perceptual abilities needed for such highly specialized skills, which can lead to frustration or simply an inability to perform the activity.

For optimal results, it is best for early childhood educators to establish an environment of student-centered learning in regards to physical education. Because young children at any given age can have vastly different motor and physical abilities from each other, it is imperative that the educator simply set standards of enjoyment, movement, and physical discovery rather than specific mastery of skills. This prevents boredom in more physically advanced children and bewilderment and demotivation in less skilled children. It is prudent for educators to provide a variety of options within every activity and game so that children can figure out what appeals and works for them at their own developmental level. This also starts children on the path to understanding themselves and evaluating choices at a young age within a fun, playful environment and begins to get their minds processing not just what to do but how to do it as well.

Educators should use simple instructions that are age-appropriate in terms of the steps and level of complexity, visual demonstrations of movements, and drills that help reinforce the skill. During practice and exploration of the new skill, educators should focus on positive feedback and evaluation to guide the children in learning. When teaching new skills, especially to toddlers and young children, instructions lasting longer than twenty seconds or that contain more than just a couple of steps will cause students to lose interest or get overwhelmed. It is typically advantageous to have very short instructional periods interspersed between longer breaks to play and try out the skills. To help manage a large group of small, active children, simple rules and expectations should be laid out with consequences for improper behavior.

Children should learn about the methods and benefits of a proper warm-up and cool-down, how to set goals to make exercise part of their daily routine, and the benefits of physical activity. Older children can learn about the effects of exercise on the heart and how to locate their pulse during and after exercise, how to stay physically active through more than just sports, and how to create a personal fitness plan.

## Sleep

Early childhood educators should talk about the importance of sleep and why parents set a "bedtime," as well as healthy sleep hygiene and establishing a sleep schedule. Children can learn about how much sleep they need and ways to improve the quality of sleep, such as physical activity and avoiding screen time before bed. Young children who may experience nightmares can benefit from learning relaxation techniques as well as talking about their fears and feelings to trusted adults.

## Stress Management

Students should be educated about stress management and exposed to techniques such as mental imagery, relaxation, deep breathing, aerobic exercise, and meditation. Children can be guided through progressive muscle relaxation and should be taught signs of excessive nervousness and stress, how to manage test and performance anxiety, and when and how to get help with excessive stress.

## Healthy Relationships

Healthy family and social relationships are important to overall health and happiness. Studies have pointed to a negative impact of parental fighting on a child's wellbeing, including sleep and exercise habits, nutrition choices, stress, and social adjustment. Early childhood educators should talk about aspects of healthy relationships such as communication, emotional support, sharing, and respect. Younger children should learn skills that are helpful in making friends, cultivating relationships, and resolving conflict, especially as they relate to peers and siblings. Cooperation, taking turns, using words rather than physical means to communicate feelings, and exploring feelings are helpful concepts to instill. Older children should begin to be exposed to dating etiquette and forming healthy romantic relationships. Educators should work to create a classroom environment of inclusion where students have an awareness of peers who may feel left out and work to include everyone. Within discussions of healthy relationships, educators should talk about accepting and appreciating diversity, including differences in cultures, religions, families, physical appearance and abilities, interests, intellect, emotions, lifestyle, and, in older children, sexual orientations. Life skills – such as having self-esteem, making decisions, calming oneself when angry or upset, and using listening skills – should be addressed.

## Hydration

Early childhood educators should teach students about the importance of hydration and signs of dehydration as well as healthy choices for fluids, with a special emphasis on water. Children and their parents should be encouraged to send kids to school with a water bottle, and classrooms or hallways should be equipped with water fountains that children can access and use with limited supervision or assistance.

## Safety Behaviors

Children should learn basic safety behaviors and the importance of following rules to prevent common injuries. Basic safety behaviors include wearing sunscreen and sunglasses when going outdoors; wearing protective gear in sports such as bicycle helmets, reflective vests, appropriate pads and cups, etc.; and using a car seat and/or always wearing a seat belt. Young children should learn about household safety such as not touching burners and not putting their fingers in electrical sockets nor opening the door to strangers. Educators should have children practice the "no, go, and tell" procedure for unsafe situations. For example, if a stranger offers the child an unknown substance, the child should know how to firmly refuse, carefully leave the situation, and tell a trusted adult. In this lesson, educators should also help children to identify trusted adults in their families and communities.

Educators can also discuss community safety measures such as using sidewalks, contacting city services (police, fire, and ambulance) in emergencies, and crossing the street safely by using crosswalks, holding hands, and looking both ways before crossing. Children should also learn about the health consequences of smoking, how to avoid secondhand smoke, and how to identify and avoid poisonous household substances. Fire safety such as "stop, drop, and roll" and emergency evacuation procedures should be rehearsed. Older children can learn about safety rules for various types of weather and how weather affects their personal safety, what different traffic signs mean, water/swim safety rules, and the importance of weighing consequences before taking risks.

## Hygiene

Young children should learn about germs and the spread of infections. Older children can learn about bacteria and viruses. The importance of washing hands (including appropriate demonstration) cannot be overstated in elementary and preschool classrooms.

Other aspects of hygiene such as covering the mouth while coughing and covering the nose while sneezing, not sharing cups, practicing clean bathroom habits, showering and bathing, and, in older children, using deodorants, antiperspirants, and facial cleansers should be included in the curriculum.

## Hygiene Stickers Remind Students to Use Healthy Practices

## Learning to Seek Health Care

Early childhood educators can play an instrumental role in the lifelong practice of seeking routine medical and dental care as well as medical support during illness and injury by setting positive attitudes towards such care and explaining the benefits to young children. Not all children will necessarily have health insurance, so information regarding local free and affordable options should be made available to parents. It is important that children learn to identify signs of illness and injury such as sore throats, headaches, stomachaches that do not go away, swelling, etc.

### Consistent Feelings of Sadness, Anxiety, Loneliness, and Stress

Just as it is important to get professional help for medical issues, it equally important to seek help with mental and emotional issues. Educators should talk about feelings and emotions and how it is normal to feel sad or anxious at various times, but that if such feelings persist, help may be necessary. Teachers can lead the class through stress management techniques to combat anxiety and talk about the role of physical activity, sound nutrition, and good sleep for mood stabilization. Young children should learn about identifying and communicating their emotions.

### Lingering Pains or Aches

Children should be instructed to tell a trusted adult when they have pains, aches, or symptoms that persist for several days so that the adult can help determine if medical attention is needed. Children can also learn basic first-aid such as how to wash a cut and put on a Band-Aid or when and how to use RICES (Rest, Ice, Compression, Elevation, and Stabilization) after an injury.

## Influence of Family, Peers, Culture, and Media on Health Behaviors

Health behaviors are heavily influenced by a child's environment, including family, friends, peers, media, and technology. These factors can shape the child's ideas of health, nutrition, and fitness, as well as influence subsequent health behaviors. It is important for educators to help children identify and cultivate positive influences while avoiding or modifying negative ones.

Educators should work with students to develop self-efficacy for healthy behaviors to help safeguard against any negative environmental influences. Children should learn about peer pressure, substance use, wearing seat belts, and how to make independent decisions and stick to them despite peer pressure or group dynamics. Discussed below are a few examples of potential environmental and situational influences.

### Family
Family factors include health insurance status, safety and injury prevention education and care, nutritional meal planning and diet composition, family dynamics and stress, family culture during leisure time such as activity vs. inactivity, child care situation, and parental and sibling modeled behavior.

### Peers
The peer group that surrounds a child can affect his or her health behaviors depending on those of the group. Example behaviors and influences include the use of helmets and seat belts, interests and activities, inclusion on sports teams or during recess and physical education, aggression and bullying or teasing.

### School and Community
Factors in this domain include things such as the availability and choices of food in vending machines, school breakfast and lunch programs, health education and screenings, first aid and AED (automated external defibrillator) access, bike paths and walking trails, parks and community fitness and sports programs, crosswalks, and non-smoking zones.

### Public Policy and Government
Tobacco and alcohol sales and policies, seat belt and helmet enforcement, child care laws, and other such regulations fall under the domain of public policy and governmental influences.

### Media
Media use and exposure can have a significant impact on young minds. Children have not necessarily developed the critical thinking skills needed to evaluate the truthfulness of media claims. Television programming and commercials, PSAs, advertising, exposure to celebrities, knowledge of current events, and consumer skills all fall under this domain.

### Technology
Technological factors including Internet access, handicap accessibility such as audio signals at crosswalks and wheelchair ramps and lifts, health technology apps, and pedometer availability can affect health behaviors.

## Motor Skills and Movement Patterns in Children

Educators should be familiar with physical and neurological development, especially in terms of motor skills and development, to provide developmentally appropriate motor movement tasks. As young

children grow and mature, they develop the ability to handle increasingly complex motor skills. Children learn to move and move to learn and, for this reason, physical activity is especially important in the classroom for young children. As children grow, their physical abilities gradually increase, and educators can begin to modify lessons and activities to continue to challenge and improve new movement patterns and abilities. What looks like "play" actually consists of meaningful movement patterns that help the child move his or her body and use large muscle groups to develop physical competency. This is known as movement education. Children should learn basic movement patterns and skills for daily life so that they can maneuver safely and appropriately in their environment in relation to other people and objects. After basic skills are mastered, more specific sport-related skills can be achieved. Movement competency is the successful ability of the child to manage his or her body in both basic and specialized physical tasks despite obstacles in the environment, while perceptual motor competency includes capabilities involving balance, coordination, lateral and backward movements, kinesthetic sense, and knowledge of one's own body and strength.

Educators should be able to assess the level at which students can control specific movements and identify patterns of physical activity that have been mastered. This information can be used to plan developmentally-appropriate movement tasks and activities. In addition, early childhood educators can be helpful in identifying students who seem to be lagging behind in age-appropriate motor abilities. In such cases, early intervention programming and resources may be beneficial.

There are three general categories of basic skills: locomotor, non-locomotor, and manipulative skills; more complex movement patterns combine skills from multiple categories. Locomotor skills – such as walking, running, jumping, and skipping – are the movement skills that children need to travel within a given space or get from one space to another. Non-locomotor skills are typically completed in a stationary position – such as kneeling, pushing, twisting, bouncing, or standing – and help control the body in relation to gravity. Manipulative skills usually involve using the hands and feet, although other body parts may be used. These skills help the child handle, move, or play with an object. Manipulating objects helps advance hand-eye and foot-eye coordination so that the child can more successfully participate in sports activities like throwing, batting, catching, and kicking.

Young children can begin to learn these skills with balls and beanbags at a less challenging level and progress to more difficult levels and activities with practice and development. Early stages usually involve individual practice first and then progress to involve partners and groups. Throwing and catching are actually quite complex skills that can be as challenging to teach as they are to learn. Early childhood educators should emphasize skill performance and principles such as opposition, following objects with the eyes, weight transfer, follow through, and, eventually, striking targets. Motor planning is the ability of the child to figure out how to complete a new motor task or action and depends on both the sensory motor development of the child as well as his or her thinking and reasoning skills.

## Motor Development
Typical motor development milestones for various age groups are as follows:

*Ages three to four:* have mastered walking and standing and are now developing gross motor skills such as single foot hopping and balancing, unsupported ascent and descent of stairs, kicking a ball, overhand throwing, catching a ball off of a bounce, moving forward and backward with coordination, and riding a tricycle. Fine motor skills begin to progress including using scissors with one hand, copying capital letters and more complex shapes, and drawing basic shapes from memory.

*Ages four to five:* tackling increasingly complex gross motor skills that require some coordination and multiple movement patterns combined together such as doing somersaults, swinging, climbing, and skipping. They also can use utensils to eat independently, dress themselves with clothing containing zippers and buttons, and begin to tie shoelaces. Mastery of fine motor skills begins to progress more rapidly, including cutting and pasting, and drawing shapes, letters, and people with heads, bodies, and arms. They tend to engage in long periods of physical activity followed by a need for a significant amount of rest. Physically, bones are still developing. Girls tend to be more coordinated while boys are stronger, but both sexes lack precise fine motor skills and the ability to focus on small objects for a long time.

**Children Enjoy Exercise with Games Like Tag**

*Age six to eight:* skating, biking, skipping with both feet, dribbling a ball. By the end of grade two, children should be able to make smoother transitions between different locomotor skills sequenced together. They can also accomplish more complicated manipulative skills such as dribbling a soccer ball with their feet and can better control their bodies during locomotion, weight-bearing, and balance. Students can begin to use feedback to hone motor skills from a cognitive perspective.

*Ages nine to eleven:* Children begin to get stronger, leaner, and taller as they enter the pre-adolescent stage and growth accelerates with the beginnings of secondary sex characteristics. Attention span and gross and fine motor skills improve. By the end of grade five, most children can achieve more performance-based outcomes such as hitting targets and can complete specialized sports skills such as fielding baseballs and serving tennis balls. They are also able to combine movements in a more dynamic environment such as moving rhythmically to music. From a cognitive perspective, they can begin to take concepts and feedback learned in other skills or sports and apply them to a new game. An example of this is increasing body stability by bending the knees to lower the center of gravity in basketball during a pick drill; this skill can also be reapplied on the ski slope. Additionally, children begin to observe peers more and can provide feedback to others.

## Promoting Physical Fitness, Responsible Behavior, and Respect in Physical Activity Settings

The youngest students enjoy being physically active for the fun of movement itself, and they particularly enjoy non-structured activities in moderate and high intensities followed by sufficient rest. By the end of second grade, students will likely voluntarily incorporate activities from physical education class to leisure time activity and, although they are not typically concerned with structured exercise or activity recommendations for health, they do recognize the physical and mental benefits of activity and they self-select game-like play they enjoy. They are able to recognize the physiologic indicators of exercise such as elevated heart rate, sweating, and heavy breathing; they have a general understanding that physical fitness improves health; and they know that there are five components of health-related fitness: cardiovascular endurance, muscular strength, muscular endurance, flexibility, and body composition.

By the end of fifth grade, students should be aware that participation in regular physical activity is a conscious decision, and they should choose activities based on both enjoyment and health benefits. At this age, they begin to develop an awareness of resources and opportunities in the school and community to support activity and may become more interested in healthy food choices, realizing that personal responsibility and their own choices can affect their health. They also become more aware of their body and voice in a complex dynamic environment with others, and have greater focus towards controlling parts of their body and their movements within an environment with others. Students should also begin to take an interest in improving aspects of fitness for better sports' performance or health indicators, and should apply the results of fitness assessments to gain a deeper understanding of their own personal fitness and health compared with peers and standards. Older students also understand that success comes with practice and effort, and they also enjoy broadening their skills and activities by learning new sports and skills based on prior mastery. They can engage in mutual physical activity with students of differing ability levels.

It is important that educators continually address the issues of personal and social behavior, especially as it relates to accepting and respecting differences in abilities, ideas, lifestyles, cultures, and choices. By the end of second grade, students should know how to follow the rules and safety procedures in physical education classes and during activities with little to no need for reinforcement. They also understand the social benefits of playing with others and how activities are more fun while interacting with other people. They should be able to effectively communicate during group activities in a respectful way, and enjoy working collaboratively with others to complete motor tasks or goals by combining movements and skills from many people together. By the end of fifth grade, students should be able to work independently or in small or large groups during physical activities in a cohesive and agreeable manner, understanding that the group can often achieve more than the individual alone. However, individually, the student should understand that he or she is also responsible for personal health behaviors and movements.

# Practice Questions

1. Which of the following would NOT be included on a list of nutrition recommendations for children?
    a. Replace higher fat foods with lower-fat alternatives
    b. Replace higher fiber foods with lower-fiber options
    c. Reduce intake of sugary beverages
    d. Replace refined foods with foods in their more natural form

2. The optimal physical education curriculum for five- to six-year-old children should focus on which of the following?
    a. Movement for enjoyment
    b. Sport-specific skills
    c. Hand-eye coordination
    d. Low intensity, endurance activities

3. Which of the following is true regarding classroom instruction of new movement skills for young children?
    a. It should occur in one long session at the beginning of the class, followed by time for children to play and attempt the skill.
    b. It should contain many small steps for the children to keep track of during play.
    c. It should be limited to short twenty-second stretches of instruction interspersed with long periods of play.
    d. It should be given in written form so children can read it at their leisure.

4. Which of the following is a healthy lifestyle habit for children?
    a. Getting eight hours of sleep every night
    b. Keeping their emotions to themselves
    c. Following safety procedures like wearing a seat belt
    d. Brushing their teeth once a day before bed

5. Educators should teach students about the importance of visiting a doctor for all EXCEPT which of the following reasons?
    a. Routine medical care and check-ups
    b. Consistent feelings of sadness, anxiety, loneliness, and stress
    c. Pains or aches that do not go away
    d. When insurance coverage changes

6. Health insurance status, safety and injury prevention education and care, nutritional meal planning and diet composition, social dynamics and stress, and culture around leisure time are all potential health behavior influences related to which factor?
    a. Family
    b. Peers
    c. School
    d. Media

7. Which of the following is true regarding motor skill development in children?
    a. Motor skill development shouldn't begin until after kindergarten.
    b. Sports skills are learned more readily than generalized body movements such as skipping.
    c. Gross motor skills are mastered before fine motor skills.
    d. Students benefit from formal movement training rather than free play.

8. Which of the following is NOT a general category of basic movement skills?
    a. Locomotor skills
    b. Sports-specific skills
    c. Non-locomotor skills
    d. Manipulative skills

9. In a kindergarten classroom, physical education should include a focus on all EXCEPT which of the following?
    a. Hitting targets
    b. Weight transfer
    c. Following objects with the eyes
    d. Running and stopping

10. Which of the following age groups is likely to be most interested in the health-based benefits of physical activity?
    a. Two- to four-year-old children
    b. Five- to seven-year-old children
    c. Seven- to nine-year-old children
    d. Nine- to twelve-year-old children

11. Which of the following are the major categories of the arts that educators should focus curricular activities on?
    a. Music, dance, theater, visual arts
    b. Music, performing arts, visual arts, sculpture
    c. Painting, drawing, woodworking, visual arts
    d. Language arts, music, theater, visual arts

12. The youngest children just beginning in art tend to create art with a focus on which of the following?
    a. Self-expression
    b. Narrative storytelling
    c. Scientific and sensory observations
    d. Creative and artistic ideas

13. Which of the following is true of art education for children?
    a. Children should focus on learning about art from their own culture and time-period.
    b. It is important for children to see professional art before creating their own works.
    c. It is important for children to study art theory before beginning their own projects.
    d. Children should experiment with a variety of methods and materials to create art.

14. Which of the following is a way for young students to easily learn rhythm in music class?
    a. Have students memorize each song on multiple instruments.
    b. Have students sit still and focus intently on the music.
    c. Have students read the lyrics before they listen to the music.
    d. Have students accompany music with simple instruments like tambourines.

293

15. Which of the following is performed by teachers and students using curriculum material or social issues?
    a. Puppetry
    b. Participation Theater
    c. Reader's Theater
    d. Theater-in-Education (TIE)

16. The main skills in theatrical arts for children include all EXCEPT which of the following?
    a. Staging
    b. Literary
    c. Technical
    d. Performance

17. A three- to four-year-old child would likely create a drawing emphasizing which of the following?
    a. The emotions expressed in their work.
    b. The figural accuracy of the drawing.
    c. The symbolic meaning of their work.
    d. The colors they use and how they look.

18. Which of the following is a technique used to make flat objects look as though they have depth?
    a. Balance
    b. Perspective
    c. Optical illusion
    d. Abstraction

19. Art serves all EXCEPT which of the following main functional categories?
    a. Religious functions
    b. Personal functions
    c. Social functions
    d. Physical functions

20. Which of the following is a principle in art that highlights the similarities in separate but related parts of a composition?
    a. Contrast
    b. Harmony
    c. Movement
    d. Balance

# Answer Explanations

**1. B:** Nutrition recommendations for children include replacing higher fat foods with lower-fat alternatives, reducing the intake of sugary beverages, and replacing more refined foods like applesauce with foods in their natural form, such as a fresh, whole apple. Answer Choice *B* is incorrect because fiber is beneficial in the diet because it increases the feeling of satiety, which can lower caloric intake, and fiber can also reduce LDL cholesterol by binding to it and helping the body excrete it. Lower fiber refined grains have the bran stripped away and should be replaced by higher fiber options.

**2. A:** The optimal physical education curriculum for five- to six-year-old children should focus on movement for enjoyment. Children at this age are motivated by fun and playing and will be active if it is fun. They are not necessarily ready to focus on sports-specific skills requiring significant hand-eye coordination. They do best with moderate- and high-intensity activities with adequate rest.

**3. C:** When teaching new skills, especially to toddlers and young children, instructions lasting longer than twenty seconds or containing more than just a couple of steps or cues will lead students to losing interest or getting overwhelmed. It is typically advantageous to have very short instructional periods interspersed between longer breaks to play and try out the introduced skills. Reading material is likely not appropriate for this age group, many of whom do not yet know how to read.

**4. C:** Following safety procedures like wearing a seatbelt is the best choice. Experts recommend that children get over nine hours of sleep per night. Also, children should brush their teeth after every meal, not just before bed. Finally, it is important for children to learn how to express their emotions in a healthy way and let a trusted adult know if they are struggling with persistent feelings of sadness or anxiety.

**5. D:** Teachers should educate students on the importance of visiting doctors for routine medical care and check-ups (every six months or so); consistent feelings of sadness, anxiety, loneliness, and stress; and pains or aches that do not go away. Research has found that even at the preschool level, talking about the importance of visiting the doctor can positively impact health behaviors in adulthood.

**6. A:** Family influences on health behaviors include health insurance status, safety and injury prevention education and care, nutritional meal planning and diet composition, social dynamics and stress, and the family's culture around leisure time.

**7. C:** Gross motor skills are mastered before fine motor skills. Students begin developing basic motor skills like walking, balancing, and manipulating objects from a very early age. They master gross motor skills before they move on to fine motor skills. Sports skills are not learned more readily than generalized body movements, because sports skills require more fine motor skills, complex motions, and cognitive abilities (e.g. locating and aiming for targets). Also, what looks like play actually helps children develop movement patterns and abilities.

**8. B:** The general categories of basic movement skills include locomotor skills like walking, running, and skipping; non-locomotor skills such as squatting and twisting; and manipulative skills such as throwing and catching.

**9. A:** In a kindergarten classroom, hitting targets is not an appropriate focus for physical education because children at this age have not mastered the fine motor abilities and complex skills to aim and hit targets. Hitting targets is more appropriate for fifth grade students. In kindergarten, activities should focus on foundational skills such as weight transfer, balance, following objects with the eyes, and basic skills like jumping and skipping.

**10. D:** Of the listed age groups, nine- to twelve-year-old students are likely to be more interested in health-based benefits of physical activity than younger children, who are primarily interested in movement for fun and enjoyment. As children mature, they gain a deeper understanding of physiology and healthy lifestyle choices and they become more interested in the health benefits of exercise.

**11. A:** Educators should focus curricular activities on the major categories of arts: music, dance, theater, and visual arts (painting, drawing, sculpture, pottery, etc.).

**12. C:** The youngest children tend to create art with a focus on the scientific and sensory aspects of the project rather than artistic creativity, self-expression, or conveying a narrative or story. They enjoy art more as a means to which explore the textures they make (for example, making texture rubbings with crayon on paper), the contrast of colors they use, and the various shapes they make as they move the drawing utensil around (although they are not making shapes for symbolic reasons, they are simply enjoying and exploring what they make when they use the supplies).

**13. D:** Children should experiment with a variety of methods and materials to create art. Educators should provide children with a wide range of materials like finger paint, glitter, and felt so that children experiment with different textures. *A* is not the best answer because art education should expose students to the historical and cultural context of art beyond that of their everyday experiences. Students can learn about famous artists and art history, but those lessons can be incorporated into creative coursework; they are not a prerequisite for student experimentation.

**14. D:** Have students accompany the music with simple instruments like tambourines. Students can easily beat along to simple songs using rhythmic instruments like tambourines, maracas, or small drums. Young children enjoy moving around more than sitting and focusing on one thing for an extended time, so learning rhythm through actions like shaking rhythmic instruments or stomping and clapping is more effective for students at this age. Also, *C* is not the best answer because many young children are not yet strong readers.

**15. D:** Theater-in-education (TIE) is performed by teachers and students using curriculum material or social issues. Participants take on roles, which enable them to explore and problem-solve in a flexible structure, yet in an educational theatrical way. In Readers' Theater, readers perform a dramatic presentation sitting on stools reading the lines typically from children's literature, enabling performance opportunities in the absence of elaborate staging or script memorization. Puppetry can be used for creative drama with either simple puppets and stages made of bags, cardboard, socks, or more elaborate, artistic materials.

**16. A:** The main skills in theatrical arts for children include literary (reading and writing the script and memorizing lines), technical (includes the staging, lighting, sound effects, etc.), and performance elements (such as the set design and the musical score). Staging is part of the technical elements.

**17. D:** A three- to four-year-old child's drawing usually emphasizes his or her color choices. At this young age, children typically do not use art for self-expression, symbolism, or realistic figural accuracy. These are all artistic skills that students develop when they are older. Young students tend to focus on sensory exploration involving color, shape, and texture.

**18. B:** Perspective is a technique used to make flat objects look as though they have depth. Balance is using size, position, color, shape and lighting in the artwork so that all of the elements are equally

present with no particular component overpowering. Abstraction is unrealistic artwork that typically has geometric lines or patterns.

**19. A:** Art has personal (self-expression, gratification, narrative functions), social (collective meaning for a group of people such as symbolic art honoring a god or political art), and physical functions (such as a pottery mug for tea) that often overlap in a project. Religious functions fall under the realm of social functions.

**20. B:** Harmony is a principle in art that highlights the similarities in separate but related parts of a composition to show how different things can actually be similar and blend together. Balance is positioning objects or using size, color, shape and lighting in a way that makes all of the elements equally present. Contrast is exemplifying differences between two unlike things such as loud and soft music, major and minor tones, fast and slow dancing movements, and light and dark colors.

Dear NES Elementary Education Test Taker,

We would like to start by thanking you for purchasing this study guide for your NES Elementary Education exam. We hope that we exceeded your expectations.

Our goal in creating this study guide was to cover all of the topics that you will see on the test. We also strove to make our practice questions as similar as possible to what you will encounter on test day. With that being said, if you found something that you feel was not up to your standards, please send us an email and let us know.

We would also like to let you know about other books in our catalog that may interest you.

## CSET Mathematics

This can be found on Amazon: amazon.com/dp/1628459158

## CSET English

amazon.com/dp/1628457198

## CSET Multiple Subject

amazon.com/dp/1628458739

## CBEST

amazon.com/dp/1628458755

We have study guides in a wide variety of fields. If the one you are looking for isn't listed above, then try searching for it on Amazon or send us an email.

Thanks Again and Happy Testing!
Product Development Team
info@studyguideteam.com

Interested in buying more than 10 copies of our product? Contact us about bulk discounts:

bulkorders@studyguideteam.com

# FREE Test Taking Tips DVD Offer

To help us better serve you, we have developed a Test Taking Tips DVD that we would like to give you for FREE. **This DVD covers world-class test taking tips that you can use to be even more successful when you are taking your test.**

All that we ask is that you email us your feedback about your study guide. Please let us know what you thought about it – whether that is good, bad or indifferent.

To get your **FREE Test Taking Tips DVD**, email freedvd@studyguideteam.com with "FREE DVD" in the subject line and the following information in the body of the email:

   a. The title of your study guide.

   b. Your product rating on a scale of 1-5, with 5 being the highest rating.

   c. Your feedback about the study guide. What did you think of it?

   d. Your full name and shipping address to send your free DVD.

If you have any questions or concerns, please don't hesitate to contact us at freedvd@studyguideteam.com.

Thanks again!

Made in the USA
Monee, IL
20 April 2021